Advances in
Clinical Social Work
Research

Advances in Clinical Social Work Research

Lynn Videka-Sherman and William J. Reid, Editors

NASW PRESS

National Association of Social Workers
Silver Spring, MD 20910

Richard L. Edwards, ACSW, *President*
Mark G. Battle, ACSW, *Executive Director*

Library of Congress Cataloging-in-Publication Data

Advances in clinical social work research/Lynn Videka-Sherman and William J. Reid, editors.
    p.   cm.
    Result of a conference entitled "Empiricism in Clinical Practice: Present and Future," held in Great Barrington, Massachusetts, on August 18–21, 1988.
    Includes bibliographical references and index.
    ISBN 0-87101-186-7
    1. Social case work—Methodology—Congresses.   I. Videka-Sherman, Lynn, 1951–   .   II. Reid, William James, 1928–
HV43.A38   1990
361.3'2—dc20   90-38698
                                                  CIP

Printed in the United States of America

Cover design by Max-Karl Winkler
Interior design by Susan Marsh Typesetting & Graphics

Contents

Preface ix

Introduction: A Time to Take Stock, *Lynn Videka-Sherman and William J. Reid* xi

1 Empiricism in Clinical Practice: Present and Future, *Scott Briar* 1

Part 1: Single-System Designs

2 Rethinking Single-Case Evaluation, *Wallace J. Gingerich* 11

Commentary: Beyond Regret: Single-Case Evaluations and Their Place in Social Work Education and Practice, *Helen Reinherz* 25

Commentary: Improving the Fit between Single-Subject Designs and Practice, *Betty J. Blythe* 29

Synthesis: Single-System Research Designs in Social Work Practice, *Bruce A. Thyer* 33

3 Single-Case Research and Traditional Practice: Issues and Possibilities, *Judith C. Nelsen* 37

Commentary: Single-System Designs in Family-Centered Social Work Practice, *Susan B. Stern* 48

Commentary: Illustrating the Value of Practice Wisdom, *Kevin J. Corcoran* 54

Synthesis: Why Don't Practitioners Use Single-Subject Designs? *Eleanor Reardon Tolson* 58

Part 2: Methodological Advances

4 Expert Systems and the Development of Knowledge in Social Welfare, *Edward J. Mullen and John R. Schuerman* 67

Commentary: Issues in the Development of Expert Systems to Enhance Decision Making in Child Welfare, *Theodore J. Stein* 84

Commentary: The Nature of Expertise in Social Welfare, *Frederic G. Reamer* 88

Commentary: Expert Systems, Socrates, and the Philosophy of Mind, *Jerome C. Wakefield* 92

Synthesis: Expert Systems in Social Welfare Practice: Questions and Concerns, *Denise E. Bronson* 101

5 Computer-Based Clinical Practice: Present Status and Future Possibilities, *Walter W. Hudson* 105

Commentary: Computer-Based Clinical Practice: An Asset or Pie in the Sky? *Deborah H. Siegel* 118

Commentary: Information Technology Supporting Empirical Practice, *Elizabeth Mutschler* 123

Synthesis: Enhancing Clinical Social Work through Microcomputers, *Anthony N. Maluccio* 127

6 Change-Process Research: A New Paradigm? *William J. Reid* 130

Commentary: Change-Process Research: No New Paradigm, but a Necessary Complement to the Old Paradigm, *Edmund Sherman* 149

Commentary: Challenges in Change-Process Research, *Enola K. Proctor* 153

Commentary: The Utility of Change-Process Research for the Education of Practitioners and Single-Case Evaluation, *Sharon B. Berlin* 159

Synthesis: Microanalysis of Intervention-Client Change Loops: The Heart of Change-Process Research, *Inger P. Davis* 163

7 The Use of Qualitative and Quantitative Data in the Development of a Clinical Program, *Sheldon D. Rose and Naomi Farber* 174

Commentary: The Interface of Qualitative and Quantitative Methods in Social Work Research, *Terri Combs-Orme* 181

Commentary: Distinguishing and Combining Qualitative and Quantitative Methods, *Charles Glisson* 189

Synthesis: Problems and Uses of Qualitative Methodologies, *Anne E. Fortune* 194

8 Modes of Practice in Developmental Research, *Edwin J. Thomas* 202

Commentary: Developmental Research: Model or Method?
Shirley Jenkins 218

Commentary: Modes of Research for the Development of
Interventions, *Jack Rothman* 222

Synthesis: The Contribution of Developmental Research,
Ronald W. Toseland 228

Part 3: Utilization of Research

9   Research Utilization: The Substructure of Belief,
Stuart A. Kirk 233

Commentary: What Is the Utilization Agenda?
Jesse E. Gordon 251

Commentary: Making Research Usable, *Robert F. Schilling* 256

Commentary: Opening the Door to Knowledge Utilization,
Craig Winston LeCroy 261

Synthesis: Research Utilization: Reflections on the Rhetoric,
André Ivanoff 265

10 Clinical Significance: Problems and New Developments,
Srinika Jayaratne 271

Commentary: Attribution Theory and Clinical Significance:
Further Issues, *Tony Tripodi* 286

Commentary: The Use of Decision Theory to Explicate the
Process of Clinical Decision Making, *Rona L. Levy* 290

Synthesis: Clinical Significance as Process and Outcome,
John G. Orme 293

11 Problems and Issues in Meta-Analysis, *Joel Fischer* 297

Commentary: Meta-Analysis: A User's Perspective,
Lynn Videka-Sherman 326

Commentary: Meta-Analysis: A Heuristic Tool for
Social Work Training, *Paula Nurius* 330

Synthesis: Meta-Analysis in Social Work, *William Nugent* 333

Part 4: Epistemology for Clinical Social Work

12 Symposium 2: On the Epistemology of Social Work Practice
Knowledge (with Apologies to Plato's Symposium),
Martin Bloom 341

Commentary: Bloom on Bloom: A Follow-up, *Martin Bloom* . . . 350

Commentary: Penetrating the Veil of Appearance in
Empirical Clinical Practice, *José B. Ashford* 352

Commentary: Thoughts on the Epistemology of Social Work
Practice Knowledge, *Cheryl A. Richey* 359

Commentary: Epistemological and Semantic Traps,
Roberta Wells Imre 366

Synthesis: The Epistemology of Social Work, *Jane F. Gilgun* 371

13 Epistemological Issues in the Development of Social Work
Practice Knowledge, *Katherine M. Wood* 373

Commentary: Epistemology and Research in Advancing
Social Work Knowledge, *Max Siporin* 391

Commentary: The Forest or the Trees? *Carol H. Meyer* 395

Commentary: Thoughts on Epistemological Issues in
Social Work, *Aaron H. Beckerman* 400

Synthesis: Themes in the Discussion of Epistemology,
Lewayne D. Gilchrist 405

14 Themes, Issues, and Prospects, *Lynn Videka-Sherman,*
William J. Reid, and Ronald W. Toseland 409

Index 423

Contributors 433

Preface

This book is the product of a conference titled "Empiricism in Clinical Practice: Present and Future," held in Great Barrington, Massachusetts, on August 18–21, 1988. The conference was sponsored by several units of the University of Albany–State University of New York, including the Office for Research, the School of Social Welfare, the Professional Development Program, and the Nelson A. Rockefeller College of Public Affairs and Policy. The American Institute for Economic Research in Great Barrington graciously donated its facilities for the site of the conference.

The conference allowed researchers who are active in solving problems related to clinical social work practice to meet in a bucolic and thought-provoking setting to discuss issues confronting and new technologies for clinical research. The sessions were stimulating and discussion oriented.

The editors of this volume are grateful to many individuals for the help they provided. Without these persons, the conference would not have succeeded so well, and this volume would not have been produced. We thank the other members of the conference planning committee—Stuart Kirk, André Ivanoff, and Susan Stern—for their illuminating and creative insights that structured the content of the conference and this volume and attracted some of the leading researchers in the country. Barbara Mollberg and Jennifer Behrens efficiently and effectively managed all the details and planning for the conference, and Marla Henriquez and Christie Romeo handled all the correspondence associated with the conference. In addition, the secretarial assistance of Marla Henriquez, Jeanne D'Allassandro, and B. J. Kelly was invaluable in preparing the manuscript.

Welcome editorial help was obtained from several graduate assistants: Janet Fitzgerald Wheeler, Lillian Segarra, and Michele Mulvaney. Several doctoral students—Jeri Burns, Cindy Penka, Nancy Smyth, and Nancy Tobler—played key roles in the conference. Others—Catherine Doyle, Joseph Englehardt, Susan R. Fessler, Stephen Jankowski, Dennis Kilgore, Joy Kyamunyogonya, June S. Pierson, Linda R. Rotering, Richard L. Schnell, Carmalita B. Scott, Katherine Skinner, and Mary F. Smith—helped with transportation and with coordinating the sessions.

Finally, we wish to thank the presentors, reactors, and chairs of the sessions. Their timely preparation of drafts and redrafts of their papers, their creative thinking, and their willingness to engage in serious discussions of controversial issues helped make the conference a great success and this book a reality.

LYNN VIDEKA-SHERMAN
WILLIAM J. REID

Introduction

A Time to Take Stock

Lynn Videka-Sherman and William J. Reid

During the past twenty years, a number of developments have made a difference in the conduct and use of research in clinical social work. The behavioral movement, which began to affect social work in the late 1960s, contributed new conceptions of scientifically based practice, as well as new methods of evaluating practice. Concurrently, the increasing emphasis on making practice accountable has spurred interest in the application of rigorous means of assessing the efforts of clinical social workers. The result has been the emergence of empirically based practice approaches that have outgrown their behavioral origins and a wide variety of techniques for the study of the effects of intervention in single cases.

More specific changes in methods have also occurred. The computer revolution has given rise to a variety of tools for informing and evaluating practice, such as expert systems methodology and computerized assessment instruments. Interest in investigating the processes of intervention by practitioners and change in clients has reemerged under the rubric "change-process research," and developmental research has proved to be an innovative and promising strategy for constructing interventions.

Some of these developments have been particularly relevant to the utilization of research. For example, the notion of "clinical significance" offers more realistic criteria by which to judge the efficacy of interventions than does the conventional standard of statistical significance, and meta-analysis has been an important tool for synthesizing the results of numerous studies. Research utilization, in the traditional sense of the utilization of research by practitioners, has itself benefited from the influx of new formulations and studies.

Finally, the debate over the epistemology of social work knowledge has enlivened the pages of social work journals during the past 15 years. The philosophical rationale of traditional research methodologies has been sharply criticized and stoutly defended. Alternative methodologies have been suggested and supported by some and dismissed by others. There has been little consensus about whether reform is needed or what shape it should take.

PURPOSE AND PLAN OF THE BOOK

This book describes and assesses these developments. It consists of papers presented at the conference titled "Empiricism in Clinical Practice: Present and Future," held at the American Institute for Economic Research, Great Barrington, Massachusetts, August 18–21, 1988. The papers, revised and updated since their original presentations, reflect the two main goals of the conference: (1) to examine the uses and limitations of empirical methods in forming the knowledge base of clinical practice in social work and (2) to review selected developments in clinical social work research, especially the newer methodologies.

The overriding purpose of the conference was to take stock of a number of aspects of this research, both old and new. Some older developments, such as single-case designs and the epistemological debate, seemed to be especially in need of appraisal. How well is single-system methodology fulfilling its promise of enabling practitioners to use empirical data to guide and evaluate their practice? What obstacles have arisen in the application of this methodology and how can they be overcome? Although the epistemological debate is perhaps unresolvable at present, is it possible to sharpen the issues and to discover a few areas of consensus? What might emerge if we brought together, as we tried to do at the conference, scholars with different points of view about the epistemology of social work?

Other developments were newer, not only chronologically but in the sense of being less familiar to researchers and scholars in clinical social work. Here the interest was not so much in assessing well-known innovations or issues but, rather, in learning more about a new development and considering its possible applications. What is an "expert systems" approach, and what is its promise for knowledge building? What can computerized assessment contribute to clinical practice?

Chapter 1, by Scott Briar, which was the keynote paper of the conference, assesses the empirical practice movement. The remainder of the book is divided into four parts. Part 1 considers applications of single-system methodology in practice situations. The extent to which this methodology is actually used by practitioners and modifications needed to encompass the broad range of practice approaches in clinical social work are among the issues considered. Part 2 presents a range of new approaches in clinical social work research—expert systems, computer-based clinical assessment, change-process research, the use of qualitative methods in experimental studies, and developmental research. Part 3 is devoted to developments in the utilization of research, including meta-analysis and the concept of clinical significance (both of which may be also considered new approaches). Part 4 is concerned with epistemological issues that have arisen in debates on the nature of social work knowledge and the kind of research needed to test and expand the knowledge base of the profession. The final chapter reviews the major themes and issues presented in the book and discusses prospects for the future.

Each of the four parts of the book is built around two or more major chapters, each of which is followed by two or three brief response articles and a synthesis of the discussion of all the articles and of the participants in the workshops. Our aim in adopting this organization was to provide a forum for debate and an in-depth examination of important topics in clinical social work research. We hope that this structure allows readers to do the same.

Chapter 1

Empiricism in Clinical Practice: Present and Future

Scott Briar

The progress of the empirical practice movement can be measured in ways other than its increasing acceptance among social work educators. One measure is the impressive expansion of the body of literature on empirical practice, including research on the effectiveness of practice. The expansion of that knowledge base reflects, of course, the substantially increased number of social work researchers, including practitioner-scientists, who are contributing to this effort. Despite these and other indicators of success, some critics have suggested that the empirical practice movement has failed to achieve its original objectives. In fact, this note was sounded in several papers prepared for the conference. Those who raise this issue tend to point to two kinds of evidence. One is the movement's failure to stimulate the widespread interest and support of practitioners. Another is the results of the studies that have been conducted on the effect of training in the empirical practice perspective, especially the use of single-subject designs, on the subsequent practice of social work students. In most of these studies, the educational intervention was limited, sometimes consisting only of one elective course. Under such conditions, one could expect only a small impact. Most of these studies also ignored the one reality about social work education of which educators are certain, namely, that most social work students consider the field practicum to be the most influential component of their education, especially so far as their subsequent practice behaviors are concerned. Therefore, until the empirical practice perspective is incorporated into the field practicum, one can expect it to have only a limited impact.

The most ambitious of these studies, both in size and the extent of educational intervention, was by Blythe (1983). The educational intervention in that study consisted of an attempt, throughout the first year of the master's degree in social work (MSW) program at the University of Washington,

Seattle, to integrate the practice, research, and practicum courses so that all direct-practice students would be prepared to evaluate the effectiveness of their practice. The least effective component of this program was the effort to integrate the practicum component, for a variety of reasons. Blythe conducted a follow-up study of six successive cohorts of graduates who were exposed to this program using a questionnaire that sought information about their utilization of specific components of the practice-evaluation technology and their attitudes toward the evaluation of practice. Although the 66 percent response rate (341 out of 573, minus 55 who could not be located) was less than one would have liked, it was substantially higher than that usually obtained in follow-up surveys of MSW graduates.

Some reviewers of this study found the results disappointing (Penka & Kirk, 1990). Slightly more than half the respondents were not using any of the tools or techniques they had been taught for the evaluation of their effectiveness, regarded by Penka and Kirk (1990) and others as a less-than-successful outcome of the educational intervention. On the contrary, as one of the early advocates of the inclusion of practice-evaluation methodologies in the education of social workers, this author was impressed with the outcomes of the study, which exceeded his expectations. His advocacy of the need for practitioner-scientists in social work has been consistently misinterpreted, and his efforts to correct this misinterpretation have been unsuccessful. The author never advocated that *all* practitioners could or should become practitioner-scientists. On the contrary, his most ambitious expectation was that a school the size of the University of Washington might prepare a handful of research practitioners a year. Blythe's survey identified a number of respondents who were attempting full-blown single-subject designs with some of their cases and even a few who were attempting to do so with all their clients. These workers clearly would be practitioner-scientists. Blythe conducted telephone interviews with 10 of the most research-active respondents.

Of greater interest, however, and more important for the future, was the finding that over 40 percent of the respondents reported using some of the tools and techniques of practice evaluation, such as specification of the objectives of an intervention in measurable terms and the measurement and monitoring of target outcomes, in their practice regularly or frequently. And the responses of these workers indicated that they employed these research tools because they found them to be useful in their practice. But the most solid point to be made about the extent of the utilization of these tools by graduates is that the rates of utilization, whether considered low or high, are much higher than they would have been if these graduates had not been trained in the use of these research tools. In other words, if Blythe's questionnaire had been administered to graduates of an MSW program that paid little or no attention to methods for evaluating the effectiveness of practice, one would expect to find significantly lower rates of utilization. Although such a study would be useful, it has become difficult to conduct it because of another development that is of considerable significance to the empirical practice movement.

In 1984, the Accreditation Commission of the Council on Social Work Education (CSWE) instituted a new set of standards for the accreditation of social work education programs (CSWE, 1984). These standards include a curriculum policy statement that specifies the standards that must be met in the curricula of educational programs and requires that the foundation curriculum must include the content necessary to provide students with the skills that will "prepare them systematically to evaluate their own practice" (p. 127). According to the commission, this objective needs to be addressed in required courses on research and practice and in the practicum. These standards apply not only to the nearly 100 MSW programs, but to the more than 360 bachelor's degree in social work (BSW) programs accredited by CSWE.

The overwhelming majority of the programs reviewed thus far have taken significant steps to satisfy these standards by revising the syllabi of courses, adding new courses, and hiring faculty members who are prepared to teach this material. There appears to be widespread agreement that these are desirable standards. Even if one assumes a low utilization rate after graduation, the effect of this development on the future progress of empirically based practice could be substantial indeed. There is, of course, one possible hazard in this development. The empirically based practice approach and the research methodology that has been associated with it may not be taught as well as some would like it to be. Therefore, it would be helpful to offer workshops on this topic at the annual meeting of CSWE so that those who teach the evaluation of practice may share their experiences and course materials. It would also be helpful to have publications that describe what should be covered to prepare students to evaluate their practice.

SUGGESTIONS FOR THE FUTURE

What needs to be done in the future to support and facilitate the benefits that could follow from this significant new opportunity? The following five concerns are suggested for inclusion in a future agenda for empirically based practice: (1) increased usefulness of evaluation tools, (2) a broadened perspective, (3) attention to developments in other areas, (4) development of better research methods, and (5) increased impact on the profession.

Increased Usefulness of Evaluation Tools

There are some indications that one of the factors that directly affects practitioners' utilization of tools for evaluating their effectiveness is whether they find them useful in their practice. There are, of course, a variety of factors that affect utility for practitioners, including organizational constraints, time, and other exigencies in the context of practice. But there is another impediment to utilization that we researchers sometimes create. As persons interested in research methodology, we have an irresistible attraction to methodological purity. We know what the perfect study should be even though we never have actually seen one. We content ourselves with shooting enough holes in any study to sink the Queen Mary. This impulse is desirable because it contributes to the definition and development of better science. But it also can inhibit students and practitioners from engaging in research because they may believe, quite reasonably, that they cannot achieve the ideal and that if they cannot, why bother to do it at all?

It is not the impulse to purity that is the problem, but how that impulse is used. We should take a cue from our colleagues in quantitative methods and research methodology in schools of public health and departments of epidemiology, who are interested in "robust methodologies." Robust methodologies are concerned with how to do the best possible research under compromised, limited, and difficult circumstances. We should use our expertise and skills in research to help practitioners find ways to do the best possible practice research within their circumstances. To do so will require some methodological innovations to maximize the usefulness of the tools and techniques we teach students and practitioners. Even if practitioners learn only how to specify measurable objectives and how to measure and monitor them, they can make significant contributions to the advancement of empirical practice. Many practicing physicians have been able to conduct significant clinical research using a few measures in controlled clinical trials—a methodology closely related to those we are trying to teach students for the evaluation of their practice.

A Broadened Perspective

Empirical practice needs to move beyond the constraints of the narrow clinical cocoon in which we researchers have, with some exceptions, encapsulated ourselves. That narrow perspective tends to bring with it an assumption that the most powerful variables in practice are to be found in the direct interaction between the practitioner and the client.

However, the weight of evidence from the body of research on the effectiveness of psychotherapy seems to suggest that whatever the effects of therapist-client interactions on outcomes, these interventions are generally not powerful. Moreover, social work practitioners are increasingly confronted with many human problems, such as child abuse, substance abuse, homelessness, severe psychiatric disability, unemployment, and family violence, that require interventions using external variables and resources, including specific social services, social support, and concrete services, that can and need to be evaluated.

Another reason for expanding the focus of empirical practice beyond a narrow clinical perspective is that CSWE's accreditation standards regarding the evaluation of the effectiveness of practice do not apply only to students of direct practice. They apply equally to students who are preparing for careers in administration, community organization, planning, policymaking, and other such roles in social work. However, little has been done to adapt and develop methods and tools with which these students can systematically evaluate the effectiveness of their practice. For example, single-subject and related methodologies can be used to conduct small-scale experiments on the effectiveness of social policy interventions, as has been done in other fields.

Attention to Developments in Other Areas

The empirical practice movement has developed its own corner of the social work curriculum without paying sufficient attention to developments in other curriculum areas that pose difficult questions, if not serious problems, for the educational and practice objectives of an empirically based approach to practice. One example is the rapid spread of systems theory as a foundation theory for social work practice. The systems perspective can be a useful heuristic framework for sensitizing social workers to the psychosocial focus that is one of the hallmarks of the profession, but one that often is honored more in the breach than in practice. However, as a theory applied to human behavior and social interaction, the systems perspective is virtually devoid of determinant predictions about human behavior and lacks the conceptual capability to generate specific, testable propositions for intervention. Nevertheless, an increasing number of social workers believes that the systems perspective is an adequate practice theory, partly because that is what they have been taught. An obvious problem is that the vagueness, generality, and indeterminancy of the systems framework does not lend itself readily to systematic efforts to evaluate the effectiveness of practice.

A second example, which poses similar problems, is the rapid spread of advanced generalist practice in MSW programs. The advanced generalist approach achieves its objectives by formulating principles and objectives of intervention at sufficiently high and broad levels of abstraction that they can be applied across levels and modes of practice. Such abstract objectives and principles pose serious problems for the development of empirically based practice and the systematic evaluation of effectiveness, and some have even suggested that it is impossible to evaluate the effectiveness of generalist social work practice for these reasons. Students who are trained in these perspectives are likely to find it especially difficult to achieve the degree of specificity required for the systematic evaluation of their practice. The broader question is this: What implications does the empirical practice perspective have for the development of the theoretical knowledge base of social work practice? These questions and problems deserve considerably more attention than they have received thus far.

Development of Better Research Methods

Further work is also needed to develop better research methods for empirical practice—not exotic ones that fascinate methodologists, but valid and reliable research tools and techniques that can be more readily and easily utilized by practitioners in developmental research. One of the most important ideas that has been introduced in the empirical practice movement is the concept of developmental research. This approach is more comprehensive and more useful to the empirical practice effort than was the evaluation model it incorporates, since practitioners can readily understand and appreciate that this approach is consistent with their view of how research can best contribute to the advancement of effective practice.

Increased Impact on the Profession

That the empirical practice movement has had little impact on the profession at large other than social work education is not surprising for two reasons. One reason is that advocates of empirically based practice have made little effort to reach the profession at large, beyond publications and sessions at a few conferences. Second, many researchers have greater access to social work education than to organized social work. If we researchers think it is important to have a greater impact on the profession at large, beyond the long-range impact through students, then we will need to consider what it would take to accomplish that goal. The nursing profession is an instructive example. Over the past 10 to 15 years, organized nursing has made a determined, systematic, national effort to persuade its membership to adopt research as one of the highest priorities of the profession. This attempt has been remarkably successful. Of course, the special circumstances that facilitated this effort in nursing are not present in social work. However, it may be possible to build on some recent initiatives of the National Association of Social Workers (NASW), such as the NASW Research Center, to increase practitioners' recognition of the empirical practice perspective and its importance for the future of the profession.

Of more immediate, as well as long-range, importance in this regard is the need for faculty members who teach this perspective to become more actively and directly engaged with practitioners and agencies in relation to students' research in their practicum placements. If students are expected to engage in practice evaluation in the practicum, then their faculty advisers will need to collaborate with the staffs of agencies to design and guide the students' work.

Empirical practice is alive and well. Moreover, we researchers are now in a position to extend and expand the infusion of an empirical practice perspective in social work education and practice by taking advantage of the opportunities now open to us. In doing so, we can make a significant contribution to the creation of more effective social work services and programs for the persons who look to us for help and support.

REFERENCES

Blythe, B. (1983). *An examination of practice evaluation among social workers.* Unpublished doctoral dissertation, University of Washington, Seattle.

Council on Social Work Education. (1984). *Handbook of accreditation standards and procedures.* Washington, DC: Author.

Penka, C., & Kirk, S. (1990). *Practitioner involvement in clinical evaluation.* Unpublished manuscript.

Part 1
Single-System Designs

Chapter 2

Rethinking Single-Case Evaluation

Wallace J. Gingerich

It is now nearly 20 years since single-case evaluation was advocated for use in social work practice (Bloom & Block, 1977; Bloom & Fischer, 1982; Fischer, 1978; Howe, 1974; Jayaratne, 1977; Jayaratne & Levy, 1979; Stuart, 1977; Thomas, 1975). Single-case evaluation has been proposed as a means of integrating research and practice (Jayaratne & Levy, 1979), a way to address issues of accountability (Gingerich, 1979; Nuehring & Pascone, 1986), and as a strategy for establishing a scientific base for social work practice (Blythe & Briar, 1985; Briar, 1977). The revised accreditation standards of the Council on Social Work Education (CSWE) now require social work programs to include content on "designs for the systematic evaluation of the student's own practice" (CSWE, 1988, p. 127). Thus, today, single-case evaluation is required of all new professionals.

Although the increasing advocacy and use of single-case evaluation reflects a remarkable change in social work practice, implementation of this new technology has by no means been complete (Robinson, Bronson, & Blythe, 1988). Most social workers who have been trained in the use of single-case evaluation find it difficult to incorporate it into their practice, and many do not use it at all (Dolan & Vourlekis, 1983; Gingerich, 1984a; Mutschler, 1984; Richey, Blythe, & Berlin, 1987). Furthermore, there is no direct empirical evidence that the use of single-case evaluation actually benefits practice (Hudson, 1987; Levy, 1981). This situation is not unique to social work practice. Behavior therapists report a similar nonuse of evaluation techniques (Swan & MacDonald, 1978; Wade, Baker, & Hartmann, 1979) and lack of evidence of the benefit to clinical practice (Hayes, Nelson, & Jarrett, 1987).

Research for this chapter was supported, in part, by grant MH18011–04 from the U.S. Public Health Service, U.S. Department of Health and Human Services.

11

What is one to make of this state of affairs? On the one hand, it is not surprising that a practice innovation as fundamental and far reaching as single-case evaluation has not been completely integrated into the routine activities of practitioners in 20 years. On the other hand, if single-case evaluation is as important to accountability and sound practice as its advocates suggest, then careful analysis and rethinking are needed.

This chapter reviews a number of identified problems that need to be addressed before it is realistic to expect that single-case evaluation will be fully integrated into social work practice. It suggests several general directions that may be pursued to develop and implement single-case evaluation procedures in standard professional practice and concludes with some reflections on what lies ahead.

PROBLEMS WITH SINGLE-CASE EVALUATION

Some of the first concerns with the use of single-case evaluation in the practice setting focused on the conflict between the objectives of service and research (Barlow, 1981; Thomas, 1978b). According to Thomas, the purpose of research is to demonstrate that an intervention produces a change in behavior, whereas the purpose of service is to bring about a meaningful change in the problem. In some instances, the experimental control required for research conflicts with clinical practice and the interests of the client. Others have countered, however, that useful evaluation can be conducted without compromising the objectives of service (Berlin, 1983; Conte & Levy, 1980; Gambrill & Barth, 1980). Although it is sometimes possible to accomplish both objectives in practice situations, in other cases, unavoidable conflicts arise, and compromises seem necessary (Barlow, Hayes, & Nelson, 1984). The debate over service and research has nevertheless been helpful in drawing attention to the different objectives of research, service, and evaluation. Clarification of the various purposes of single-case evaluation will help researchers and practitioners develop more realistic, useful, and justifiable evaluation methods and procedures.

A second set of concerns has to do with the applicability of the techniques of single-case evaluation to different approaches to social work practice. Single-case evaluation may not fit well with nonbehavioral (Nelsen, 1981) or psychodynamic approaches (Saleebey, 1979). Furthermore, most of the techniques that have been proposed have been unnecessarily restricted to quantitative or "hard" empirical methods (Reid & Davis, 1987; Ruckdeschel & Farris, 1981). Although there have been several notable efforts to apply single-case techniques to nonbehavioral practice (Broxmeyer, 1978; Corcoran, 1985; Dean & Reinherz, 1986; Nelsen,

1978, 1981; Sodervick, 1975), the real issues and concerns have yet to be addressed (Ivanoff, Blythe, & Briar, 1987). The assumption seems to have been that techniques that work in one setting or type of practice will also be useful in other settings—if only the practitioner will use them. But evaluation in the context of different frameworks of practice may require different methods and techniques.

Another set of problems with single-case evaluation is purely pragmatic. Students and practitioners have repeatedly stated that they find it difficult to do single-case evaluation because it is time consuming, because clients do not cooperate with the requirements of evaluations, and because agencies do not provide the necessary supports (Dolan & Vourlekis, 1983; Gingerich, 1984a; Levy, 1981; Mutschler, 1984) These appear to be valid criticisms. Many of those who voiced them were presumably sympathetic to single-case evaluation and were frustrated over their inability to implement it in their practice. Although single-case evaluation may have value in an abstract or theoretical sense, practitioners will not use it if it does not address important recognized needs. Consequently, we researchers need to consider the practical aspects of implementing single-case evaluation in normal social work practice.

Finally, some have suggested rightly that insufficient attention has been given to the dissemination and implementation of the technology of single-case evaluation in practice (Robinson, Bronson, & Blythe, 1988). Furthermore, it is unlikely that single-case evaluation will be fully used unless issues related to its dissemination, adoption, and implementation are addressed.

SUGGESTED DIRECTIONS

Clearly, single-case evaluation has not solved all the problems it was intended to solve. Despite the considerable body of available techniques and methods and practitioners who are interested in using them, knowledge of single-case evaluation and how to implement it is still often inadequate for the job. Nevertheless, the experience of the past 20 years is a good basis on which to begin to rethink single-case evaluation and how it may be developed and implemented more completely in practice. Potentially useful directions to consider include clarifying the goals and objectives of single-case evaluation, developing practice-based single-case evaluation methods and techniques, and assessing the utility of evaluation for practice.

Practice Requires Evaluation, not Research

A review of the literature suggests that clear distinctions are not made between research and evaluation and the relationship of each of these to single-case evaluation. In addition, there is no consensus on what single-case evaluation is and how and when it should be used. For example, the tendency to use the terms "single-case evaluation," "single-subject research," "single-subject designs," "time-series analysis," "clinical evaluation," and "empirical clinical practice" interchangeably is unfortunate because it leads to confusion, unrealistic expectations, and ineffective implementation.

As Thomas (1978a) and Barlow, Hayes, and Nelson (1984) suggested, the purpose of *research* is to develop scientific knowledge. For single-case research, the purpose is to demonstrate a causal connection between an intervention and an outcome. In contrast, the purpose of *practice* is to bring about an improvement in a client's situation. Decisions about what intervention to use, when to introduce it, when to change it, and when to withdraw it are based on what is considered best for the client and what will maximize the outcome. Following these definitions, Thomas (1978a) correctly noted that the requirements of research and service sometimes conflict, making it inappropriate to conduct research in a service setting.

Evaluation refers to the determination of whether a desired outcome was achieved. Minimally, evaluation requires that outcomes be discernible and that they be analyzed in relation to the desired level of performance. Evaluation also includes an implicit assessment of change, that is, whether the client's functioning is different from what it would have been had there been no intervention. Evaluation is not exclusively a research or practice process. As Thomas (1978a) and Barlow, Hayes, and Nelson (1984) noted, the distinctions between research, practice, and evaluation are primarily a matter of goals and purposes. The techniques and activities involved in the three processes are similar; it is the degree to which the interests of service or research are served by the activity that characterizes it as research, practice, or evaluation.

Single-case evaluation refers to the use of single-subject designs, behavioral assessment techniques, and a wide range of other research and evaluation procedures to determine if a desired outcome for a single client (or a client system) has been achieved. Single-case evaluation is distinguished from other practice-evaluation strategies by its focus on a single case or single system. Single-case evaluation does not require a particular design or assessment method.

From a perusal of standard texts on practice, it is clear that evaluation, presumably some form of single-case evaluation, is an integral part of virtually all approaches to practice. Evaluation is needed to decide whether to continue or modify an intervention and when to terminate it. In fact, it would be difficult to conceive of practice without evaluation. There is less agreement, however, on whether standard practice should include research. On the one hand, Gambrill (1983) and Fischer (1978) suggested that practitioners should make systematic inferences about the effectiveness of their interventions. On the other hand, Hollis (1972) and Reid (1978) seemed to imply that research, although necessary, should be conducted in a research context, not as part of standard practice.

The foregoing analysis suggests that the practice of social work requires evaluation, but not research. Competent practitioners should be able to provide reasonable evidence of the extent to which their clients have benefited from treatment. They need not provide rigorous scientific evidence of a causal connection between their interventions and the observed changes. It is interesting to note that one study (Eldridge, 1983) found that many practitioners engage in an intuitive type of self-evaluation in which they try to infer which interventions produced the observed outcomes.

Although practitioners need not conduct research as a part of their practice, they and the profession are in critical need of empirically based interventions. Later reviews of practice-outcome research (Reid & Hanrahan, 1982; Rubin, 1985) were more encouraging than were earlier ones (Fischer, 1973; Wood, 1978), yet it is probably accurate to say that today, social work practice is based largely on "practice wisdom," rather than on empirically tested interventions. The inherent difficulties involved in developing and testing social work interventions and the scant resources devoted to research and development suggest that it will be a long time before it can be claimed that social work practice is empirically based.

The expectation that practitioners develop empirically based models as part of their regular practice (Blythe & Briar, 1985; Briar, 1977) does not seem to be a realistic solution to this problem, as some recent formulations seem to have acknowledged (Ivanoff, Blythe, & Briar, 1987). Most practitioners do not have the necessary specialized training in research. Furthermore, they and the agencies in which they work generally are not rewarded for developing and testing new practice models; they are rewarded for providing competent professional services.

The problem of how best to develop a scientific base for social work practice is difficult and one that is beyond the scope of this chapter. However, several elements of a solution seem clear. First, clinical research centers, similar to those found in medical schools, should be established, and their mission should be to develop and test new interventions using developmental research methods (Thomas, 1984). Second, bona fide clinician-researchers who are expert both in research methods and in clinical theory must be trained at the doctoral level. Third, it must be acknowledged that both undertakings will require substantially higher levels of funding if the goal of a scientific base for social work practice is to be achieved.

Clarification of the nature and purpose of evaluation in practice should lead to a moderation of the expectation that practitioners should conduct research as a part of standard practice. Nevertheless, it is reasonable to expect practitioners to evaluate their practice, that is, to assess whether the desired outcome was achieved. To do so, practitioners will need methods and techniques that are suited to their particular practice situation.

Develop Practice-Based Evaluation Techniques

If evaluation is an integral part of practice, then it seems reasonable that the orientation to the development of evaluation methods and techniques should be practice based, rather than research based. That is, instead of starting with a research perspective, complete with research terminology, methods, and techniques, the problem should be approached from the perspective of practice, and the needs and requirements of practice should be addressed. For example, one might ask, How is evaluation currently being carried out in practice? What are the functions of evaluation in practice? What aspects of the evaluation methodology need further development? What are the practical constraints on evaluation in normal practice? How much evaluation is enough? In other words, what is needed is a more ethnographic approach to studying the nature and function of evaluation in normal practice. The intent is to develop an understanding and appreciation of the nature and purpose of evaluation as it is currently done, so that future developments in single-case methodology can build on and enhance current practice, rather than impose unfamiliar and sometimes incompatible methods.

Consistent with this practice-based orientation, evaluation methods and techniques need to be systematically designed and developed along the lines Thomas (1984) suggested for designing interventions. A full exposition of design and development is not possible here, but some particularly important considerations should be highlighted. Design and development would begin with a thorough description and analysis of existing evaluation procedures and an analysis of problems and desired innovations. During the design phase, a range of different methods and procedures would be generated that addresses the requirements for evaluation within the particular practice model. In the development phase, successive iterations and refinements of the evaluation procedure would be tried in practice settings, so the procedure could be refined and made usable. Once an evaluation procedure was fully developed, it then would be formally evaluated to determine its impact on the process and outcomes of practice. Only when an evaluation procedure demonstrated its usefulness and feasibility would it be prepared for diffusion and adoption.

The techniques for carrying out evaluation are likely to be somewhat specific to the practice approach being used and therefore should be designed and developed within the context of the specific practice model. This is a common idea in practice theory. For example, although all practice models require some form of assessment, the purpose, content, and procedures are different for different approaches. Likewise, although all models incorporate interviewing, each approach uses the interview differently and employs different techniques. This is not to say that there are not similarities across approaches in how assessment and interviewing are carried out, but the differences would seem to be important to the success of the practice model. Thus, the "uniformity myth" of single-case evaluation should be abandoned, and practice-specific methods and techniques should be developed.

One possible result of the development of practice-based single-case evaluation is that specific methods and techniques for different practice situations may evolve. For example, in the field of prevention, in which it is not possible to know how the client would have been had there been no intervention, Bloom (1983) suggested that the assessment of change can be done indirectly by comparing the client's functioning during treatment with norms for clients in similar situations. Bloom (1987) later referred to this comparison of the observed outcome with the predicted outcome based on theory as theoretical significance.

A growing body of techniques may be useful for the development of practice-based single-case evaluation. With respect to design, retrospective baselines provide one alternative when preintervention baselines are not possible (Green & Wright, 1979). In other situations, it may be preferable to take a postintervention baseline, that is, to ask the client at the end of treatment to rate his or her functioning before treatment (Howard, 1980). Sometimes useful results can be obtained without a baseline (Broxmeyer, 1978; Thyer, 1986). Thyer and Curtis (1983) proposed a potentially useful alternative called "the repeated pre-post design" in which measures taken immediately before and after intervention sessions are used to assess change during the course of treatment. Still another alternative is the natural multiple baseline design (Hayes, 1985).

Similar progress has been made in the area of assessment in single-case evaluation. Nelsen (1981) and Bloom and Fischer (1982) suggested a broad range of strategies and techniques for measurement, many of which are applicable in normal practice settings. In addition, Hudson (1982) and Corcoran and Fischer (1987) presented many practical scales for use in evaluation.

Although most single-case evaluation techniques are quantitative, a qualitative perspective seems to be useful as well (Ruckdeschel, 1985). Such a perspective places more importance on the context of evaluation and the meanings that clients and practitioners attribute to the outcomes of treatment and to the evaluation process. As one example of a qualitative technique, Reid and Davis (1987) suggested the use of structured recording and the logical analysis of events to assess change in a client. Kazdin (1981) advocated case studies as another qualitative approach to single-case evaluation. With respect to process-outcome questions, Nelsen (1984) noted that the use of intermediate goals is a way to evaluate the process of change.

Ultimately, however, it is not sufficient to talk about evaluation methods and techniques apart from a therapeutic approach and an identified population of clients. The unique requirements of different practice situations require that evaluation methods and techniques be designed and developed specifically for the setting in which they will be used.

Assess the Utility of Single-Case Evaluation

Although single-case evaluation seems to offer promise for more effective and accountable interventions, there is still no evidence other than opinion and testimonials to support this claim. Clearly, such evidence is a weak basis on which to advocate that clinicians should evaluate their practice and may be one reason why many practitioners do not routinely do single-case evaluation. Reports from practitioners that evaluation takes more time than it is worth, does not give them the kind of information they need, or only confirms what they already knew may well be valid. It simply is not known whether single-case evaluation pays off for practitioners or clients.

Hayes, Nelson, and Jarrett (1987) described a functional approach to evaluating the utility of clinical activities, specifically psychological assessment, for treatment. They defined *treatment utility* as the degree to which an activity is shown to contribute to a beneficial outcome of treatment. For example, an assessment procedure has utility if it can be shown that the outcome of treatment was positively influenced by the use of the procedure. Likewise, a single-case evaluation procedure would have treatment utility if it could be shown that the use of the procedure improved the outcomes for the client in some way.

Following Hayes, Nelson, and Jarrett (1987), a variety of questions are relevant for assessing the treatment utility of single-case evaluation. For example, what is the effect of the use of different assessment strategies on the outcome of treatment? What is the effect of the use of assessment data on the outcome? What is the effect of baselining, or taking a retrospective baseline, on the outcome? Do monitoring and graphing the client's functioning during treatment have an impact on the outcome? Do single-case evaluation techniques or methods interact differentially with different client groups, for example, or do children respond differently from adults? Do clients with high cognitive functioning respond differently from low-functioning clients? Do clients with targeted behavioral outcomes respond differently from clients with targeted cognitive or affective outcomes? The answers to these questions would help determine which single-case evaluation techniques are useful and with which clients.

Assessing the treatment utility of single-case evaluation will indicate not only whether such an assessment has a beneficial impact on outcome, but it will improve our understanding of the intervention process itself. For example, if it can be shown that repeated assessment improves outcomes, then one would need to ask how (Hayes, Nelson, & Jarrell, 1987) Is it because practitioners engage in different behaviors (such as more praising), or is it because self-assessment changes the client's awareness or interest in the outcome and thus serves as a reinforcer for change?

It is instructive to note that assessing the treatment utility of single-case evaluation (a functional assessment) is different from assessing its scientific adequacy or rigor (a methodological assessment). For example, procedures that lack scientific rigor may have clinical utility (as clinicians have been known to claim) or, conversely, procedures that have scientific merit may lack clinical utility (as clinicians have also been known to claim). Thus, projective tests may make clinicians more effective in treatment (perhaps because of what the clinicians observed during testing), even though the devices themselves are unreliable. Similarly, single-case evaluation could have a beneficial impact on treatment outcomes even though the actual results of the evaluation are not scientifically valid. Thus, it may be discovered that having clients monitor and graph their behavior enhances the outcomes of treatment even though the procedure itself does not give a valid indication of the outcomes. The point is not that scientific rigor is not needed in single-case evaluation— it certainly is for some purposes—but that treatment utility is a different issue with different requirements.

A thorough consideration of the issues of treatment utility should lead practitioners and researchers to be more specific about just exactly what it is that we hope to accomplish with single-case evaluation. Do we expect evaluation to improve practice? If so, how? Do we expect single-case evaluation to show that our interventions are effective, that is, that we are accountable? Or, do we expect single-case evaluation to provide a scientific base for practice? While all these objectives are good and valid, they are not necessarily compatible with each other, nor does realizing one objective ensure that the others will be met. Being more specific and clear about the objectives we have for single-case evaluation should help us assess its various utilities (treatment, accountability, scientific) more adequately and be more realistic in our claims about its benefits.

FINAL THOUGHTS

This chapter has suggested that single-case evaluation be thought of as a practice process, that evaluation techniques should be systematically designed and developed from a practice perspective, and that the utility of single-case evaluation should be assessed. If these suggestions are followed, some noticeable changes will occur in single-case evaluation techniques. First, more practical and usable evaluation techniques will be developed that fit naturally within normal practice and provide concrete, identifiable benefits for clients and practitioners. Second, evaluation will increasingly be thought of as a practice process and less as a research process or exercise in accountability. Third, single-case evaluation will take on a variety of forms, depending on the populations of clients who are served, the goals of treatment that are targeted, and the methods of practice that are used.

It is also likely that computerized tools, such as a "clinician's assistant," will soon be developed to facilitate and support single-case evaluation. Such a system could be implemented on a small laptop computer and would help the practitioner carry out single-case evaluation. Making use of expert systems technology (Gingerich, 1988; Schuerman, 1987; see also Chapter 4, this volume), the system could advise the practitioner on the setting of realistic goals for treatment and the selection of suitable strategies for assessing the goals. The system could then prompt the practitioner to enter data on the outcomes for a client, graph those data, and assess changes according to clinical or statistical criteria. Although the system would contain quantitative data on outcomes, it might also contain case notes in a structured format like that proposed by Reid and Davis (1987). The system might even advise on the intervention to be used (Goodman, Gingerich, & de Shazer, 1989) and prompt the practitioner to continue, modify, or terminate treatment on the basis of changes in the data. Once data on the outcomes for a large number of clients have been accumulated, metaanalytic techniques (Corcoran, 1985; Gingerich, 1984b) could be used to analyze which interventions seem to work best with which clients. It is not difficult to see how such a system could go a long way toward providing the kind of data management, analysis of change, and reporting needed to implement single-case evaluation in everyday practice.

Considerable progress has been made since single-case evaluation was first advocated two decades ago. Basic knowledge and skills have been gleaned from a variety of professional fields and techniques have been developed, yet many challenges lie ahead. Single-case evaluation is about to leave the security and optimism of its youth, move into new environments, and adapt its theory and methods to be compatible to those new environments. In the process, practice and evaluation are certain to change, and both, it is hoped, will be the better for it!

REFERENCES

Barlow, D. H. (1981). On the relation of clinical research to clinical practice: Current issues, new directions. *Journal of Consulting and Clinical Psychology, 49*, 147–155.

Barlow, D. H., Hayes, S. C., & Nelson, R. O. (1984). *The scientist practitioner: Research and accountability in clinical and educational settings.* New York: Pergamon Press.

Berlin, S. B. (1983). Single-case evaluation: Another version. *Social Work, 19*, 3–11.

Bloom, M. (1983). Single system designs for preventive practitioners. *Journal of Social Service Research, 6*(3/4), 17–28.

Bloom, M. (1987). Theoretical significance. In N. Gottlieb, H. A. Ishisaka, J. Kopp, C. A. Richey, & E. R. Tolson (Eds.), *Perspectives on direct practice evaluation* (pp. 105–121). Seattle: University of Washington School of Social Work.

Bloom, M., & Block, S. R. (1977). Evaluating one's own effectiveness and efficiency. *Social Work, 22*, 130–136.

Bloom, M., & Fischer, J. (1982). *Evaluating practice: Guidelines for the accountable professional.* Englewood Cliffs, NJ: Prentice-Hall.

Blythe, B. J., & Briar, S. (1985). Developing empirically based models of practice. *Social Work, 30*, 483–488.

Briar, S. (1977). Incorporating research into education for clinical practice in social work: Toward a clinical science in social work. In A. Rubin & A. Rosenblatt (Eds.), *Sourcebook on research utilization* (pp. 132–140). New York: Council on Social Work Education.

Broxmeyer, N. (1978). Practitioner-research in treating a borderline child. *Social Work Research & Abstracts, 14*, 5–10.

Conte, J. R., & Levy, R. L. (1980). Problems and issues in implementing the clinical-research model of practice in educational and clinical settings. *Journal of Education for Social Work, 16*, 60–66.

Corcoran, K. J. (1985). Aggregating the idiographic data of single-subject research. *Social Work Research & Abstracts, 21*, 9–12.

Corcoran, K. J., & Fischer, J. (1987). *Measures for clinical practice: A sourcebook.* New York: Free Press.

Council on Social Work Education. (1988). *Handbook of accreditation standards and procedures.* Washington, DC: Author.

Dean, R., & Reinherz, H. (1986). Psychodynamic practice and single system design: The odd couple. *Journal of Social Work Education, 22,* 71–81.

Dolan, M. M., & Vourlekis, M. M. (1983). A field project: Single-subject design in a public social service agency. *Journal of Social Service Research, 6,* 29–43.

Eldridge, W. D. (1983). Conceptualizing self-evaluation of clinical practice. *Social Work, 28,* 57–61.

Fischer, J. (1973). Is casework effective? A review. *Social Work, 18,* 5–20.

Fischer, J. (1978). *Effective casework practice: An eclectic approach.* New York: McGraw-Hill.

Gambrill, E. D. (1983). *Casework: A competency-based approach.* Englewood Cliffs, NJ: Prentice-Hall.

Gambrill, E. D., & Barth, R. P. (1980). Single-case study designs revisited. *Social Work Research & Abstracts, 16,* 15–20.

Gingerich, W. J. (1979). Procedure for evaluating clinical practice. *Health and Social Work, 4,* 104–130.

Gingerich, W. J. (1984a). Generalizing single-case evaluation from classroom to practice. *Journal of Education for Social Work, 20,* 74–82.

Gingerich, W. J. (1984b). Meta-analysis of applied time-series data. *Journal of Applied Behavioral Science, 20,* 71–79.

Gingerich, W. J. (1988). *Expert systems and their potential uses in social work.* Paper presented at the Annual Program Meeting, Council of Social Work Education, Atlanta, GA.

Goodman, H., Gingerich, W. J., & de Shazer, S. (1989). BRIEFER: An expert system for clinical practice. *Computers in Human Services, 5,* 53–68.

Green, G. R., Jr., & Wright, J. E. (1979). The retrospective approach to collecting baseline data. *Social Work Research & Abstracts, 15,* 25–30.

Hayes, S. C. (1985). Natural multiple baselines across persons: A reply to Harris and Jenson. *Behavioral Assessment, 7,* 129–132.

Hayes, S. C., Nelson, R. O., & Jarrett, R. B. (1987). *The treatment utility of assessment.* Ann Arbor: Institute for Social Research, University of Michigan.

Hollis, F. (1972). *Casework: A psychosocial therapy* (2nd ed.). New York: Random House.

Howard, G. S. (1980). Response-shift bias: A problem in evaluating interventions with pre/post self-reports. *Evaluation Review, 4,* 93–106.

Howe, G. S. (1974). Casework self-evaluation: A single subject approach. *Social Service Review, 48,* 1–24.

Hudson, W. W. (1982). *The clinical measurement package.* Homewood, IL: Dorsey Press.

Hudson, W. W. (1987). Future directions in clinical evaluation. In N. Gottlieb, H. A. Ishisaka, J. Kopp, C. A. Richey, & E. R. Tolson (Eds.), *Perspectives on direct practice evaluation* (pp. 37–54). Seattle: University of Washington School of Social Work.

Ivanoff, A., Blythe, B. J., & Briar, S. (1987). The empirical clinical practice debate. *Social Casework, 65,* 290–298.

Jayaratne, S. (1977). Single-subject and group designs in treatment evaluation. *Social Work Research & Abstracts, 13,* 35–42.

Jayaratne, S., & Levy, R. (1979). *Empirical clinical practice.* New York: Columbia University Press.

Kazdin, A. E. (1981). Drawing valid inferences from case studies. *Journal of Consulting and Clinical Psychology, 49,* 183–192.

Levy, R. L. (1981). On the nature of the clinical-research gap: The problems with some solutions. *Behavioral Assessment, 3,* 235–242.

Mutschler, E. (1984). Evaluating practice: A study of research utilization by practitioners. *Social Work, 29,* 332–337.

Nelsen, J. C. (1978). Use of communication theory in single-subject research. *Social Work Research & Abstracts, 14,* 12–19.

Nelsen, J. C. (1981). Issues in single-subject research for behaviorists. *Social Work Research & Abstracts, 17,* 31–37.

Nelsen, J. C. (1984). Intermediate treatment goals as variables in single-case research. *Social Work Research & Abstracts, 20,* 3–10.

Nuehring, E. M., & Pascone, A. B. (1986). Single-subject evaluation: A tool for quality assurance. *Social Work, 31,* 359–365.

Reid, W. J. (1978). *The task-centered system.* New York: Columbia University Press.

Reid, W. J., & Davis, I. P. (1987). Qualitative methods in single-case research. In N. Gottlieb, H. A. Ishisaka, J. Kopp, C. A. Richey, & E. R. Tolson (Eds.), *Perspectives on direct practice evaluation* (pp. 56–74). Seattle: University of Washington School of Social Work.

Reid, W. J., & Hanrahan, P. (1982). Recent evaluations of social work: Grounds for optimism. *Social Work, 27,* 328–340.

Richey, C. A., Blythe, B. J., & Berlin, S. B. (1987). Do social workers evaluate their practice? *Social Work Research & Abstracts, 23,* 14–20.

Robinson, E. A. R., Bronson, D., & Blythe, B. J. (1988). An analysis of the implementation of single-case evaluation by practitioners. *Social Service Review, 62,* 285–301.

Rubin, A. (1985). Practice effectiveness: More grounds for optimism. *Social Work, 30,* 469–476.

Ruckdeschel, R. A. (1985). Qualitative research as a perspective. *Social Work Research & Abstracts, 21,* 17–21.

Ruckdeschel, R. A., & Farris, B. E. (1981). Assessing practice: A critical look at the single-case design. *Social Casework, 62,* 413–419.

Saleebey, D. (1979). The tension between research and practice: Assumptions of the experimental paradigm. *Clinical Social Work Journal, 7,* 267–284.

Schuerman, J. R. (1987). Expert consulting systems to social welfare. *Social Work Research & Abstracts, 23,* 14–18.

Sodervick, G. J. (1975). *The application of a single-subject design in a psychosocial approach to casework treatment.* Unpublished doctoral dissertation, Smith College, Northampton, MA.

Stuart, R. B. (1977). Research in social work: Social casework and social group work. In A. Minahan (Ed.-in-Chief), *Encyclopedia of Social Work* (17th ed., pp. 1106–1122). New York: National Association of Social Workers.

Swan, G. E., & MacDonald, M. L. (1978). Behavior therapy in practice: A national survey of behavior therapists. *Behavior Therapy, 9*, 799–807.

Thomas, E. J. (1975). Uses of research methods in interpersonal practice. In N. A. Polansky (Ed.), *Social work research: Methods for the helping professions* (pp. 254–284). Chicago: University of Chicago Press.

Thomas, E. J. (1978a). Generating innovation in social work: The paradigm of developmental research. *Journal of Social Service Research, 2*(1), 95–116.

Thomas, E. J. (1978b). Research and service in single-case experimentation: Conflicts and choices. *Social Work Research & Abstracts, 14*, 20–31.

Thomas, E. J. (1984). *Designing interventions for the helping professions.* Beverly Hills, CA: Sage Publications.

Thyer, B. A. (1986). Single-subject designs in clinical social work: A practitioner's perspective. In H. R. Johnson & J. E. Tropman (Eds.), *Social work policy and practice: A knowledge-driven approach* (pp. 292–309). Ann Arbor: University of Michigan School of Social Work.

Thyer, B. A., & Curtis, G. C. (1983). The repeated pre test-post test single-subject experiment: A new design for empirical clinical practice. *Journal of Behavior Therapy & Experimental Psychiatry, 14*, 311–315.

Wade, T. C., Baker, T. B., & Hartmann, D. P. (1979). Behavior therapists' self-reported views and practices. *Behavior Therapist, 2*, 3–6.

Wood, K. (1978). Casework effectiveness: A new look at the research evidence. *Social Work, 23*, 437–458.

Commentary

Beyond Regret: Single-Case Evaluations and Their Place in Social Work Education and Practice

Helen Reinherz

Chapter 2 illustrates the distance that the social work profession has traveled and the balanced view it has achieved in assessing the place of single case evaluation among the available strategies of social work research (Reinherz, Regan, & Anastas, 1983). In that chapter, Gingerich no longer laments that practitioners who have been trained in the method do not, cannot, or will not use single-case evaluation techniques in their daily practice (see also Gingerich, 1984; Richey, Blythe, & Berlin, 1987). He has laid that issue to rest and has moved forward to consider its practical utility as a tool for specific practice contexts.

Moving forward, Gingerich has suggested that we researchers look carefully "in vivo" in specific fields of practice to see *what modifications* need to be made to single-case design to enable practitioners to carry out useful evaluations molded by the need of the clientele and setting, rather than by "scientific rigor." Such thinking moves researchers well beyond the repetitive debates about whether single-case design is research or practice and whether its use constitutes a disservice to one or both. This is a much-needed correction to the mystique that single-case evaluation is a universal panacea for demonstrating the effectiveness of practice or a simplistic solution to a complex problem that is incapable of capturing the nuances of treatment.

There are three interesting issues raised by the chapter that provide opportunity for further discussion and amplification, however. They are (1) furthering the contributions that single-case evaluation can make in the training and educational process in social work, (2) differentiating single-case evaluation techniques from specific practice theories, and (3) clarifying the legitimate role of research and evaluation for practice.

SINGLE-CASE EVALUATION AS A TEACHING TOOL

Others can address the utility of the concurrent teaching of behaviorally oriented social work with single-case evaluations. The experience at Simmons College School of Social Work has convinced this author and some of her colleagues that the teaching of the single-system design method has enhanced the clinical learning of psychodynamically trained social work students in a seminar on the use of single-system designs with individual, family, or group cases (Dean & Reinherz, 1986). In their evaluations of the course, the students have attested to the importance of the process, particularly the careful specification of goals, the challenge of creating measurements (however imperfect) of interventions and outcomes, and the capacity to examine their work from many vantage points. The process of measurement they have used has included content analyses of audiotapes, standardized measures, self-anchored scales, and diaries. Visual documentation of the clinical process, shared with clients at times, has allowed the students to monitor the process and progress of cases.

Particularly in the context of psychodynamic practice, there were concerns about the feasibility of the single-system "method" and its acceptability to other faculty members, students, clients, and the traditional social work community in greater Boston in which the students' training took place. The process has been instructive in that all the clients have agreed to participate and many clients have expressed positive opinions (Campbell, 1988). Other faculty members, especially in the field, have been interested and helpful. The personnel of agencies first reacted to presentations by students and teachers by questioning the obtrusiveness of the measures and the appropriateness of using techniques that require the disclosure to clients of their participation in "research." However, many of these concerns have been rapidly resolved. The techniques practiced in these seminars have been flexible in that both qualitative and quantitative techniques have been taught (Reid & Davis, 1987).

A formal evaluation of the seven-year program is now being conducted. However, it can be said that the students' progress in the course work, as noted by the teachers of clinical methods, has been substantial. Several teachers have incorporated examples of single-case evaluation into their syllabi. Currently, all first-year courses on clinical methods introduce the single-case evaluation method.

Beyond providing opportunities for clinical students, who may often think in global terms, to develop more appropriate, often intermediate or instrumental goals (Nelsen, 1984), there are additional advantages to clinical work of the participation in single-case evaluations. For example, students have highlighted the capacity to follow in detail their and their colleagues' cases over two semesters. Learning is thus increased tenfold for each participant in the seminar.

At Simmons College, the hope is not so much that all the students will continue to perform the single-systems techniques with every client in their practice, but that the students will continue to use the processes they learned in the course. Thus, it is hoped that in their subsequent practice, the students will continue to delineate goals, select appropriate interventions to achieve their goals, and continue to monitor the clients' progress and their own in implementing the interventions.

PRACTICE AND RESEARCH METHODOLOGY

It is useful to be able to call on many methods in the pursuit of the goals of research. Students or practitioners who do single-case evaluations have many options from among which to choose in the gathering of data. The strongest evidence always comes from multiple strategies. One of the earliest published examples of the use of the single-system method with a nonbehavioral orientation was by Broxmeyer (1978). Although the theoretical base was psychodynamic, measurement consisted of specifying behaviors, actions, and expressed feelings. Thus, in a psychodynamically based treatment situation, the counting of specific acts and behaviors; content analyses of expressions of affect and of clinical manifestations, such as a dying patient's "letting go" or an older adolescent's growing assertiveness; and developing sense of individual "identity" may be studied within a specific case (Dean & Reinherz, 1986). It is the belief of the faculty members who have taught the seminar on single-systems methods at Simmons College that both quantitative and qualitative measurement techniques can be applied in a nonbehavioral framework.

As Gingerich said so well, adaptations can be made for the needs of different agencies and clients. For example, a child's progress in learning self-control in the classroom and at home can be measured concretely by the number of "time-outs" in the class, by a behavioral scale filled out by the teacher and parent, and by the number of class assignments the child completes, as well as by the child's increased verbalization in interviews and growing oral expression of anger. Other measures, both qualitative and quantitative, can be developed for family therapy groups, for parents of hospitalized patients, for alcoholics, and for adolescents. Hence, part of the creativity of the method is the ability to select the most appropriate measurement tools (Bloom & Fischer, 1982).

DOES PRACTICE NEED RESEARCH?

Finally, on one issue, this author disagrees with Gingerich. Gingerich stated in Chapter 2 that "the practice of social work requires evaluation, but not research." This statement, it seems, was an overstatement of the obvious to make a point about the immediate priority to the profession of providing evidence of *benefit*—of the *progress* of treatment. It is true that much social work practice is based on "practice wisdom," not the results of empirical research. Nevertheless, although evaluation is needed, so is research. Practitioners do not have to be burdened with the mandate to produce the major or basic research for the profession. However, they must be helped to use new information generated through developmental research by the research centers and practitioner-researchers in the profession. Research is disseminated to practitioners in many ways, including continuing education classes, the comments of experts, and reading. Knowledge building for the use of the profession and for the enhancement of interventions must continue. Therefore, Gingerich's suggestion about creating more research centers for the scientific study of practice and the provision of ample funds for them should be adopted.

REFERENCES

Bloom, M., & Fischer, J. (1982). *Evaluating practice: Guidelines for the accountable professional.* Englewood Cliffs, NJ: Prentice-Hall.

Broxmeyer, N. (1978). Practitioner-research in treating a borderline child. *Social Work Research & Abstracts, 14,* 5–10.

Campbell, J. A. (1988). Client acceptance of single-system evaluation procedures. *Social Work Research & Abstracts, 24,* 21–22.

Dean, R., & Reinherz, H. (1986). Psychodynamic practice and single system design: The odd couple. *Journal of Social Work Education, 22,* 71–81.

Gingerich, W. J. (1984). Generalizing single-case evaluation from classroom to practice. *Journal of Education for Social Work, 20,* 74–82.

Nelsen, J. C. (1984). Intermediate treatment goals as variables in single-case research. *Social Work Research & Abstracts, 20,* 3–10.

Reid, W. J., & Davis, I. P. (1987). Qualitative methods in single-case research. In N. Gottlieb, H. A. Ishisaka, J. Kopp, C. A. Richey, & E. R. Tolson (Eds.), *Perspectives on direct practice evaluation* (pp. 56–74). Seattle: University of Washington School of Social Work.

Reinherz, H., Regan, J. M., & Anastas, J. W. (1983). A research curriculum for future clinicians: A multimodel strategy. *Journal of Education for Social Work, 19,* 35–41.

Richey, C. A., Blythe, B. J., & Berlin, S. B. (1987). Do social workers evaluate their practice? *Social Work Research & Abstracts, 23,* 14–20.

Commentary

Improving the Fit between Single-Subject Designs and Practice

Betty J. Blythe

In clarifying the goals and objectives of single-case evaluation, Gingerich observed that it is unreasonable to expect practitioners to conduct research as part of their standard practice (that is, to develop scientific knowledge about practice), but that it is reasonable to expect that they evaluate their practice (that is, assess whether the desired outcome was achieved). Initially, this author thought that although this distinction is important, it is not new. In checking the literature, however, she found that the distinction between the goals of research and evaluation has been clarified only in the past few years (see, for example, Ivanoff, Blythe, & Briar, 1987). What was even more surprising was that, until recently, the language used to describe single-case evaluation emphasized the goal of research and focused on the methodology of single-subject design (for examples, see Bloom, 1983; Levy, 1981) and the generation of research findings by practitioners (Nelsen, 1981). Gradually, terms like "single-case evaluation" (Gingerich, 1984), "empirically based practice" (Siegel, 1985), and "practice evaluation" (Richey, Blythe, & Berlin, 1987), have come to be used more frequently, but single-subject design methods are still used to define these terms and to describe the goal as the integration of research and practice.

Since the stated goal of single-case evaluation has shifted somewhat, but there is some evidence of a continuing emphasis on research and the jargon used to describe single-case evaluation sometimes reflects an apparently unconscious research agenda, it may be helpful to think carefully about how single-case evaluation is described. When this author talks to students or practitioners about evaluating practice, she usually says that it involves specifying goals for clients; developing ways of measuring these goals; routinely applying these measurement strategies to determine if clients are attaining the goals; and then using this information to decide whether to continue, discontinue, or revise the intervention plan. The goal or purpose is to monitor the client's progress

toward the attainment of goals (goals can involve prevention, maintenance, or change) and to adjust the intervention plan accordingly.

As Gingerich noted, many social work scholars have been advocating
the use of this method for nearly two decades with limited success in
increasing its actual use to evaluate practice. Perhaps too much effort has
been directed toward an inappropriate goal for all practitioners—the
routine generation of scientific information about social work interventions while conducting daily practice. Many potential "converts" may
have been lost because of the requirement that only rigorous single-case
studies were acceptable. Or many practitioners may not have been
interested in developing scientific knowledge, but would have been
motivated to learn how to monitor their work with clients. As S. Briar
(personal communication, September 1, 1981) noted, just getting practitioners to specify goals carefully and to monitor the attainment of goals
would be a substantial improvement in practice, regardless of whether
the practitioners conducted single-subject research.

In defining the purposes of evaluation, Gingerich stated that
"evaluation also includes an implicit assessment of change, that is,
whether the client's functioning is different from what it would have
been had there been no intervention." To this author, the introduction
of this concept is akin to trying to establish a causal connection between
an intervention and an outcome. Rather, she believes that practitioners
should be concerned with change in a client in relation to the client's
previous functioning and to the expressed goals of treatment. Although
this statement may seem to be splitting hairs, it is necessary to think
carefully not only about the purpose of evaluation, but about how that
purpose is achieved.

Whatever words are enlisted to describe single-case evaluation and its
purpose, much less emphasis should be placed on single-subject designs as
crucial tools. When working with a client or client unit, a particular design
evolves largely according to the treatment plan. Hence, the designs are
really of secondary importance. In fact, spending so much time talking
about single-subject designs and then discovering that less elaborate designs are more applicable to practice may have slowed the field down. It was
often unrealistic to suggest to students and practitioners that they select a
design at the beginning of their work with a new client or client group, and
their attempt to do so led them to try to force their intervention plan to
conform to the design. In such cases, the criticism that single-case evaluation interferes with practice is justified. Allowing the design to evolve as the
treatment phases change (such as from assessment [baseline] to the first
intervention or from one intervention strategy to another) seems to make
more sense, fit better with routine social work practice, and be more

acceptable to most practitioners. In short, it was not completely accurate to say that practitioners were fortunate to have a research tool, single-subject methodology, that allowed them to evaluate practice. With the benefit of hindsight, one can now say that the field was fortunate to have the concept of the continual and routine monitoring of a client's progress toward reaching the goals of treatment.

The research tools that are important or helpful in getting practitioners to monitor clients' attainment of goals are measurement tools rather than the methodology of single-subject design (Blythe & Tripodi, 1989). Such concepts as reliability and validity, for example, help practitioners assess clients' presenting problems, specify goals, and develop appropriate ways of measuring the attainment of goals. Concepts and principles of measurement can aid other areas of practice as well, such as monitoring the implementation of interventions. But these tools need to be discussed within the framework of practice if they are to help practitioners.

Gingerich argued that the profession needs to develop practice-based evaluation techniques, rather than rely on ones that are research based, but he did not describe what practice-based single-case evaluation would entail, who would carry out this monumental task, and who would fund it. Perhaps the answer lies in something as simple as getting practitioners more involved in developing or selecting these techniques. For a long time, researchers and academicians have been prescribing what practitioners should do. It is no surprise, then, that they have emphasized scientific knowledge in talking about the purpose of single-case evaluation and in identifying appropriate tools.

One example of a practice-based single-case evaluation tool that Gingerich presented for the field of prevention is comparing a client's functioning during treatment with norms for clients in similar situations to assess change in a client in contrast to "how the client would have been had there been no intervention." The use of norms would seem to make the task more complicated than it need be. Rather, the client's functioning should be compared to the goal established for the client. Whether one is trying to prevent child abuse or marital conflict or keep such conditions as alcoholism or schizophrenia in remission, one can define the presence or absence of these problems and identify suitable goals for clients without looking at norms. In fact, the norms probably will not fit the client or may not be available. It seems simpler and better to develop client-specific goals, with input from the client and significant others when appropriate, and then to assess the client's functioning in reference to these goals.

Echoing a recommendation by Levy (1987), Gingerich's suggestions about examining the treatment utility of practice evaluation are interesting, and it would be helpful to have the answers to these questions. It is hoped that practitioners will be involved in such studies, if for no other reason than to guard against most researchers' tendencies to ask esoteric questions that examine relationships between variables and that sometimes cloud the primary question of concern: "Is evaluating practice useful to practitioners?"

REFERENCES

Bloom, M. (1983). Single system designs for preventive practitioners. *Journal of Social Service Research, 6*(3/4), 17–28.

Blythe, B. J., & Tripodi, T. (1989). *Measurement in direct social work practice: Guidelines for practitioners.* Newbury Park, CA: Sage Publications.

Gingerich, W. J. (1984). Generalizing single-case evaluation from classroom to practice. *Journal of Education for Social Work, 20,* 74–82.

Ivanoff, A., Blythe, B. J., & Briar, S. (1987). The empirical clinical practice debate. *Social Casework, 65,* 290–298.

Levy, R. L. (1981). On the nature of the clinical-research gap: The problems with some solutions. *Behavioral Assessment, 3,* 235–242.

Levy, R. L. (1987). Single subject research designs. In A. Minahan (Ed.-in-chief), *Encyclopedia of social work* (pp. 588–593). Silver Spring, MD: National Association of Social Workers.

Nelsen, J. C. (1981). Issues in single-subject research for nonbehaviorists. *Social Work Research & Abstracts, 17,* 31–37.

Richey, C. A., Blythe, B. J., & Berlin, S. B. (1987). Do social workers evaluate their practice? *Social Work Research & Abstracts, 23,* 14–20.

Siegel, D. H. (1985). Effective teaching of empirically based practice. *Social Work Research & Abstracts, 21,* 40–48.

Synthesis

Single-System Research Designs in Social Work Practice

Bruce A. Thyer

Chapter 2 by Gingerich and the reactions to it by Reinherz and by Blythe clearly indicate that the use of single-system designs (SSDs) has truly come of age in social work practice. In the articles, two respected practitioner-researchers from a broadly defined "empiricist" stance and a well-known social scientist who has studied psychodynamic practice have agreed on a number of significant themes. Among these themes are the following:

Foremost is the consensus that SSDs *are* a valuable tool to assist social workers in monitoring the effectiveness of their practice. Reinherz clearly demonstrated that the use of SSDs is not only compatible with, but also may augment, the teaching of psychodynamic therapy. By using SSDs, psychodynamic therapists may obtain data regarding the efficacy of social work services and enhance their clinical assessment and intervention skills (Dean & Reinherz, 1986; see also Broxmeyer, 1978; Hansen & Shireman, 1986). It has been demonstrated as well that SSDs may be employed successfully by practitioners from a variety of theoretical orientations, including task-centered practice (Tolson, 1977), communication theory (Nelsen, 1978), strategic therapy (Szykula & Morris, 1986), paradoxical treatment (Kolko & Milan, 1983), and transactional analysis (Erskine, Clinton, & Olmstead, 1975). Such examples should lay to rest the notion that SSDs may be incorporated successfully only into behavior analysis and therapy.

The authors all note the important distinction to be made regarding the purposes of SSDs. In clinical settings, it is clearly far more practical to use such designs to answer the question, Did the client/system improve over time? (these answers constitute the process of evaluating practice) than to implement designs that are capable of addressing the question, Did the client/system improve *because of social work treatment?* This latter endeavor is more properly referred to as "practice experimentation," in which sufficient controls are built into the design to permit reasonably high internal validity. Such ambitious endeavors usually require designs involving multiple baselines or withdrawal phases and are too intrusive to be routinely used in clinical settings, as Thomas (1978) pointed out.

There is a consensus that the exigencies of practice should direct the use of SSDs and that the various requirements of some designs (for instance, lengthy baselines, removal phases, and multiple baselines) should not dictate the course of treatment and clinical decision making. Toward this end, it was noted that various innovative designs may be utilized in evaluating practice less intrusively and more flexibly and still permit the practitioner to determine if clinical improvements are occurring. One example is the B design, in which the systematic measurement of a client's problems are begun at the same time as formal treatment, so that a baseline phase is avoided. Another example is the A-B design that includes a retrospective baseline, information for which is obtained from a client's reports or archival data, and avoids the delays in starting treatment associated with baseline phases. The simple A-B design, although low in internal validity (one cannot conclude with certainty that treatment was the agent responsible for clinical improvements), permits one to answer the relatively simpler question, Did the client improve during the course of treatment? The A-X design is probably the most realistic approach, with X representing multiple interventions applied over the course of treatment. Other examples of practical SSDs that are helpful in ascertaining change in a client are the repeated pretest-posttest design (Thyer & Curtis, 1983), probe designs (Curtis & Thyer, 1983), and natural multiple baseline designs (Hayes, 1985).

Among the many areas that require further development is the major issue of treatment utility—the empirical demonstration that practitioners who routinely use such designs serve their clients better (or more effectively or efficiently) than do those who do not use them. It is now well recognized that students cannot be trained to use SSDs and expected to apply them routinely in practicum or postgraduate practice if the social work agencies do not expect or support such use or if the other staff members in agencies are not familiar with such designs or do not encourage the new graduates to apply them.

Advocates of SSDs need not be unduly defensive about the lack of data on the treatment utility of these designs or the data regarding the relatively poor generalization and maintenance of practice-evaluation skills after graduation. The technology of such designs is relatively new, and the passage of time and the conduct of the relevant studies will resolve the questions about treatment utility. An empirical analysis of the organizational and staff contingencies that support or discourage the routine use of SSDs in agency-based practice will uncover ways of promoting their

application. Campbell's (1988) study clearly demonstrated that the practices associated with SSDs (such as baselining, the operational measurement of a client's problems, repeated assessments, and removal phases)
have been accepted by mental health clients far more often than a reliance
on practitioners' opinions alone. Furthermore, Campbell's conclusion (p.
22) that "concern over client reactions to the use of single-system evaluation procedures does not appear to be a valid reason for not using them"
mitigates one type of criticism of the use of SSDs.

It should be noted that social work education and treatment are
replete with conventionally accepted practices that lack treatment utility; the use of process recordings, psychosocial histories, and ego
assessments are but a few examples. If SSDs are criticized because there
are no data on their treatment utility, it seems appropriate to direct such
criticisms to these older, more established practices. Application of the
two-edged sword of considerations of treatment utility may prove
uncomfortable to the wielder of the blade. Likewise, there are little data
to show that students make much use after graduation of other subjects
they have been taught (nomothetic research, human behavior, or social
policy, for example), which again counters somewhat the extensive
literature on the lack of employment of the techniques of SSDs in
practice. Although it is not a satisfactory defense for continuing to teach
SSDs in schools of social work, it will suffice until practitioner-researchers, such as Gingerich, Blythe, and Reinherz, provide the relevant
empirical data.

Finally, it should be noted that from the beginning of professional
social work, there were advocates of an empiricist approach, which is
congruent with the contemporary application of SSDs and their related
practices, including the operational description of clients' problems, the
repeated assessment of these problems over time, and the reliance on
information provided by individual clients, not the aggregated data of
faceless groups. Consider the following quotations from Richmond (1917),
the founder of social casework: "Special efforts should be made to
ascertain whether abnormal manifestations are *increasing* or *decreasing* in
number and intensity, as these often have a practical bearing on the
management of the case" (p. 435). "To say that we think our client is
mentally deranged is futile; to state the observations that have created this
impression is a possible help" (p. 335). "In work with individuals, averages mean very little" (p. 163).

SSDs are clearly congruent with both historical and contemporary
professional standards of practice and ethics. Their expanded employment
may result in the circumstance envisioned by Richmond in 1917: "Good
work creates a demand for more work of the same grade, thus exerting an

influence which tends, as it spreads, to change for the better the conditions under which social work is done" (p. 362).

REFERENCES

Broxmeyer, N. (1978). Practitioner-research in treating a borderline child. *Social Work Research & Abstracts, 14*(4), 5–10.

Campbell, J. A. (1988). Client acceptance of single-system evaluation procedures. *Social Work Research & Abstracts, 24*(2), 21–22.

Curtis, G. C., & Thyer, B. J. (1983). Fainting on exposure to phobic stimuli. *American Journal of Psychiatry, 140,* 771–774.

Dean, R., & Reinherz, H. (1986). Psychodynamic practice and single system design: The odd couple. *Journal of Social Work Education, 22,* 71–81.

Erskine, R. G., Clinton, L., & Olmstead, A. E. (1975). Graphs as measures of care. *Transactional Analysis Journal, 5,* 255.

Hansen, L. B., & Shireman, J. F. (1986). The process of emotional divorce: Examination of theory. *Social Casework, 67,* 323–331.

Hayes, S. C. (1985). Natural multiple baselines across persons: A reply to Harris and Jenson. *Behavioral Assessment, 7,* 129–132.

Kolko, D. J., & Milan, M. A. (1983). Reframing and paradoxical intention to overcome "resistance" in the treatment of delinquent youths: A multiple baseline analysis. *Journal of Consulting and Clinical Psychology, 51,* 655–660.

Nelsen, J. C. (1978). Use of communication theory in single-subject research. *Social Work Research & Abstracts, 14,* 12–19.

Richmond, M. E. (1917). *Social diagnosis.* New York: Russell Sage Foundation.

Szykula, S. A., & Morris, S. B. (1986). Strategic therapy with children: Single-case study demonstrations. *Psychotherapy, 23,* 174–180.

Thomas, E. J. (1978). Research and service in single-case experimentation: Conflicts and choices. *Social Work Research & Abstracts, 14*(4), 20–31.

Thyer, B. A., & Curtis, G. C. (1983). The repeated pre test-post test single-subject experiment: A new design for empirical clinical practice. *Journal of Behavior Therapy & Experimental Psychiatry, 14,* 311–315.

Tolson, E. (1977). Alleviating marital communication problems. In W. J. Reid & L. Epstein (Eds.), *Task-centered practice* (pp. 100–112). New York: Columbia University Press.

Chapter 3

Single-Case Research and Traditional Practice: Issues and Possibilities

Judith C. Nelsen

Doing a single-case study does not require major modifications in some practitioners' usual ways of working with clients. In behavioral, cognitive-behavioral, and task-centered treatment, practitioners and clients generally identify a limited number of specific target problems that are observable, at least to the clients. They most often work toward change in one of these problems at a time. The idea of regularly monitoring change is so built into these models that asking clients to participate in measurement or having a second party observe a client's behavior at times does not seem out of line.

"Traditional" practitioners use any of a number of other practice models, including the psychodynamic psychosocial model; the problem-solving approach; various couple and family treatment models, such as communications, structural, or systemic; or a variety of group-practice approaches. Even many generalist and eclectic practitioners use an amalgam of these approaches. Clearly defined case goals are seen as desirable in such models, but quite a few interrelated goals may be set. Several goals may be worked on at the same time, and work on any goal may be intermittent. The requirement of single-case designs that the practitioner intervene to try to help the client achieve measurable change in one target area at a time is not easily compatible with these ways of working. In traditional practice, the goals that are set should be observable enough that the practitioner, the client, or a third party can recognize whether they are being achieved, else how could any judgments be made of the client's progress or lack of progress? But in arranging to have a client take objective measurements or someone else observe a client, the traditional practitioner who attempts to do single-case research may also encounter problems.

Nevertheless, on the basis of experience with teaching and doing single-case research, this author believes that traditional practitioners who make the effort can learn much that is useful to their clinical work and can give much back to the field. Their efforts also tend to heal the schism that is sometimes felt between behavioral or task-centered practitioners and others by making traditional practice more empirically based and accountable.

This chapter examines three tasks with which traditional practitioners tend to have trouble when they do single-case research: deciding what problem to measure at what point in a case, facilitating the carrying out of measurements, and having one family member observe another to monitor change or as a reliability check. In each area, common difficulties are identified and possible solutions are presented. Also examined are ways in which the struggle with these issues can strengthen the practitioner's work with clients, provide opportunities for unique contributions to the profession's knowledge base, or both.

DECIDING WHAT TO MEASURE

Picture an average traditional practitioner, who uses the psychosocial model to treat individual clients or the structural model to treat families. Seek to make this person identify what changes he or she expects to see in a given case, that is, to spell out specific goals for this client or client system. Part of the response should duplicate what a behavioral or task-centered practitioner would say: The client's presenting problems should be ameliorated to the degree possible. However, the traditional practitioner often does not expect to work on these problems for a while or may plan never to work on them directly. For example, in a psychosocial case, the client's presenting problem may be an excessive amount of anxiety. The practitioner, believing the client is anxious because of too high expectations of himself or herself, may suggest working on the goal of lowering the client's self-expectations with the hope that if it is achieved, the client will be less anxious. In a structural case, the child's misbehavior that brought the family into treatment may never be directly worked on. But correcting the parents' faulty alliance may be an important goal if the practitioner thinks the child's behavior is a response to it. Elsewhere (Nelsen, 1984), this author labeled as "instrumental" those treatment goals, such as the client's lowered self-expectations or the parents' alliance, that are expected to lead toward the "final" goal: to resolve the clients' presenting problems. In a different traditional case, a practitioner's first goal may be simply to get a resistant teenager to come in regularly for sessions. Such a goal, representing an apparently necessary condition simply for work to proceed, can be called "facilitative." Traditional practice models often rely on practitioners helping clients achieve a whole series of facilitative and instrumental goals to reach the final goals (positive changes in presenting problems) the clients ultimately seek.

That work may be directed toward any of these different types of goals, and the presumed interrelatedness of the goals need not pose problems for the traditional practitioner who is planning to do single-case research. There can even be some benefits. The practitioner's thinking about the network of goals in a case could be a valuable exercise. Progress toward any final, instrumental, or facilitative goal could be measured, the latter types perhaps even more easily if the final goals are global or long term. Labeling the variable to be measured a "change goal" or "change target," rather than a "target problem," as is usual in single-case research on behavioral practice (Bloom & Fischer, 1982), allows practitioners and clients to maintain a positive focus on what is to be achieved, rather than a negative focus on what is wrong. Finally, a possibility allowed by this conceptual scheme is that the goal sought may involve change in someone or something other than the primary client. For example, if a boy's troubles in school are apparently compounded by a teacher's scapegoating him, an instrumental goal in the case and change target for the research may be to change the *teacher's* behavior. Such an option frees one from a "blame the client" mentality with which practice researchers have been charged (Kagle & Cowger, 1984).

One clear negative potential does exist. Those who measure clients' or others' progress toward instrumental or facilitative goals may not bother to check whether the final case goals that are supposed to follow from them have ever been reached. Of course, ethically, all practitioners should be accountable for clients' final goals being met, whether or not they are doing single-case research. Ironically, however, this negative potential also suggests an important contribution that traditional practitioners can make to social work's knowledge base. In a single-case project, the traditional practitioner can often look at whether given interventions lead to the achievement of a given instrumental goal *and* whether achievement of this instrumental goal is followed by improvement in a presenting problem. A client's progress toward a facilitative goal should also represent the achievement of some readiness for other changes, the occurrence or nonoccurrence of which can then be monitored.

The point about instrumental goals and their connections to final goals may be illustrated with a student's multiple baseline study. In two cases, the student is intervening to try to help a mother and her children express feelings, anger particularly, about the parents' recent divorce. The student is keeping track of the family members' progress toward expressing these feelings in the family sessions (an instrumental goal). She is also arranging that someone monitor the child's acting-out behavior, which was, in both cases, the reason why the family sought help. If this study establishes both sets of connections (interventions followed by movement toward the instrumental goal, followed by movement toward the final goal), an important piece of traditional practice theory will have been empirically validated. Most traditional practice models desperately need such empirical testing of their practice assumptions that are, by and large, commonly accepted but only based only on theory and clinical experience.

Many settings allow for the possibility of such multiple baseline studies across clients, particularly when many clients with the same or similar presenting problems are seen. For example, if confrontation in meetings with family members is thought to break through alcoholics' denial and if the alcoholics' admission that they have a problem is seen as a crucial step toward their abstinence, these posited interconnections could be tested across clients. According to the structural family treatment model, a cross-generational family coalition is a common problem when children act out. The model suggests how to restructure the generational hierarchy and asserts that doing so will help the child (Umbarger, 1983). Testing these connections in a multiple baseline study across clients should not be difficult.

Many traditional practitioners experience another kind of problem in choosing a change target for a single-case project. The research designs force them to decide which goal or change target they intend to help the client work on next, to allow time to establish a baseline, and then to intervene to try to help the client achieve measurable change. Establishing a stable baseline can be troublesome in any practice model. But traditional practitioners are also used to working on several goals at a time or some goals intermittently. They may decide when to help the client work on a particular goal, depending on the client's apparent readiness to do so, responsiveness, and other factors. The research requirement of having to choose to work on one goal consistently for a time may simply force more planful attention to such issues as the client's readiness. Occasionally, however, it leads a practitioner to push a client to achieve changes in regard to a goal that is not appropriate at the time or at all. For example, a psychodynamically oriented student whose female client was not making much progress seized on the client's comment, "My house is in disorder, nothing is getting done" to propose (luckily only to the supervisor) that an improvement in the client's housekeeping should be the change target in a single-case research project. In fact, the client's comment was most likely a symbolic message about how she felt the treatment was going. Later, the student discovered, while probing further, that housekeeping was not one of the client's real concerns. One solution to this kind of problem is to make sure that traditional practitioners who have never done single-case research talk fully with their clients about what goals the clients want to work on when change is to be monitored. Another is that such practitioners try to review their tentative choices of change targets beforehand with someone who is neither naive nor anxious about practice or about the research method.

ARRANGING FOR MEASUREMENT

Once a reasonable change target has been chosen, the traditional practitioner must arrange for measurement. Several types of measures can lead to difficulties. Sometimes the practitioner will be measuring a process variable, one of the most difficult to define operationally and count. Process measures are used when change is sought in clients' behavior within the treatment session, representing movement toward an instrumental or facilitative goal. For example, the change target may be for parents to form an alliance, a couple to blame each other less, an individual to talk more about feelings, or group members to give each other more support. A different set of problems often arises for the traditional practitioner whose client will be asked to participate in self-monitoring, something the client is not used to doing and the practitioner may feel awkward asking for.

Their first attempts to use process measures may be enough to discourage traditional practitioners from ever again trying single-case research. There is the initial difficulty of operationally defining a variable that may have seemed clear and distinctive when they first identified it. "Clients' statements about their feelings," a favorite of students, is a case in point. Sophisticated analyses reveal that clients often say "I feel" when they mean "I think," as in the statement, "I feel she shouldn't have done that." They may talk about physical feelings that the student who is interested in emotions wants to exclude, such as "feeling tired," but the distinctions are not always clear. Are "feeling out of it" and "feeling nervous" statements about physical or emotional feelings? Then there are such issues as whether the client should be given credit for acknowledging feelings the worker has directly solicited ("Were you annoyed?" "A little") or feelings about situations far in the past ("I used to hate it when my mother did that") or in the future ("I'll be so pleased when I graduate"). The question of what to include and what to exclude from one's operational definition becomes more and more complex.

To limit these difficulties, the practitioner may choose to measure a one-dimensional variable and as simple a one as is relevant. Books that offer access to process measures that others have developed and tested (Greenberg & Pinsof, 1986; Grotevant & Carlson, 1987; Kiesler, 1973) may also be of help. Furthermore, it is essential for the practitioner to listen to several tapes after developing a tentative operational definition so that he or she can identify problems or gray areas. Other people can help or at least serve as sounding boards in the struggle for a clearer operational definition. The outcome should be to develop guidelines that are as unambiguous as possible for original and second coders to use. As one positive, struggling with an operational definition of a process measure helps the practitioner understand more clearly just what it is he or she hopes the client will do. In addition, thinking about what to include and exclude often highlights issues of what is valid to expect for the particular client. For example, with a client who rarely discloses feelings, the practitioner may want to give credit for a "feeling statement" of any kind, physical or emotional, past, present, or future. For a client who tends to intellectualize by talking about feelings in the past, only a present feeling may do.

Deciding on the unit of attention so one can obtain frequency counts with a process measure is also complex. The practitioner who wants to count something like the client's feeling words may become over-whelmed with determining the frequency after a successful intervention. Imagine how many words a talkative client might have used in a 50-minute session and the tediousness of counting them if many of the words were about feelings! The practitioner who wants to count statements of a particular kind is left to struggle with what a statement is. Clients tend not to talk in complete sentences, if that is the definition. Changes in topics are hellish to determine. And so on. It is usually easier either to count words (of whatever definition) in a random sample of interview segments or to divide the tapes into intervals of perhaps 5 minutes and check for the presence or absence of the target variable in each interval.

A series of other problems often arise when traditional practitioners ask clients to self-report. For one thing, unless the single-case study is begun within the first few sessions, the client was probably not led to expect that formal self-monitoring would be part of the treatment. When the practitioner suggests it, the client has a right to know why. Ideally, the practitioner is able to say what the benefits would be, the client is enthusiastic, they decide what will be measured and how, and the client completes the measurements. Sometimes the process unfolds just about this way. But more likely, it does not.

If the practitioner uses the word "research" in explaining the request for measurement, the client may become wary and rightfully want to know more. Even if all the client's questions are answered in a reassuring manner, an achievement the neophyte practitioner-researcher often cannot manage, the research process has intruded into the treatment. The ways it has done so are not always superficially evident, yet the practitioner must attend to them to prevent damage both to the treatment and to the validity and reliability of the measurements.

As one response, clients who are unused to self-monitoring may resent the practitioner asking them to put in so much effort, especially if they consider it unnecessary or useful only for the practitioner's research, not for them. Or clients may want to please the practitioner by improving in the area monitored but may be anxious that they will find it hard to achieve the desired change. With a client who expresses any such feelings openly, the practitioner can convey understanding, allow the client to choose whether to self monitor, reassure the client that there is no pressure to accomplish the change without help, and suggest how the self-monitoring could be useful to the treatment. Certainly, practitioners should always ask clients how they feel about being asked to self-report. Those clients who do not express their feelings openly may still unintentionally give clues by what they say. A secretly resentful man may bring up content about how people are always pushing him around for their own purposes. A woman may speak angrily about how her husband made her do something she did not want to do. An anxious client may begin talking about a time in childhood when her mother had too high expectations of her. Such comments at least give the practitioner another opening to ask about the client's possible hidden feelings about self-monitoring. Some clients who do not give such clues or who do so without the practitioner picking them up simply fail to bring in the self-reports. Some even leave treatment rather than face the practitioner again.

Finally, the client who self-monitors and improves during the baseline period because of reactivity causes different problems. The reactivity may spoil the practitioner's project. Or if the practitioner extends the baseline waiting for it to stop, the client may have to endure disappointment and a possible sense of failure from seeing the improvement decline over time.

Traditional practitioners who are new to single-case research need support and guidance to negotiate self-monitoring with clients so they can avoid or minimize these problems. One possible solution is to start a project involving self-monitoring early in a case before the client is used to proceeding without it. Another is to discuss with a supervisor or consultant how a particular client may react to self-monitoring and what to do to facilitate a favorable response, perhaps even role playing some alternatives. Certainly, practitioners should be encouraged to ask about clients' feelings, to watch for symbolic messages suggesting anger or anxiety, and to figure out ways to assuage these feelings. Finally, clients may be warned that positive changes caused by reactivity may not last, but they can be regained.

Practitioners probably also need a chance to verbalize their own anxieties about the research beforehand in a safe environment. They are entitled to feel concerned that their project may have been aborted because the client will not self-monitor, about the possibility that the client will be angry or upset, and about how they will respond. Of course, it is easier to handle all these problems effectively after one has gone through the process a few times, a fact that may offer some solace.

The benefits gained from self-monitoring can also persuade practitioners to use this procedure again as part of another single-case study or simply as an assessment or intervention tool. Most obviously, the information learned can help them plan treatment and give surer proof of the results than is available otherwise. In many instances, clients use the greater self-awareness of their functioning to gain motivation for change or more self-control. Finally, as an unintended consequence, practitioners who talk with clients about the clients' feelings in response to being asked to self-report may become more skilled at probing and sensitively handling clients' responses to the practitioners' actions in general or to other events in treatment. These matters should be discussed frankly whether single-case research is being done or not.

HAVING ONE FAMILY MEMBER OBSERVE ANOTHER

The possibility of asking one family member to observe another for a single-case study arises in two instances. One is when the person whose behavior is to be monitored cannot do so because of age, disability, or unwillingness but another family member is able and willing. The most common examples are a parent observing a child or any competent family member observing another who is retarded or seriously emotionally ill. The second impetus for asking one family member to observe another occurs when the one to be observed is self-monitoring some aspect of his or her own behavior that occurs when other family members are present and the second observer will provide a reliability check.

Presumably any adult or adolescent to be observed should be asked to give consent unless he or she is mentally incompetent. For the traditional practitioner, obtaining such consent raises the same issues as when clients are asked to monitor themselves. Will the person to be observed feel angry or anxious but not admit to any feelings and then perhaps sabotage the observation, the treatment, or both? This individual may not even be the primary family member the practitioner is seeing. For example, the practitioner may be working to help the mother of a teenager develop better parenting skills. There may be no direct opportunity to deal with the feelings of the teenager who is to be observed. Of course, family members who do the observing can be anxious or can sabotage the reporting, too. Here, as before, a careful anticipation and airing of feelings is in order, whenever possible. Finally, when clients who have agreed to self-monitor are asked to let someone else observe them as a reliability check, the importance of this observation for the research must be clarified so the client does not think the practitioner doubts his or her veracity.

Even if a person understands why the practitioner wants the information, subjecting oneself to another family member's observation can have negative implications. There is an implicit message of infantilization: The observer is more capable of reporting back to the practitioner what is really going on or, in the case of a reliability check, the person who is doing the self-monitoring can be believed only when someone else double checks. Even children of elementary school age and retarded or mentally ill family members who have any sense of what is happening can feel some humiliation or anger. Furthermore, the family member whose behavior is being observed is, of course, the one whose behavior is ultimately expected to change as a result of the interventions used. Many family therapists (see, for example, Satir, 1983; Umbarger, 1983) rail against this "identified patient" focus. They believe it can result in everyone pressuring the identified family member to change his or her behavior instead of encouraging a focus on family-wide issues that may be strongly influencing that behavior.

At least when a child or teenager is observed, the practitioner will probably ask other family members to change their behavior in regard to this person as part of the treatment. Asking one member of a marital pair to observe another, either for primary data or as a reliability check on self-monitoring, clearly places the "identified patient" focus and expectations for change on the one who is being observed. This is anathema for most traditional practitioners unless the marital partner being observed is voluntarily seeking to change himself or herself and sees the partner's observations as simply assistance with the research project.

A possible solution to some of these difficulties is to make the process reciprocal or at least to spread it around the family a bit. In the multiple baseline project mentioned earlier, in which children's acting out behavior was to be monitored before and after the family discussed the parents' divorce, one of the cases required the mother and an older brother to observe a 9 year old's aggressive behavior. The family was promised that later, they could observe and work on changing some behavior of the older brother and perhaps even something the mother did that was troubling to other family members. In fact, the issue of who was later going to observe whom doing what became a humorous focus for family discussions at times.

Each marital partner in joint counseling can be asked to monitor one of his or her own behaviors to be changed in treatment while observing a behavior the spouse is self-monitoring. In such a case, neither partner is being made into an "identified patient." Some healthy competitiveness in each spouse's efforts to change may even ensue. A less fortunate outcome is the spouses' disagreement on counts, a possibility that can adversely affect both the apparent reliability of the self-reports and the marital treatment. An interesting issue also arises when both spouses are asked to monitor an interaction that occurs between them, such as how many arguments they have. In either instance, different counts may lead the practitioner to conduct some fruitful discussions of what constitutes an argument, a supportive act by one spouse, or whatever else is being observed. In one of this author's cases, a wife counted only 2 instances of a husband giving her praise all week while the husband counted 10. It turned out the praise did not "register" if the husband said something like, "That's a nice dress." The praise had to be more elaborate and refer to one of her behaviors or personal characteristics before she could "hear" it, a fact that was vitally important for the husband to know. In another case, the husband credited the couple with having had an argument every time his wife said something he perceived as critical of him, even though he did not tell her this at the time or respond to the criticism. Clarifying these different perceptions was important for both couples and was a side benefit of doing the research.

CONCLUSIONS

Having described some common problems that traditional practitioners encounter in doing single-case research, the author would like to reaffirm the importance of their making the effort. Traditional practitioners should be just as careful as those who use behavioral or task-centered models to define clear treatment goals and to see whether they are being accomplished. It is not enough for them to complete one course on single-case research or one unit on single-case studies in a general research course and perhaps do some behavioral measures as an anomaly with one of their clients. They must do single-case research *within the context of their preferred ways of practicing* to learn that objective measurements and single-case experimental designs are just as relevant to their traditional practice as to any other. Traditional practice will benefit from this scrutiny, not because it will lose its identity to become just like behavioral or task-centered practice but because its asserted connections between particular interventions and goals and between particular instrumental and final goals must be tested empirically. Much traditional practice will stand that test. And the field needs to find out as soon as possible what will not.

REFERENCES

Bloom, M., & Fischer, J. (1982). *Evaluating practice: Guidelines for the accountable professional.* Englewood Cliffs, NJ: Prentice-Hall.

Greenberg, L. S., & Pinsof, W. M. (Eds.). (1986). *The psychotherapeutic process: A research handbook.* New York: Guilford Press.

Grotevant, H., & Carlson, C. (1987). Family interaction coding systems: A descriptive review. *Family Process, 26,* 19 74.

Kagle, J., & Cowger, C. (1984). Blaming the client: Implicit agenda in practice research? *Social Work, 29,* 347–351.

Kiesler, D. (1973). *The process of psychotherapy: Empirical foundations and system of analysis.* Chicago: Aldine.

Nelsen, J. C. (1984). Intermediate treatment goals as variables in single case research. *Social Work Research & Abstracts, 20,* 3–10.

Satir, V. (1983). *Conjoint family therapy.* Palo Alto, CA: Science & Behavior Books.

Umbarger, C. (1983). *Structural family therapy.* New York: Grune & Stratton.

Commentary

Single-System Designs in Family-Centered Social Work Practice

Susan B. Stern

Applying single-system designs to practice with families presents challenges to those interested in the evaluation of family therapy. This article identifies some issues that family researchers and teachers of practice evaluation must grapple with and suggests ways to advance evaluation of family-centered social work practice.

From observations of the number and popularity of family therapy courses in the curriculum of schools of social work, as well as discussions with practitioners and academic colleagues, it would seem that social work services are increasingly being delivered from a family systems perspective. This perspective has given rise to a variety of family therapy schools or approaches to intervention that are well accepted and considered effective by many practitioners. However, the empirical evaluation of these approaches lags behind their usage. Despite the promise of systems-based family treatment, there is little or no evidence of effectiveness for many "brands" (methods) of family therapy. (The word *brands* is used purposely because of the cover of the November–December 1983 issue of the *Family Networker* that depicted family therapy as a big business that comes with brands, charismatic leaders, and the like, all wrapped in an attractive package.) Gurman, Kniskern, and Pinsof (1986) found in their evaluation of 15 prominent brands of family therapy that, of 150 possible brand-by-problem combinations, outcome research had been done on only 35 (23 percent) and probable evidence of efficacy existed for only 13 (9 percent).

Even when systems-based family therapy has demonstrated apparent effectiveness, it is seldom clear how changes are achieved or maintained. A distinctive feature of family therapy is the belief that a change in the pattern of interaction in the family system will result in a change in

This chapter is partially based on a paper presented with William J. Reid at the 1988 Annual Program Meeting of the Council on Social Work Education, Atlanta, GA.

the behavior of individual family members and the overall functioning of the family. However, the few evaluative studies of family therapy have usually focused only on ultimate outcome criteria or change in the presenting problem. Little attention has been paid to the hypothesized connections between change in these outcomes and changes in the family's patterns of interaction (Stern & Reid, in press).

Nelsen noted in Chapter 3 that in a structural/strategic case, for example, a child's misbehavior, the reason for which the family sought treatment, may be addressed only by correcting the parents' faulty alliance. However, it would be rare for such an alliance actually to be measured. Since understanding how change occurs in families is necessary to develop effective interventions, the failure to measure the alliance hampers the ability of practitioner-researchers to test the validity of theories underlying systems-based family treatment. What is more disturbing, the child's misbehavior may not actually be measured because it is assumed that the behavior will naturally change if the goal of strengthening the parents' alliance is achieved. Nelsen considers strengthening the parents' alliance an example of an instrumental goal, which must then be linked to the final goals. The emphasis on instrumental goals is a useful way for researchers and practitioners of family therapy to conceptualize the goals related to changes in family processes or interactions, whether one means structural changes à la Minuchin (1974) or changes in patterns of communication à la Satir (1967). In addition to measuring outcome goals that are directly related to the family's presenting problem, Nelsen's approach highlights the need to monitor baseline levels of family interaction and progress toward change in family processes.

THE MULTIPLE TRACKING DESIGN

The multiple tracking design, a single-system design, was developed by this author and Reid specifically to address the relationship between change in family processes and problems (Stern & Reid, in press). Single-system methodology, with its continuous measurement, is well suited to addressing the following two issues simultaneously: (1) the contribution of family systems processes to the maintenance of and change in problems and (2) the role of therapeutic intervention in affecting both family processes and problems (instrumental and outcome goals).

The multiple tracking design is based on a simple AB design (probably the one most natural to practice) with a follow-up and a booster (Barlow & Hersen, 1984). It emphasizes attention to the measurement of presenting problems and systems-level variables and the careful tracking of how they covary. At a minimum, one problem and outcome goal and one systems-level variable or instrumental goal should be measured. Ideally, the measurement of systems variables would include change in the marital subsystem (when one exists) and change (for better or worse) in the functioning of individual family members other than the identified client. The model does not dictate what to measure; it dictates only at what levels measurement should take place, which allows the practitioner-researcher to choose the measures that are most relevant to his or her case and to test assumptions that are germane to the specific model of family therapy being used. A strength of this design is that the model is user friendly. It lends itself to different approaches to family therapy, including the structural, behavioral, and communications approaches. If it was used by practitioner-researchers of various orientations, it could begin to yield some information on hypotheses and questions like these:

1. Is change really necessary in the family system to ameliorate specific problems, and, if so, how much change is required? Since family therapists would predict that change in the system must occur before a problem can be lessened or overcome, they could look for this type of relationship in their data, both visually in graphic displays and through time-series analysis. For example, in one case, two adolescent sisters complained of headaches that the therapist hypothesized were maintained by faulty patterns of family communication. Following a medical checkup to rule out physical causes, the family was treated using Satir's (1967) communication model. Tapes of the sessions were coded by two of the therapist's fellow students for changes in the targeted communication patterns. However, although communication among the family members did improve, this change in the system did not lead to a decrease in headaches. One wonders whether biofeedback or relaxation training with or without family treatment would have been more effective for the sisters. In another case (Stern & Reid, in press), a decrease in child abuse occurred only following interventions to change the family structure despite previous parent training, which supports the need for changes to occur in the family system.

2. Is it necessary to maintain changes in the family system to avoid the recurrence of a problem? With a booster and follow-up, one may expect some backsliding after treatment is terminated, with a reversal following the booster session (Barlow & Hersen, 1984). However, family therapists may argue that if second-order change has occurred, it would not reverse and that a change in the system is necessary for the maintenance of the change in a problem. One can examine a number of possibilities in this regard by constructing a grid of the various combinations for change in problem and system variables at the termination

of treatment and at the follow-up. For example, if change occurs in both variables at the termination of treatment but only change in the presenting problem is maintained at the follow-up, perhaps a change in the system is not necessary to avoid the recurrence of a particular problem (Stern & Reid, in press).

3. What is the connection between specific family treatment interventions and changes in family processes? The key, of course, is well-specified interventions and monitoring of the family's response to the intervention. One problem that often arises is the lack of specificity of many family therapy interventions.

On the one hand, these ideas sound simplistic, as if all practitioner-researchers need to do is to operationalize and measure family problems, family process, and their interventions. On the other hand, this author is continually astonished at the complexity of measuring family interaction and systemic interventions. Yet, the critical issue and stumbling block in research on family therapy remains this measurement task. Practitioner-researchers find it most difficult to operationalize and evaluate exactly those family-interaction variables in which they are most interested, a point that will be discussed more fully in the next section.

TEACHING STUDENTS AND PRACTITIONERS TO EVALUATE FAMILY PRACTICE

In teaching single-system evaluation to students who were specializing in a family systems concentration, the author emphasized the concept of a practitioner-experimenter (see Carter, 1970), which symbolizes the relationship of evaluation to practice. Since the practitioner-experimenter is primarily a practitioner, the idea is to fit evaluation to good practice, not vice versa. Despite this author's encouragement to evaluate family treatment as they typically practiced it, with few exceptions, the students' projects were behavioral. Although the students might discuss the systems aspects of their cases, they did not systematically measure and evaluate systems variables. Rather, they often used these variables to explain why the behavioral treatment did not work. For example, in treating an agoraphobic young woman who had an enmeshed relationship with her mother, one student utilized behavioral interventions solely. Not surprisingly, the client's mother sabotaged the treatment. The author assigned every available article on single-system designs with nonbehavioral and family practice and continually made suggestions about how to evaluate family treatment and operationalize and measure key constructs. However, faced with the obstacles inherent in the measurement of family systems variables, the students preferred the easier option of conducting a behavioral project despite their commitment to a systems-based family therapy approach.

Nelsen presented many suggestions for conducting single-system evaluations with nontraditional practice such as taping interviews, developing coding schemes, and using goal-attainment scaling—all of which are valid measurement approaches. Practitioner-researchers can approximate measurements of patterns of interaction among family members by counting "I" statements (communication patterns) and the frequency of parental cooperation (family structure). One must still ask whether family researchers can satisfactorily measure family interaction variables such as alliances and detouring. The answer seems to be that we are not completely capturing the richness of family process. Studying the individual psychotherapy process literature on the client-therapist relationship may suggest new ways to look at relationships in families, at least at a dyadic level. Despite the differences between families and other types of small groups, group interaction research may be particularly suited to the study of process in families.

While adapting measurement strategies from other fields of study may enhance social work practice research, we should not overlook what family therapists themselves have to offer by way of evaluation. Although as practitioner-researchers we teach fitting designs to the case, we have not emphasized fitting measurement to what family therapists naturally do to study change in family processes. If we were to study how family therapists actually evaluate practice, one might, for example, observe a group of five social workers behind a one-way mirror hypothesizing about how the parents are detouring conflict through their acting-out child and monitoring the weekly changes in the marital dyad's ability to deal directly with disagreement and its effect on the child. Would an 80 percent rate of agreement among the five family therapists on the changes that occurred be acceptable data to plot on a graph? In structural family therapy, in which enactment is a key intervention, therapists read the enactment feedback and frequently make clinical decisions about the family members' reactions to the restructuring interventions. Enactments could serve as mini-experiments of selected systems variables. For example, if a young boy was acting up in the session, the parents could be directed to take charge of their son's behavior and get him to sit down. Other mini-experiments could take the form of communication/problem-solving episodes within a behavioral-systems approach.

Without rejecting traditional measurement strategies, we practitioner-researchers should be creative in turning to other ways of knowing that are natural to practice and not consider these methods less rigorous. If we could learn how to measure process variables and the achievement of instrumental goals as imaginatively and as well as we measure problems and the attainment of outcome goals, we might begin to understand the links between problems and process changes in family therapy and the role of treatment in those changes. Again, one is reminded of a cover of *Family Networker* (July-August 1985 issue) with the caption "Let Us Sell No Intervention Before Its Time." One fears that the warning came too late. We may not want to have the product recalled, but, as practitioner-researchers, let us at least try to understand how it works.

REFERENCES

Barlow, D. H., & Hersen, M. (1984). *Single-case experimental designs: Strategies for studying behavior change.* New York: Pergamon Press.

Carter, R. D. (1990). *The practitioner as experimenter.* Unpublished manuscript, University of Michigan, Ann Arbor.

Gurman, A., Kniskern, D., & Pinsof, W. (1986). Research on the process and outcome of marital and family therapy. In S. Garfield & A. Bergin (Eds.), *Handbook of psychotherapy and behavior change* (3rd ed., pp. 565–624). New York: John Wiley & Sons.

Minuchin, S. (1974). *Families and family therapy.* Cambridge, MA: Harvard University Press.

Satir, V. (1967). *Conjoint family therapy.* Palo Alto, CA: Science & Behavior Books.

Stern, S. B., & Reid, W. J. (in press). Evaluating problems and systems change in family therapy: A multiple tracking design. *American Journal of Family Therapy.*

Illustrating the Value of Practice Wisdom

Kevin J. Corcoran

The professional opinions of Nelsen and this author on empirical practice have crossed before. For example, Nelsen (1981) articulated some of the difficulties in applying the empirical model of nonbehavioral interventions, while this author (Corcoran, 1985) argued its ease. We have both made the same error of using the term *"nonbehavioral,"* since it is inappropriate to define an entire range of treatments by what they are *not*. Just as racial minorities are not defined as "nonwhite" and men are not defined as "nonwomen," these interventions should not be defined as "nonbehavioral." Nelsen's use of the term "traditional practice" is a more descriptive phrase and is a more accurate term for the daily activities of much clinical social work. The content of Nelsen's chapter suggests that it is fairly easy to apply empirical clinical practice to traditional practice.

With regard to Chapter 3, on single-case research, this response underscores two of Nelsen's important observations and two opinions about which this author has some reservations. It also illustrates how Nelsen's chapter provides a conclusion that is pertinent to the advancement of empirical clinical practice in social work.

SALIENT OBSERVATIONS

Among Nelsen's important assertions was that single-case *evaluation* is relevant to and achievable by traditional clinicians in their everyday practice. This point was evident in her focus on "change targets," as well as on the need to start the empirical evaluation at the beginning of treatment. The relevance and availability of empirical evaluation were also manifest in Nelsen's keen understanding of traditional practice. One illustration was the symbolic manifestation of the treatment impasse that was found in the client's statement, "My house is in disorder, nothing is getting done."

Second, Nelsen's focus on the need for practitioners to conceptualize and establish instrumental goals to facilitate the final goals of treatment advances the model of empirical clinical practice. Like other concomitant opinions (Safran, Greenberg, & Rice, 1988), hers cogently asserted that clinicians need to establish a working hypothesis of how each client will change. This hypothesis must be based on theory and must incorporate the moderating, intervening, and dependent variables that pertain to each client in the social environment. In other words, Nelsen articulated how social workers will increasingly draw on relevant information from other areas, namely, human behavior and the social environment.

Nelsen's two important contributions—her illustration of the relevance of single-case evaluation for traditional practice and the need to hypothesize the process of each client's change—underscore that empirical clinical practice is not ego dystonic to the activities of traditional social work clinicians. Nevertheless, Nelsen may be "preaching to the choir." Her message needs to be heard by the practitioners who do not even come to the "church." That is, the strengths of Nelsen's article will not be fully realized by groups of researchers, but await the open-minded reading by traditional practitioners.

AREAS OF RESERVATIONS

This author has reservations about two points that Nelsen made. First, Nelsen may be, as many others are, overly optimistic about the development of empirical evaluations of traditional, or even nontraditional, practice. Many educators have asserted that the Council on Social Work Education's (CSWE, 1988) requirement that schools of social work teach students to evaluate their practice will increase the prevalence of single-case research. However, one must bear in mind that the standard mandates that students be exposed to the material—not necessarily trained in *doing* practice evaluation. Contrary to the tunes sung by the choir of researchers, participation in a couple of research courses, or even a single unit or required reading from a practice course, is not going to result in social workers' routine evaluation of their practice. More must be done if future practitioners are truly to engage in empirical practice. Until the content of empirical practice pervades numerous courses on practice and thus becomes part of practice instructors' ways of doing social work, the development of empirical practice will continue to be syncopated and restricted to a few (see, for example, Gingerich, 1984).

Nelsen was clearly aware of this situation when she argued for expanding the content on empirical evaluation and making it a requirement of various social work courses. To this end, perhaps the content should not simply be removed from research courses or added to clinical practice courses, but put into the field curriculum; thus, students would learn, as Nelsen illustrated, how empirical evaluation facilitates effective practice. Until this happens practice evaluation is integrated with practice and field courses, students' knowledge of practice evaluation will make Ebbinghaus's curve of retention look like a bottom line.

The second point with which this author takes issue is Nelsen's view of empirical evaluation as single-case research. As Gingerich argued in Chapter 2, and others have argued elsewhere (Barlow, Hayes, & Nelson, 1984), empirical evaluation has more utility for practice than for research. From his clinical experience, this author believes that sophisticated single-subject research designs are simply too cumbersome to use in everyday practice. Thus, the role of empirical evaluation must be less ambiguous and must be restricted to a part of effective practice.

CONTRADICTORY NOTE FROM THE CHOIR

Nelsen was correct in her observation that "traditional practice models desperately need such empirical testing of their practice assumptions." This observation is true not only for many theories of practice, but also for assumptions about the value of the model of empirical clinical practice. What Nelsen observed regarding traditional practice also applies to the empirical model, namely, that beliefs about the value of the model are "by and large commonly accepted but only theory based." For example, we researchers assert that the empirical model will help practitioners do good social work, but we have no empirical evidence. Alternatively, we believe that empirical evaluation will provide usable feedback, with little empirical evidence.

The absence of research support for the benefits of the empirical model did not prevent major revisions in CSWE's standard for accreditation. Many of us "know" that the empirical model is valuable. We "know" that it actually can help practitioners. And we "know" that it is a beneficial addition to social work education. We "know" these things from our own form of "practice wisdom"—in essence, an "educational wisdom" that is based on our experiences, self-observation, and inductive reasoning, and on some implications from research. As Nelsen stated, she believes, "on the basis of experience with teaching and doing single-case research, . . . that traditional practitioners who make the effort can learn much that is useful to their clinical work and can give much back to the field."

Despite this author's agreement with this statement, he believes that it is based on a method parallel to "practice wisdom." Despite the "desperate need" for research to test the assumptions of the empirical model of practice, our "educational wisdom" has advanced the knowledge of single-case evaluation and will continue to do so. Consequently, we researchers are inherently contradictory in our criticism of practitioners' use of practice wisdom. If this method of knowledge development is acceptable to us, such that it influences what we do as educators and researchers, then practice wisdom is also an acceptable method for developing knowledge of traditional clinical practice.

REFERENCES

Barlow, D. H., Hayes, S. C., & Nelson, R. O. (1984). *The scientist practitioner: Research and accountability in clinical and educational settings.* New York: Pergamon Press.

Corcoran, K. J. (1985). Clinical practice with nonbehavioral methods: Strategies for evaluation. *Clinical Social Work Journal, 3,* 78–86.

Council on Social Work Education. (1988). *Handbook of accreditation standards and procedures.* Washington, DC: Author.

Gingerich, W. J. (1984). Generalizing single-case evaluation from classroom to practice settings. *Journal of Education for Social Work, 20,* 74–82.

Nelsen, J. C. (1981). Issues in single-subject research for nonbehaviorists. *Social Work Research & Abstracts, 17*(Summer), 31–37.

Safran, J. D., Greenberg, L. S., & Rice, L. N. (1988). Integrating psychotherapy research and practice: Modeling the change process. *Psychotherapy, 25,* 1–17.

Synthesis

Why Don't Practitioners Use Single-Subject Designs?

Eleanor Reardon Tolson

A young mother murders her child and tries to take her own life. She is admitted to the psychiatric unit of a hospital. Her husband sobs as he shows the social worker pictures of his adorable, now-deceased 2-year-old daughter. His grief is palpable, and the social worker blinks back tears. The young woman, it turns out, is a twin, and her twin sister and her husband insist on seeing the social worker immediately. They understand that schizophrenia runs in families and that identical twins are particularly vulnerable. They seek reassurance. Later in the day, an emergency interview is scheduled with another young woman and her parents. This woman is a psychiatric outpatient with a history of serious suicide attempts. Each attempt has been preceded by an expressed wish to terminate treatment. The woman has terminated treatment again today. It is hoped that involving her parents will provide some protection. The family interview ends with the patient agreeing to continue treatment. Although her psychiatrist is reassured, the social worker is not. "You worry too much," the psychiatrist tells the social worker in an effort to comfort her.

Contact with patients and families is punctuated by the usual agency/institution entanglements. Two psychiatrists fight during a staff meeting. A colleague is unhappy with her raise. Another colleague plots about obtaining a tenured appointment in the psychiatry department. Paperwork must be completed. Appointments with families of new patients must be made. The day is nearing an end. The phone rings. The second patient of the day is unconscious after one more attempt to terminate her grief permanently. Will the social worker join the psychiatrist in the emergency room? The social worker has no role in the emergency room. She is there to comfort the psychiatrist. She excuses herself as soon as he is able to release her. Returning to her office, she finds a note indicating that an adolescent patient wants to see her immediately, a note that is only one of many from this young woman who is diagnosed as having a hysterical conversion reaction. The social worker is annoyed. Labeling her annoyance "countertransference" does not help. She asks the unit nurse to tell the patient that she will see her tomorrow and goes home.

This day in the life of a social worker illustrates some of the forces that obstruct the use of single-subject designs (SSDs). First, there is little time. Second, the emotional burden is draining. Third, the necessity to respond to human need is far more important and appealing than the necessity to measure the effectiveness of treatment. Fourth, and most important, there is little need to track data in this setting. The woman who killed her child will respond to medication or she will not. Her husband will be able to resume his life and make appropriate decisions for her care or he will not (it is possible that he will require outpatient treatment during which including his emotional state will be important). Unfortunately, no subtle measurements were necessary to determine whether the family interview with the depressed client was effective.

Of course, it is dangerous to generalize from a sample of one. There is, however, a small amount (too small) of data that describes what a group of social work students do in practice. Tolson and Kopp's (1988) study, for example, revealed that students saw a substantial number of clients for brief periods, that a substantial number of their clients were extremely poor, that the clients presented an average of 5.2 problems, and that these problems varied widely. Furthermore, although the students used a large variety of interventions, the largest subset of them were of the traditional type. All these characteristics either hinder or minimize the usefulness of SSDs. Brief treatment works against repeated measurement, the sine qua non of SSDs. Furthermore, it appears that brief treatment should be the treatment of choice (Tolson, 1988; Videka-Sherman, 1988). It is likely that much service to poor clients entails the provision of resources, an intervention that is not particularly difficult to measure. The necessity to ameliorate many problems, often in a short period, leaves little time for considering issues of measurement and design. The large variety of problems confronted indicates that an equally large number of rapid-assessment instruments is needed. Finally, the use of traditional interventions makes it difficult to use experimental SSDs.

Do all these obstacles and all the evidence that social workers do not use these designs in practice mean that we empirically minded practitioners should abandon our aspirations to engage clinicians in evaluating their practice? Of course not. They do indicate that measurement efforts must be compatible with and useful to practice. We have behaved like a small boy with a hammer (SSDs being the hammer), insisting that SSDs are useful across the board. In fact, we need to determine which methods of evaluation are useful in which settings, with which clients, and with which problems. SSDs are most useful in settings in which practitioners work with their clients over at least several weeks to resolve problems that have observable components and that occur frequently.

CAN SSDs AID AND ABET PRACTICE?

It is axiomatic that the type of research design employed must fit the question addressed, including the state of knowledge about the question and, in clinical work, the seriousness of the question. There are three questions that are consistently asked by clinicians and for which data are useful. They will be identified along with the appropriate teaching arena.

What Is the Problem and What Is Causing It? Assessment

Usually, the target problems that are the foci of treatment can be at least broadly identified by obtaining information in the course of the interview (client's verbal description). Sometimes it is necessary to gather more systematic data to refine the definition of the problem or to determine the cause of the problem. For example, intervention with an older woman who was experiencing great anxiety was unsuccessful until the woman was asked to complete a self-report instrument several times each day. These data revealed that the troubling levels of anxiety were experienced early in the morning, which allowed for a more focused intervention. In cases in which there is no clear antecedent to or cause of the problem, it is often useful to ask the client to keep a diary describing the circumstances in which the problems occur. A diary of this type is usually essential to the use of cognitive interventions, for example.

Obviously, data of this sort have nothing to do with research designs. They do not require a baseline and may not be obtained until intervention has proved unsuccessful, as in the case of the woman with anxiety. Obtaining such data is part of effective practice and should be taught in practice courses. To teach students to gather data, practice teachers must be able to teach them to identify the information that they need and the variety of means available for obtaining it, such as self-reports, standardized instruments, observation, and diaries or logs.

Is the Client Getting Better? Accountability

The second use of data is to determine whether the client or the problem is improving. The vast majority of social workers are concerned about whether the desired changes are occurring with their clients. Such concern is not only an ethical imperative; data will probably be necessary to avoid malpractice suits in the future. As a result, it is essential that students be taught to track changes.

This use of data may be described as the use of a B design. A fancier form is the AB design. In a B design, there is no baseline, but repeated measurements are employed. The term "B design" connotes repeated observational measurement. Some problems do not require a B design, while the parameters of other problems cannot be captured with a B design.

In many cases, it is preferable to use a procedure like Reid's (1978) problem specification. In this procedure, the manifestations of a problem are identified, along with some indication of their frequency, duration, or severity, when appropriate. The client is questioned about changes in these manifestations during each interview. Problem specification has the following advantages: (1) it can be shaped to fit any problem, (2) the appropriate type and source of data can be determined for each manifestation and sometimes will be systematic and repeated observations, and (3) this procedure does not have any hint of "research." A resource problem, for example, is measured with a B or AB design as being simply present or absent. Tracking a resource problem with this design is both unnecessarily complicated and inadequate. Using problem specification, the conditions that must be met to resolve the problem would be identified, and the extent to which they are fulfilled would provide a measure of accountability. This process may be illustrated with a housing problem. The specifications could be that the housing must (1) cost less than $350 per month, (2) have two bedrooms, and (3) must be within walking distance of public transportation. Obviously, the specifications permit a more meaningful measure of whether the client's needs have been met than a simple statement that an apartment was found. Needless to say, the problem-specification procedure does not preclude repeated observational measures (in research terms, *problem specification* can be described as the operational definition of the problem and solution).

How to gather data for the purposes of accountability should be taught in the practice courses and in the field. The means of determining accountability should be identified in every practice text that is written (it is hoped that reviewers of such texts will regularly comment on this aspect of the practice approach). The difficulty with teaching data collection to determine a problem and accountability in practice courses and in the field is that few of the faculty members who teach these courses are sophisticated about how to collect data. Thus, we clinical researchers must begin to teach practice courses and teach field supervisors if we are going to have an impact on the practice of students—the future generation of professionals.

Does This Intervention Work? Generation of Knowledge

The generation of knowledge is the only purpose for which attention to designs is necessary. It requires the use of experimental SSDs like the withdrawal design or the multiple baseline. This content is probably most appropriately taught in a course on research or in a research component of a course on practice. The question is, of course, Is it reasonable to expect practitioners to engage in the generation of knowledge? It is easy to identify the negative factors: the lack of time, agency support and rein-forcement, and interest; more pressing concerns; and so on. There are, however, some compelling reasons for engaging practitioners in such endeavors. First, it is likely that virtually every practitioner has developed an effective intervention strategy for a particular problem that, if tested and disseminated, would contribute to the profession's knowledge base. Sometimes this clinical wisdom is stored in one person in an agency, and much of it is lost when the person moves on.

Second, the requirement to do experimental SSDs sometimes produces knowledge. For example, a student who was placed on a medical-surgical unit of a hospital was required to use such a design. Settings like hers provide no end of obstacles, the most serious of which is the short-term stays of patients, coupled with the fact that a first-year student is at the field site only 2 days each week. After much struggle, the student decided to work with three alcoholic patients on a detoxification unit using a multiple-baseline design. The goal was to get each patient to make an appointment for the outpatient treatment of alcoholism. This goal applied to all patients on the unit, but few of them complied. The student conducted the usual intake interview and informed all three patients that they were expected to make an appointment for outpatient treatment. She waited a different number of days for each patient to do so (a staggered baseline) and then employed her intervention, a brief confrontational speech. The intervention worked: All three patients made an appointment for outpatient treatment. Unfortunately, none of them kept the appointment and, even more un-fortunately, the student concluded, therefore, that her intervention was unsuccessful. This small experiment showed two things: (1) that the in-tervention succeeded in helping clients make the first step and (2) that another intervention is needed to make the second step—keeping the first appointment. These are potentially important findings, given the costs of alcoholism to individuals, their families, and society.

The third compelling reason for clinicians to engage in SSD research to generate knowledge concerns the development of the practice ap-proaches. This purpose is related to Chapter 3, on SSDs in traditional practice. The biggest obstacle to the use of these designs in traditional practice is undoubtedly the lack of specification of the treatment approach. Treatment approaches that cannot be specified cannot be deliberately replicated. The limitations to replication call into question the usefulness of trying to teach them, let alone test their effectiveness. The act of using experimental designs requires that some aspect of traditional treatment be specified so that it can be reinserted in the withdrawal design or offered to others in the multiple baseline design. The ability to identify the procedures that are necessary to enable clients to identify their feelings, for example, would be an enormous boon to the development of the traditional approaches.

An additional advantage to teaching SSDs is only indirectly related to the clinical situation. It appears that in the process of learning these designs, students improve their clinical skills. They become better able to identify specific problems, goals, and interventions, and their inferential thinking is challenged.

This examination of the need for data in practice suggests that students should be taught SSDs, but that they should be expected to use them only in limited circumstances. These circumstances include the use of a B design (as part of problem specification) for demonstrating accountability when the problem or the manifestation of the problem is best captured by repeated observational measurements and the use of the experimental designs when it is desirable to test the effectiveness of a particular intervention. As Briar indicated in Chapter 1, researchers' expectations regarding the percentage of students who will use SSDs have probably been unrealistic. It seems, however, that it is not the percentage of students that is in question but, rather, the percentage of cases with which the students will use the designs. This author's ambition is that all practitioners will use (1) problem specification with all problems and with all clients, (2) B designs with all problems or manifestations of a problem that are best captured by repeated measurement and when the amount and frequency of therapeutic contact permits repeated measurement, and (3) experimental SSDs when they have discovered a new intervention strategy, an event that will probably not occur more than three times, on average, in their careers.

How can these aims be accomplished? First, all students must be taught good, basic practice skills—the specification of a problem, goal, intervention, and so on. Second, all students should be taught these skills in practice courses, and all practice texts should contain problem specification or some similar procedure. Third, all students should be taught to use experimental SSDs and the circumstances in which they should be employed. Fourth, all students should be taught with an empirical orientation; that is, they should learn methods that have been demonstrated to be effective, they should learn that demonstrated effectiveness is one of the most important criteria for selecting an intervention, and they should be required to use record-keeping systems that enable them to identify cases and problems with which they are ineffective so they will be motivated to use and to test new interventions (Videka-Sherman & Reid, 1985). Fifth, we should articulate the expectation that students will, during their professional careers, generate knowledge. Sixth, one of our professional organizations—NASW or CSWE—should provide special recognition for practitioners who generate knowledge, just as ACSW provides recognition for clinical competence.

If we social work educators are serious about educating empirically minded practitioners, perhaps we should start by organizing ourselves to promote the achievement of the foregoing objectives. Attaining them will require influencing practice teachers, field instructors, and the professional organizations.

REFERENCES

Reid, W. J. (1978). *The task-centered system.* New York: Columbia University Press.

Tolson, E. R. (1988). *The metamodel and clinical social work.* New York: Columbia University Press.

Tolson, E. R., & Kopp, J. (1988). The practicum: Clients, problems, interventions, influences on student practice. *Journal of Education for Social Work, 24,* 123–134.

Videka-Sherman, L. (1988). Meta-analysis of research on social work practice in mental health. *Social Work, 33,* 325–338.

Videka-Sherman, L., & Reid, W. J. (1985). The structured clinical record: A clinical education tool. *The Clinical Supervisor, 3,* 45–61.

Part 2

Methodological Advances

Expert Systems and the Development of Knowledge in Social Welfare

Edward J. Mullen and John R. Schuerman

This chapter considers the development of expert systems in social welfare and the implications of this technology for the development of knowledge in the field. It begins with an introduction to expert systems and some basic concepts underlying their construction. Next, it describes a project to develop an expert system in which the authors have been engaged. Then it considers some issues that have arisen in the authors' work on the nature of decision making in social welfare and the ways in which knowledge and skills enter into those decisions.

An *expert system* is a computer program designed to give advice on decisions. The program asks the user a series of questions about a case and then makes recommendations for action. A variety of such systems are being used in industrial and commercial applications and in medical diagnosis. Expert systems come from the field of artificial intelligence. They attempt to capture the knowledge and skills of human experts in a way that is usable by others. These systems differ in a number of ways from classical, algorithmic computer programs. They are said to be "knowledge based," rather than "data based." In an algorithmic computer program, it is usually possible to describe exactly what the program does with a set of input data. In an expert system, on the other hand, there are a number of different "routes" through the program, and how the data are manipulated is determined very much by the character of the data.

The authors wish to acknowledge the help of their coworkers in the Chapin Hall Child Welfare Decision Making Project, Matthew Stagner and Penny Johnson. Other staff at Chapin Hall also contributed valuable suggestions.

WHY EXPERT SYSTEMS IN SOCIAL WORK?

Before one invests in the technology of expert systems and encourages the development of systems, it is important to consider to what extent, if at all, expert systems make sense for facilitating decision making in social work and social welfare. The temptation to embrace a powerful new technology simply because of its success in other fields should be avoided. Will this technology fit the types of problem situations that social workers typically face?

Expert systems are appropriate when the problem is relatively complex and hence requires considerable human expertise. The knowledge should not be of the "commonsense" type, but should be acquired through professional training and experience. Furthermore, the knowledge should exist in representable form; that is, it must be subject to analysis and be amenable to explication. This requirement leads to the issue so often encountered by social work researchers regarding the extent to which a knowledge base exists that supports social work interventions.

The task of acquiring and verifying social work knowledge may present a challenge that expert systems developers have not yet encountered in other domains. There are many social work problems for which expert systems technology is not appropriate because of insurmountable difficulties in representing the domain of knowledge. The application of expert systems technology to social work expertise is reminiscent of earlier attempts to apply evaluation research methods to the assessment of social work intervention. It may again be found that large areas of social work intervention are without a well-developed knowledge base.

Shortage of Experts

Expert systems are generally developed because of a shortage of expertise or a desire to unburden experts of routine decision making and to release their energies for more creative tasks. It seems that in social work, there is great need for expert systems on this count. Professional social work experts are in short supply, especially social workers who are highly trained in specialized areas of practice. Also, busy professionals could use their expertise more fully if they could be relieved of some detailed decision making.

There is an increasing shortage of professional social workers in many public and private social agencies. Large public child protective agencies are an example. Although expert systems could not and should not replace professional decision making in such settings, they could support decision making by less highly trained staff. Thus, they would not replace the expertise of highly trained staff, but they would greatly expand the use of expert knowledge in an efficient form. Safeguards would need to be built in, however, such as ensuring that more highly trained experts review the recommended decisions.

Possible Applications

Social work expert systems could support a range of practice decisions. They could be used to conduct various types of assessments, including assessments of needs and problems and classification. They could also be used to advise on intervention, as in the system described later in this chapter.

Expert systems could also be used to train social work practitioners. For example, while in training, social workers in child protective services could interact with an expert system that was designed to assess the risk of future abuse or neglect. Trainees could work with a case in which there was an allegation of abuse or neglect and test their expertise against the "thinking" of the expert system. The details of the system's "thought processes" would be available to the trainees. The trainees could ask why the system is asking a question, and once the system reached a conclusion about the level of risk of harm, the trainee could ask the system for an explanation or justification of the conclusion. The system would present its justification, usually describing the rules and the sources of its facts. In sessions with students, the authors have observed that interaction between the class and an expert system with regard to a case example can stimulate class discussion about why requested information is relevant, as well as the soundness of the system's inferences.

KNOWLEDGE REPRESENTATION

One of the core problems in artificial intelligence is that of knowledge representation. *Knowledge representation* is concerned with how knowledge is stored in the mind or in a computer and how this information is structured to facilitate symbolic processing. *Symbolic processing* refers to nonnumerical computations involving concepts and relationships among concepts. A knowledge-representation system includes syntax (conventions for combining symbols to form expressions) and semantics (specifications for inferring meaning). A number of formalisms exist for coding knowledge, including production rules, predicate logic, and structured objects (generalized graphs, semantic or associative networks, and frames). The challenge of knowledge representation in the development of an expert system

is to find a way to codify what an expert knows. Three such schemes—
production rules, networks, and frames—facilitate codification.

Production Rules

Most current expert systems are "rule based," that is, their knowledge
is contained in a large number of rules. Rules consist of one or more "ifs"
and one or more "thens." The rules are manipulated by a part of the
program called the "inference engine." The inference engine asks questions of the user and tries to invoke ("fire") the rules; that is, it determines
whether the ifs of a rule are true and if they are, it declares the thens of the
rule to be true also. Attempts are made to make the rules as simple as
possible, since the complexity of a system arises from the large number of
rules and their interactions. Interactions among the rules occur when a
then of one rule is an if of another rule. A system of rules is often compared
to a decision tree, but it can be much more complex. The development of
an expert system involves collaboration between a "knowledge engineer"
and a specialist in a subject to uncover the rules used to make decisions.
The knowledge engineer is responsible for coding the knowledge of an
expert into the form of rules.

Networks

Decision trees and production rules can be thought of as representing
relationships among constructs. Another way of representing relationships is with semantic networks (or associative networks). Semantic
networks are derived from early work that built on general graph theory.
An early application of semantic networks was the representation of
meaning in language.

A semantic network is a set of nodes or concepts that are connected
in various ways to other nodes. The connections may represent definitions,
logical deductions, empirical relationships, or heuristic or intuitive associations. The net may have no particular "beginning" or "end." Despite
early enthusiasm, researchers in artificial intelligence found semantic
networks to be theoretically and practically deficient (Brachman, 1979).

Frames

Frame-based languages evolved in an attempt to remedy the deficiencies of rule-based systems. Frames are similar to prototypes in that they are
structures for representing classes of objects (for example, the class "child")
and typical members of the class. A frame has "slots" that describe and

structure the properties associated with the class of objects and are used to store information about particular instances of the frame. A slot can have a default value, the value for a typical member of the class. For example, the slot "state of health" in the frame "child" may have the default value "good." Frames represent an important aspect of human thinking: We all have templates in our minds for common objects and situations that carry assumptions about what those objects and situations are like. These assumptions are revised as we learn more about particular situations.

Frames are organized into hierarchies or lattices. For example, the frame "person" may have the frame "child" under it. Frames that are lower in the hierarchy inherit the slots and defaults of those above them. The user of a frame-based program specifies "instances" of the frames, that is, particular cases. These instances inherit the slots of all their parent frames, including the default values of those slots.

Certainty

Human knowledge and human decision making have various degrees of certainty. It is important that expert systems capture this characteristic of decision making. One way that expert systems represent the uncertainty and ambiguity in decision making is through "certainty factors." In the authors' programs, certainty factors are attached to facts and rules. When a user is asked for a fact, the certainty of that fact is also requested in the form of a number between zero and one, loosely similar to a probability. A rule also has an associated certainty, which is used to determine the certainty of the rule's thens if the rule is used. When the rule is used, the inference engine combines the certainties of the ifs of the rule with the certainty of the rule to determine the certainty of the thens.

How uncertainty should be handled in expert systems is a matter of considerable debate and investigation. The procedures the authors have adopted are relatively simple, and it is possible that more complex handling of uncertainty will be required for truly sophisticated social welfare systems.

Dependency Information

Facts also have associated "dependency information," which provides support for why the facts exist. This dependency information consists of data on how the assertion was derived and how it can be justified. A derivation is a statement of the inferencing path that led to the fact. For example, the system may conclude that Mary is at high risk of harm from a rule that states, "If a perpetrator admits inflicting physical punishment on a child, then the child is at high risk of harm." The derivation of the assertion, "Mary is at high risk of harm" would be the combination of the fact that the perpetrator admits inflicting physical punishment on the child and the rule that used the fact to reach the conclusion.

The derivation does not explain why a fact exists, only how the fact entered the knowledge base. In contrast, a justification is a statement of the logical base for the fact. In the foregoing example, a perpetrator could retract his or her admission of inflicting physical punishment on the child. If the system was programmed not to retract the assertion that the risk of harm was high in such circumstances, then the assertion would remain in the knowledge base, derived as before, but no longer justified or logically supported by other facts.

The authors have found that a system's ability to provide dependency information is important. An expert system that is able to reach a conclusion but is unable to reveal how the conclusion was reached or why the conclusion is valid would not be satisfying. For example, if it is concluded that a child is at risk of harm, it would be useful to be able to determine how that conclusion was reached (derivation) and why the assertion is true (justification).

CASE EXAMPLE: THE CHAPIN HALL STUDY

The authors' work on expert systems has been conducted in the context of a project with the Illinois Department of Children and Family Services (IDCFS). The objective of the project was to develop detailed descriptions of the decision-making processes of workers in the department. Examples of such decisions include whether to remove an abused or neglected child from his or her home and, if so, where to place the child. Both rule-based and frame-based expert systems have been used as research tools in developing these descriptions.

IDCFS is an agency with a relatively low percentage of highly trained and experienced workers. It is a high-volume setting responsible for investigating an increasing number of allegations of abuse and neglect. The decisions that are made about families and children are clearly critical and have serious consequences. If expert systems could be developed for some of these decisions, they could result in considerable benefits.

The authors did not examine all the decisions that must be made in the course of all child welfare cases, in part because of the limitations of resources. But some decisions did not seem to lend themselves to modeling with expert systems. For example, the decision to accept a report of abuse or neglect at the State Central Registry seems to be less a matter of expertise than of resources (for example, staff who are available to answer the call) and routine screening based on a few explicit criteria.

In another decision—the determination of services to be provided to children and families—it was found that the necessary knowledge structure for developing an expert system was not present. The provision of some services, such as referral to income maintenance agencies or assistance in obtaining medical care and housing, is straightforward. It is the softer services, those that are aimed at psychological change (changes in attitudes and family interactions), that are more problematic. Counseling services are frequently prescribed, but the authors have been unable to uncover the principles that govern the prescription of these services. The objectives of counseling are often not well connected with the major responsibilities of the child welfare agency, such as protection of the child from harm. Thus, although counseling seems to be a valued service, the rationale for its use is not clearly understood. In addition, the outcomes of counseling are uncertain. To put it another way, knowledge of how to get a parent to stop abusing a child is incomplete. In this and similar situations, it seems inappropriate to attempt to develop expert systems, since the human expertise appears to be incompletely developed.

Stages of Development of an Expert System

The development of an expert system takes considerable time. Citrenbaum, Geissman, and Schultz (1987) and Geissman and Schultz (1988) suggested a four-stage approach: the determination and specification of the problem, the initial prototype, the expanded prototype, and the delivery system. Similarly, Marcot (1987) proposed a four-stage process: creating a prototype, developing a first-generation rule set, testing and expanding the rule set to the second generation, and testing that second-generation rule set. The process of developing expert systems is obviously similar to the research process.

Specification of the problem. As in other areas of research, the process begins with specification of the problem, which in work on expert systems means the identification of the knowledge area or domain for analysis. What knowledge is needed; that is, what is the requirement of the knowledge base? Is the development of the expert system technically feasible? In the broader field of the development of expert systems, this is the stage in which a search is made for similar systems that have already been developed and successfully implemented. In social work, few systems exist, so early work must be done without much guidance. In such circumstances, the development of systems during the early stages may more properly be considered developmental research than knowledge engineering. The acquisition of knowledge is generally a routine process in industry and finance. However, in social welfare, the process is not expected to be routine; rather, it may require considerable research to understand the substance and form of knowledge used by social welfare experts.

The authors focused on important decisions made by the IDCFS staff during the investigation and follow-up service phases on cases in which there were allegations of child abuse or neglect. The focus was limited to an examination of cases only in Cook County. Furthermore, only the more significant decisions that affected cases in important ways relevant to the ultimate provision of services would be modeled.

Development of a prototype. In this stage, experience is first gained with the problem area. This stage is similar to exploratory research in which the researcher works with a small aspect of the subject matter hoping to sharpen the definition of the problem and formulate hypotheses. The expert system developed at this stage normally addresses only part of the problem domain and lacks sophisticated technical apparatus. At this point, the task is to grasp a small portion of the expert's knowledge and how the knowledge is used. During prototyping, the developer determines the types of decisions or problem situations with which the expert deals. The knowledge engineer tries to gain a better understanding of the dimensions of the knowledge area and to demonstrate the technical feasibility of an incompletely developed system. As is often the case in exploratory research, it is during this stage that the developer examines whether the domain is too broadly defined and needs narrowing.

Two prototypes of expert systems have been developed to assess the risk of harm, and others have been developed for the decision to substantiate or not substantiate an allegation of abuse or neglect and the decision to take protective custody. These prototypes are being tested and elaborated. The more advanced stage, which is yet to come, will require careful verification and validation of the prototypes. Testing of the systems on site is even further away.

The principal method of knowledge representation has been if-then rules. Some rules are simple in form with a single if clause or pattern. Others are more complex and contain several ifs. An example of a rule is the following:

If this caretaker has
a drinking or drug problem OR
a psychiatric problem OR
a chaotic lifestyle OR
poor intellectual functioning,
Then this caretaker's functioning is poor.

Frames have also been used to represent knowledge in the IDCFS project. For example, one of the risk-of-harm expert systems defines the frame "case" to represent all cases considered by the system. The frame "case" has a number of slots, including "case number," "number of children," "caretaker's prior history of mental illness," and so forth. Subtypes of the frame "case" (called "child" frames in the language used) have been defined. For example, there is a child frame called "abuse cases" and another called "neglect cases." These child frames inherit all the slots of the parent "case" frame. In addition, they have slots that define characteristics of either abuse cases or neglect cases. Further, the frame "abuse cases" has child frames called "sex abuse cases" and "physical abuse cases." These frames inherit all the slots and facets of the top frame "case," as well as the frame "abuse cases." Other slots that are appropriate to either sex abuse cases or physical abuse cases are defined as well. Many of these slots are given default values that are also inherited. For example, the "county" slot of the frame "case" has the default value "Cook," which is inherited by all the child frames.

Instances of the frames "physical abuse cases," "sex abuse cases," and "neglect cases" are defined. These instances have specific values assigned to their slots. The expert system that has been developed asks the user for values of a slot if the slot is without a value and the value is needed to reach a conclusion.

Expansion and testing of the prototype. During this stage, the expert system is elaborated and refined. The full range of knowledge areas required by the problem is developed. Complex problems would normally result in the development of several expert systems relevant to various aspects of the problem. Technical enhancements are included, such as user-friendly interfaces. This phase is like laboratory research in that the work normally consists of refinement in a controlled environment. During this phase, the system's accuracy, adequacy, and precision are examined. This task involves the measurement of the accuracy and fineness of the predictions generated by the rule set, as well as the extent to which the system encompasses most of the problems in the knowledge domain.

Testing the system on site. The final stage in the development of an expert system is field testing. Will the system work efficiently and effectively in a range of environments to which it is to be applied? In this phase, the focus is on the end user. The system is delivered in a form that will operate without problems in the field. Will the intended user be able to use the system with real problems? When development has been completed, the system should have been fully verified and validated— conditions not yet reached in social work applications (Marcot, 1987).

ISSUES IN CONSTRUCTING EXPERT SYSTEMS

Some issues have been raised by the authors' work that are important for decision making and the development of knowledge in social welfare.

Construction of a Story

In the process of gathering data about a case, people construct a story that incorporates the facts of the case. It seems to be important that the story is coherent and consistent. Problems are caused by facts that are contradictory or that otherwise do not fit into a story. Thus, people have various ways of dealing with inconsistent facts, including discounting them or simply ignoring them. They also want the story to be more or less complete, so they tend to fill in the story with assumptions about facts that they do not know about.

Explanation. One of the functions of story construction is to explain the case. One wants to know what happened but also wants to be able to say something about why it happened. In this culture, understanding causality is important. Of course, the causes of things can be understood at many levels, and one could pursue the sources of human behavior to the level of chemical reactions in the brain. In stories that caseworkers construct about clients, explanations tend not to be deep. Thus, explanations that caseworkers give for the abuse of a child are often simple, for example, that the child was acting up or the caretaker was frustrated by things going on in his or her life. Sometimes deeper explanations are given, but the chain of explanation is usually short.

Researchers do not understand very well what is meant by "understanding." For us, understanding is constructing a story that is coherent and consistent and that provides at least some explanations. It is not clear how much understanding a computer program aimed at decision making needs to have. The programs the authors are developing have little understanding in the sense just suggested. They ask a lot of questions and associate a decision with particular sets of facts. (In these programs, not all sets of possible facts have decisions associated with them. In this respect, they are not unlike human decision makers who may not know what to do in a particular situation.) It is possible to build checks into the programs for contradictory or inconsistent information and to ask the user to clarify matters. Beyond that, the programs do weigh some facts more heavily than others, sometimes to the point of ignoring certain information. Thus, they do not construct a full, coherent, explanatory story of the case.

In the field of artificial intelligence, programs are being developed that understand stories and fill in details, making assumptions about missing information when necessary (Shank, 1984). Such programs are able to draw conclusions about unknown motivations, events, and outcomes. The authors' programs do not do that, and it is not certain that they need to. It is possible that many decisions in a field such as child welfare do not require deep understanding. Perhaps it is better simply to specify certain combinations of facts and associate preferred actions with each of those sets. Human situations contain lots of inconsistent and missing facts. The human tendency to try to resolve those contradictions and gaps may be misguided in certain circumstances. Perhaps the program should be oblivious to some contradictions.

Commonsense Understanding

The problem of common sense is connected to the issue of story construction in expert systems. Common sense refers to all the things one has learned since birth that are buried in one's mind and not thought about until one has to use them. Common sense is really not common in that it differs from one person to another. Two people may have different "common senses," although obviously there is an overlap, particularly among those in the same culture who have similar life experiences. A certain amount of common sense can be programmed into an expert system. That is, it is sometimes discovered that a piece of common sense has entered into a decision and that a rule that incorporates that idea can be written. But it is not clear how much common sense programs need to make decisions in child welfare. A few thousand pieces of common sense could theoretically be programmed into a system, but that may not be enough, and thus it is possible that the need for common sense will overwhelm efforts to build adequate programs.

Contextual Factors

When this project was begun, the authors were greatly concerned about the effects of "contextual" factors on social welfare decisions. Contextual factors include considerations that are external to the facts of a particular case. Such considerations include organizational and political constraints on decisions, the availability of resources (including the worker's time and energy), and caseload factors (the size and composition of the caseload of the worker, office, and agency). Such factors undoubtedly affect real decisions, and some could be included in a decision-making model and in an expert system. The legitimacy of contextual factors depends, to a certain extent, on the particular decision to be made. For example, it seems inappropriate to allow the availability of resources to enter into decisions about the risk of harm to a child, but when decisions are made about the type of placement to be used, resources need to be taken into account.

The problem with some of these factors is that their influence is often more unpredictable than are case-specific issues; that is, their effects depend on the worker or the office. Although separate systems could be developed for each worker (who would change from time to time), the authors are aiming for something more general. Thus, many of these contextual factors could be thought of as sources of "error variance," causes of variations in decisions from the systematic bases the authors are trying to uncover.

When contextual considerations crop up in discussions with experts, they are subjected to critical scrutiny, that is, to questioning about whether they are systematic elements that should be taken into account in the decision-making process. Sometimes these contextual elements are not generalizable and therefore are not appropriate to include in such systems. When contextual issues are generalizable, they are included.

Depth of Social Work Knowledge

The issue of just how complicated or "deep" knowledge in social work is has many implications, some of which have to do with the future of expert systems in the field. If the knowledge is relatively simple, then questions can be raised about whether expert systems are really needed in the field. Of course, the process of developing expert systems may still serve useful purposes even if a system is never used for decision making. It may help systematize knowledge, in which case the system could be used for training and perhaps for monitoring practice. But if decisions are not complex, then a computer program to help make them is unlikely to be used in practice.

The authors cannot really approach the question of the overall depth of social work knowledge, since they are working on well-defined decisions in a limited field, child welfare. At most, they can discuss their initial impressions of how complicated certain decisions in that field are. These decisions do not appear to be very complicated; perhaps it should be said that they are "moderately" complicated. A moderate number of decisions need to be made in the course of a child welfare case; the number of factors entering into each decision ranges from small to moderate, and the "depth" of the decision tree for any decision is usually small. The complexity of an expert system is sometimes measured in terms of the number of rules (although that is an arbitrary measure, since a single rule can be complex). So far, the authors' systems contain at most a few hundred rules.

In short, it does not seem that a large and complex body of knowledge is involved in making these decisions. This observation raises the issue of the relative importance of knowledge and skill in the work of a child welfare caseworker. It is possible that the worker's skill in interviewing and investigating a case is a more important part of the job than is the actual making of decisions, however agonizing those critical decisions are. Thus, obtaining the relevant facts of a case may be more difficult than making a decision from those facts. So far, the authors' programs do not provide guidance about how to find information; they assume that the user has the information they ask for. Modeling the skills of interviewing and investigating would be a far more difficult task than modeling the decision-making process.

The matter of skill has often come up in criticisms of expert systems, although in a different form than was posed here. The critics have suggested that real experts do not make decisions by using a set of rules, but take action on the basis of skills that are deeply ingrained (Dreyfus & Dreyfus, 1984, 1985). When they were novices, experts may have used rules, but they have long since discarded the rules as the basis of action. Experts can give reasons for their actions if pressed, but the reasons do not come close to capturing the skills involved. This notion of skill comes close to the idea of "intuition" but goes beyond it. Whether this aspect of skill, the skill used in making a decision, is a serious problem for expert systems in social welfare is still not clear and seems to be an empirical issue. Even though experts may not use rules anymore, it may be possible to approximate their behavior to a high degree of accuracy with a set of rules.

Validation

If and when full-scale expert systems are developed in social welfare, it will be necessary to subject them to verification, that is, to determine whether they are adequate for the purposes for which they were designed. Of course, the correctness of outcomes is a concern throughout the developmental process. Hence, the sensibleness of each rule and the logical consistency of the set of rules must be considered. Once a reasonably large system is developed, it is subjected to what may be called "laboratory testing"; that is, the developer tries to think up combinations of input data that could make the system fail, just as the designer of an airplane part subjects the part to all manners of stress. Once a complete system has survived such laboratory testing, it must be given a more formal test.

The testing of an expert system usually proceeds by trying it out on numerous cases on which one or more experts have rendered decisions. Like a human consultant, a computer system will make mistakes, so the adequacy of the system is measured by the proportion of cases in which the system gives the same recommendation as do the majority of experts. Question can be raised as to whether a comparison with experts is the appropriate test of an expert system in social welfare. But other issues arise in the evaluation process.

The first problem concerns the specification of the relevant universe of cases for the system. This problem is likely to be more serious for expert systems in social welfare than for those in other arenas, such as medicine. The system on which the authors are working concerns decisions made in the investigation of allegations of child abuse and neglect in Cook County. But that is a large universe; it includes children of various ethnicities, races, social classes, and cultures. It seems desirable to specify more narrowly the universe of cases on which the system is to work. Such specification is likely to be difficult, requiring the uncovering of various assumptions and biases in the system.

As was just mentioned, the adequacy of an expert system is usually expressed in terms of a percentage of correct recommendations. However, a common problem is encountered in the use of fallible techniques in individual cases. Although the system may be 90 percent correct overall, in an individual case, it is either 100 percent right or 100 percent wrong. (When referring to a correct recommendation, the authors assume a certain kind of decision with certain kinds of outcomes, but do not assume that one decision is good and the other bad. Rather, they assume that if one knew the outcomes that would ensue from each alternative, one could rank them clearly in terms of their benefits and harms. The decision to take protective custody of a child is an example of such a decision.) The decision to use less-than-certainly-effective techniques in an individual case is based on the weighing of the probability of success, the availability of alternative approaches, and the costs of the various possible errors.

This line of reasoning suggests that it would be desirable to have some idea about the kinds of cases on which the system falters. Hence, it seems that the aim of an evaluation of an expert system should not just be to determine the proportion of cases for which the system gives correct decisions but to uncover the system's limitations. Specifying the relevant universe of cases is part of specifying limitations, but within the intended universe, the system may do poorly on certain kinds of cases, and the character of those cases should be specified.

These observations could also be made about the evaluation of new social work interventions. That is, the evaluation of new interventions may be thought of as involving a determination of the relevant universe and a specification of the limitations of the intervention with the purpose of finding out the kinds of cases for which the intervention does not work. In the case of expert systems, it should be possible to find in the system those features (such as sets of rules) that give rise to the limitations and to consider possible ways to remove the limitations, something that often is not easily done with an intervention.

The analogy with the evaluation of interventions is an appropriate place to take up the issue of the standard of correctness against which an expert system should be judged. As was noted, the usual practice is to compare the system's performance against that of an expert or experts. This practice obviously is not entirely satisfactory; it would be more desirable to test the system's recommendations with empirical evidence on the outcomes of actions taken as a result of the recommendations, just as one evaluates an intervention by looking at its outcomes.

So one should attempt to uncover the limitations of the system in terms of the kinds of cases on which it makes the wrong decision and should conduct that investigation by examining the outcomes of actions taken as a result of the system's recommendations. This line of investigation leads to a new set of problems. First, there is the problem of defining what is meant by a "kind of case." One could mean a particular set of input data, that is, a specific configuration of responses to questions that the system asks. However, in the case of the system on which the authors are now working, there are hundreds of millions of possible configurations of data (the data consist primarily of categorical variables, such as the child's age, that are reduced to categories). Hence, the "kind of case" must be taken as meaning some set of possible configurations of input values. How small or large those sets should be is a problem. The smaller they are, the more useful to a person in deciding whether to use the system for the case at hand. But many small sets will be difficult for the evaluator to handle. Determining the boundaries of the sets is also a problem. One of the classical functions of theorizing is to specify "meaningful" or "relevant" sets of configurations of data. But work with expert systems clearly reveals the limitations of existing theories. In particular, the focus on minute details that is required in the development of expert systems is not supported by theories that are at a global level of specification.

Hence, the evaluator should examine the outcomes of recommendations for a reasonably large number of relatively small "kinds of cases." Of course, to do so correctly, one needs some comparison cases in each cell, cases on which actions other than those recommended by the program were taken. Now one encounters the classic small cell problem. Where is the evaluator going to find enough cases to perform an adequate test within each kind of case? The tests will have to be done over time, so there will also be problems of sample loss, not to mention problems of measurements, specification of outcomes, and so on. And who is going to pay for this huge undertaking? These observations about the problems of evaluating expert systems have relevance for the assessment of empirically based practice in general.

EXPERT SYSTEMS AND PRACTICE RESEARCH

During the past three decades, experimentation was valued as a source of information about practice. The work on expert systems again focuses attention on practitioners' knowledge, or "practice wisdom," assuming that it is worthwhile. The development of expert systems requires that practitioners be seen not only as partners with researchers in the development of knowledge, but also as the source of knowledge.

The development of expert systems involves a scrutiny of the bases of decisions and other professional activities and requires that the developers get as close as possible to the observable phenomena underlying decisions. The process of moving from observation to judgment and decision is thus laid out in great detail. This process can then be criticized and, it is hoped, improved.

However, if the authors' initial experience is found to be typical, it may be discovered that there are many areas of practice in which expert knowledge is not deep or is illusive. Of course, from the standpoint of knowledge development, this lack of knowledge provides great opportunities. Those domains in which knowledge is found to be thin or nonexistent could become the focus of knowledge-building research. Essentially, the scenario would be to use expert knowledge when it exists and to start building knowledge in areas in which it is thin or lacking. Of course, as has been discussed, there is still the considerable task of determining the extent to which expert knowledge is valid.

In those areas in which knowledge is relatively deep, the attention to knowledge representation that is required in the development of expert systems may also contribute to the expansion of knowledge. The linear representation typically found in the hypothetico-deductive paradigm does not easily fit the complexity of the decision-making processes used by practitioners. Linear combinations of factors, even with nonlinear and interactive terms, may be inadequate to represent many of these processes. As was indicated, even simple approaches to the design of expert systems (such as systems of rules) may not work, as in the authors' attempts to represent counseling decisions. Part of the problem lies in the importance of story construction, common sense, and contextual factors for many decisions. The question is, How can one adequately represent a knowledge base such as that found in social work practice—knowledge that is highly intuitive, contextual, uncertain, and responsive? It is a type of knowledge that needs to be both generalizable and applicable to particular dynamic person-situation contexts. In this regard, there is much to be learned from research on knowledge representation that is being conducted in such disciplines as computer science, cognitive psychology, and philosophy.

REFERENCES

Brachman, M. (1979). The practitioner as theoretician. *Journal of Education for Social Work, 9, 7.*

Citrenbaum, R., Geissman, J., & Schultz, R. (1987, September). Selecting a shell. *AI Expert,* pp. 30–39.

Dreyfus, H. L., & Dreyfus, S. E. (1984). From Socrates to expert systems: The limits of calculative reasoning. *Evaluation and Program Planning, 4,* 207–218.

Dreyfus, H. L., & Dreyfus, S. E. (1985). *Mind over machine.* New York: Free Press.

Geissman, J. R., & Schultz, R. D. (1988, February). Verification and validation of expert systems. *AI Expert,* pp. 26–33.

Marcot, B. (1987, July). Testing your knowledge base. *AI Expert,* pp. 42–47.

Shank, R. (1984). *The cognitive computer.* Reading, MA: Addison-Wesley.

Commentary

Issues in the Development of Expert Systems to Enhance Decision Making in Child Welfare

Theodore J. Stein

Mullen and Schuerman's work on expert systems is an extension of a line of investigation that has intrigued social work researchers since the late 1950s. Two questions lie at the core of the problem that they are addressing: What are the factors that influence decision making in social work (in this case in child welfare)? Can the decision-making process be formalized through the development of models to guide the practitioner? The need for models to facilitate rational decision making is as great, if not greater, today as it was in the past, and the task of developing models is somewhat easier.

RATIONAL MODELS OF DECISION MAKING

The profession has long assumed that professional education equips the practitioner to make the difficult choices that are confronted in practice. There is little empirical support for this contention. Even if it were true, it would not apply to child welfare settings. As Mullen and Schuerman correctly pointed out in Chapter 4, few child welfare practitioners, supervisors included, have graduate degrees in social work, and relatively few have bachelor of social work degrees. Most practitioners acquire knowledge of their jobs through in-service training programs, consultation with supervisors, and on-the-job experience.

Professional ethics and concern for clients' rights demand that decision making be as objective as possible—that the personal bias that research has shown strongly influences social workers' decision making must be reduced if not eliminated (Stein, Gambrill, & Wiltse, 1976; Stein & Rzepnicki, 1984). In addition, the amount of litigation against child welfare agencies and their employees is growing rapidly (Besharov, 1985; Stein, 1987). There is more litigation in child welfare than in any other area of social work practice. Malpractice suits, charges of criminal liability, and class-action suits against agencies demand the development and implementation of procedures to rationalize decision making.

The foregoing supports an argument for the development and use of decision-making models when choices are based, to the extent possible, on objective facts organized in a rational manner. It does not, however, argue specifically for the use of computers to facilitate training and decision making. Whether expert systems are a viable alternative (or a useful adjunct) to traditional approaches to in-service training and whether computers will be helpful to practitioners for organizing information and making decisions are empirical questions.

THE DATABASE

Identifying the database that social workers use for decision making has been one of the most difficult tasks confronting researchers. This problem, as Mullen and Schuerman pointed out, is not confined to social work but exists in other disciplines.

A central problem in specifying the database for decision making in child welfare has been the lack of shared purpose in the field, which has encouraged the pursuit of personalized agendas. For example, before 1980 and passage of the Adoption Assistance and Child Welfare Act, it was relatively easy to place a child in foster care. Foster care was used for a variety of reasons: (1) to provide treatment, since it was assumed that foster care was therapeutic for a child (Kline & Overstreet, 1972); (2) to punish parents whose behavior, although not necessarily injurious to a child, was repugnant to social workers and other members of the community (Mnookin, 1977); (3) to reduce a series of unspecified risks, when concern for a child's safety was reinforced by vague laws and a standard for decision making that focused the decision maker's attention on making long-range predictions (Goldstein, Freud, & Solnit, 1979); and (4) to give parents respite in the hope that children could be reunited with their families of origin (Kadushin & Martin, 1988). It takes little imagination to conceive of the multiplicity of "databases" that could be brought to bear to answer the questions that arise from these diverse purposes. In addition to theories of social work practice and of child development, social workers had to factor in their assumptions about what any juvenile court judge would tolerate, to account for normative practices within their agencies, and to consider the availability of resources before making a decision. It would have been amazing had research uncovered consistent principles of decision making.

The identification of a database has been simplified in recent years. Individual discretion has been replaced, to a large extent, by statutes, agency policies, and procedural manuals that set forth with precision what workers are to do and by professional standards for practice that narrow the range of variables to be considered in making choices. For example, vague laws that allowed children to be placed in foster care because they were not receiving "proper parental guidance" are being replaced in many states by the requirement of evidence that a child has been harmed or will suffer harm because of parental actions. Narrowing the conditions for removal and requiring that social workers articulate the nexus between parental behaviors and a child's condition reduce greatly the variables to be considered in decision making and facilitate the creation of a database.

Issues

One of the difficulties in developing models for decision making in child welfare that would be generally applicable across settings is accounting for site-specific variables, which Schuerman and Mullen referred to as "contextual factors," such as the availability of resources, the culture in an agency, and the erratic decision-making behavior of juvenile court judges.

Some of the factors that simplify the creation of a database create problems in producing general models for decision making. To the extent that precision in state policies and procedures and changes in the statutory basis for adjudicating a child who has been abused or neglected make it easier to outline the variables that influence decision making in any city or state, they make it difficult to generate models that would be applicable across jurisdictions. Thus, although it may be easier to identify the variables that are salient to decision making than in the past, the substantive rules in any model will likely vary across states and within states that have county-run child welfare systems.

Implementation

It may be easier to develop expert systems than to implement them in practice settings. The numerous problems in this regard include the ability and willingness of administrators to allocate funds for necessary hardware and software, the resistance of staff to efforts to routinize their work, the possibility that staff members will resist computerized decision making because they view computers as a way for administrators to monitor their behavior, and concerns about the confidentiality of clients.

REFERENCES

Besharov, D. J. (1985). *The vulnerable social worker: Liability for serving children and families*. Silver Spring, MD: National Association of Social Workers.

Goldstein, J., Freud, A., & Solnit, A. J. (1979). *Before the best interests of the child*. New York: Free Press.

Kadushin, A., & Martin, J. A. (1988). *Child welfare services* (4th ed.). New York: Macmillan.

Kline, D., & Overstreet, H. M. (1972). *Foster care of children: Nurture and treatment*. New York: Columbia University Press.

Mnookin, R. H. (1977). Foster care: In whose best interest? *Harvard Educational Review* (reprint series 9), pp. 158–197.

Stein, T. J. (1987). The vulnerability of child welfare agencies to class action suits. *Social Service Review*, 61, 636–651.

Stein, T. J., Gambrill, E. D., & Wiltse, K. T. (1976). *Children in foster homes: Achieving continuity of care*. New York: Praeger.

Stein, T. J., & Rzepnicki, T. L. (1984). *Decision making in child welfare services*. Boston: Kluwer-Nijhoff.

The Nature of Expertise in Social Welfare

Frederic G. Reamer

All social workers want to be experts. We would like to be able to claim, with confidence, that we know how to rid clients of depression, eliminate poverty, contain crime, and accurately predict who is certain to abuse children. Only a few, including perhaps those who fear any form of determinism, even its most benign form, would want it any other way.

When we are in command of our senses, however, we know better than to expect such proficiency. We know that despite our ambitious efforts to uncover the mysteries of problems such as crime, poverty, depression, and child abuse, the secret still eludes us. The grand sum of our knowledge to date is such that we understand some of the causes of life's problems in some circumstances and that some of our interventions are effective some of the time. Sometimes we are even able to document these phenomena empirically. MacIntyre (1981) put it well:

> For the central function of the social scientist as expert advisor or manager is to predict the outcomes of alternative policies, and if his predictions do not derive from a knowledge of law-like generalisations, the status of social scientist as predictor becomes endangered—as, so it turns out, it ought to be; for the record of social scientists as predictors is very bad indeed, insofar as the record can be pieced together. (p. 85)

This statement is only partly true, of course. Life is really like a medium-size standard deviation. Thus, we social workers understand a modest amount about a lot of problems, a great deal about a few, and abysmally little about a few others. One wonders, then, what room there is for a so-called expert in social welfare.

Not that there is any shortage of people who claim to be experts. Many well-educated individuals profess—with robust arrogance and hubris—that they know just about all there is to know about a subject, but they really have a weak grasp of matters. More and more, the words of Nicholas Murray Butler (quoted in Andrews, 1989), the late philosopher and president of Columbia University, ring true: "An expert is one who knows more and more about less and less" (p. 88).

Given these sentiments, should one not summarily dismiss this notion of "expert systems" in social welfare? Is the proposal to fashion sophisticated, artificially intelligent technology to make decisions in social welfare simply another ill-conceived, sleight-of-hand maneuver?

This author thinks not, for reasons that will be set forth shortly. Although it would be preferable to choose another, more modest, name for this technology, the core of Mullen and Schuerman's proposal should not be rejected.

It is no secret that there is great—and sometimes ugly—disagreement in the profession about the proper place of empiricism and computer technology. At one extreme are those for whom empiricism seems beyond criticism. At the other extreme are those who are hostile to any effort to quantify what social workers do. Those who have been caught in the cross fire, in their meek efforts to sort it all out, have been stunned by the bite of some of the dialogue.

Fortunately, Mullen and Schuerman have taken a different tack in their observations about the application of research tools to practice. They are more concerned with knowledge in the broad sense than with empirical data in the narrow sense. Although they would probably concede that their knowledge-based expert system must depend ultimately on some data-based empirical research, their discussion understandably does not venture into that netherworld of debate between the logical empiricists and the skeptics. Their goal is more immediate: to explore the ways in which social workers' day-to-day and night-to-night judgments can be aided by computer programs designed to give advice on decisions that must be made in practice.

After an initial fear that Mullen and Schuerman's chapter would be filled with naive claims about the application of automated, empirically based knowledge to the whole range of social workers' customary decisions, this author was greatly relieved to discover that Mullen and Schuerman have a similar understanding of the limitations of expert systems and that they believe "there are many social work problems for which expert systems technology is not appropriate because of insurmountable difficulties in representing the domain of knowledge. . . . [Expert systems] would not replace the expertise of highly trained staff, but they would greatly expand the use of expert knowledge in an efficient form."

To their credit, Mullen and Schuerman see expert systems as an adjunct to the difficult decisions social workers are called on to make. Expert systems are neither a crutch nor a panacea; instead, they are a tool to help practitioners think about the complex professional world as systematically and coherently as possible. Mullen and Schuerman view expert systems as an organizing device, as a sophisticated prompt, and as an unusually tactful challenger of the conclusions about professional practice that we social workers reach on our own.

For the most part, this author agrees with this view. What should be avoided, however, is the unrealistic elevation of expectations that occurs too often whenever the word *expert* is bandied about. Neither social workers nor anyone else should believe that the introduction of expert systems means that the computer that houses them is omniscient and truly objective. As is all too well known, the machine's calculations mainly reflect the conceptual biases of human beings. The machine is only as smart as those who enter data into it, and most people are not all *that* smart when it comes to understanding—truly understanding—the human condition. Thus, the danger is that social workers will think they can routinely suspend their own judgments because the machine knows best. This danger is especially apparent with students. Having taught social work research methods and data analysis for many years, this author is still struck by the frightening impressionability of novices who are all too willing to believe—sometimes with remarkable conviction—that the computer contains inherent insight and that its wisdom far exceeds its users'.

What practitioners *should* come to understand clearly is that expert systems can—if they are introduced into social welfare organizations skillfully and constructively (no mean challenge)—help guide their thinking and their organization of complicated information. Expert systems can even suggest plausible courses of useful action. But they do not possess what David Hume, the eighteenth-century Scottish philosopher, described as the ability to derive an "ought" from an "is," that is, the ability to move from purely descriptive statements of fact (or apparent fact) about the world to normative judgments about what ought to be done (Searle, 1969). Expert systems certainly can help practitioners think more systematically about the predictors of child abuse, mental illness, and marital conflict. But no expert system can make value judgments. No machine can decide whether it is morally acceptable for a worker to lie to a child paternalistically about his abusive parent's intentions, to hospitalize a moderately confused street person against her wishes, or to breach a promise of confidentiality given to a client who has threatened to harm his spouse. Empiricism has its limits, which are seen most clearly when one is faced with complex ethical judgments (Reamer, 1990). No one yet has figured out a surefire way to operationalize concepts, such as right and wrong or duty and obligation, and the human race has been trying hard to do so at least since Socrates' time.

When we social workers honestly appraise the status of our knowledge, we have to admit that it is in the middle range. It is far beyond primitive and far short of perfect. It is much like what Brodbeck (1968) aptly dubbed "imperfect knowledge"—when one has only a limited grasp of the nature and magnitude of the complex variables that fill one's world. Social work theories about human behavior are much more like amorphous clouds than like precision clocks, as Popper (1965) stated decades ago. As Popper (1950) said, "We shall never get anything like 'the whole truth.' Our theories are not descriptions of nature, but only of some little feathers which we plucked out of nature's garb, more or less accidently" (p. 193).

Nonetheless, practitioners must do what they can with what they have, and if the cumulative knowledge the profession now possesses can be brought to bear on practitioners' decisions and lend greater order to their judgments, that will be all for the better. But let us be careful not to oversell the product, lest we lead professionals to believe that their fallible but wonderful and unique human judgment should be rejected in favor of expert systems' orderly printouts. After all, it is up to us to generate the important questions in the first place, and this function certainly cannot be assumed by automated technology. Although our ability to produce the right question is itself circumscribed, it is a profound ability nonetheless. As John Tukey once observed (quoted in Rose, 1977), "Far better an approximate answer to the right question, which is often vague, than an exact answer to the wrong questions, which can always be made precise" (p. 23).

REFERENCES

Andrews, R. (1989). *The concise Columbia dictionary of quotations*. New York: Columbia University Press.

Brodbeck, M. (1968). Explanation, prediction, and "imperfect" knowledge. In M. Brodbeck (Ed.), *Readings in the philosophy of the social sciences* (pp. 363–398). New York: Macmillan.

MacIntyre, A. (1981). *After virtue*. Notre Dame, IN: University of Notre Dame Press.

Popper, K. (1950). Indeterminism in quantum physics and in classical physics, Part II. *British Journal for the Philosophy of Science, 1*, 173–195.

Popper, K. (1965). *Of clouds and clocks: An approach to the problem of rationality and the freedom of man* (Annual Holly Compton Memorial Lecture). St. Louis, MO: Washington University.

Reamer, F. G. (1990). *Ethical dilemmas in social service* (2nd ed.). New York: Columbia University Press.

Rose, R. (1977). Disciplined research and undisciplined problems. In C. H. Weiss (Ed.), *Using social research in public policy making*. Lexington, MA: Lexington Books.

Searle, J. R. (1969). How to derive an "ought" from an "is." In W. D. Hudson (Ed.), *The is/ought question*. New York: St. Martin's Press.

Expert Systems, Socrates, and the Philosophy of Mind

Jerome C. Wakefield

An expert system is a computer program designed to capture a form of human expertise in a set of programmable rules for making decisions. The rules are typically obtained by interviewing experts about the rules that they follow when they make the relevant decisions. Because each step in a computer program must be clearly specified, constructing an expert system requires a precise understanding of how the mind of the expert works. Thus, expert systems is much more than a technology; it is really a new form of theory construction, in which the subject matter is the detailed functioning of the mind of the expert. The theory (in the form of a computer program) is empirically tested by comparing its performance to that of the expert being modeled. If it were possible routinely to construct expert systems that mimic human expertise, computers could perform tasks that now require human intelligence, with momentous consequences for society.

Because it is easy to get swept away by the grand theoretical and practical aspirations of the expert systems field, Mullen and Schuerman's unusually balanced appraisal in Chapter 4 is all the more refreshing. Mullen and Schuerman's lucid consideration of both the problems and potential of expert systems in social work stands in contrast to the overly optimistic predictions that typically emanate from the artificial intelligence community. The reality is that despite prodigious efforts, the expert systems field has so far generally failed in its goal of modeling human-level intelligent performance (Dreyfus & Dreyfus, 1986). There are occasional successes under constrained conditions, and many programs approach a level of minimal though brittle competence, but not full expertise. In sum, "All attempts to use facts, heuristic principles provided by experts, and inferences to produce expertise in areas where experts exhibit holistic understanding have failed" (Dreyfus & Dreyfus, undated, p. 7).

Why is it so difficult to model expertise with computer programs? As will be discussed later, the assumption that expertise consists of rules may be the Achilles' heel of expert systems. If *rule* is understood broadly as any instruction in which specified data determine a specified decision, then all current types of expert systems consist of sets of rules. (I do not consider here the new "neural net" systems, which do not attempt to model existing human expertise with rules, but, rather, attempt to build up their own form of expertise from scratch; success with neural nets has been extremely limited.) Mullen and Schuerman attempted to distinguish "rule-based" systems from other kinds of expert systems, but their distinction is really among different types of rules. As Dreyfus and Dreyfus (undated) put it, "An analysis of the programming techniques underlying all current expert systems shows they essentially involve using rule-like principles to make inferences from banks of data" (p. 4).

This commentary considers some obstacles to the computer modeling of expertise by sets of rules. These obstacles are important not only because they place limits on the expert systems that may be constructed, but because they suggest ways that actual expert systems may unexpectedly go wrong in their decision making. A diagnosis of the problems with expert systems also has general intellectual implications because it concerns the limitations of certain approaches to the mind. Thus, these observations are relevant to many areas of professional concern, including practice and education, as shall be emphasized at the end.

SOCRATES AND THE FAILURE TO FIND RULES

As Dreyfus and Dreyfus (1984) first suggested, the two basic assumptions underlying expert systems methodology can be traced back to Socrates. They are, first, that possessing expertise is a matter of possessing knowledge in the form of a set of rules and, second, that an expert is capable, with prompting (as in a Socratic dialogue), of explicitly formulating the rules that constitute his or her expertise. Socrates applied this methodology to the study of virtuous traits, such as wisdom, moderation, and courage, which he considered a kind of "expertise in living" that enables one to live a happy life. He did so by trying to identify people who might possess the appropriate virtues and thus the corresponding knowledge; then, by engaging in a dialogue with them about their virtue, he tried to formulate their knowledge into rules that could be taught to others. Socrates thus played the role of what the expert systems industry now calls the "knowledge engineer," who interviews the expert and formulates the expert's knowledge into a set of rules.

Socrates failed in his quest for the rules underlying virtue. Both his methodology and his failure may be illustrated with passages from a Platonic dialogue, *Laches*. In the dialogue, two generals, Laches and Nicias, are consulted by some fathers who want to know how to train their young sons to be courageous. The generals are consulted because they are assumed to be experts on the nature of courage. When Socrates enters the discussion, he first states the basic assumption of the knowledge engineer that "what we know, we must, I suppose, be able to state" (Plato, 1973, p. 30), and then asks Laches, "What is courage?" Laches responds:

> Good heavens Socrates, there is no difficulty about that; if a man is willing to remain at his post and to defend himself against the enemy without running away, then you may rest assured that he is a man of courage. (p. 31)

Socrates points out that there are several problems with this definition. First, people can be courageous even though they are retreating, if they are fighting while they are retreating and if the retreat is for strategic purposes. So, standing one's ground is not really a necessary condition for courage. Furthermore, it is arbitrary to limit the definition to cases of courage in battle; people can be courageous in political, personal, or professional relationships, as well. At best, Laches has provided an example of courage, rather than a rule by which courage can be universally recognized.

Laches recognizes Socrates' examples as genuine cases of courage and concedes that his definition is incorrect. He then formulates a more general account: "Well then, I think [courage] is a sort of endurance of the soul" (p. 34). That is, courageous people endure in their action despite pressure and pain. Socrates points out that this new criterion is not sufficient. Some people possess foolish endurance; they do not care enough about pain or danger to take sensible care of themselves, and thus may needlessly sacrifice their lives. Endurance may even be shown in the performance of a cowardly act, such as running from a battle despite physical pain and entreaties from one's comrades. Endurance may be due to recklessness, foolhardiness, obliviousness to danger, and resolute cowardice, none of which indicate courage.

Laches finally admits, in frustration and bewilderment, that he is unable to formulate the rule that he uses when he makes his expert judgments about courage:

> I am really getting annoyed at being unable to express what I think about courage in this fashion. I still think I know what courage is, but I can't understand how it has escaped me just now, so that I can't pin it down in words and say what it is. (p. 37)

After a lengthy investigation, Socrates concludes that neither Laches nor Nicias can actually state the knowledge they supposedly possess: "Then we have not discovered, Nicias, what courage is" (p. 47).

Socrates' problem with Laches illustrates perhaps the greatest single obstacle to the success of expert systems methodology. When knowledge engineers try to get experts to state the rules that they follow, they often find that the experts do not know any such rules. Even with insistent Socratic prompting, experts cannot make explicit their expert knowledge, and when they do formulate rules under the pressure of questioning, the rules often prove to be inadequate to explain their performance.

There are three ways of explaining these facts. The explanation that Socrates embraced is that "experts," like the two generals, do not actually possess the expertise they claim to possess. This explanation is unlikely as a general solution, given that many of the greatest experts in fields ranging from railroad scheduling to chess playing have had no better luck formulating their expertise into rules than did Laches and Nicias. A second explanation is that the rules are complex and have become unconscious from habitual use. This explanation is also unlikely, given that endless discussion and fine tuning do not seem to reveal the rules that the expert is supposed to know unconsciously. The third possibility is that expertise does not consist entirely of a set of rules and that the expert systems approach is based on a mistaken conception of human nature.

PROBLEMS WITH THE RULE APPROACH

There are many reasons for doubting that expertise can be formulated as a set of rules. First, to formulate the rules that make up an expert system, one must be able to describe all the possible kinds of data that the system's rules must take into account. However, expertise involves the ability to adjust to unexpected circumstances and to see the relevance of novel facts. Because what is relevant to a decision is not entirely predictable, expert systems tend to break down when novelty is involved. The appropriate response in a novel situation may be obvious to any person, but it may be beyond the expert system's capabilities because the novel circumstances were not anticipated when the system was being programmed.

As Mullen and Schuerman noted, a human expert has the entire world of common sense at his or her disposal and acts in the context of that vast amount of background knowledge. Only a limited amount of commonsense wisdom, over and above domain-specific rules, can be built into expert systems. Thus, expert systems are prone to be smart if the relevant information is limited, but foolish if broader commonsense considerations play a role. Consequently, expert systems are likely to have more success in domains that are relatively independent of common sense, like recognizing geological formations that contain petroleum or identifying substances on the basis of spectral sequences. However, no field requires common sense more than does social work. The expertise to deal successfully with a client's problems is not isolatable from a broad, everyday understanding of people and their environments.

Common sense is especially important because of a feature of human meaning systems often called "holism." The cognitive system operates as a whole, in the sense that any belief anywhere in a person's meaning system can affect any other belief if the right cognitive connections exist. Consequently, it is generally impossible to isolate decisions about one topic from the overall knowledge of the decision maker about things in general. Yet, it is precisely such an isolation that knowledge engineers attempt.

Human beings, unlike expert systems, are extremely sensitive to the overall "Gestalt" or meaning of a decision situation. Once an overall meaning is imparted to a situation, the details take on new meaning, and seemingly incidental facts may turn out to be critical. One may call this fact—that any unpredictable detail may be critical in light of an overall sense of the situation—the "Sherlock Holmes effect"; Holmes was forever finding some small clue that no one else would consider to be relevant and showing that it had direct and dramatic bearing on the case at hand. Sets of rules lack such flexible contextual understanding. Consequently, expert systems will sometimes fail in situations in which most human decision makers would succeed.

EXPERTISE AS EXPERIENCE-BASED SKILL

It is difficult to comprehend what human expertise may be if it is not a matter of rules. One possibility is that expertise is a mental version of bodily skills, such as walking, driving an automobile, or piano playing. Such skills display the kind of holistic and flexible responses that are required of the expert. At least at a phenomenological level, skills do not seem to work like rule systems, even though rules and reflection are involved in the early stages of learning a skill. Early in learning to play the piano, for instance, one learns such rules as that one should hit a certain key to get a certain musical note. But the virtuoso is no longer aware of such choices; he or she has a direct relationship with the production of the music, and hitting the right key is not a separate act of choice but a fluid part of playing. This skill of hitting the right key at the right time in the right way, given a particular context and a particular audience, would be hard, indeed, to capture in a set of rules.

Although no fully adequate theory of either skill or expertise exists, Dreyfus and Dreyfus (1984, 1986) presented an interesting account of the development of skills as a model for the development of expertise. Their approach is a useful beginning point for reflection and one that explains some of the problems with rule systems just described. Guided by studies of the acquisition of skills in such varied fields as chess, nursing, driving, and piloting a fighter plane, Dreyfus and Dreyfus suggested that the acquisition of skills can be divided into five stages and that rules are a relatively primitive form of decision making used only in the early stages.

At the heart of Dreyfus and Dreyfus's account of expertise as skill is the claim that as experiences build up, the perceptual organization of the learner evolves so that he or she sees new things. According to Dreyfus and Dreyfus, the novice begins by responding to context-independent features of the situation that can be recognized without special knowledge. The novice has no "feel" for the situation, so he or she must use rules concerning such context-independent features to guide action. With experience, the learner becomes capable of making new discriminations and of perceiving context-relative aspects of situations that he or she would not have noticed before. This ability enables the learner to apply rules of greater subtlety involving the newly perceived aspects. Next, as the learner becomes capable of recognizing many relevant aspects and features of situations, the amount of data becomes overwhelming, and a simple set of rules is too unwieldy. At this point, the learner starts to approach tasks in two stages. First, the learner perceives a situation as a whole, rather than as a bundle of features and aspects as before, and immediately sees the situation in terms of an overall need, goal, or problem that organizes his or her subsequent activity and limits the relevant considerations that have to be taken into account. This holistic perception is based not on rules, but on a direct sense of the situation shaped by the similarities between the current situation and situations encountered in the past. Then, within the constraints set by the overall perception of a central goal or need, the learner applies the rules that are relevant to that kind of situation and forms a specific plan.

Finally, with more experience and talent, the use of rules for formulating specific courses of action wanes. Instead of first seeing the overall situation in terms of a goal and then deliberating about how to carry out the goal, the expert immediately perceives the situation in terms of the action that is needed. The expert has an immediate sense of the relevant similarities and dissimilarities between the present situation and a myriad of past situations and acts on this sense without having to decompose the situation into features or aspects. He or she simply perceives the situation in terms of what needs to be done, and this perception is shaped by a history of concrete encounters. Thus, expertise at the highest level is totally independent of rules:

Normally, the instruction process begins with the instructor decomposing the task environment into context-free features which the beginner can recognize without benefit of experience. The beginner is then given rules for determining actions on the basis of these features, like a computer following a program. . . .

The expert performer—except, of course, during moments of break-down—understands, acts, and learns from results without any conscious awareness of the process. What transparently *must* be done *is* done. People do not usually make conscious deliberative decisions when they walk, talk, ride a bicycle, drive, or carry on most social activities. . . .

It seems that a beginner makes inferences using rules and facts just like a heuristically programmed computer, but that with talent and a great deal of involved experience, the beginner develops into an expert who intuitively sees what to do without applying rules. (Dreyfus & Dreyfus, 1984, pp. 222-226)

If Dreyfus and Dreyfus are correct, then it is easy to see why experts—including Laches and Nicias—cannot state the rules by which they operate. There simply are no such rules. The expert operates by directly recognizing appropriate similarities between the current situation and thousands of previously encountered cases.

The notion that expertise consists of the ability to perceive holistic relations between the current problem and a vast array of previously experienced situations has implications for professional education. One implication is that theory-based education may be a necessary foundation, but it is severely limited in its power to produce practice expertise. A reassuring implication is that social work's focus on field experience as a central part of education is appropriate to the goal of educating practitioners.

APPLICATION OF EXPERT SYSTEMS TO SOCIAL WORK

Having considered obstacles to the success of expert systems, this chapter concludes on a more optimistic note, with a brief comment on some potential contributions of expert systems methodology to social work. None of the limitations of rule-based expert systems implies that the formulation of an expert system is without value. Despite the obstacles to expert systems' achievement of true expertise, even the critics acknowledge that it is possible for expert systems to attain a level of competence that is sufficient to make them illuminating and worth-while instruments: "The computer can do better than the beginner, and can even exhibit useful competence" (Dreyfus & Dreyfus, 1984, p. 221). One can still learn a lot about how people think from the sorts of interviews conducted in constructing an expert system, even if total success is not achieved and even if the results do not represent the highest level of expertise. Imperfect systems can be useful as a support to human decision making, as long as they are not relied on as the sole decision-making authority.

What, then, might expert systems do for clinical research? An expert system is an attempt to model somebody's way of thinking. Because of the power of computers, such models can be much more elaborate than is the typical written theory. However, to create an expert system, one has to display Socratic relentlessness in questioning the expert, drawing distinctions, and formulating new rules to take account of discovered exceptions. Expert systems methodology is thus qualitative empirical method ology systematically and doggedly pursued. Therein lies its promise as a new and more precise model for the empirical study of practice and as an educational tool that will demand more critical and research-minded thinking from students in formulating their cases.

The most obvious application of expert systems to social work is in the modeling of the skills of the expert practitioners, but expert systems methodology could just as easily be used to understand the target of the intervention, rather than the intervener. The possibility of using expert systems methodology to model clients' skills seems to have been overlooked in previous discussions of expert systems, yet such modeling would have manifold benefits. All people are experts on how they go about running their lives. One may even say that clients are experts on how they are self-defeating and why they fail to cope better with their environment, to the degree that their mental processes are involved in their problems. Clinical interviewing is aimed at enabling clinicians to construct models of clients' functioning. Expert systems methodology could be used to systematize the clinical interviewer's task and provide the interviewing process with structure and rigor. This modeling could be done jointly with clients, so that clients could help us to understand the rules they are using in grappling with their environments. The limitations of expert systems would not be fatal to this enterprise because even a partial improvement in our understanding of clients could be extremely important.

Conceptualizing practitioners, in part, as "knowledge engineers" attempting to understand the rules that their clients follow could challenge social workers to be much more precise in their formulations of cases. It also could provide an opportunity for sidestepping the dogmatisms of the various therapeutic theories to which practitioners adhere. The use of a "client-centered" expert systems approach to practice that is informed by an integrative theoretical framework could enable us to achieve the long-sought ideal of a nondogmatic idiographic formulation of each client's meaning system. Such a formulation could be tested in the course of practice and used to suggest interventions. Thus, expert system methodology could be used as a model for both idiographic practice research and practice itself. This is an optimistic vision of how expert systems may contribute to clinical practice, education, and research and bring clinical research and clinical practice closer together. Even if the product of such an attempt should prove to be flawed, we, our students, and our clients would surely benefit from the rigors of the process.

REFERENCES

Dreyfus, H., & Dreyfus, S. (undated). *Ethical aspects of expert systems.* Unpublished manuscript.

Dreyfus, H., & Dreyfus, S. (1984). From Socrates to expert systems: The limits of calculative rationality. *Technology in Society, 6*, 217–235.

Dreyfus, H., & Dreyfus, S. (1986). *Mind over machine: The power of human intuition and expertise in the era of the computer.* New York: Free Press.

Plato. (1973). Laches. In *Plato: Laches & Charmides* (R.K. Sprague, Trans.). New York: Bobbs-Merrill.

Synthesis

Expert Systems in Social Welfare Practice: Questions and Concerns

Denise E. Bronson

Mullen and Schuerman's effort to explicate and program the decision-making processes of experienced social workers in a child welfare agency raises fundamental questions about four issues. These issues are (1) the nature of practice wisdom, (2) the methodology of developing expert systems, (3) the limitations of expert systems software, and (4) the value of these systems for practice.

THE NATURE OF PRACTICE WISDOM

Two characterizations of practice wisdom emerged in the discussion of expert systems. First, Mullen and Schuerman described practice wisdom as a set of "if-then" rules and "stories" that guide decision making by practitioners. In this conceptualization, practitioners can be prompted to analyze and describe the procedures they use to make clinical decisions. For example, through intensive interviewing, Mullen and Schuerman were able to determine how social workers made decisions regarding out-of-home placements for children by asking the workers what information was important to the decision and how it was processed. In their view, practice wisdom is retrievable.

Wakefield presented a different characterization of practice wisdom. He suggested that there may be a level of practice wisdom that is not retrievable, since the expert cannot articulate what information is used in the process. Decision making at this level moves beyond simple if-then rules and stories and reflects the "art" of social work. Intuition plays an important role in this conceptualization.

Whether one believes that expert systems can be developed is highly dependent on which conceptualization of practice wisdom one accepts. For those who think that good social work is an "art" largely based on intuition, expert systems are impossible; they can never reflect the intricacies of practice and at best can only weakly approximate the decision making of an experienced practitioner. On the other hand, those who maintain that practice wisdom can be collected from social workers and codified see expert systems as tools for modeling practice wisdom. The first position accepts and encourages inexplicit decision making, while the second fosters specificity and precision.

METHODOLOGY OF DEVELOPING EXPERT SYSTEMS

Assuming that practice wisdom can be retrieved and codified, the question arises of how to approach the design and development of an expert system. Mullen and Schuerman's approach involved identifying a specific practice problem, selecting staff who are experienced in handling it, developing a prototype based on the experts' explanation of their decisions, testing the system, and redesigning the system if necessary. Mullen and Schuerman stressed that expert systems elevate the importance of practice wisdom by attempting to model practitioners' decision-making processes and the conclusions they draw. If the endeavor is successful, the computer will reach the same decision as the "expert" practitioners and will use the same information to reach its conclusion.

Other models for developing expert systems that reduce the importance of individual experts were proposed during the ensuing discussion. For example, an empirical model was suggested that consists of the following four steps:

1. Articulate a decision-making strategy and have practitioners implement it.

2. Monitor the implementation of the strategy.

3. Evaluate the outcomes of the decision.

4. Develop an expert system around strategies that produced desirable outcomes.

Reamer and Wakefield supported the importance of empiricism in developing expert systems. Reamer questioned whether there are identifiable experts in social work and proposed an empirical model to reduce the reliance on experienced practitioners. Wakefield noted that an empirical method may be more precise.

Concerns about selecting social work "experts" prompted additional suggestions for developing expert systems. One suggestion proposed defining decision rules after decisions are made to eliminate the necessity of consulting with experts. Another suggestion was to base programs on practitioners with demonstrated competence, rather than on "model" social workers. Still another recommendation was to develop expert systems that consolidate the knowledge of several individuals. Mullen and Schuerman agreed, noting that systems that focus on the commonalities among experts usually capture more generalizable knowledge.

LIMITATIONS OF EXPERT SYSTEMS

Despite the generally favorable attitude toward continuing the work on expert systems, several critical concerns were expressed. Reamer cautioned that social workers should not have unrealistic expectations for expert systems, since these systems are neither omniscient nor omnipotent. Wakefield warned that expert systems really model the end product of decision making, not necessarily the process. Thus, it is possible that eventually the computer will make a serious mistake that could have disastrous results.

Stein questioned the extent to which a system developed in one setting can be used in another, that is, the generalizability of expert systems. If, for example, the program uses information about an agency's or state's policies, use of the system will be limited to situations in which those policies are in effect. Similarly, shifting theoretical orientations and service objectives may limit the generalizability of the system over time. Given the expense of developing a system, this is a serious issue.

A related question concerns the inclusiveness of expert systems. Mullen and Schuerman noted that common sense and contextual factors often figure into decisions about practice. Whether this type of information can or should be included in expert systems was addressed in some manner by each of the commentators.

THE VALUE OF EXPERT SYSTEMS FOR PRACTICE

Despite the reservations expressed, the benefits of expert systems were also emphasized. First, Mullen and Schuerman noted that the process of developing expert systems allows researchers to study how practitioners make sense of information about clients by forcing them to specify what they do. In addition, the process of making expertise explicit identifies the strengths and weaknesses of practice knowledge that were not evident before.

Second, Mullen and Schuerman contended that the process of developing expert systems elevates the importance of practice wisdom in social work knowledge. Although some of the commentators questioned whether it is desirable to do so, given the current state of practice knowledge and the profession's inability to solve many problems, others argued that any procedure that stimulates thinking about practice wisdom and attempts to codify it is important.

Third, another benefit of expert systems that was identified concerned the methodology used to retrieve practice knowledge. Reamer stated that expert systems are really tools to guide systematic and coherent thinking about practice problems. Stein argued that the process of examining practice decisions may be the most important contribution of expert systems. He noted that helping practitioners to explicate their decision making rationally will allow them to articulate their decisions better—a particularly useful skill for child welfare workers who often need to justify their decisions in the courtroom. No doubt, social workers in other areas are called on to defend their decisions and can benefit in the same way.

Finally, Wakefield asserted that the development of expert systems can be used to guide future practice. For example, a discussant noted that in the field of management, the design of expert systems has emphasized the skills needed for retrieving information. Similarly, in social work, these systems help to identify what information about clients the social worker should collect to make sound decisions about practice. Mullen added that once social workers know what information is important, they may find that the decision making is easier.

In their final comments, Mullen and Schuerman stressed the importance of research to validate expert systems and reinforced their position that social work has much to learn from this effort. Their work demonstrates that the process of developing expert systems forces social workers to address many fundamental questions about the nature and value of practice wisdom. It remains to be seen whether the process of developing expert systems or the product itself is the most useful contribution of this work.

Chapter 5

Computer-Based Clinical Practice: Present Status and Future Possibilities

Walter W. Hudson

At the heart of any clinical practice is a fundamental empiricism that cannot be ignored. When needy people seek help for their problems from social agencies and human service practitioners, that act alone sets into motion the business of collecting data. The important facts that must be collected about nearly every client include information about the nature of the client's problem, the onset and duration of the problem, who else may be involved, the kinds of resources that might be available to help solve the problem, what efforts have thus far been made to deal with the problem, and the nature of any deficits or weaknesses that must be overcome. In short, there is no question that clinical practice is intensely empirical by its very nature.

Although the conduct of clinical practice is always an empirical enterprise from the outset, the empiricism of practice varies tremendously with respect to its quality and precision. Human service providers are under a constant vigil to find ways of improving the quality of information that is used to evaluate the nature and extent of clients' problems. They are also under a constant vigil to discover whether the services provided to clients produce visible or measurable gains.

Over the past decade, there has been a growing acceptance of applied measurement theory as one viable means of collecting information about the presence, frequency, duration, or magnitude of clients' problems. This acceptance has been seen in the increased use of standardized measurement tools in social work practice, as well as the heavier reliance on the use of structured interviews, problem checklists, and a variety of assessment devices that were rarely even considered only a few years ago (Edleson, 1985; Hudson, 1982; Levitt & Reid, 1981).

Although great strides have been made through the use of standardized assessment scales and other data-gathering tools to improve the quality of information obtained about clients and their problems, difficulties have been encountered. The oldest and still most heavily relied on data-gathering tool is the unstructured clinical interview. Its great appeal is its simplicity and ease of use; you do not have to score it, and you can interpret it according to any fancy or whim that may strike you. These attractive features make it one of the most unreliable and least valid data-gathering devices.

At the other extreme are highly structured measurement tools that have excellent reliabilities and validities. However, one must administer, score, and interpret them according to rigid rules that require, by comparison, a great deal of time and effort. Consequently, there is a constant tradeoff between the use of efficient and inexpensive unstructured interviews, on the one hand, and more costly and time-consuming standardized tools, on the other hand.

Therefore, it would seem that significant improvements in the quality of clinical empiricism involve the fundamental task of finding ways to improve the use of standardized assessment devices. The computer is one means of accomplishing that task. To understand the potential value of using a computer, one should first examine the procedures and problems that are associated with traditional methods of gathering clinical information.

PAPER-AND-PENCIL METHODS OF GATHERING DATA

Many human service practitioners are now using standardized assessment tools to gather a rich variety of information about their clients and their clients' problems. One example is the practitioner who routinely uses the Index of Marital Satisfaction (IMS) scale (Hudson, 1982) to evaluate the degree of discord within a dyadic relationship. Obviously, the practitioner must acquire a supply of blank IMS forms and store them in a convenient place for ready use. When the practitioner and the client decide that the IMS scale should be completed, the practitioner must get a copy of the scale from the storage area and give it to the client. The client must then complete the scale. When the client fills out the scale the first time, the practitioner must explain the purpose of the scale and discuss its use during the course of assessment and treatment. When the client has completed the IMS scale, the practitioner must then score the scale and render an interpretation of the obtained score. Often he or she will report the score to the client and then explain its meaning.

If the practitioner and the client plan to use the IMS scale repeatedly to monitor changes in the level of the client's marital discord, the IMS must be administered, scored, and interpreted each time. However, if the practitioner also chooses to produce a graphic representation of the changes with respect to the level of the client's problem, he or she must obtain or prepare a blank chart or graph and then record the IMS scores on it every time they are obtained from multiple administrations of the scale. It should not be overlooked that each copy of the completed IMS scale, as well as the chart containing the graphed scores, will likely be stored in the client's record folder.

None of these steps individually takes much time or effort by the client or the practitioner. Yet altogether they represent professional time that cannot then be devoted to delivering service. At least that is one view of the matter. Some believe that such a use of time is an integral part of the treatment process and therefore cannot be ignored or omitted. Regardless of one's position in this matter, the use of formal assessment tools requires the expenditure of professional time. That fact becomes significant if the example is extended to many practitioners who use a variety of different assessment devices with numerous clients.

The only reasonable conclusion one can draw is that a commitment to improved clinical empiricism involves a commitment to the consumption of time and monetary resources. If that commitment is exercised through the use of traditional paper-and-pencil methods of assessment and evaluation, it will ultimately be a large one. Several investigators have clearly demonstrated that it is a difficult commitment for many practitioners and human service organizations to make (Blythe, 1983; Cheatham, 1986; Gingerich, 1984; Welch, 1983).

ADVANTAGES OF MICROCOMPUTERS

One possible way to improve the empiricism of clinical practice is to use a microcomputer. Although computers are not without problems, some of which will be mentioned later, there is much to recommend them. They are now relatively inexpensive. Today one can purchase an extremely powerful microcomputer with color graphics and telecommunication for under $2,000, the price one used to pay for an electronic typewriter. Needless to say, a computer will do much more than will an electronic typewriter. Computers are useless, however, unless one has software tools that will cause them to perform useful work. That is not a serious problem, because there are now available powerful low-cost software tools that can be used to conduct many tasks that practitioners and researchers must perform. Database managers, word processors, spreadsheet programs, filing systems, and many other tools can be used to design computer-based systems for use in practice, research, and administration.

Computer-Assisted Social Services

Because of the enormous variety of software tools currently available, it is difficult to describe the use of microcomputers in terms of the many software tools that one might use. Instead, the Computer-Assisted Social Services (CASS) system is used here to illustrate the capacity of the microcomputer. CASS is a general-purpose practice tool that is available for use on IBM or compatible computers that have a hard disk and DOS 3.0 or greater (Hudson, 1990).

Storing and Producing Assessment Devices

Because of the massive storage capacity of the computer, one can virtually eliminate traditional storage areas for maintaining printed copies of a greater number of assessment tools. For example, the CASS program is delivered with 22 different assessment scales that are immediately ready for use. Practitioners who use systems such as CASS no longer need to maintain a supply of assessment tools if the computer is used to administer and score them.

The capacity to store and use 22 assessment devices is not very impressive. However, a unique feature of the CASS program is its ability to accommodate an unlimited number of scales, checklists, structured interviews, and other measurement devices. In other words, the program is user extendable. One may add to the system as many available assessment tools as one wishes, and one may create as many tools as are needed or desired.

Design Flexibility

Because of the flexibility of the computer, it is possible to use a tremendous variety of different assessment tools. Thus, by using the domain-sampling model of measurement, one can employ an almost endless variety of unidimensional and multidimensional scales. One often needs a wide range of additional measures, such as single-item self-anchored scales, checklists, semantic differentials, rating scales, and so on (Hudson, 1988). The CASS program not only will accommodate such a variety of assessment tools, it will permit the user to create new ones for use with clients. A future version of the program is planned that will incorporate the use of high-resolution graphic scales for use in working with young, preliterate children and others who have pronounced language difficulties.

Administering Assessment Devices

A computer can also be made to administer assessment devices to clients. That is, it can easily present any number of items to a client and then capture and save the client's response to each item. Naturally, the computer should have the capacity to present brief or extended instructions to the client about how any particular assessment scale should be completed.

The CASS program, for example, will present instructions for completing any assessment device. It will then present each of the items contained in the assessment scale, allow the client to respond to each item, and then save the responses for future use. There is no limit to the amount of instruction or the number of items in any assessment device that can be installed within the CASS program.

Scoring Assessment Scales

The mathematical capability of the computer is well known and plays a central role in achieving improved clinical empiricism through the ability to score and interpret completed assessment scales. For example, the CASS program actually scores each scale while the client is responding to it. Thus, by the time the client has entered his or her response to the last item, the final score on the scale has already been obtained.

As was indicated earlier, one of the difficulties of using standardized assessment tools is that these tools must be scored and interpreted according to rigid rules, such as scoring formulas, which can be simple or complex. Although practitioners can easily learn to calculate the required scores, they can just as easily make numerical errors in solving the simplest scoring formulas. Unfortunately, a simple numerical error may produce a disastrously misleading result. The computer does not make such mistakes.

But there is more to improving clinical empiricism than computing the correct score on a test or scale. Not only can the practitioner make mistakes in calculating a score, the client can make mistakes in responding at the keyboard or with a pencil and paper. Practitioners often check the responses on paper-and-pencil scales to see that each item is completed and contains an acceptable response. However, they find it difficult to ensure that each response is acceptable, and they find it all but impossible to determine whether a particular response is highly discrepant from the others.

Computers can check such things routinely. For example, the CASS program ensures that each response falls within the range specified by the particular scale, and it will not accept a response to an item that falls outside the permissible range. The program also performs another important function. It checks the response to each item to determine whether it is consistent with the responses to all other items (this feature can be turned on or off as desired). If it detects an inconsistent item, it automatically presents the item once more to the client; it does not force a consistent response, but enables the client to correct any error in the first trial. Moreover, it does so in such a manner that the client is often not aware that the item has been presented a second time.

Just as a client may answer an item by writing a 2 when intending to write a 4, for example, he or she may press the wrong key when using a computer. Thus, range and consistency checking are important capacities that should be included in any assessment procedure. They are difficult to carry out using paper-and-pencil methods, but they can be done routinely and effortlessly with a computer. Features such as these tend to produce more accurate information that has reliabilities somewhat higher than those obtained from paper-and-pencil administrations of assessment devices (Hudson, Nurius, & Reisman, 1988; Stocks, 1990).

Interpreting Assessment Scales

Scores on assessment devices are usually reported as numbers. However, numbers have no meaning in themselves; they must be interpreted. For example, it is of no benefit to tell a client that she scored, say, 46 on the IMS scale unless she is also told what that score means. Although practitioners can learn to properly interpret assessment scores, they may vary considerably in the way they choose to interpret such scores. Computers, on the other hand, can be given interpretive information about each assessment device so they can provide a consistent interpretation of each obtained score to the practitioner and the client.

The CASS program, for example, enables the practitioner to store up to 900 different diagnostic files that are used to support the interpretation of scores obtained on any scale. Each file may contain five different interpretations of scores for a total of up to 4,500 diagnostic statements that are based on the scores from any assessment device that is stored within the system. Standard interpretations of scores are provided for the 22 scales that are shipped with the CASS program.

Preparing Graphs

It is simple to prepare a graph that depicts the scores obtained by a client through repeated assessments of one or more specific problems.

Such skills are now routinely taught to students in many professional schools, and the task is considered to be a modest one by those who are familiar with the techniques.

Nonetheless, the preparation of graphs takes time, and the graphs must be updated and maintained. This is a trivial chore for the computer; the CASS program routinely presents a graphic report of a client's progress with the stroke of a few keys at any time such a report is desired. Such graphs can be viewed on screen, or they may be printed out for permanent storage in the client's record folder. Furthermore, the CASS program has eliminated the chore of updating and maintaining graphs. That is, each time the client completes an assessment scale, the graph for that scale is immediately updated and is ready to be viewed with the new score that has been added to it.

The preparation and updating of graphs are important capabilities. Although numerical scores that are obtained from reliable and valid assessment tools constitute the core of improved empiricism in clinical practice, it is the graphic representation of change in a problem over time that provides the practitioner and the client with the most valuable evaluative information about their work together. Simple graphs are perhaps one of the most powerful monitoring tools available. Yet, they are among the least used tools in social work practice. One reason for their underutilization is the time required to prepare, update, and maintain them. The computer can eliminate this problem and hence can lead to their greater use.

Using Single-Case Design

The investigation of scientific hypotheses about the effectiveness of specific packages of intervention is accomplished through the use of controlled observations about a client's response to treatment as the conditions of treatment are altered or varied according to careful plans. Single-case experimental designs constitute a set of scientific tools that may be used to enhance the quality of practice and to investigate scientific hypotheses.

As with simple graphs, single-case designs are not difficult to depict in graphic representations. Yet, they, too, are severely underused even by those practitioners who have been trained to use them. Some of the reasons for the failure to make better use of single-case designs are related to distinctions between the aims of practice and the aims of science (Hudson & Bronson, 1988). Others have to do with the deliverability of a technology (Nurius & Hudson, 1988b), an area that the computer can help to enhance.

In others words, the computer can accommodate a tremendous variety of single-case designs with little effort by the practitioner and none by the client. The CASS program, for instance, has the capacity to accommodate any single-case design of up to 12 phases for virtually every assessment device that any client completes. Moreover, the worker can create a different design for each client and each assessment scale. Once the practitioner specifies the parameters of the design, the design will be shown for every graph that is subsequently produced. Naturally, the practitioner can modify the design when necessary.

Because of the ease with which single-case designs can be used in a computer-based assessment system, practitioners may make better use of these clinical tools in the future. Equally important, such computer capabilities may lead to the increased participation by practitioners in clinical research. Such an outcome would mark a significant advance in clinical empiricism and could result in increased uses of research methods and findings in the future.

Agency Forms, Social Histories, and Clinical Questionnaires

A significant portion of the assessment work of practitioners is accomplished through the use of forms, social histories, and a variety of clinical questionnaires. The computer can be a powerful aid in administering and completing such questionnaires. For example, the CASS program will accommodate an unlimited number of forms, social histories, and clinical questionnaires that can be completed independently by the client together with the practitioner or by the practitioner during an interview with the client.

Basically, all CASS does is present the items of a questionnaire to a respondent and then permit the respondent to enter the requested information. There are, however, several advantages to using a computer for this purpose. First, the information is stored permanently for immediate retrieval and use. A wide variety of blank social history forms and clinical questionnaires need not be printed and stored in traditional paper-and-pencil form. Furthermore, one no longer has the problem of translating poor handwriting, and a new questionnaire can easily be lengthened, shortened, or otherwise modified according to experience obtained in testing and using it. Most important, the use of a computer-based clinical system eliminates the frustration that organizations have endured for years over the inconsistency with which important documents, such as social histories and clinical questionnaires, have been completed. The forms management feature of CASS is actually a type of relational database system. This means that a great deal of repetitive data entry can be eliminated and CASS, through its forms management capabilities, can even write summary reports for the practitioner or others who need them.

Tests and Examinations

Assessment scales, histories, and questionnaires are only part of the measurement systems that practitioners often are called upon to use with their clients. Another important class of measurement tools is tests and examinations that are often used to examine cognitive, intellectual, and motor skills and are indispensable in certain kinds of mental health and medical service institutions. As with assessment tools, tests and examinations can be easily administered, scored, and interpreted with the use of a computer.

The CASS program incorporates such a feature and allows for the inclusion of an unlimited number of tests of any length. Depending on how the user instructs the system, it will administer and score an entire test or compose a test of the desired length on the basis of a larger pool of items supplied by the user. It will administer any item that can be characterized as having an exact "right answer." For those who work with school-related performance and behavioral problems, formal testing may be an essential component of diagnosis and treatment planning, and the computer can be a powerful aid in such work.

Confidentiality and the Security of Data

Human service professionals must be greatly concerned about respecting the rights of clients to privacy and confidentiality. The capacity of a computer to store great quantities of information about people is frequently seen as threatening. There are basically two sources of concern. One has to do with the abuse of information, which traditionally has been dealt with by training practitioners. The second has to do with the security of obtained information: who has access to it.

It is not difficult to secure computer-based information. The computer can protect sensitive information through the use of such devices as passwords and data encryption. The CASS program uses both. Each copy of the program is licensed for use by one practitioner who is given a unique password. No one can gain access to that practitioner's records without the particular password and access to the practitioner's physical copy of the software. (The student version of the program does not protect data on clients because students and records are regulated under the supervision of classroom and field practicum instructors, who must have access to client records at all times.)

Suppose, for example, that you own a copy of the CASS program, you know a colleague's password, and you even have a diskette containing all the information about several of his or her clients. You would still not be able to gain access to those data. Neither could you use a word processor or other decoding program to read those records. The CASS program uses a sophisticated encryption algorithm to protect information on clients. In fact, it is easier for someone to break into an office and steel filing cabinets to pilfer folders of records than it is to decrypt and read a protected record of a client prepared by the CASS.

Other Desirable Features

There are many other functions or services that a computer-based assessment system could incorporate. For example, the CASS program has a full range of file and case management functions that include writing and reviewing case notes, encrypting and decrypting sensitive documents that should be included in a client record, and other management functions that enable practitioners to open and close case records, transfer case records from one practitioner to another, and prepare special case rosters for use by administrators and managers.

In other words, the CASS is not a limited-function program to administer and score assessment scales. Rather, it is an extensive system that provides the basis for operating a completely computer-based practice. It will manage an entire caseload, and it will do so for each practitioner in a social service agency or organization. It will even allow a practitioner to integrate a word processor, spread-sheet program, database manager, filer program, and other frequently used software to support a variety of practice-related functions. Neither should CASS-like systems be seen as useful exclusively for practice. Indeed, they can be employed as the only needed data-gathering tool for the conduct of small, moderate, or even quite large clinical research projects (Stocks, 1990). For example, CASS can administer any number or size of research questionnaires as well as administer and score the assessment scales that make up the body of research data one seeks.

The major point, of course, is that the microcomputer is capable of providing a tremendous number of professional service functions for use by practitioners working in a variety of human service environments. Use of and familiarity with currently available clinical software systems will generate new ideas for even more powerful service supports to practitioners and their clients.

PROBLEMS IN USING COMPUTERS IN PRACTICE

The current microcomputer technology is sufficiently powerful to make it a readily available tool for use by practitioners in nearly every type of social service setting. Furthermore, as was mentioned earlier, the cost of computers and computer supplies is no longer prohibitive, and a single microcomputer can serve five to 10 practitioners and hundreds of clients. In addition, a great deal of clinically relevant software is now available, and more is being developed every day. Although the cost of such software varies considerably, many fine products are available at modest prices. Therefore, the major problem associated with the use of computers has to do with the training of practitioners, supervisors, managers, and data entry personnel in their use.

One cannot merely launch into the productive use of a microcomputer without considerable training. At a minimum, practitioners must know how to operate the computer and must learn the command structure of any particular software system they plan to use (Hudson & Nurius, in press; Nurius, Hooyman, & Nicoll, 1988; Nurius & Hudson, 1988a; Nurius, Richey, & Nicoll, 1988). Beyond that, they must also understand the substantive technology that is implemented by the particular software system.

The failure to account for these three training needs can produce keen disappointments with computer applications. However, if these training needs are met, the computer can be an extremely beneficial tool in the conduct and evaluation of professional practice. These and other problems associated with the use of computers have been addressed elsewhere (see, for example, Bronson, Pelz, & Trycinski, 1988; Glastonbury, LaMendola, & Toole, 1988; Hudson & Bronson, 1988; Hudson & Nurius, in press), and the reader is encouraged to become familiar with them.

TRAINING STUDENTS TO USE COMPUTER-BASED ASSESSMENT SYSTEMS

For microcomputers to be an important and powerful aid to the conduct of clinical practice and to the enhancement of clinical empiricism, students must be taught how to use microcomputers and relevant clinically oriented software systems. To promise such training, a student version of the CASS program has been produced for use in classroom and field practicum training (schools may purchase the student version for a modest fee and are then permitted to copy and distribute it to all students without additional fees). The student version does nearly everything that the professional version of the software does. The major restriction of the student version is that it may be used with a maximum of 20 clients. Those who are interested in obtaining and using the student version of CASS may write to the publisher for acquisition information (WALMYR Publishing Co., PO Box 24779, Tempe, AZ 85285-4799).

FINAL THOUGHTS

Given the available microcomputer technology and the fact of the microcomputer revolution, it seems inevitable that computers will play an increasingly important role in clinical practice. They will serve direct practice functions and will certainly enhance clinical empiricism. Moreover, as the research evidence has made clear, computers often produce more accurate clinical information than is obtained from either interviews or paper-and-pencil administrations of assessment devices (Hudson, Nurius, & Reisman, 1988; Stocks, 1990).

Although new computer hardware and technology are being developed and released on a nearly continuous basis, we social workers have not yet exhausted the capacity of the current generation of machines, and most of us have not even seen the newer systems. Yet, as professionals we must carefully consider how we will avail ourselves of this potentially powerful and maturing tool.

It is difficult to envision the computer capability that will become increasingly available, but the future "intelligence" of machines will be considerable, to say the least. For example, in 1988 it was announced that engineers at Arizona State University invented a computer chip that learns from its own mistakes. Once that technology is refined, one shall see true "thinking machines" within a decade. What this will mean for applications such as those discussed here is difficult to fathom.

A final thought will strike many in our profession as unsavory, indeed. It is the suggestion that a significant group of human service professionals must learn or be trained to understand and use computer technology for the express purpose of designing and developing clinically relevant software systems. As horrible as it may seem to some, it is important that many of us learn how to program computers, and professional degree programs must consider how they will relate to such training. That is the only way that we social workers will ever have full command of this technology in the service of our clients and the work we must do to help them.

REFERENCES

Blythe, J. (1983). An examination of practice evaluation among social practitioners. *Dissertation Abstracts International, 44,* 1952A–2607A.

Bronson, D. E., Pelz, D., & Trycinski, E. (1988). *Computerizing your agency's information system.* Beverly Hills, CA: Sage Publications.

Cheatham, J. (1986). *The effects of client, agency, and practitioner factors on the practice evaluation of social practitioners.* Unpublished doctoral dissertation, Florida State University, Tallahassee.

Edleson, J. L. (1985). Rapid assessment instruments for evaluating practice with children and youth. *Journal of Social Service Research, 8*(3), 17–31.

Gingerich, W. (1984). Generalizing single-case evaluation from classroom to practice setting. *Journal of Education for Social Work, 20,* 74–82.

Glastonbury, B., LaMendola, W., & Toole, S. (Eds.). (1988). *Information technology and human services.* London: John Wiley & Sons.

Hudson, W. W. (1982). The clinical measurement package. Homewood, IL: The Dorsey Press.

Hudson, W. W, (1986). Measuring clinical outcomes and their use for managers. *Administration in Social Work, 11*(3/4), 59–72.

Hudson, W. W. (1990). *Computer assisted social services.* Tempe, AZ: WALMYR Publishing.

Hudson, W. W., & Bronson, D. (1988, April). *Computer-based social work assessment.* Paper presented at the Advances in Research for Social Work Practice Symposium of the School of Social Work, State University of New York, Buffalo.

Hudson, W. W., & Nurius, P. S. (in press). *Computer assisted practice: Theory, methods and software.* Belmont, CA: Wadsworth Publishing.

Hudson, W. W., Nurius, P. S., & Reisman, S. (1988). Computerized assessment instruments: Their promise and problems. *Computers in Human Services, 3*(1/2), 51–70.

Levitt, J. L., & Reid, W. J. (1981). Rapid assessment instruments for practice. *Social Work Research & Abstracts, 17*(1), 13–19.

Nurius, P. S., Hooyman, N., & Nicoll, A. E. (1988). The changing face of computer utilization in social work settings. *Journal of Social Work Education, 24*(2), 186–197.

Nurius, P. S., & Hudson, W. W. (1988a). Computers and social diagnosis: The client's perspective. *Computers in Human Services, 5*(1/2), 21–36.

Nurius, P. S., & Hudson, W. W. (1988b). Workers, clients and computers: An integrative paradigm. In B. Glastonbury, W. LaMendola, & S. Toole (Eds.), *Information technology and human services.* London: John Wiley & Sons.

Nurius, P. S., Richey, C. A., & Nicoll, A. E. (1988). Preparation for computer usage in social work: Student consumer variables. *Journal of Social Work Education, 1*(Winter), 60–69.

Stocks, J. T. (1990). *Validation of a computer-administered instrument for the repeated measurement of depression.* Unpublished doctoral dissertation, Florida State University, Tallahassee.

Welch, G. (1983). Will graduates use single-subject designs to evaluate their casework practice? *Journal of Education for Social Work, 19,* 42–46.

Commentary

Computer-Based Clinical Practice: An Asset or Pie in the Sky?

Deborah H. Siegel

The systematic measurement of clients' problems and progress throughout treatment is a necessary and laudable goal for all social workers. The use of computers to help reach this goal has received significant attention in the social work literature (Butcher, 1985; Forrest & Williams, 1987; Geiss & Viswanathan, 1986; Glastonbury, 1985; Nurius & Hudson, 1988).

In Chapter 5, Hudson described the many valuable ways in which computers can help clinicians and their clients define target problems clearly and track changes in those problems over time. Together, these uses of the computer could create a minirevolution in the way clinical social work is practiced.

In the excitement over the potential of computers to enhance clinical practice and the management of information in agencies, it is tempting to overlook some of the issues involved in their use. These issues fall into three interlocking areas: (1) the potentially deleterious consequences of the use of computers, (2) questions about how realistic it is to anticipate that computers will influence most social workers' practice, and (3) epistemological issues.

POTENTIALLY DELETERIOUS CONSEQUENCES

Undoubtedly, as Hudson pointed out, some clients make mistakes when recording their answers on paper-and-pencil assessment devices, and using a tool such as the Computer-Assisted Social Services (CASS) to present questions to clients can help reduce this possibility. One must keep in mind, though, that sitting in front of a computer keyboard can be an intimidating experience for the uninitiated. Expecting clients to interact with a computer may exacerbate feelings of inadequacy and incompetence. Perhaps the CASS should not be used with easily overwhelmed clients or those who have deficits in literacy skills (Nurius & Hudson,

1988). In these cases, it may be more appropriate for the worker to read items from the questionnaire to the client.

Computers can convey the aura of an impersonal, bureaucratized, mechanistic approach to clients. Clients often come to social work agencies in pain and crisis, craving human warmth and connectedness. Agencies that use the CASS routinely with most clients may lose sensitivity to this fact. Thus, the routine use of the CASS could become yet another example of how agency policies and procedures can place administrators' and workers' needs before consumers' needs.

The CASS's capacity to check immediately the consistency of responses to items as the client completes a questionnaire on the computer raises two concerns. The computer's instant feedback may lead the client to feel criticized, defensive, suspicion, or some other unproductive and uncomfortable emotion. Second, the social worker's preoccupation with gathering accurate data in this way may reflect a naive wish for "hard" clinical data when such data are not obtainable. The statistics that social workers use for analysis may be vastly more sophisticated than the data they have to work with; that is, workers may, in essence, be killing a flea with an elephant gun. The use of statistical analyses can obscure the fact that quantified psychological and social data are often merely suggestive, not conclusive. Checking the statistical range and consistency of a client's responses may be a somewhat grandiose way of handling the kinds of clinical data that social workers usually encounter in their daily practice. Furthermore, statistics may be used inappropriately on clinical data that do not meet prerequisite mathematical assumptions. When a statistic is just the punch of a button away, the practitioner may be tempted to compute it "for the hell of it." Hudson recognized that the appropriate use of the CASS technology requires a certain expertise.

Social workers must also be cautious about overselling the usefulness of computerized data-gathering tools and minimizing the value of the unstructured interview. Standardized questionnaires tell the client to answer professionals' questions; they do not enable clients to tell their stories in their own terms. Thus, essential information may be lost. Structured assessment tools have much to offer as a supplement to—not as a substitute for—so-called unstructured interviews. When they are used selectively and in conjunction with unstructured interviews on a case-by-case basis, they round out the practitioner's repertoire of interventions.

REALISTIC EXPECTATIONS

It seems reasonable to assume that any rational social worker would embrace a labor-saving device. But several factors cast shadows on the likelihood that social workers as a group will embrace computer-based clinical practice any time soon.

Graphs are an underutilized tool in clinical social work practice, according to Hudson, because of "the time required to prepare, update and maintain them." Computers will, of course, make graphs available more readily. But one must question the assertion that the reason social workers do not use graphs more often is that graphs are hard to draw. It is much more likely that the major stumbling blocks to their use are the lack of appreciation for them as a therapeutic tool; the failure to think about client's problems in quantifiable terms; and the failure to help clients gather data on their thoughts, feelings, and behaviors. The availability of programs like CAS in and of itself does not address these impediments to empirically based practice.

Similarly, it is encouraging that a personal computer program can accommodate a single-system design with up to 12 phases. But it is rare to find a practitioner who does a B design, much less an AB, reversal, or multiple baseline design. The available computer technology seems to have surpassed the typical social worker's ability to use it effectively and completely. The situation is akin to having a microwave oven and no food to cook in it. And contrary to what Hudson suggested, what gets in the way of the wider use of single-system designs in clinical practice is probably not the absence of computerized analysis procedures, but clinicians' and agencies' lack of commitment to and skill in using those designs and the designs' inapplicability to the realities of daily clinical practice. In short, the availability of computers to augment clinical practice does not necessarily mean that computers will be used in that way.

An additional concern is whether social workers have the capacity to use all the information they generate with computers. Agencies could print out thousands of graphs and analyses that may never be read or used, simply because the sheer quantity is overwhelming and incentives to invest energy in that activity are weak. One envisions storage rooms piled high with years of unexamined printouts.

Few, if any, major innovations in social work practice take hold without the support of social work curricula. Where in bachelor's and master's programs in social work there is room to be made for teaching the skills necessary for the intelligent use of CASS-type tools? What should be dropped from the curriculum? How can classroom and field instructors integrate computer-based practice into their teaching? These questions must be addressed before computer-based practice can acquire a firm foothold in the mainstream of the profession.

The last, and perhaps most potent, reason to question the computer's influence on social work practice is that social workers, like most people, tend to resist change. Charles Glisson, a colleague of this author, once said that his grandma refused for years to replace her wood stove with an electric range, arguing that the newfangled contraption would not cook as well, would only break down, and would be useless when the electricity went out. It is easy to think of analogous arguments that social workers might offer against the use of computers in their clinical practice.

EPISTEMOLOGICAL CONCERNS

It is true, as Hudson asserted, that "at the heart of any clinical practice is a fundamental empiricism that cannot be ignored." It is also true that there is usually a fundamental mystical component in clinical endeavors, whether intuition; relationship, or some other intangible, elusive, hard-to-measure phenomenon. Social work empiricists must acknowledge, therefore, that some essential aspects of the assessment of and change in clients may not be measurable, given the limitations of the five senses and of existing measurement instruments. Even a reliable and valid measure may not detect clinically significant change. At present, computers are as inept as humans in removing the complexities, ambiguities, value conflicts, and ambivalence that characterize social work practice. We must not let the illusion of science delude us.

Hudson was correct when he stated that a worker can interpret the results of an unstructured interview "according to any fancy or whim that may strike" and that standardized assessment scales and other data-gathering tools can improve the quality of information obtained from clients. However, whim and fancy can just as easily affect one's view of "hard" data. For example, although the client may show dramatic improvement on the Index of Self Esteem (Hudson, 1982) from intake to termination, it is up to the clinician and the client to determine if this improvement is real, reflects a socially desireable response bias, the "hello, good-by" effect, or something else.

A nagging, perhaps inescapable, epistemological concern is whether computers will "improve the empiricism of clinical practice," as Hudson maintained, or lead social workers off on a number-crunching tangent. Will they lead social workers into a realm of esoteric chest thumping? Computer analyses of data from structured questionnaires will yield valuable information only insofar as those data are clinically relevant to a particular client and are valid and reliable. Clinical practice can be empirically based without the use of computers—even when the clinician chooses not to gather quantified data in every case. Empirically based practice at its best treats the gathering of quantifiable data as just one component of responsible clinical work. One also can be empirical by following the canons of logic in one's clinical thinking; being critical and self-aware about assumptions and interpretations; expecting concrete, observable, measurable evidence of change in a client; and using research findings to inform one's decision making.

CONCLUSION

Such tools as the CASS are exciting because they can enhance social work practice. But the availability of these tools will not rescue social workers from the tendency to rely primarily on subjective judgment and intuition as guides for assessment and evaluation. The profession must first embrace empirically based practice; only then can the CASS's potential contributions be realized. As a supplement to empirical clinical practice, the CASS has much to offer. In this sense, as Katherine Wood suggested at the conference, Hudson's chapter could have been more accurately titled "computer-assisted" rather than "computer-based" social work practice. At present it is unlikely that the computer, rather than human judgment and interpersonal interaction, will form the heart of clinical social work.

REFERENCES

Butcher, J. N. (Ed.). (1985). Special issue on psychological adjustment. *Journal of Consulting and Clinical Psychology, 53.*

Forrest, J., & Williams, J. (1987). *New technology and information exchange in social services.* London, England: Policy Studies Institute.

Geiss, G. R., & Viswanathan, N. (1986). *The human edge: Information technology and helping people.* New York: Haworth Press.

Glastonbury, B. (1985) *Computers in social work.* London, England: Macmillan.

Hudson, W. W. (1982). *The clinical measurement package.* Homewood, IL: Dorsey Press.

Nurius, P. S., & Hudson, W. W. (1988). Computer-based practice: Future dream or current technology? *Social Work, 33,* 357–362.

Information Technology Supporting Empirical Practice

Elizabeth Mutschler

In a review of computer applications, Gambrill and Butterfield (1988) concluded that social workers will not make use of empirical data related to practice unless computer activities are made accessible and enticing and are broken down into achievable steps. They described how computers can facilitate the gathering, organizing, and processing of data; how this information can be used for assessment, treatment, insurance reporting, utilization review; how information technology can be employed in the computer-based education of clients, case planning and monitoring, and the graphic presentation of data; and how computerized assessment and prediction can facilitate clinical decision making.

Chapter 5, by Hudson, illustrates Gambrill and Butterfield's view that computers can be seen as a bridge that practitioners may use to gain access to empirical data regarding practice questions. Hudson focused specifically on how computers may assist the practitioner in assessing clients and gave a detailed example of the Computer-Assisted Social Services (CASS) system that he developed. Hudson's extensive experience in developing software for clinicians reflects the learning and increased sophistication of the profession in this field. The CASS emerged from a simple computerized version of a range of paper-and-pencil measures into a comprehensive assessment package, including computerized social histories; a range of clinical questionnaires; and scoring, interpretation, and graphing of the assessment results. During the past few years, this author has worked with students and with a range of agencies to develop and implement computerized tools for clinical practice. This commentary continues the discussion in Chapter 5 by focusing on some issues that have arisen in using computers in clinical practice. To address these issues, the author uses a conceptual model developed by Keen (1980). Computerized client information systems frequently focus on the tasks of practitioners. But such computerized tools are not used in a vacuum; they must accommodate individual, organizational, and technological factors in relation to the specific tasks of the decision maker. Keen's model describes three factors that facilitate or impede the adoption of computerized information systems: the users, the information technology, and the organizational context.

THE USERS

Tasks

The tasks of social workers may be described as being on a continuum from structured to semistructured to unstructured. Structured tasks are generally repetitive and routine, with established and well-explicated procedures. Semistructured or unstructured tasks may be made at irregular intervals and tend to be confronted anew each time they arise because of their complexity. The data obtained through the CASS can support structured as well as unstructured tasks. Much of the information gathered through the computerized intake assessment (for example, whether a client is eligible for specific services) is related to structured tasks; routinely used forms are already a component of the intake procedures, and the required information is well defined. Unstructured tasks are frequently related to treatment planning, implementation, and termination. In this area computerized data are generally used to support decisions about tasks, but not as a substitute for clinical decisions (Gingerich, in press; Schuerman, 1987). For example, computerized graphs can document changes in a client in specific areas, but the client and social worker need to decide in each case when the termination of treatment is appropriate.

Training of Users

Hudson stressed the importance of training students and practitioners to use computer technology and of participation by professionals in the development and testing of clinically relevant software programs. Similarly, several studies (Greist & Klein, 1981; Hedlund, Vieweg, & Cho, 1985; Mutschler & Cnaan, 1985) have demonstrated that practitioners are more likely to use computer systems if they contribute to the design and implementation of the computers and if the computer tools are responsive to the needs of clinicians. Keen (1980) pointed out, however, that the development and implementation of information technology are parts of an evolving process. Users frequently learn about the potential of a computerized system only after some initial experience. The database and the design of the system, therefore, have to be flexible enough so they can be responsive to the skills and evolving needs of the users.

ORGANIZATIONAL FACTORS

The influence of organizational factors and their interactions with the characteristics of the tasks and users, although frequently ignored in the literature and in practice, may have profound influences on the applications of computers for practice. For example, computer systems may not be used effectively because the organization's control-and-reward system provides no incentive to users. The organization also is affected by the available technology, level of technical expertise, and the appropriateness of the hardware and the software.

Hudson pointed out that human service organizations have been frustrated by the great inconsistencies in the data that are collected. Computerized social histories and questionnaires can provide consistent and comprehensive data for clinical and administrative decision making. However, organizations have to develop procedures to maintain the discretion of practitioners, respect client's rights, and protect the confidentiality of the obtained information.

Especially in the initial phase of the development of a computer system, an organization may expect immediate "hard" benefits and cost savings from computer applications. Although a computerized client-assessment-and-monitoring system may not save actual dollars or personnel, it will often provide significant qualitative benefits, such as more complete, more accessible, and more accurate data on clients (Hedlund, Vieweg, & Cho, 1985; Mutschler & Cnaan, 1985).

TECHNOLOGY

Hudson described the potential of the currently available on-line microcomputer technology for clinical practice. Relatively easy-to-use software packages allow for the development of a standardized database on clients, as well as for tailor-made programs for the needs of specific units of agencies or groups of clients. As social workers learn to use information technology in their day-to-day practice, there will be a trend toward "end-user computing" (Larsen, 1987). That is, computers will no longer be the property of computer professionals, but will be in the hands of those who actually perform the work of the human service organization. Data entry and the generation of reports, for example, will increasingly be performed by professionals (and may perhaps be done by the clients themselves) interacting with their terminals, rather than remote clerical staff.

Although the introduction of computer technology can help practitioners to gather empirical data, it may also raise practitioners' concerns about the misuse of client data, the interpretation of assessment data, and the effect of the technology on their role as professionals (Greist & Klein, 1981).

CONCLUSION

Many writers in the field agree with Henderson (1986) that human service professionals no longer have the choice *not* to use computers. However, the extent to which social work practitioners will use computers to gain access to empirical practice data will depend (1) to a lesser degree on technological advances, because the available hardware and software are more than adequate for most data-processing needs in clinical practice; (2) to a large degree on whether the organizational environment facilitates or inhibits the use of computers as a direct, clinical tool; and (3) most on knowledgeable social work practitioners who can creatively participate in keeping the emerging information technology responsive to the needs of clients and clinical practice.

REFERENCES

Gambrill, E., & Butterfield, W. (1988). Computers as practice and research tools. *Social Work Research & Abstracts, 24*, 4–6.

Gingerich, W. J. (in press). Expert systems: New tools for professional decision making. *Computers in Human Services*.

Greist, J. H., & Klein, M. H. (1981). Computer programs for patients, clinicians, and researchers in psychiatry. In J. B. Sidowski, J. H. Johnson, & T. A. Williams (Eds.), *Technology in mental health care delivery systems* (pp. 165–166). Norwood, NJ: Ablex Publishing.

Hedlund, J. L., Vieweg, B. V., & Cho, D. W. (1985). Mental health computing in the 1980s: General information systems and clinical documentation. *Computers in Human Services, 1*, 3–33.

Henderson, J. C. (1986). Emerging trends and issues in decision support systems and related technologies: Implications for organizations. In G. R. Geiss & N. Viswanathan (Eds.), *The human edge* (pp. 92–107). New York: Haworth Press.

Keen, P. G. M. (1980). Decisions support systems: A research perspective. In G. Fick & R. H. Sprague (Eds.), *Decision support systems: Issues and challenges* (pp. 24–37). New York: Pergamon Press.

Larsen, J. (1987). Implementing computers in mental health settings. In J. H. Greist, J. A. Carroll, H. P. Erdman, M. H. Klein, & E. C. Wurster (Eds.), *Research in mental health computer applications: Directions for the future* (pp. 110–122). Rockville, MD: National Institute of Mental Health.

Mutschler, E., & Cnaan, R. A. (1985). Success and failure of computerized information systems: Two case studies in human service agencies. *Administration and Social Work, 9*, 67–79.

Schuerman, J. R. (1987). Expert consulting systems in social welfare. *Social Work Research & Abstracts, 23*, 14–18.

Enhancing Clinical Social Work through Microcomputers

Anthony N. Maluccio

The purpose of the chapter by Hudson, Siegel, and Mutschler was to explore the use of microcomputers in clinical social work practice. Chapter 5, by Hudson, described the benefits of computer-based assessments and illustrated the use of computers by presenting the Computer-Assisted Social Services (CASS) system, an interactive software program that provides social workers with various tools for assessing, monitoring, and evaluating clients' problems over time.

Hudson's key themes were as follows:

• Social work practice is empirical in nature in that it involves, from the outset, gathering information about the client.

• The quality of the data that are being collected is a major concern. The most common approach in social work research is to use the unstructured interview, which is the least reliable and valid and the most time-consuming approach. At the other extreme are various formal measurement tools; although these tools have excellent reliability and validity, they are more difficult to use and tend to be narrowly focused.

• The microcomputer is one prominent means of improving the quality of clinical empiricism. There are powerful computer systems that can assist social workers in this task.

Siegel indicated that she was intrigued by the potential of microcomputers for clinical practice. Playing devil's advocate, however, she delineated a number of issues in the following areas:

• potentially deleterious effects (for example, computers may prove intimidating to clients as well as to practitioners)

• the reluctance of the professional community to embrace the use of microcomputers in clinical practice (for instance, the machine can create graphics, but practitioners do not necessarily think in terms of graphics)

• epistemological concerns (empiricists tend to react negatively to the "mystical" component of clinical practice, yet there is a need to appreciate this nonempirical dimension).

Mutschler emphasized the importance of keeping the computer program small enough so it is manageable for practitioners, building on the ideas and suggestions of practitioners, and teaching practitioners how to use it. She highlighted and illustrated the following uses and benefits of microcomputers in a mental health setting:

• supporting clinical assessment, teaching skills, and providing homework assignments for treatment purposes

• structuring certain tasks, such as the determination of clients' eligibility for services

• promoting the involvement of clients in the helping process.

BENEFITS AND OBSTACLES

The consensus was that the use of microcomputers holds much promise for enriching clinical practice in a variety of ways. Thus, microcomputers can

• increase the reliability and validity of data collection for assessment and treatment planning

• organize data into a configuration that can help determine patterns and trends

• monitor the progress of treatment

• make more efficient use of resources, including the time and energies of clients and practitioners

• involve clients and practitioners in a more interactive process

• encourage clients and social workers to think and use their cognitive resources more actively.

Various potential obstacles also need to be recognized in efforts to promote the use of microcomputers in social work practice and education. Foremost among these impediments is the fear that the machine may replace the practitioner, or at least reduce the practitioner's role, professional discretion, and creativity.

Other concerns included these:

• Computers may be useful in gathering and handling more information, but there is a danger of information overload.

• Many practitioners, faculty members, and students tend to be fearful of technology, or at least hesitant to use it in their work, in part because they see it as a threat to human interaction.

• In general, faculty members are not sophisticated in computer technology.

• It is difficult to use microcomputers for complex social problems that cannot be easily partialized.

IMPLICATIONS FOR EDUCATION AND PRACTICE

In light of the potential benefits and obstacles, the following sugges-tions were offered for expanding the use of microcomputers in clinical practice and social work education:

• Faculty members and field instructors should be helped to become comfortable with and knowledgeable about computers. To apply com-puter technology in teaching or practice, they must first learn the basics of using computers, such as how to use the command structure.

• Faculty members and field instructors should be given the oppor-tunity to develop guidelines and to practice skills in using microcomputers in direct practice with clients. They should address issues such as these: With whom should computers be used and for what purposes? When should computers be used in lieu of some other tool or approach?

• Educators and practitioners should be helped to understand that the introduction of any tool into the helping process becomes an inter-vention in itself. Therefore, the timing of its introduction must be con-sidered carefully and the influence of the tool on the process and outcome of helping efforts must be recognized.

• Educators and practitioners should delineate the criteria for deter-mining the kinds of information needed with different types of clients or problems and at different points in the treatment process. Different purposes require different kinds of information.

• Faculty members should learn how to introduce microcomputers into practice courses. At present, this technology is used primarily in research courses, so the relevance for clinical practice may not be clearly conveyed to students.

• Researchers should identify available scales (such as assessment scales) and delineate their differential uses in practice, as well as create new scales that are responsive to the concerns of practitioners.

Chapter 6

Change-Process Research: A New Paradigm?

William J. Reid

To establish a respectable empirical basis for practice, it is necessary to determine connections between treatment processes and outcomes. This knowledge is an essential part of the answer to the often-posed master question guiding intervention research: What works with whom, how, and under what conditions?

Although controlled experiments can theoretically provide the best data on process-outcome relations, practical and ethical constraints on experiments necessitate a reliance on the naturalistic study of these relations. This type of study has been referred to as "process-outcome research" (Orlinsky & Howard 1978). In the 1980s, several researchers (Elliott, 1983b; Greenberg, 1986; Kiesler, 1983; Safran, Greenberg, & Rice, 1988) attempted to formulate a type of process-outcome research that focuses on the processes of change during the period of contact between the professional helper and the client system. This focus has generated considerable interest, and for good reason, since it has brought together a number of conceptions and methods of inquiry that hold considerable promise, if not the key, for understanding the intricate connections between practice events and changes in client systems.

This chapter reviews this development, which has been referred to as "change-process research" (Greenberg, 1986; Kiesler, 1983). It first clarifies what is meant by change-process research, puts this research into a historical context, and then identifies themes in this type of research and selected issues raised by it.

WHAT IS CHANGE-PROCESS RESEARCH?

Change-process research focuses on the processes of change that occur during the course of psychosocial treatment. "Treatment" and "service" are used throughout as generic terms to include psychotherapy, counseling, and clinical social work with individuals and families. These change processes encompass what practitioners, clients, and others do to effect change, how change is brought about, and what kinds of changes occur as the service unfolds. They are studied as they occur in the course of treatment or of episodes of treatment (for example, within sessions or between one session and the next).

It is useful to distinguish change-process research from related forms of inquiry. As a type of process-outcome research, change-process research can be distinguished from studies that do not interrelate process *and* outcome variables. For example, process studies that examine differences in the intervention methods of practitioners at different levels of experience would not be change-process research. By the same token, studies of the outcomes of a given intervention would not be included if they failed to examine associations between intervention and outcome. Finally, not all process-outcome studies would be considered "change process." Excluded, for example, would be studies that correlated summary measures of intervention for a group of cases with summary measures of outcome, as has been done in studies that correlate ratings of the empathy of practitioners with the outcomes of clients at termination (see, for example, Sloan, Staples, Cristol, Yorkston, & Whipple, 1975).

For research to be considered "change process," there must be, at a minimum, measures of process, which can be defined as the instrumental activities of the practitioner or the client during treatment, *and* measures of change in the client following closely in time. These measures, which usually involve within-interview changes in the client's affect, behavior, and cognitive states, have been identified as "suboutcomes" (Greenberg, 1986) or "intermediate outcomes" (Rosen & Proctor, 1978), since they presumably are connected to more significant changes in the client's life. Measures of process and change then need to be interrelated in analyses of the process of change. Summary measures of process and outcome are not excluded, but, if they are used, they serve as additional variables, rather than the main focus. To round out the definition, change-process research is better seen as a method of inquiry than as a way of classifying studies; that is, a study may incorporate a change-process focus in a design that also includes other research strategies.

HISTORICAL CONTEXT

Change-process research is by no means a new development. It evolved as part of the process studies of such pioneers as Lasswell (1938), Rogers (1942), Dollard and Mowrer (1947), and Snyder (1947). By the mid-1950s, enough had been published to warrant a review of the "considerable body of literature on content analysis of recorded interviews" (Auld & Murray, 1955, p. 378). Many studies in this review would be included in most contemporary definitions of change-process research. An early focus was on clients' responses following different types of interventions by practitioners (Bergman, 1951; Snyder, 1947). Two later examples of this type of research were studies by Dittes (1957) and Speisman (1959). In a single-case study, Dittes rated the therapist's permissiveness in each session and correlated these ratings with per-session physiological measures of the patient's anxiety—his galvanic skin reaction (GSR). Dittes found a positive (.51) correlation between the therapist's permissiveness and the frequency of GSRs.

Speisman tested the hypothesis that deep interpretations would lead to greater resistance by a patient than would superficial interpretations. The interpretations were rated according to their depth, and the patient's resistance in his or her responses following the interpretations were similarly measured. In addition to obtaining support for the hypothesis, Speisman found that the patient's level of resistance failed to influence the therapist's next response.

A somewhat different early example, one that foreshadowed current systemic views of treatment, was a study by Lennard and Bernstein (1960), who applied measures derived from systems theory in an intensive study of four cases. Various measures of communication between the therapists and the patients were obtained and interrelated. The most significant change-process findings were obtained from patients' ratings of their relative satisfaction with each session. The patients were found to be more satisfied when both they and the therapists were more talkative, when the therapists' comments were more specific and effective, when the therapists asked fewer questions, and when the patients changed the subject fewer times.

In social work, one of the earliest examples of change-process research was a study by Hollis (1968), the profession's foremost pioneer in process research. The study compared in-session communications of continuers and discontinuers. Few differences were found between these two types of cases with respect to the overall profiles of the practitioners' or the clients' communication, as assessed by the Hollis classification system. However, a qualitative analysis of the sequences of the practitioners' and the clients' responses indicated that continuing clients were more likely than discontinuing clients to initiate reflective observations, whereas discontinuing clients were more likely to receive lengthy reflective communications from the practitioners.

In a later example, Davis (1975) examined the client's immediate reaction to the practitioner's use of procedures of direct influence. Negative reactions were more common than positive ones, on the whole, although the role of negative responses varied considerably according to the practitioner. Negative in-session reactions to advice notwithstanding, the clients reported, in a posttreatment interview, that they were either satisfied with the amount of advice they received or wanted more.

Although varied in methodology, these examples all contain the essential elements of change-process research: an analysis of the interrelation of treatment events (process) and change in clients during the course of treatment. Other examples of change-process research in the past three decades may be found in the comprehensive review of process research by Marsden (1971) and Orlinsky and Howard (1978, 1986).

Despite its lengthy life span, change-process research has been a minor theme in clinical research, which has been largely oriented to treatment outcomes. When attention has been given to process, the emphasis has been on the classification or description of practitioners' activities or to relations between summary measures of intervention and outcome. In social work, for example, the bulk of process research has consisted of studies of such phenomena as the nature of practitioners' interventions, diagnostic and other factors that influence practitioners' activities, practitioners' styles, variations among phases of the case or of the interview, and the relation of summary process measures to outcomes at termination (Fortune, 1981).

However, a review of recent work in process research as a whole—both empirical studies and methodological essays—suggests that the star of change-process research is definitely on the rise. Such studies and essays have been features in several books (Greenberg & Pinsof, 1986b; Rice & Greenberg, 1984b; Weiss & Sampson, 1987) as well as numerous journal articles (see, for example, Elliott, 1983a, 1983b, 1985; Greenberg, 1986; Safran, Greenberg, & Rice, 1988). Moreover, at the conclusion of their authoritative review of process-outcome studies, Orlinsky and Howard (1986) recommended that more attention be paid to change over the course of treatment: "A greater focus on micro-outcomes should make it possible to trace the specific changes that occur in a patient's life and personalities to events and patterns occurring in therapy sessions" (p. 370). Furthermore, a cadre of researchers whose works have been cited here have formed a network of investigators who are involved in continuing programs of change-process research.

It is clear that change-process research is currently "hot." Probably, more of it can be expected. Recent efforts have resulted in a clearer conceptualization of this form of inquiry, have systematized its methodology, have heightened its respectability, and have introduced new techniques. Whether all or any of these efforts represents a "new paradigm" or a shift in paradigms, as Elliott (1983a) and Rice and Greenberg

(1984a) argued, is another question, one to which this chapter shall return after some of the contemporary developments in change-process research have been examined in greater detail.

CURRENT PERSPECTIVES

What follows is an attempt to set forth some of the central ideas and methods that characterize contemporary change-process research. Not all change-process studies incorporate all these features, nor do all change-process researchers accord them top priority. Nevertheless, taken together, these aspects form a profile of the new look in change-process research.

View of Treatment

At the foundation of present-day change-process research is a systemic conception of treatment. In the traditional views, which have dominated not only clinical research but theories of practice, practitioners provide therapeutic input to which clients respond. In fact, the very words *treatment* and *therapy* suggest that someone, namely, a *professional*, is doing something to someone else, namely, a *client* (often called a *patient*). Having accepted this medically oriented view as a given, process researchers accordingly gave priority to the study of the practitioner's technical operations and attitudes—interpretations, empathy, reflection, and so on. Various attempts were made to construct exhaustive classifications of practitioners' activities, but little attention was paid to the therapeutic activities of the client, whose behavior was viewed as being a "response" to the practitioner's input, as one might view a patient's response to a drug. In contemporary change-process research, treatment is viewed as "therapist and patient systems in a circular, mutually influencing, ongoing interaction" (Gurman, Kniskern, & Pinsof, 1986, p. 625). In this process of mutual influence, the practitioner no longer has a monopoly on the role of change agent. The client also is seen as an active change agent; thus, both the practitioner and the client engage in change activities. Furthermore, systems of change can be enlarged through the involvement of other helpers, support networks, and so on.

"It Is the Client Who Changes"

This conception of treatment places more emphasis on the client as both the agent and object of change. Although change-process research has continued the tradition of examining interactive processes between the practitioner and the client, the client has moved to center stage in most studies. As Rice and Greenberg (1984a) put it, "the central focus in the new paradigm is on the client rather than the therapist. It is the client who changes, and we are trying to understand how that change comes about" (p. 21). Accordingly, recent change-process studies have focused on such client-oriented processes as experiencing, the development of insight, states of mind, and shifts in mood. Antecedent variables may be drawn from the client's preceding communications, as well as from the practitioner's, and, of course, from their interaction.

In this respect, there has been a subtle but important shift of emphasis from earlier change-process studies. Earlier studies (for example, Davis, 1975; Dittes, 1957; Hollis, 1968; Speisman, 1959) tended to focus on the client's immediate reaction to certain classes of techniques by practitioners (such as perminniveness, interpretation, reflection, and advice giving). In this kind of study, the client's response is used to evaluate the effects of the practitioner's intervention: How well does the intervention take? In recent studies, the tendency has been to center on the processes of change experienced by the client. Obviously, in a treatment context, the practitioner is an important source of change, but interest is directed instead toward the mechanisms and patterns of change in the client. Thus, in Rice and Saperia's (1984) study of clients' in-session work on problematic reactions, the findings led to a client operations model consisting of the steps that clients use to move toward the resolution of their problems. The model is used as a basis for considering how the practitioner can facilitate the client's efforts to change. Similarly, in a single-case study, Reid and Strother (1988) devised a typology of a couple's extraordinarily successful problem-solving efforts, and Sherman and Skinner's (1988) focus was on the relationship between the client's linguistic processes and "experiencing" within the session.

o's and i's

Therapeutic systems involving practitioners, clients, and others are, of course, brought into being to effect changes in the clients' lives. Increasingly, these changes are viewed as a process in which conventional distinctions between intervention and outcome lose their simplicity. To take an example from this author's work on the task-centered model, if the practitioner and a family work collaboratively in the session to develop a task that the family then does at home, the implementation of the task can be seen as both part of the process of resolving the problem and as the outcome of the previous task-development process, depending on how one wishes to construe events in this chain of cause and effect (Reid, 1985, 1987a, 1987b; Reid & Davis, 1987). As Greenberg and Pinsoff (1986a, p. 19) put it, the "Big O" of a summary outcome measure at termination has been replaced by many "little o's." One might add that the "Big I" of the practitioner's intervention as it appears in summary measures becomes a lot of "little i's" contributed by both practitioners and clients in a collaborative process. It then becomes possible to depict change-process research as a study of strings of intermixed i's and o's.

Context

Moreover, particular i's and o's must be understood within the context of the sequence in which they occur. The characteristic function of a given i or o must be seen in relation to this context. Thus, as Elliott (1983b) observed:

> Research on empathy in which empathy ratings are averaged across interviews or cases are insensitive to the possibility that empathy may play a crucial role only at certain moments in a helping relationship—for example, following a new and highly intimate disclosure. (p. 114)

To clarify what Elliott and other change-process researchers mean by context, it is important to keep in mind that any rating of a treatment event is affected by its context. In fact, "context units" and context rules are standard features of any content-analysis scheme. Thus, a practitioner's comment, "You felt your anger rising" would be given a high or low rating of empathy in a conventional scheme, depending on what the client had just communicated. Change-process researchers do not want to be limited to the use of context simply to classify or rate an event; rather, they want to use it to understand more precisely the conditions under which it occurs. Their approach presumably would not rule out aggregating events if their contexts could be used to make meaningful discriminations—for instance, empathy following the disclosure of intimate information versus other kinds of empathy. Elliott (1983b), for example, called for building a taxonomy of contexts.

Chunks, Events, and Single Cases

In conventional process-outcome studies, researchers have typically used representative samples of entire courses of treatment or core samples (such as third interviews). Some aggregation of process variables (average empathy ratings or the proportion of directive interventions, for example) has then been related to some terminal outcome measure. The more cases, the better, has been the usual assumption. For change-process researchers, this strategy is likely to be seen as unproductive. Averages of process variables that are devoid of their contexts at best provide weak measures, usually too weak to override the multiplicity of factors that make up measures of outcome at termination. In fact, the failure of this strategy to produce consistent results for promising variables such as empathy (Mitchell, Bozarth, & Krauft, 1977) was an important stimulus for the change-process movement.

Change-process researchers favor the intensive study of smaller units that are selected because they are likely to contain informative data about change processes, rather than for their representativeness. Intensity is achieved not only through the use of multiple measures (Elliott, 1983a) but also through the simultaneous investigation of different levels of systems that are captured by the event (for example, the "speech acts" of each participant, as well as the levels of interaction or relationship of all participants (Greenberg, 1986). These units may be referred to as "events" (Davis & Reid, 1988; Elliott, 1983b; Greenberg, 1986; Reid, 1985), "episodes" (Greenberg, 1986), or "good moments" (Mahrer & Nadler, 1986). Greenberg and Pinsof (1986a) suggested "chunk" as a generic term. Chunks may be sampled across cases or within single cases. When more complete coding is done, studies may be restricted to single cases (Elliott, 1983a). Perhaps the most frequently used unit is the "change event" (Greenberg, 1986), which captures a "change effort" directed at a client's problem or state, identified by some behavior of the client ("client marker"), such as the expression of conflict. The event consists of change-oriented behavior by both the practitioner and the client and terminates in some identified outcome.

As one example, Rice and Saperia (1984) studied three events from three cases. Each event involved the client's efforts to solve a problematic reaction. The processes of resolving the problem that were observed in the practitioner-client communications were coded and analyzed. Elliott (1984) studied four "insight events" from four different cases using 22 different measures of behavior by therapists and clients in an approach he referred to as "comprehensive process analysis." In another study (Elliott, 1983a), he applied the approach to a single-insight event consisting of only a few lines of practitioner-client interaction. Once selected, events can be and usually are analyzed in terms of smaller units—the practitioner's and client's responses, for example. Events can be selected by various means; perhaps the most usual is to have practitioners, judges, or clients select events following sessions or at the end of treatment.

Sources and Analysis of Data

Change-process studies follow the tradition of process research in their reliance on tapes and typescripts of treatment sessions. In keeping with their focus on change in clients, they make greater use of phenom-enological data obtained from clients, for example, through interviews, questionnaires, or clients' reactions to replays of treatment sessions. Coding schemes are used to classify process events, and standard reli-ability procedures for assessing reliabilities are followed.

Analytic methods reflect a mix of quantitative and qualitative ap-proaches, often in the same study. On the quantitative side, simple correlational methods are often used to relate different events in treatment, such as practitioner and client variables. Although change-process re-search involves the analysis of phenomena over time, only limited use has been made of quantitative models developed for this purpose, such as time-series analysis or sequential analysis. As a rule, analytic techniques are not advanced (for instance, the eyeball interpretation of graphs or the use of standard statistical procedures that ignore autocorrelation). Al-though sequential analysis (Cousins & Power, 1986) has been viewed as a potentially valuable tool by change-process researchers (Elliott, 1983b), its promise has yet to be realized. At least one application produced disappointing results (Hill, Carter, & O'Farrell, 1983).

A common approach has been to employ qualitative methods (sometimes referred to as "clinical analysis") to extend and supplement quantitative methods (Elliott, 1983a; Hill, Carter, & O'Farrell, 1983; Luborsky, Singer, Hartke, Crits-Christoph, & Cohen, 1984; Rice & Saperia, 1984). A major use of qualitative methods is to identify patterns of behavior or interactions during interviews that were not addressed by quantitative techniques. In some instances, the more important findings indeed originate from the qualitative analysis of interview material. A distinctive qualitative methodology for the analysis of such material has yet to be developed. As it stands, the qualitative analysis of patterns in treatment sessions is pretty much what strikes the trained eye and informed mind in going over a recording of an interview.

Special Approaches

A variety of special approaches, which typically contain both quantita-tive and qualitative components, have been developed or adapted by change-process researchers. These approaches range from general research models to data-collection techniques. Several approaches have been in-fluential or seem particularly promising.

Task analysis. Task analysis has been used since the 1940s to study competencies and problem solving in industrial psychology, education, and other fields. As adapted by Greenberg (1984), Rice and Saperia (1984), and Safran, Rice, and Greenberg (1988), the method calls for the intensive analysis of change events to specify the problem-solving processes used by clients and practitioners. In this method, the client's problem-solving tasks are described, together with the practitioner's interventions that are appropriate for their solution. The investigator conducts a rational task analysis in which he or she tries to set forth a range of possible strategies to solve the problem. This "thought experiment" helps the researcher to conceptualize ways in which the problem could be solved. The study of actual problem solving—empirical task analysis—is the next step. The conduct of successive rational and empirical analyses, each building on the other, leads to a fuller picture of the problem-solving strategies. The stage is then set for studies that compare successful and unsuccessful resolutions of problems and that relate the performance of tasks to the outcomes. As more is learned about which kinds of efforts to resolve problems work best, the practitioner's interventions can be modified accordingly to enhance the problem-solving process.

In one example, already mentioned in another context, Rice and Saperia (1984) used a task-analytic approach to develop a performance model for the client's resolution of affective/behavioral problems within the context of client-centered therapy. In a more complex example, Greenberg (1984) used the approach to develop a performance model for resolving conflicts using the two-chair technique in the context of gestalt therapy.

By combining change-process and developmental research strategies, the task-analytic approach has a good deal to contribute to the building of intervention models. Actually, the approach schematizes and specifies some key operations used in developmental research (Thomas, 1984). How task analysis is used to build more effective practice models is hazy, however, in the expositions and examples available thus far.

Interpersonal process recall. Originally developed as an educational technique (Kagan, 1975), interpersonal process recall (IPR) has been adapted by change-process researchers, notably Elliott (1984). With IPR, clients essentially view (or listen to) tapes of treatment sessions in which they have participated. Immediately after this reexperiencing of the original events, the clients are asked for their reactions, which may take such forms as rating the helpfulness of specific interventions by practitioners or giving their perceptions of change events.

Symptom-context methods. Developed by Luborsky et al. (1984), the symptom-context method is applied to sessions in single cases. The method examines factors in the session (the context) that may account for the presence of specified behavior (symptoms) by the client. Different contexts are compared to trace causal patterns, for example, contexts preceding an increase in the symptom with those preceding a decrease or those in which the symptom does not occur. Contextual factors may include the practitioner's intervention, the client's behavior, or the interaction between the practitioner and the client. For example, in a study of a single long-term case, Luborsky et al. (1984) investigated variables that predict shifts in the depressive states of a client within a session. Using tapes of the therapy sessions, the researchers measured the presumed explanatory variables (such as helplessness and hostility) before and after some 14 shifts, divided between increases and decreases in the patient's depression. Although changes in the therapist-patient relationship before the shifts were judged to be influential, the researchers centered their analysis and conclusions on which alternative theories of depression could best explain the shifts. The method can be extended to study factors that may explain any behavior of a client in a session.

Identifying "client states." According to Marmor, Wilner, and Horowitz (1984), "client states are observable recurrent patterns of behavior that have both verbal and nonverbal components" (p. 195). For example, in the study of a client, one state identified was "artificial and engaging with behaviors that included animation, histronic verbalization and gestures, and quick speech." A different state was "self-disgust," manifested by such behavior as "looking away, lowered voice, slow speech, playing with hair." These states, according to Horowitz (1979), relate to the client's images of himself or herself and others, including the therapist. In studies to date, states have been initially identified by therapists and operationalized by researchers. (A typical brief case contains about seven states that recur during the course of treatment.) Given definitions and indicators of the states, reliability judges have been able to identify and locate them, including their beginning and end points, with a satisfactory degree of reliability.

Practitioners can intuitively recognize such "states of mind" in their clients. The achievement of this group of researchers has been to develop ways of conceptualizing these states of mind and measuring them reliably. Although meaningful correlates of them have yet to be identified, it is obvious they could be used as measures of suboutcome or as equivalents of the "symptom" in the symptom-context method devised by the Luborsky group (1986).

Testing hypotheses. The Mt. Zion Psychotherapy Research Group has developed a method of hypothesis testing in single-case studies of change processes (Weiss & Sampson, 1987). Essentially, hypotheses, usually based in psychoanalytic theory, are posed and tested through an examination of events that meet the criteria relevant to the hypotheses. These events include both the therapist's and patient's behaviors during the session. Professional clinicians judge verbatim typescripts with careful reliability checks and with a control of the material given to them to avoid biases. Over the past decade, several studies that have used this approach have yielded a variety of interesting findings (see, for example, Weiss & Sampson, 1987). One study, for example, examined the "transference demands" of patients that therapists respond in a certain way—by being authoritative, hostile, romantic, and so on. Considerable support in one case study was obtained for the hypothesis that the patient would experience relief if the therapist moved to disconfirm the beliefs underlying the demand. This support was seen as lending credence to Freud's later theories that such demands were based on pathogenic expectancies; that is, in these transference situations, patients *expect* the therapist to behave in certain ways on the basis of earlier experiences, but really do not want them to behave in those ways.

ISSUES

The developments in change-process research raise a number of issues, some of which have already been mentioned. The remainder of this chapter focuses on these issues in depth.

What Is New?

The "new look" in change-process research was heralded by Rice and Greenberg (1984a) as a "new research paradigm" and by Elliott (1983a) as the "beginning of a Kuhnian-type paradigm-shift in therapy process research" (p. 51). This may be yet another instance in which Thomas Kuhn's name was taken in vain.

Although there have been new developments, it is hard to view them as amounting to a paradigm in the sense of a set of widely shared assumptions and procedures. Certainly, it is hard to see them as a shift in paradigms. As Orlinsky and Howard (1978) pointed out, the entire field of psychotherapy research is in "a preparadigmatic state." It is hard to have a "paradigm shift" if you do not have a paradigm to shift from.

Rather than a new paradigm, there has been an evolution in a number of developments over a substantial period, one that dates back to the beginnings of psychotherapy research. Some of these developments have recent origins, but others have been around a long time. The result has been new emphases: the focus on change events; the restyling of various techniques, such as task analysis and IPR, for the study of change-processes; and the emergence of change-process research as a growth industry.

But as has been characteristic of change-process research in the past, there is still a diversity of research approaches, sampling strategies, and coding schemes, not to mention differences in treatment theories, methods, and analytic procedures. A stable set of research conventions, followed by a substantial number of investigators, have yet to emerge that would establish the presence or even the beginnings of a "paradigm." This point was recently acknowledged by Safran, Greenberg, and Rice (1988) in relation to one of the cornerstones of change-process methodology: "There is no consensus in the field regarding the nature of appropriate intensive analysis design" (p. 12).

Linking Process and Change

How successful have change-process researchers been in demonstrating links between process and change? This question shall be considered within a framework that provides certain meanings for process and change and that articulates their interrelationship. If process is taken to mean change-related activity, then virtually all the practitioner's in-session activities can be seen as "process." The changes the practitioner experiences as a person or professional is not of interest in this research. On the client's side, however, matters are less clear-cut. Certain behaviors of clients appear to be analogous to the practitioner's change-generating activities. For example, the client may explore difficulties, solve problems, and communicate about emotionally laden concerns, but such efforts are perhaps better seen as "client process," rather than "client change," since they may not necessarily result in any benefit to the client. Other activities may be viewed as having both process and change aspects. As noted earlier, a successful task can be both an instrument to solving a problem and evidence that progress (a suboutcome) has been achieved. Still other measures of the behavior of a client are more reflective of change than of process, such as expressing relief from anxiety or depression in the session. Ideally, all these variables—practitioner and client process and client change in the session—should be interrelated and linked to measures of the outcome at termination. For example, the practitioner might instigate problem-solving by the client in the session, which might enable the client to come up with a solution. Successful repetitions of this pattern should have an effect on the eventual outcome.

No study in the literature made all these various distinctions or examined the resulting interrelationships—an undertaking that is perhaps too much to expect in the current state of the art. Yet these distinctions provide a framework against which any given study can be examined. Typically, in change-process studies, only a few connections are demonstrated. For example, in the single-case study by Hill, Carter, and O'Farrell (1983), sequential analysis was used to link the counselor's response modes (practitioner process) to the client's response modes (client process). A few interrelationships were found. The response most likely to lead to generative responses by clients—those related to "experiencing" and "insight"—was, ironically, the practitioner's "silence." Although these response modes of the client reflect some change along with process, complete measures of change were obtained by having the client complete questionnaires after each session in which she provided evaluative data, including a listing of positive and negative events in the session. Qualitative analyses of these data suggested, among other things, that the client made the most progress (for instance, experiencing) when the therapist was active and informative. That finding did not square with the role of silence as seen in the sequential analysis. Outcomes at termination and follow-up were obtained. Although the findings were not specifically related to the in-session process or change measures, they were consistent with the change-process analysis, which suggested that the effects of treatment had been limited. The study, conducted by a senior change-process researcher using state-of-the-art methodology, is typical in its presentation of a mixture of interesting but inconsistent and fragmentary quantitative data, welded together with a qualitative analysis whose pathways to the evidence in the case are not always clear.

On the other hand, the data and analysis do present a picture of a change process in the case that is considerably sharper and better evidenced than one finds in a conventional case study. For example, data on the client's response modes clearly document the conclusion that the client spent the bulk of the sessions on describing the problem but gained little insight into it. Also, it was apparent from the data that the first portion of each session was dominated by her description of the problem ("storytelling") until intervention by the practitioner moved her toward a more meaningful focus on her feelings and behavior. The discrepancy between this finding and the generative power of silence that was apparent in the sequential analysis can be resolved by considering silence as part of a longer string of change-process events. Although silence may have been the immediate stimulus for the client's experiencing or insight, it presumably was preceded by confrontational activity by the therapist. This point also illustrates the difficulty in applying sequential analysis or any quantitative approach to the study of change-process strings, especially when the context is not taken into account.

Perhaps the most significant substantive contribution of change-process research thus far has emerged from the intensive analysis of "insight events" in psychotherapy (Elliott, 1983a, 1984; Greenberg, 1984; Rice & Saperia, 1984). Task analysis, comprehensive process analysis, and qualitative analysis have been among the more fruitful methodologies employed. These analytic methods have led to detailed and useful accounts of the processes by which clients achieve self-understanding and how practitioners help them do so. Of particular interest has been the identification of cognitive and emotional processes and a delineation of their sequencing. Rice and Saperias's (1984) study provides a specific illustration. In that study, clients who experienced an upsetting reaction, such as anger at others, often then had a "reaction to their reaction," for instance, a feeling that their anger was unnatural. If they continued to stay focused on the original upset, they made more headway than if they shifted to the secondary reaction. By the same token, practitioners were more facilitative if they helped the clients stay with the original focus than if they allowed or encouraged the clients to shift to the secondary reaction. In the example, and generally, a major achievement of change-process research has been to delineate change processes as they occur in the client, with an emphasis on the client's active contribution to these processes.

Although intriguing and possibly important, such findings are based on the sort of collage of quantitative measures and qualitative analysis illustrated by Hill, Carter, and O'Farrell (1983). The exploratory "discovery-oriented" nature of their results is fully acknowledged by change-process researchers, who project more "rigorous" (and more conventional) studies to verify the yield of hypotheses and insights obtained from their more intensive investigations. It is not clear, however, how this future research agenda would overcome the limitations (the lack of sensitivity to context, myths of the uniformity of processes, and so forth) that gave rise to recent developments in change-process research.

For the time being, and perhaps for some time to come, it may make sense to regard the tentative links between process and change that have been produced by this body of research as one kind of provisionally valid knowledge, which may be "harder" than much of what is available. But, while using it, researchers also can be critical of it and work toward improving the methodology on which it is based.

Generalization

Throughout its history, change-process research has produced many interesting findings but precious little in the way of general knowledge, such as practice principles. Recent developments suggest a narrowing of scope to even smaller and less representative samples of practice. Yet this direction makes sense for understanding the complexities of change processes. It is possible that the strategy of replicating small-scale studies can build a microtheory of the behavioral, affective, and cognitive processes of change in clients that all human service professionals can draw on. But the development of knowledge by this means will occur slowly in small increments.

Meanwhile, researchers may need to rethink their notions about generalization in the development of knowledge for clinical practice. They may need to place less emphasis on constructing empirically validated practice principles and more on generating valid findings that can help harden knowledge that is of direct relevance to practice. Research-based knowledge is better seen as one part of a general configuration of different kinds of knowledge than as a "foundation" for theory or practice.

Applicability to Social Work

However one wishes to construe this knowledge, it must be recognized that its range of application to social work is limited by the types of practice and populations studied—largely psychodynamic or client-centered therapies with middle-class clients who are articulate and well motivated.

How a client's insight developed or how a practitioner may best handle the client's transference demands may be useful to some social workers, but most probably would consider these findings to be more of intellectual than of practical interest. For the purposes of social work, knowledge of a client's change processes needs to be tested with working- and lower-class populations, especially with clients with a low or dubious motivation for any kind of help. Moreover, the emphasis in change-process research on one-to-one treatment needs to be broadened to include families and other social systems.

If change-process research is to be more relevant to social work, then more research of this kind needs to be undertaken by social work researchers. Few studies of this kind have been done in social work. Furthermore, despite process studies that were stimulated by the work of Hollis, the production of process research in general has declined and shows little sign of a resurgence. For example, in recent years, few social work doctoral dissertations (which are predictors of trends in research) have been devoted to any form of process research (Reid & Strother, 1986).

Social work's emphasis in recent years on outcome evaluation and empirical practice has been salutory. A push toward more—or perhaps just some—study of change process need not be a deflection of this emphasis. In fact, change-process studies should augment efforts to develop demonstrably effective practice models.

REFERENCES

Auld, F., & Murray, E. J. (1955). Content analysis studies of psychotherapy. *Psychological Bulletin, 52,* 377–395.

Bergman, E. (1951). Counseling method and client responses. *Journal of Consulting Psychology, 5,* 216–222.

Cousins, P. G., & Power, T. (1986). Quantifying family process issues in the analysis of interaction sequences. *Family Process, 25,* 89–106.

Davis, I. P. (1975). Advice-giving in parent counseling. *Social Casework, 56,* 346–347.

Davis, I. P., & Reid, W. J. (1988). Event analysis in clinical practice and process research. *Social Casework, 69,* 298–306.

Dittes, J. E. (1957). Galvanic skin response as a measure of patient's reaction to therapist's permissiveness. *Journal of Abnormal and Social Psychology, 55,* 295–303.

Dollard, J., & Mowrer, O. H. (1947). A method of measuring tension in written documents. *Journal of Abnormal and Social Psychology, 42,* 3–32.

Elliott, R. (1983a). Fitting process research to the practicing psychotherapist. *Psychotherapy: Theory, Research & Practice, 20,* 47–55.

Elliott, R. (1983b). That in your hands: A comprehensive process analysis of a significant event in psychotherapy. *Psychiatry, 46,* 113–129.

Elliott, R. (1984). A discovery-oriented approach to significant change in psychotherapy: Interpersonal process recall and comprehensive process analysis. In L. N. Rice & L. S. Greenberg (Eds.), *Patterns of change: Intensive analysis of psychotherapy process* (pp. 249–286). New York: Guilford Press.

Elliott, R. (1985). Helpful and nonhelpful events in brief counseling interviews: An empirical taxonomy. *Journal of Counseling Psychology, 32,* 307–322.

Fortune, A. E. (1981). Communication processes in social work practice. *Social Service Review, 55,* 93–128.

Greenberg, L. S. (1984). A task analysis of interpersonal conflict resolution. In L. N. Rice & L. S. Greenberg (Eds.), *Patterns of change: Intensive analysis of psychotherapy process* (pp. 67–123). New York: Guilford Press.

Greenberg, L. S. (1986). Change process research. *Journal of Consulting and Clinical Psychology, 54,* 4–9.

Greenberg, L. S., & Pinsof, W. M. (1986a). Process research: Current trends and future perspectives. In L. S. Greenberg & W. M. Pinsoff (Eds.), *The psychotherapeutic process: A research handbook.* New York: Guilford Press.

Greenberg, L. S., & Pinsof, W. M. (1986b). *The psychotherapeutic process: A research handbook.* New York: Guilford Press.

Gurman, A., Kniskern, D., & Pinsof, W. M. (1986). Research on the process and outcome of marital and family therapy. In S. L. Garfield & A. E. Bergin (Eds.), *Handbook of psychotherapy and behavior change: An empirical analysis* (3rd ed., pp. 565–624). New York: John Wiley & Sons.

Hill, C. E., Carter, J. A., & O'Farrell, M. K. (1983). A case study of the process and outcome of time limited counseling. *Journal of Counseling Psychology, 30,* 3–18.

Hollis, F. (1968). Continuance and discontinuance in marital counseling and some observations on joint interviews. *Social Casework, 49*, 167–174.

Horowitz, M. J. (1979). *States of mind.* New York: Plenum Press.

Kagan, N. (1975). *Interpersonal process recall: A method of influencing human interaction.* Unpublished manuscript.

Kiesler, D. (1983). *The paradigm shift in psychotherapy process research.* Unpublished manuscript.

Lasswell, H. D. (1938). A provisional classification of symbol data. *Psychiatry, 1,* 197–204.

Lennard, H. L., & Bernstein, A. (1960). *The anatomy of psychotherapy.* New York: Columbia University Press.

Luborsky, L., Singer, B., Hartke, J., Crits-Christoph, P., & Cohen, M. (1984). Shifts in depressive state during psychotherapy: Which concepts of depression fit the context of Mr. Q's shifts? In L. N. Rice & L. S. Greenberg (Eds.), *Patterns of change: Intensive analysis of psychotherapy process* (pp. 157–192). New York: Guilford Press.

Mahrer, A. R., & Nadler, W. P. (1986). Good moments in psychotherapy: A preliminary review, a list, and some promising research avenues. *Journal of Consulting and Clinical Psychology, 54*, 10–15.

Marmor, C. R., Wilner, N., & Horowitz, M. J. (1984). Recurrent client states in psychotherapy: Segmentation and qualification. In L. N. Rice & L. S. Greenberg (Eds.), *Patterns of change: Intensive analysis of psychotherapy process* (pp. 194–210). New York: Guilford Press.

Marsden, G. (1971). Content analysis studies of psychotherapy: 1954 through 1968. In A. E. Bergin & S. L. Garfield (Eds.), *Handbook of psychotherapy and behavior change: An empirical analysis* (pp. 345–407). New York: John Wiley & Sons.

Mitchell, K. M., Bozarth, J. K., & Krauft, C. C. (1977). A reappraisal of the therapeutic effectiveness of accurate empathy, nonpossessive warmth, and genuiness. In A. S. Gurman & A. M. Razin (Eds.), *Effective psychotherapy: A handbook of research* (pp. 482–502). New York: Pergamon Press.

Orlinsky, D. E., & Howard, K. I. (1978). The relation of process to outcome in psychotherapy. In S. L. Garfield & A. E. Bergin (Eds.), *Handbook of psychotherapy and behavior change: An empirical analysis* (2nd ed., pp. 283–330). New York: John Wiley & Sons.

Orlinsky, D. E., & Howard, K. I. (1986). Process and outcome in psychotherapy. In S. L. Garfield & A. E. Bergin (Eds.), *Handbook of psychotherapy and behavior change: An empirical analysis* (3rd ed., pp. 311–381). New York: John Wiley & Sons.

Reid, W. J. (1985). *Family problem solving.* New York: Columbia University Press.

Reid, W. J. (1987a). Evaluating an intervention in developmental research. *Journal of Social Service Research, 11*, 17–39.

Reid, W. J. (1987b). The family problem solving sequence. *American Journal of Family Therapy, 14*, 135–146.

Reid, W. J., & Davis I. P. (1987). Qualitative methods in single-case research. In N. Gottlieb, H. A. Ishisaka, J. Kopp, C. A. Richey, & E. R. Tolson (Eds.),

Perspectives on direct practice evaluation (pp. 56–74). Seattle: University of Washington School of Social Work.

Reid, W. J., & Strother, P. (1986). *The clinical study in social work dissertations*. Paper presented at the Annual Program Meeting, GADE, Fordham University, New York, NY.

Reid, W. J., & Strother, P. (1988). Super problem solvers: A case study. *Social Service Review, 62,* 430–435.

Rice, L. N., & Greenberg, L. S. (1984a). The new research paradigm. In L. N. Rice & L. S. Greenberg (Eds.), *Patterns of change: Intensive analysis of psychotherapy process* (pp. 7–24). New York: Guilford Press.

Rice, L. N., & Greenberg, L. S. (Eds.) (1984b). *Patterns of change: Intensive analysis of psychotherapy process.* New York: Guilford Press.

Rice, L. N., & Saperia, E. (1984). Task analysis of the resolution of problematic reactions. In L. N. Rice & L. S. Greenberg (Eds.), *Patterns of change: Intensive analysis of psychotherapy process* (pp. 29–65). New York: Guilford Press.

Rogers, C. R. (1942). Electrically recorded interviews in improving psychotherapeutic techniques. *American Journal of Orthopsychiatry, 12,* 429–435.

Rosen, A., & Proctor, E. K. (1978). Specifying the treatment process: The basis for effectiveness research. *Journal of Social Service Research, 2,* 25–43.

Safran, J. D., Rice, L. N., & Greenberg, L. S. (1988). Integrating psychotherapy research and practice: Modeling the change process. *Psychotherapy, 25,* 1–17.

Sherman, E., & Skinner, K. (1988). Client language and clinical process: A cognitive-semantic analysis. *Clinical Social Work Journal, 16,* 391–405.

Sloane, R. B., Staples, F. R., Cristol, A. H., Yorkston, N. J., & Whipple, K. (1975). *Psychotherapy versus behavior therapy.* Cambridge, MA: Harvard University Press.

Snyder, W. U. (1947). A comparison of one unsuccessful with four successful nondirectively counseled cases. *Journal of Consulting Psychology, 11,* 38–42.

Speisman, J. C. (1959). Depth of interpretation and verbal assistance in psychotherapy. *Journal of Consulting Psychology, 23,* 93–99.

Thomas, E. J. (1984). *Designing interventions for the helping professions.* Beverly Hills, CA: Sage Publications.

Weiss, J., & Sampson, H. (1987). The Mount Zion Psychotherapy Research Group. *The psychoanalytic process: Theory, clinical observation and empirical research.* New York: Guilford Press.

Change-Process Research: No New Paradigm, but a Necessary Complement to the Old Paradigm

Edmund Sherman

So much can be said about Chapter 6, by Reid, because of all the new information it contains and the many implications of this information. However, space precludes a detailed discussion, so this article focuses on four different aspects of that chapter: (1) what it has to say about the nature and methods of change-process research, (2) whether change-process research is a new paradigm, (3) Reid's conception and actual use of change-process research in social work, and (4) the implications of all three issues for future research in clinical social work.

ISSUES

Reid's article is a fine, thorough review of the developments in this emerging methodology. One major intention of the method is to introduce in-therapy or in-treatment outcomes as an alternative to the standard design that uses posttreatment and follow-up measures of outcome. Reid captured this shift in emphasis in his description of change-process research "as a study of strings of intermixed i's [little interventions] and o's" (little outcomes) in place of O (big outcome). It should be added that these little o's are not apt to be summative because the emphasis is on finding patterns, rather than on aggregates or rates.

Since the thrust of this research is different from the traditional research, the question becomes, Does this shift in emphasis or thrust represent a paradigm shift? On this question, this author agrees with Reid that it does not, and Reid makes a good case for his view that change-process research is more an evolution of a number of developments dating back to the beginnings of psychotherapy research than a shift in paradigms. On the other hand, his conclusion that a "push toward more— or perhaps just 'some'—study of change process need not be a deflection of [the salutory] emphasis" on evaluation and empiricism in social work is an understatement, even with the added thought that such studies "should augment efforts to develop demonstrably effective practice models."

They would not only augment such efforts, they are a necessary *complement* to the evaluative empirical thrust. The power of change-process research is that it shows much more specifically and operationally what the practitioner does that appears to be related to change within the context of intervention. It is the "stuff" of practice. Much more detailed attention must be paid to the intervention process itself, and it must be done in context. Thus, a holistic and dialectical perspective on aspects of practice that have been systematically ignored by linear, sequential, and discontinuous quantitative research methods is called for. The very focus on how the client or client system *uses* the social worker's intervention or agency service and how the *client* experiences the change process is an important shift in emphasis, if not paradigm, and a shift much more in line with social workers' often-repeated statements about clients helping themselves. The conventional research view of social workers (or their interventions) as the presumed agents in a linear, cause-effect sequence is a gross simplification, as Reid amply demonstrated in the chapter and in his research.

Reid's conception of the place of change-process research in clinical social work is the most interesting and promising aspect of his article. Reid noted that there is an emphasis on one-to-one treatment in change-process research, to which this author would add that it is practically the exclusive emphasis (a check of the two most comprehensive compendia in the recent literature on psychotherapy process research by Rice and Greenberg [1984] and by Greenberg and Pinsof [1986] confirmed this impression). This one-to-one perspective fits well with the profession's long-standing but inter-mittent interest in casework process research. It is this perspective and the relevant methods and tools from the literature on process in psychotherapy that this author has found helpful in his research on the change process in casework (Sherman & Skinner, 1988). This has been a far easier task than has Reid's, because Reid has had to translate procedures that are essentially geared to intrapersonal client change processes to the interpersonal change processes of couples and families.

Reid makes the valid point that the emphasis on one-to-one treatment in change-process research needs to be expanded to include families and other social systems and that it needs to be applied to working- and lower-class populations, particularly those with dubious motivations for any kind of help. It should be stated, however, that Reid and his colleagues *have* broadened change-process research to include the interpersonal client systems of couples and families—and they have done it effectively.

Just in passing, it should be noted that in their systematic study of a couple's problem-solving activities in task-centered treatment, Reid and Strother (1988) found that tasks generated or modified by the client contributed more to change than did tasks generated by the social worker. It would seem that it was the investigators' more holistic attention to context and their focus on the experience of change in clients that enabled them to make this observation, which would have been unlikely from a more conventional worker-to-client linear perspective. It is also interesting that in the ongoing task-review work within the treatment model, there was an opportunity for interpersonal process recall, a procedure described by Elliott (1984) in his article on a discovery-oriented approach to change events in psychotherapy. The recall by the clients in their review of tasks provided data for both process research and the enhancement of treatment in the task-centered mode.

In their article on event analysis in process research in a family treatment situation, Davis and Reid (1988) asked, "So what is new in all this?" They then answered, "What is new is that all events are empirically grounded, of a low order of inference, recorded, and thus verifiable" (p. 302). Fifteen years ago, in the field of psychology, Cronbach (1975) called for a more even balance between the conventional empirical hypothesis-testing research and what he called "intensive local observation [psychotherapy research]." Just as Cronbach made the claim for psychology, so we social workers can make the claim for clinical social work now. Single-subject design has moved us somewhat in that direction, but change-process research contains a much greater specificity at a fine-tuned operational level of complexity and subtlety than does the recent single-subject research in clinical social work. However, it seems that this "new kid on the block" will enhance single-subject research considerably in the future.

Although change-process research does not represent a paradigm shift, it may be the necessary shift in balance in clinical social work research that Cronbach called for in psychology. Just as an overdetermined focus on solutions to a defined target problem in practice often becomes *the* problem, an overdetermined focus on "bottom-line" outcome studies has become a problem for the kind of clinical social work research that could further knowledge about the intricacies of the actual process of practice. This statement does not mean that evaluative outcome studies should be shortchanged; rather, the two enterprises have to go on concurrently and even jointly in the same research projects.

There may be a philosophical difference between the two types of research—a recurrence of the old issue of process versus outcome in practice. For example, those in the functional school of casework were suspicious of the prescribed or premature determination of goals or outcome; functionalists like Ruth Smalley and Jessie Taft believed that the ends or goals should emerge from the process, not the other way around. Now, it seems that the leading exponents of change-process research are from the client-centered and experiential schools of therapy, with cognitive-constructivist additions, but they are, indeed, process oriented in practice. By contrast, the task-centered model is highly goal and outcome oriented, with goals and related tasks quickly and systematically applied in each situation. So, the model is not really in the process tradition. Yet, Reid has been able, pragmatically and effectively, to adapt a number of the ideas and procedures from this process-oriented form of research to his goal-oriented model of practice. So in saying, somewhat tentatively, that perhaps there should be a push toward some, if not more, change-process research, Reid is being too modest about the place of such research in clinical social work research in general and about his creative use of this research in particular.

REFERENCES

Cronbach, L. J. (1975). Beyond the two disciplines of scientific psychology. *American Psychologist, 30,* 116–127.

Davis, I. P., & Reid, W. J. (1988). Event analysis in clinical practice and process research. *Social Casework, 69,* 298–306.

Elliott, R. (1984). A discovery–oriented approach to significant change in psychotherapy: Interpersonal process recall and comprehensive process analysis. In L. N. Rice & L. S. Greenberg (Eds.), *Patterns of change: Intensive analysis of psychotherapy process* (pp. 249–286). New York: Guilford Press.

Greenberg, L. S., & Pinsof, W. M. (1986). *The psychotherapeutic process: A research handbook.* New York: Guilford Press.

Reid, W. J., & Strother, P. (1988). Super problem solvers: A case study. *Social Service Review, 62,* 430–445.

Rice, L. N., & Greenberg, L. S. (Eds.). (1984). *Patterns of change: Intensive analysis of psychotherapy process.* New York: Guilford Press.

Sherman, E., & Skinner, K. (1988). Client language and clinical process: A cognitive-semantic analysis. *Clinical Social Work Journal, 16,* 391–405.

Challenges in Change-Process Research

Enola K. Proctor

The promise of change-process research is evident in its definition: the analysis of the interrelation of treatment events and change in clients or the study of strings of intermixed i's (interventions) and o's (outcomes) (Hertel, 1972; Reid, Chapter 6, this volume). The substance of social work practice also may be viewed as a string of intermixed i's and o's. To inform practice, research must shed light on the relationships between those i's and o's. Thus, change-process research is perhaps unique in its ability to clarify, test, and refine the connections between the process and outcomes of treatment.

Whatever the potential of change-process research to grapple with these fundamental hypotheses of practice, its conduct and impact on practice remain limited. Drawing on the trends reviewed by Reid in Chapter 6, this article identifies and briefly discusses three issues that are central to the quality of change-process research.

RELEVANCE OF FOCUS

The substantive focus and scope of many process studies to date has been narrow. Traditional studies of psychological and psychotherapeutic processes focus on microscopic within-session events, such as the utterances of speech and silences (Greenberg, 1986) whose relevance to social welfare issues and relation to ultimate outcomes (presenting problems) has not been clear. Such topics and units for analysis may have obscured the relevance of change-process research to social work, thereby limiting its conduct and the apparent applicability of its results.

The scarcity with which social workers conduct process studies suggests that these traditional foci do not excite them or, perhaps more accurately, do not excite the external funders upon whom researchers often depend to conduct this intensive and hence expensive research. Change-process research may not be "hot" because it is not perceived as relevant. Often missing is a focus on changes in clients, their situations, and their behaviors that are relevant to the presenting problems. Thus, the challenge to change-process researchers is to select carefully the substantive focus of process studies and to clarify its relevance to pressing social work issues.

Research can be both relevant and specific in unraveling the process of change. The key is to ensure that the variables of focus are related, within some theoretical rationale, to real-world problems and the means to resolve them. Process researchers in psychology have made some recent progress in this regard. Mahrer and Nadler (1986) identified a "provisional list" of 11 "good moments," or points when clients manifest evidence of therapeutic process, movement, improvement, or change; this list generated a number of suggested avenues of pursuit by process researchers. The topics derive from and are relevant within the framework of psychological conceptions of behavioral change; therein lies their significance and the promise of their identification for directing the activity of process researchers.

Social work may develop a different list. The profession has documented the importance of such factors as the client's commitment to change, reduction in anxiety as a precursor to new self-understanding, trust between minority clients and majority workers, and enhancing women's sense of competence and awareness of options. When these states and behaviors are pursued in helping, they serve as outcomes in the process of change. When their contribution to the attainment of ultimate outcomes is clear, that is, when they are viewed as essential in resolving the client's presenting problems, then their relevance for study and the relevance of change process for the profession are evident. The conduct and applicability of process research can be enhanced by the identification and explication of the relevance of valid, reasonable, and representative outcomes for focus.

INCORPORATION OF CONTEXTUAL FACTORS

Too often, change-process research has perpetuated the myth of uniformity by, in the words of Greenberg (1986), "aggregating process, as though all process during sessions or across therapy is the same" (p. 7). Just as researchers have matured beyond this myth in our understanding and testing of interventions, it is important to appreciate the limits to generalizing the process of change. In all likelihood, the process differs across various populations of clients and presenting problems. Even the helping relationship varies according to the client, the problem, and situational factors (Proctor, 1982). An important challenge, then, is to specify the process in terms of contextual variables.

In commenting on the tendency to focus on process, Meyer (1987) observed, "Every modality that confines its treatment processes to transactions without reference to context carries risks, primarily of failure in effectiveness over time, but also of losing connectedness to the institution of social work" (p. 403). For social work to demonstrate its expertise in the fields of practice, population groups, or problem areas, social work researchers, including change-process researchers, must attend increasingly to these substantive issues.

How may contextual issues be included in the agenda of change-process research? One obvious means is to study the process of change with specific population groups, presenting problems, or practice settings. Through inclusion criteria, subjects can be limited to a homogeneous group. The processes of change in different populations can be compared by employing comparative group designs or multiple baseline single-subject designs. Such research may enhance the understanding of these processes for specified populations and problems. For example, decision-making processes may differ for populations and problems (for example, elderly people who are contemplating institutional placement versus pregnant teenagers who are deciding whether to keep their babies) or settings (acute medical care versus outpatient mental health settings).

QUESTION-METHOD CORRESPONDENCE

Ensuring the appropriateness of the methodology to research questions is a third challenge. The questions addressed by change-process research require unraveling the multiple ingredients of change. Most theoretical orientations to practice view the process of change as complex, in that attainment of any goal or outcome involves prerequisite changes and processes (Rosen, Proctor, & Livine, 1985). Thus, the questions for change-process research are complex. Indeed, one may see so little change-process research because the questions are so comprehensive that their investigation appears formidable. Yet methodologies must correspond to the scope and complexity of questions.

The first methodological requirement for change-process research is specificity in operationalization and measurement. Both the intervention process and the outcomes must be operationally or molecularly (Hertel, 1972) defined and measured. Behavioral specification and precise measurement of the ingredients of the process are essential for replication, for the clear understanding of what occurred, and for the subsequent utilization of knowledge. Yet many studies fail to specify what constitutes a faithful rendition of treatment and what departures fall within an acceptable range (Kazdin, 1986). To contribute to knowledge about the process of change, researchers need information about the level of the intervention and how variations in its dosage, timing, and intensity relate to changes in a client's behavior.

Second, multifactorial designs are necessary to explore the patterns and interrelationships among elements of the process. Designs must be capable of assessing, minimally, the presence of interventions and outcomes and the relationships between interventions and outcomes, as well as the relationships among various outcomes. Snapshot, simplistic designs are not sufficient to capture the complexity of questions posed in change-process research. Many older process studies focused on single variables, to the exclusion of patterns (Greenberg, 1986). Many social work process studies concentrated more on the occurrence and patterning of i's, such as the social worker's sustainment, reflection, and structuring, with scant attention to the consequent o's. Conversely, some process studies in the client-centered perspective have emphasized outcomes for clients to the exclusion of the activities of social workers that influence those outcomes. The study of relationships among variables and patterns of change requires, at a minimum, factorial designs and multivariate levels of data analysis to permit the study of the effects of interactions (Parloff, 1986).

Also important is measurement that is specific to the sequences, states, and phases of change (Hertel, 1972; Mahrer & Nadler, 1986). Global summary scores over a span of an interaction are not instructive to understanding the order of events or the sequence of patterns. Promising methods, although infrequently used in social work, include the sequential analyses of variables, which can shed light on the contingencies between the social worker's and client's behaviors (Russell & Trull, 1986) and clarify the direction of influence. Sequential analysis requires time markers in the recording of behavior, or at least rules for making decisions that permit the alignment and sequencing of behavior for coding and analysis protocols for coding (Cone & Foster, 1982; Gottman, 1980).

Finally, a variety of individual and group designs should be considered and used in change-process research. Single-subject designs, though not widely viewed as a tool in change-process research, can clarify sequences of events; indeed, one of the strengths of single-subject designs is their ability to capture the course of change over time. Yet few single-subject studies have measured change in a client within an interview. The further removed measurement is from the worker-client contact, the less likely results are to reveal events in the actual process of change. Of course, relating immediate measures to more distant reactions over time will enhance the understanding of how the process generalizes or occurs (analogous to learning curves) over time. The potential of single-subject designs for analyzing the relationships among multiple outcomes has not been realized.

However, single-subject designs have not been the best source of information about what treatments work with what clients with what problems. Comparative group designs are increasingly advocated for their potential to shed light on subtle differences in intervention processes under various circumstances. Meaningful comparisons can be drawn of clients, phases, interventions, and desired outcomes. Although the primary focus of comparative designs has been on outcome, their major contribution may be an interim comparison of treatment processes, revealing similarities and differences in how treatments are implemented (Kazdin, 1986). Comparative studies also can reveal the differential effects of the same intervention on various groups of clients. Basham (1986) viewed comparative designs as being more instructive to the treatment process than is the meta-analysis of single-treatment studies.

Although opponents and proponents of various methodologies abound, allegiance to any particular design is not the issue. Rather, the design should be determined on the basis of its appropriateness to answer the research question. In a developmental approach, the products of one set of studies, however limited, can build incrementally upon those from earlier studies. The design and focus of those studies can and should vary.

The conduct of change-process research is conceptually and methodologically challenging. The quality of its products may be enhanced by explicating the relevance of its focus to social welfare concerns, by attending increasingly to contextual issues to enhance the generalization of results, and by ensuring that designs and measures are adequate to test the interrelationship of process events.

REFERENCES

Basham, R. B. (1986). Scientific and practical advantages of comparative design in psychotherapy outcome research. *Journal of Consulting and Clinical Psychology, 54*, 88–94.

Cone, J. D., & Foster, S. L. (1982). Direct observation in clinical psychology. In P. C. Kendall & J. N. Butcher (Eds.), *Handbook of research methods in clinical psychology* (pp. 311–354). New York: John Wiley & Sons.

Gottman, J. M. (1980). Analyzing for sequential connection and assessing interobserver reliability for the sequential analysis of observational data. *Behavioral Assessment, 2*, 361–368.

Greenberg, L. S. (1986). Change process research. *Journal of Consulting and Clinical Psychology, 54*, 4–9.

Hertel, R. K. (1972). Application of stochastic process analysis to the study of psychotherapeutic processes. *Psychological Bulletin, 77*, 421–430.

Kazdin, A. E. (1986) Comparative outcome studies of psychotherapy: Methodological issues and strategies. *Journal of Consulting and Clinical Psychology, 54*, 95–105.

Mahrer, A. R., & Nadler, W. P. (1986). Good moments in psychotherapy: Preliminary review, a list, and some promising research avenues. *Journal of Consulting and Clinical Psychology, 54,* 10–15.

Meyer, C. M. (1987). Content and process in social work practice: A new look at old issues. *Social Work, 32,* 401–404.

Parloff, M. B. (1986). Placebo controls in psychotherapy research: A sine qua non or a placebo for research problems. *Journal of Consulting and Clinical Psychology, 54,* 79–87.

Proctor, E. K. (1982). Defining the worker-client relationship. *Social Work, 27,* 430–435.

Rosen, A., Proctor, E. K., & Livine, S. (1985). Planning and direct practice. *Social Service Review, 59,* 161–177.

Russell, R. L., & Trull, T. J. (1986). Sequential analyses of language variables in psychotherapy process research. *Journal of Consulting and Clinical Psychology, 54,* 16–21.

The Utility of Change-Process Research for the Education of Practitioners and Single-Case Evaluation

Sharon B. Berlin

In Chapter 6, Reid did an enviable job of pulling together the main elements of change-process research—its history, essential attributes, utility, and limits—with precision and clarity. Although there is increasing recognition that these methods are well suited for addressing questions that are central to the clinical enterprise, the emergence of this research approach probably does not represent a new research paradigm or a shift in paradigms. It does, however, increase the ability of researchers to investigate additional levels of clinical phenomena. It is especially important because it permits a whole new slant on the opportunities and possibilities of empirically based clinical practice.

VALUE OF CHANGE-PROCESS RESEARCH

Beyond focusing on the extent to which the client's target problem is changing over time, as have the traditional single-case investigations, the change-process perspective also focuses on how the client is changing—what is going on as he is getting stuck, surging ahead, or sliding back into the thick of his original dilemma. Although it has been said that single-case research methods are tools that practitioners can use to understand better how the treatment is going or how change is occurring, these methods yield only partial information. For example, they can be used to find out that according to a client's estimate of her depressed mood, she is now more depressed or less depressed or that her mood has been stable over some given period. They also may allow researchers to determine that such changes coincide with interventions and then to infer that the intervention has something to do with the change. However, they do not indicate anything about how the client actually got to the change—what she did, thought, felt, struggled with, and took from the interaction that resulted in a meaningful shift in mood.

One can learn a lot about how to assist clients with certain kinds of change by studying how change unfolds—by discerning the internal and external steps or patterns that clients take as they move from insight to effective action; from knowing something on an intellectual level to knowing it in a more visceral, emotional sense; or from cycling around in a familiar dysfunctional relationship to opting for something more constructive and different. In these terms, what one does as a clinician is based on an understanding of what it is that clients do when making an adaptive shift.

An additional characteristic—a virtue—of change-process research, particularly task analysis, is that it utilizes information from multiple sources. Task analysis focuses the researcher on theory, clinical wisdom, and rigorous observation. All these sources of knowledge are viewed as legitimate, complementary, and necessary aspects of full understanding. Moreover, task analysis brings together research strategies for exploration and verification.

Rice and Greenberg (1984) argued that through the use of task analysis, one can locate relatively consistent patterns of change across clients and within a given kind of change event (such as resolving problematic reactions or intrapersonal conflicts) and within a relatively similar therapeutic context (gestalt therapy interventions, for example). The research goal of locating such patterns is ambitious and requires, among other things, a lot of time, a huge tolerance for tedium, and an ability to maintain clarity in the midst of ambiguity. Although the goal is important and worthy for researchers in clinical social work, it is unlikely to attract the efforts of practitioners. However, when applied to a single case, change-process methods offer a feasible way to gain a great deal of information that is of immediate practical value. This application is something that practitioners may well be interested in.

EDUCATING STUDENTS IN CHANGE-PROCESS METHODS

In the same way that training clinical students in single-case research will help them to become more precise, grounded clinicians even if they do not perform complete single-subject investigations case by case, training clinical students in change-process methods will aid them in becoming more explicit and multiply informed clinicians even if they do not carry out complete change-process investigations every time.

This notion of the educational potential of change-process methods comes largely from this author's experience in conducting a small-scale task-analytic study of cognitive therapy for depression (Berlin, Mann, & Grossman, in press) and from taking a group of clinical students who were enrolled in a class on the process of psychotherapy through the steps of task analysis. Briefly, in carrying out the steps of the task-analysis method, the researcher does the following:

• articulates his or her general theory (which is based on formal theory and clinical experience) about how change occurs in a given domain

• focuses his or her search for knowledge on a specific kind of change task or event and operationalizes the marker and resolution for that event

• relies on the general theory to explicate a rational or "idealized" delineation of the steps the client is expected to take in resolving the particular change event

• specifies the interventions that promise to support or prompt change in the client

• locates the change event (from marker to resolution) in transcripts of the session and uses a coding system (see Greenberg, 1986) to observe the extent to which the client's performance conforms to or deviates from the rational mode.

All along, the researcher collects outcome data, the little o's that convey how much the original problem is changing, and uses this information to fill out or corroborate the client's record of change. Finally, the researcher revises the rational model to incorporate the observed differences in the client's operations and uses the revised performance model as the basis for additional observations. Depending on the scope and purpose of the investigation, the revised performance model may either be a model of change for an individual client or a model that reflects patterns of change for a number of clients.

The author and her associates have focused their investigation on the question of how depressed women work their way toward cognitive-emotional change within the context of cognitive therapy. To date, they have constructed performance models of change in clients for two interrelated kinds of therapy events or subtasks: (1) generating more constructive appraisals and using them as a basis for action and understanding, or searching for the general theme underlying situation-specific appraisals to understand one's more basic, core assumptions, and (2) generating more constructive core assumptions and using them as a basis for action and understanding. These performance models are based on data from sessions with six clients and are the second revisions of the original rational models. Additional examples of the events will have to be examined before the performance models can be revised further and developed into a set of warranted and testable hypotheses about the processes of cognitive-emotional change.

In the meantime, the author has learned a great deal—just from asking herself to think through and spell out her view of how change occurs for these kinds of events, from closely attending to nuances in the clients' expressions and trying to discern how individuals approach and incorporate difference or move away from it, and from sometimes catching herself getting in the way of forward movement and sometimes assisting it in a right-on-the-mark kind of way. She believes that all these experiences have contributed to her becoming a more theoretically grounded, observant, attuned practitioner.

The second source of optimism about the educational potential of task analysis comes from having tested it in a small master's degree–level research/clinical course on the process of psychotherapy. In the context of receiving intensive guidance and multiple examples in the classroom and focusing only on the minimum essential steps of task analysis, the students analyzed their work with a single client with good results. With only a little extra creativity, it was possible for them to use these methods to track the processes of change for a range of social work interventions beyond the traditional psychotherapeutic encounter. Always, the basic job was to articulate the components of their general theoretical perspective, identify the critical change tasks or events that were to be investigated and spell out the idealized or theoretical version of how those tasks are resolved, and observe actual occurrences of clients working toward the resolution of the tasks in question so the theoretical model of change could be revised and improved. Most important, this educational exercise highlighted what the students knew and did not know about how change occurs and imparted a curiosity and enthusiasm for further investigation.

Although optimism about the potential of task analysis and other change-process methods seems warranted, the virtues of these methods should not be oversold. Change-process methods are fraught with pitfalls, especially measurement difficulties and the possibility of falling into a bottomless abyss of subjectivity. However, the hope is that these methods will be added to other imperfect and useful knowledge-generating tools.

REFERENCES

Berlin, S. B., Mann, K. B., & Grossman, S. F. (in press). Task-analysis of cognitive therapy for depression. *Social Work Research & Abstracts*.

Greenberg, L. S. (1986). Change process research. *Journal of Consulting and Clinical Psychology, 54*, 4–9.

Rice, L. N., & Greenberg, L. S. (Eds.). (1984). *Patterns of change: Intensive analysis of psychotherapy process*. New York: Guilford Press.

Microanalysis of Intervention-Client Change Loops: The Heart of Change-Process Research

Inger P. Davis

This article focuses on three issues that were raised by the presentations of Reid, Sherman, Proctor, and Berlin and the audience's reactions to them at the conference. These issues are (1) the meaning and measurement of changes during the therapeutic process (i's and o's) in comparison with the traditional summated measures of outcome and intervention (I's and O's); (2) the pros and cons of the practice researcher having or not having a theory to guide the selection of therapeutic process episodes, chunks, events, or other units of analysis; and (3) the usefulness, cost, and potential gains of the change-process method of inquiry for clinical practice, research, and professional education.

MEANING AND MEASUREMENT OF CHANGES

In Chapter 6, Reid presented the major characteristics that distinguish change-process research. The first characteristics are the practitioner-client interaction system as the target for study and the greater emphasis on the client as an agent of change. Interventions and change outcomes within and between sessions (i's and o's) are seen as strings of intertwined events that occur in a flowing process throughout the course of treatment. Because this process cannot be microanalyzed in toto, segments are selected through attention to the context in which change occurs. Just as the clinician's interventions are context driven (chosen during moments when the client is ready for them), the change-process researcher selects the contexts in which change is likely to happen. This selection is seen as a beginning step toward being able to discriminate between contexts that produce effects and those in which not much is happening. The selected segments (coding units) may be of various sizes, events, chunks, or single cases, as Reid elaborated. A final characteristic is the application of a mix

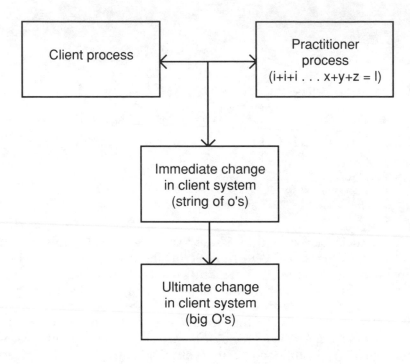

Figure 1.

of many qualitative and quantitative measures. Figure 1 (a diagram by Reid that was not included in Chapter 6) captures several of these characteristics.

Although all the presenters agreed that change-process research is neither new nor a paradigm, the nature of some of the comments reflects how difficult it is to replace a traditional "give-and-receive," "expert-patient" view of treatment with a true systemic perception. In any event, the topic of the i-I and o-O links was addressed primarily from the angle of what the client or the practitioner (and others) do to effect change and much less from the perspective and the mutual systemic interaction between the client and the practitioner that is a hallmark of change-process research. Thus, in terms of Figure 1, the discussion was often centered *within* the client or the practitioner boxes more than on the set of arrows between the three top boxes. This tendency to focus on either the client or the therapist may be a carryover of habitual thinking from past paradigms of process and outcome research in which attention was given—as Reid pointed out—to the practitioner's activities or to associations between summary measures of interventions and the client's reactions or changes in a session or after treatment. However, a good deal of discussion was also devoted to the connections between the two boxes symbolizing the immediate and ultimate changes in the client system (the o-O link).

Concept of Negative Change

The concept of negative change was discussed from several perspectives and ultimately viewed as important for the I-O link as for the incremental client-practitioner changes that occur during treatment. Although there is a natural tendency to focus on (if not savor) the positives, professional responsibility mandates that, as practitioners, we at least do not harm the client—that no malevolent interaction spiral exists between the client and the practitioner and hence no negative O results.

As far as the o's are concerned, the picture is complex. Here, immediate positive and negative reactions are often intertwined. Many practitioners have aroused a client's ire one week to learn the next week that, after mulling it over, the client accepted and processed the practitioner's message in whatever interventive cloak it was couched. In many instances, clients may not be able to arrive at a positive O except by zig-zagging through the mix of positive and negative o's. However, one needs to take a close look at the episodes/chunks of therapeutic process surrounding the negative o's to make sure that they are there for reasons intrinsic to the client's unique past and present experiences and coping abilities, not because of a string of misconstrued, inept i's.

What has just been said does not imply that ineptness—"missing-the-mark" type interventions—are or necessarily could be avoided. After all, practitioners are human beings. Even under the best circumstances, culminating in lasting, profound changes in the client's psychosocial functioning, some of what the practitioner did, exuded, or otherwise channeled into the therapeutic process will probably fail to connect or will have a negative effect on the client's efforts to change. One psychotherapist (Bugental, 1988) observed that most cases have some elements of success, as well as of failure. Occasional limited failures in the day-to-day work with clients may not lead to the failure of therapy as a whole, but they may, in subtle ways, "make the work less productive than it might otherwise be" (Bugental, 1988, p. 533). From his practice experience, Bugental identified two sources of therapists' failure with clients, namely, therapists' hesitation to invest as fully in the therapeutic process as their clients need and the betrayal of the clients that comes from treating them as less than human beings and more as problems, diagnostic categories, types, and so on.

Rounding off the discussion of negative change in clients, the following are examples of past and recent research that included and measured both positive and negative outcomes: Dollard and Mowrer (1947), Hunt and Kogan (1952), Kogan, Hunt, and Bartelme (1953), Strupp (1980a, 1980b, 1980c, 1980d), and Elliott (1984). Berlin presented another example from her study of the change process in cases utilizing cognitive therapy for depression. In her study, the events selected for analysis included resolution events, as well as episodes in which the client derails, "spins out" so to speak, onto another track leading nowhere. A comparison of these two types of resolution events, in the context of the therapist's attempts to keep the client on track, will generate new understanding of the nature of this interplay, it is hoped.

Concern was expressed over how one may capture possible *sleeper-effect* changes (O's) that emerge after treatment is terminated and monitor the durability and robustness of the string of o's and the observed O change when a case is closed. Berlin observed that the extent to which clients "plough" the learning and changes emanating from the therapeutic process into their lives to cope with problems as they reoccur seems to be as important as is the specific reduction in depressive mood or the resolution of marital conflict when a case is closed. And just as the treatment process itself (whether short or long term) is the context for in-session change, contextual factors in the client's family, workplace, or other environments appear to have a lot to do with how and how well changes in a client hold up over time.

Issues surrounding the *measurement* of o's in addition to traditional composite measures of change outcomes (O's) generated lively give-and-take discussion. Is it necessary to obtain measures of the client's and therapist's behaviors from each session, in addition to the global outcome measures? Reid saw both types of measures as being highly desirable, but clients should not be viewed as inexhaustible suppliers of data. A trade-off needs to be made between the possible overloading of the client system, the limited resources for collecting data, and the need for and usefulness of the data, which depend on the specific questions under study. Since the taping of sessions has become more common, the researcher has the option to apply many types of process-analysis measures without burdening the client with numerous measurement devices. The application of fine-grained analytic procedures, however, is labor intensive and time consuming; thus, resources may allow only the analysis of highly select samples of process segments, episodes, events, and so forth. One proposed alternative source of data for measuring changes in clients is diaries kept by clients.

Standardized measures may be available, but if they have been developed for and validated with motivated, self-revealing middle-class clients, they cannot appropriately be used with taciturn, acting-out adolescents. Therefore, change-process researchers frequently create and add their own case-specific instruments to the ever-growing pool of one-shot measures. This situation raises yet other methodological issues, such as severe limitations on the cumulative effects of this body of research and the extent to which studies can be compared.

A second major issue, the role of theory in the conduct of change-process research, was discussed mainly in relation to points raised by Proctor. Proctor suggested that change process research will gain by becoming increasingly theory-driven, which, among other things, will facilitate and guide the selection of variables to be focused on in a given inquiry. Unfortunately, time did not allow a fuller exploration of the relevance of different levels and kinds of theory to change-process research. Therefore, a few points of observation are added here.

It is probably impossible for social work practitioners *not* to be guided by theory in some, albeit rudimentary, form. In clinical practice encounters, practitioners always have at least some raw notion how and why their own and their clients' behaviors interconnect in certain contexts to bring about the kind of change in clients they would or would not like to see. The raw notion perhaps better described as practice wisdom gleaned from past successes, failures, and aesthetic experiences, to use Siporin's (1988) terminology, becomes a subtle component in the practitioners' infusions in the therapeutic process. That is, clients, no doubt, pick up some positive cues from the practitioners' nonverbal messages, stemming from the gratification practitioners experience when their clients "see the light" or some negative cues when practitioners recoil (without detriment to the clients, it is hoped) when their clients "tread water" or even get off the track altogether. In other words, this aesthetic transformative process culminates in a mutually experienced sense of completion, when the client's full engagement in the therapeutic process leads to situational changes in the client's life (Siporin, 1988).

Mixed in with these elusive interactional experiences (part art, part science, part skills) one also hopes to find that the practitioner adeptly draws on theories of human development, social psychology, personality, and ecology, among others, to grasp the client's unique intrapersonal and interpersonal circumstances and to select and time specific interventions tuned to the phases of the therapeutic encounter. The change-process researcher sighs with relief if the practitioner, who has agreed to expose tape-recorded sessions to the change-process analysis, is a purist, who, from the pool of behavioral, cognitive, psychodynamic, task-centered, or problem-solving practice models, has selected, mastered, and remained faithful to only one model. The chaotic theoretical contexts created by an eclectic practitioner represent another challenge, one that process researchers of any kind may want to approach gingerly for the time being. It takes more than the mastery of fractions and division to figure out how, how much, and in what ways the multiple theories selected by the practitioner actually guide or contribute to the practice process.

Thus, a decision to let theory guide practice and research is immediately followed by the question, What theory? As was indicated, there are many to choose from, considering both the theories the practitioner claims to have been guided by and those that were actually applied and were clearly evidenced in the therapeutic process. Many practitioners use and master practice models with distinct theoretical underpinnings, such as the cognitive, psychodynamic, task-centered, and problem-solving models, and it is possible to select episodes from the therapeutic process and study change in a client in the context of characteristic features of a particular model. However, the question is, How many x, y, z's can change-process researchers allow to be mixed in with the i's before they have to conclude that the composite adds up to an amorphous blob, not worthy of being counted as an I?

The problem of appropriate operational definitions of the I, or intervention integrity, not only may render the testing even of a mini-practice theory premature, but also may undermine the confidence with which findings of significant associations between I's and O's can be accepted unless the i's and o's are also reliably and validly accounted for. The I-O link must be established before it is determined what I stands for, and that can only be done by appropriate measures of i's.

The question of how theory is or should be related to change-process research depends on the purpose of the research activity. Are researchers guided by and do they test theoretical propositions, or are they engaged in unravelling the early bits and pieces of what some day may add up to a practice model or a practice theory? Some answers may be found by looking at a common formulation of the steps of change-process research: the microanalysis of interactional change events; the creation of a preliminary performance model specifying "ideal" intervention strategies as responses to given "change markers" of clients; the analysis of new sets of change events similar to the ones from which the model was developed and from subsequent revisions in the model; and the formulation of a more advanced performance model, which is replicated on different types of cases, by different practitioners, and so forth. The steps described so far rely primarily on the ability to identify the therapeutic events and on an accurate fine-grained description and analysis of observable behaviors along many dimensions. Moving from the performance to the operational-model stage requires a higher level of abstraction—one or more theories to incorporate the psychological processes underlying the observable client-therapist behaviors (Elliott, 1984; Rice & Greenberg, 1984a). It is only at the later stages that the models become clinically and theoretically robust enough to be exposed to more traditional group-comparison designs, at which point it makes sense to set hypothesis-testing goals for the change-process research.

A middle road may be taken between discovery and hypothesis-testing designs by using change-process research to establish associations among variables, as Proctor proposed. Mahrer (1988) made a similar suggestion by describing two approaches to discovery-oriented research, the first aiming to provide a close discovery-oriented look at psychotherapeutic events and phenomena and the second "to discover the relations among psychotherapeutic conditions, operations, and consequences" (p. 697). Mahrer spelled out the five procedural steps involved in the former and the three steps of the latter approach. Inquiries into the interconnections among conditions, operations, and consequences seek answers to these three general questions formulated by Mahrer (1988):

> 1. Given this *operation*, carried out under this condition, what are the consequences? That is, if the therapist does this operation, when the patient is being this way, what will happen?
> 2. Given this *consequence*, what conditions can achieve this consequence? That is, what can the therapist do to effect this desired consequence?
> 3. Given this *condition*, what operation can achieve this consequence? That is, when the patient is this way, what does the therapist want to achieve, and what does the therapist do to achieve this consequence? (pp. 699–700).

Questions like these are mulled over by reflective practitioners in their everyday professional lives. As was pointed out earlier, other similarities between practitioners and process researchers stem from the fact that the process researcher's mind-set, tools, and operations run parallel to the practitioner's. However, the practitioner has the rudder in hand, and one or more clients are on board who are more or less engaged in the joint activities involved in propelling the boat ahead or at least keeping it afloat. The process researcher, on the other hand, is loaded down with gear for a camera crew (but usually without the supportive crew) and is trying to stay close enough to let one camera lens zoom in to capture special moments, while letting another widen to scan the immediate and distant surroundings, ranging from turbulent waves to a calm, glassy sea. Another difference may be that when the ship is safely ashore, the practitioner and client or clients part with shared feelings of having completed their mission, a productive or not-so-productive journey, as the case may be, but, it is hoped, with a sense that it was worth the effort and worth repeating when circumstances call for it again. The process researcher, on the other hand, realizes as the taping machinery is dropped on the floor that as rough as it might have been to capture what went on, the trip itself was nothing but the beginning. Miles of tapes will patiently lie there waiting to be microanalyzed.

In any case, as Strupp (1989) noted, a therapist can do little with a finding that one form of therapy appears to be slightly more effective than another in terms of outcomes for clients. Practitioners need systematically observed findings that give details of the links between the aforementioned conditions, operations, and consequences of the interplay between the client and the practitioner. And such findings are more likely to be derived from the minutiae of change-process research than from traditional group-comparison studies that present aggregated data, in which the idiosyncracies of practitioners and clients are largely wiped out.

Mahrer (1988) made a persuasive case for the conclusion that hypothesis-testing research has contributed little to confirming or disconfirming theories or to adding to a cumulative body of knowledge of psychotherapy. However, discovery-oriented research holds great promise for blending theory, practice, and research by conceptually challenging researchers to learn the secrets of psychotherapy and to discover what is discoverable.

Overall, one has to conclude that, so far, contributions to practice from either type of process research remain more a promise than a reality. And change-process research, as presented in the non–social work literature, may have even less relevance to social work practice than to other forms of interpersonal helping because change-process studies have largely been conducted with middle-class, majority clients, who are only partly representative of the caseloads of social workers. The detailed account of the client-practitioner process, essential to change-process research, is often hard to obtain with many social work clients, such as chronically mentally ill people or those who are homeless. And a tape recorder will often scare away an illegal alien, a child-abusing parent, a runaway youth, a drug addict, or others who intermittently have stepped onto the wrong side of the law. In so-called court-ordered therapy, researchers get some interactional process going and obtain at least the information that the judicial system is entitled to, but probably not much that will be meaningful for a fine-grained analysis of the interaction process. As anyone who has actively worked with clients under these difficult conditions knows, even the most compassionate, empathic, skillful therapeutic operations often result in pseudoengagement by clients and meager outcomes at best. Many clients bear too heavy a load of early losses, emotional and physical deprivations, hurts, and despairs to be able to grab hold of the tools the practitioners offer to change the direction of the downward spiral in which they have become trapped.

Thus, although labor intensive, expensive change-process research holds the promise of yielding findings that are meaningful to practitioners about the interplay among conditions, operations, and consequences of the client-practitioner collaboration, it should be used selectively and with the full understanding and participation of clients. And it should, of course, include the use of multiple measures of change and interventions to allow the optimal triangulation of quantitative and qualitative data. Furthermore, change-process research is but *one* tool in the armamentarium of social work research that is needed to unlock the undiscovered in the client-practitioner process that can be used alone or in conjunction with other methods of inquiry.

The question of how and when change-process research is the method of choice, and at what price, depends to a large extent on which priorities are set for research. No consensus on what these priorities ought to be was arrived at, at the conference. One suggestion, proposed by Edwin J. Thomas, was that the first priority should be to examine the association between an overall intervention packet (I) and an ultimate change outcome (O), not to explore i's. Process research is important, but it should not displace or take priority over an emphasis on outcome research involving the I's and O's. However, if time and resources are available, it would be interesting to examine the i's.

Finally, change-process research is a valuable educational tool, a point barely touched on in the professional literature. Many graduate students have expressed enthusiasm about the gain in in-depth understanding of the therapeutic process that emerges from the microanalysis of taped sessions from their practicum cases or those of others. Naturally, the level of sophistication of this form of research varies greatly among students, whether they are microanalyzing process events that are singled out for study because they meet a priori selection criteria or analyzing "informative events" that represent something new that is of interest beyond the particular case (Davis & Reid, 1988; Reid, 1985). The mastery of the complexities of informative-events analysis or of many of the change-process studies included in Rice and Greenberg (1984b) can probably be expected only of doctoral-level students.

In sum, change-process research is valuable for investigating selected topics of clinical social work practice and as a learning tool for graduate and postgraduate professional education. It deserves to be exposed to continued experimentation in research as well as in education to be molded into a shape that fits the commitments and mission of social work.

REFERENCES

Bugental, J. F. T. (1988). What is "failure" in psychotherapy? *Psychotherapy, 25,* 532–535.

Davis, I. P., & Reid, W. J. (1988). Event analysis in clinical practice and process research. *Social Casework, 69,* 298–306.

Dollard, J., & Mowrer, O. H. (1947). A method of measuring tension in written documents. *Journal of Abnormal and Social Psychology, 42,* 3–32.

Elliott, R. (1984). A discovery-oriented approach to significant change in psychotherapy: Interpersonal process recall and comprehensive process analysis. In L. N. Rice & L. S. Greenberg (Eds.), *Patterns of change: Intensive analysis of psychotherapy process* (pp. 249–286). New York: Guilford Press.

Hunt, J. M., & Kogan, L. S. (1952). *Measuring results in social casework* (rev. ed.). New York: Family Service Association of America.

Kogan, L. S., Hunt, J. M., & Bartelme, P. F. (1953). *A follow-up study of social casework.* New York: Family Service Association of America.

Mahrer, A. R. (1988). Discovery-oriented psychotherapy research, rationale, aims, and methods. *American Psychologist, 43,* 694–702.

Reid, W. J. (1985). *Family problem solving.* New York: Columbia University Press.

Rice, L N., & Greenberg, L. S. (1984a). Future research directions. In L. N. Rice and L. S. Greenberg (Eds.), *Patterns of change: Intensive analysis of psychotherapy process* (pp. 289–300). New York: Guilford Press.

Rice, L. N., & Greenberg, L. S. (Eds.). (1984b). *Patterns of change: Intensive analysis of psychotherapy process.* New York: Guilford Press.

Siporin, M. (1988). Clinical social work as art form. *Social Casework, 69,* 177–185.

Strupp, H. H. (1980a). Success and failure in time-limited psychotherapy: A systematic comparison of two cases: Comparison 1. *Archives of General Psychiatry, 37,* 595–603.

Strupp, H. H. (1980b). Success and failure in time-limited psychotherapy: A systematic comparison of two cases: Comparison 2. *Archives of General Psychiatry, 37,* 708–716.

Strupp, H. H. (1980c). Success and failure in time-limited psychotherapy: With special reference to the performance of a lay counselor (comparison 3). *Archives of General Psychiatry, 37,* 831–841.

Strupp, H. H. (1980d). Success and failure in time-limited psychotherapy: Further evidence (comparison 4). *Archives of General Psychiatry, 37,* 947–954.

Strupp, H. H. (1989). Psychotherapy: Can the practitioner learn from the researcher? *American Psychologist, 44,* 717–724.

Chapter 7

The Use of Qualitative and Quantitative Data in the Development of a Clinical Program

Sheldon D. Rose and Naomi Farber

Planning a control-group experiment to evaluate a clinical program requires more than a research design. It involves the development of numerous program and organizational structures without any one of which the experiment cannot be successfully carried out. The purpose of this chapter is to illustrate how to use various kinds of data to develop one of these structures, the treatment program. The examples presented here draw on experiences generated and decisions made during the three years it took to develop a program that was used in a set of interrelated experiments reported by Tallent, Rose, and Tolman (1989), Tolman and Rose (1989), and Whitney and Rose (1989).

PROGRAM DEVELOPMENT

The goal-oriented activities to which the leader introduces the members and in which she or he involves them is referred to as the program. Important among these activities are orientation, assessment, and intervention. The focus of this chapter is on the intervention components of program. However, the logic for decision making was the same for the other elements.

The intervention components to be included in or added to the treatment program had to have a theoretical link to ameliorating the presenting problem (stress, in this example) of the target population. The following theories guided the selection of the initial procedure that was linked to the following procedures noted in parenthesis: operant theory (reinforcement procedures), social learning theory (in particular, the modeling sequence), cognitive-behavioral theory (cognitive restructuring, self-instructional training, and generalization training), small-group theory (procedures for inducing cohesion and stimulating broad participation), and problem-solving theory (problem-solving procedures).

Most of these theories that linked strategies with the more effective management of stress could be combined into one broad-based cognitive-behavioral theory called stress inoculation (Meichenbaum, 1977). By adding the small-group strategies, the authors developed a still-broader treatment theory called "the multimethod group approach" (Rose, 1989).

Furthermore, the connection between each procedure and stress reduction had to have some empirical support under some conditions with some populations. The more support, the stronger the argument for including the procedure in the package. To establish both theoretical and empirical linkages, the authors did a library search of all programs dealing with the issues involved in stress. Those programs that had some empirical foundation were integrated into a comprehensive training manual (Rose, Tolman, & Tallant, 1985). The new procedures were added to those procedures that had already demonstrated a relationship to outcome. Since a series of studies aimed at increasing assertive behavior by means of the modeling and reinforcement strategies had already been completed, cognitive restructuring, relaxation training, and numerous group exercises to deal with stress were added. Because stress-management training was a group program, all procedures had to be used in such a way as to promote intense interaction among the members. Once the program was in place, it was continually being adapted. The adaptation was a product of the analysis of data collected in the pilot studies.

THE PILOT PROGRAM

Before the actual experiment, each group could be, in a sense, regarded as a data-based case study. As many as five pilot groups were conducted per experiment. As shall be demonstrated, pilot groups are necessary for developing a program, training the leaders, selecting measurements, developing recruitment strategies, and so forth. As data are collected, the final form of the program and the testing, organizational, and recruitment structures are gradually approximated.

Collecting Data to Make Decisions

Qualitative and quantitative data were collected in each of the pilot studies to provide the basis for making decisions about the program's elements, their timing, measurement strategies, and the training of leaders. Quantitative data were collected by means of scales and other precoded responses to highly structured questions or schedules of observation. These data permitted narrow-range comparisons and the testing of hypotheses. Qualitative data were obtained by means of open-ended questions and semistructured observations; the limited structure permitted a wider range of responses and observations. The partial structuring prevented idiosyncratic responses without any known context. As a result, qualitative data suggested new variables, hypotheses about relationships, and insight into the nature of the experience. As the reader will note, the distinction between qualitative and quantitative is not absolute. Most data would be placed on a scale between the two extremes.

Procedures for Obtaining Quantitative Data

The procedures for collecting quantitative data that were used in the preexperimental phase were pre–post self-report measures, postsession questionnaires for all members (those questions that requested a scaled response), and systematic observations by observers (who spoke, how often, and to whom). Although these procedures are thought of as quantitative, they were used in the preexperimental phase in the same way as was information gathered in less prestructured ways. They were regarded as one of many sets of information to be considered when making decisions. There was usually no statistical testing.

The specific pre–post measures were selected after a review of the literature in which stress was measured. A test was considered only if a theoretical link of the measure to the concept had been established. Tests with high degrees of reliability, validity, and sensitivity to change in other studies, as well as theoretical consistency with the prevailing theory of the study, were retained in the experiment. Several measures were later eliminated because they showed little evidence (sensitivity) of pre–post change in the pilot studies. The measures that met the criteria were the SCL-90-R (Derogatis, 1982), the Profile of Mood States (McNair, Lorr, & Droppleman, 1971), the Hassles Inventory (Kanner, Coyne, Schaeffer, & Lazarus, 1981), and the Physiological and Behavioral Stress Inventory (Decker, Williams, & Hall, 1982). Unfortunately, all these measures are self-reports, with all the known limitations of such measures.

The degree of change tells little about the ongoing group process or of members' subjective responses to the elements of the program and their satisfaction with the program as a whole. Furthermore, the literature generally suggests that the level of members' attraction to other members of the group is a good estimate of a group's cohesion. The postsession questionnaire was used to determine the response of members to the foregoing issues in each session. A similar questionnaire was given to the leaders. Questions on attraction to the group, attraction to the leader, satisfaction with the session, the feeling of control, the helpfulness of the other members, and the usefulness of the program as a whole and of specific elements of the program were asked at the end of every session. Each question could be answered on a seven-point scale.

The group results of the postsession questionnaire were discussed with the clients at the beginning of the subsequent session for two reasons. First, if one asks for data but does not show clients how it is used, the clients' cooperation in the future use of the instrument tends to be reduced. Second, the group discussion is an opportunity to explore discrepancies in the clients' self-reports.

Observers were used during the group session to record which members participated and, sometimes, with whom they communicated. Participation has been shown to be significantly correlated with outcome in assertiveness training groups (Rose, 1981). From time to time, more complex observational systems were used, but because the findings from these elaborate systems were seldom reliable without long and costly training, they were eventually dropped as being cost ineffective.

Other data also were collected. They were the rate of homework completion, which also was significantly correlated with outcome in the Rose (1981) study, and the rate of attendance, on the assumption that if one does not attend, changes one way or another are not the result of the group experience.

Procedures for Collecting Qualitative Data

The qualitative data were collected through the following procedures:
• partially structured exit interviews with members who dropped out of the group
• partially structured interviews with leaders who described critical events that occurred in the group
• partially structured interviews with observers who made impressionistic observations of what the leaders did and the critical incidents in the group
• two open-ended questions on the postsession questionnaire.

Exit interviews of those who left the group early were attempted in the pilot studies. In these interviews, open-ended questions were asked about events or conditions in the group that contributed to the dropouts' early departure. In general, the dropouts were hard to reach and unusually taciturn about their experiences. Those few who were willing to talk at length provided helpful information about the general group approach and the specific application of the program in their groups.

The postsession questionnaire contained two open-ended questions. The members were asked to describe what they found useful and what they would like to change in each session. These open-ended questions often suggested areas that were not covered in the more structured questions but that were, nevertheless, relevant to the members.

Using the Data in Program Development

The foremost use of the data was to determine whether a procedure should be maintained as is, modified, or dropped and where that element should be placed in the program package. The purpose of the pre–post measures (in most cases behavioral or attitudinal self-report checklists) was to estimate changes in the levels of stress and in the management of stress in the pilot groups. Clinical relevance was determined, in part, by how many people showed change and how much change was demonstrated. It was interpreted, in part, on the basis of the impressions of the leaders, observers, and members in their respective semistructured interviews. The interpretation of the causes of change was made on the basis of impressions gained from the in-depth qualitative procedures. The relevance of other decisions was determined against the background of whether a group was generally successful (the members showed gains on most tests, and the gains were of a reasonable size).

With regard to the data from the interviews and the postsession questionnaire, a procedure did not have to be satisfying to or be found useful by all participants. However, critical comments in as few as two groups by at least several people in each group made a given procedure at least a candidate for modification. Suspect procedures and the relevant data were presented to the group for further comment and later to the team of leaders and research assistants and to the observers for a decision.

Finally, the project director, leaders, research assistants, and observers reviewed as a group all these data. On the basis of their discussion, they arrived at a tentative decision regarding emendations, but this decision was reconsidered periodically when new data came in. Although some elements were added, the program was somewhat shortened. All the leaders' presentations were reduced to five minutes or less. Activities such as meditation exercises and discussions of diet and how it impinges on stress that focused too long on one person were restricted. (The members were referred elsewhere for this information or given handouts.) Time-management training was dropped because it was not of interest to enough clients. Those individuals who required help in time management or any other topic that was dropped from the program were encouraged to raise their concerns in the group. If others were interested, the group was permitted to add the procedure. Finally, it was decided that role plays were to be kept short in the early sessions and that longer role plays would be allowed in later sessions, but none would be longer than five minutes.

Data are used to make decisions not only about program development but about the timing and distribution of each of the elements in the program. It was assumed that cohesion-building strategies should be implemented early in the treatment but given little attention in the middle and end sessions. The members' early high attraction to each other seemed to result in their more readily accepting suggestions by their peers and the leader. Moreover, the members in highly attractive groups indicated that they felt more strongly reinforced by positive feedback and could more readily accept negative feedback than did those in the less attractive groups. All the other interventions seemed to work better if interpersonal attraction, as determined by the postsession questionnaire, was quickly built up.

The distribution of relaxation training was changed so this training was a small part of every session. This decision was made at the suggestion of some group members and reaffirmed by others, who found too much relaxation training at one time not as useful as relaxation training and practice distributed over time.

REFERENCES

Decker, T., Williams, J., & Hall, D. (1982). Preventive training in management of stress for reduction of physiological symptoms through increased cognitive and behavioral controls. *Psychological Reports, 50,* 1327–1334.

Derogatis, L. R. (1982). Self-report measures of stress. In L. Goldberger & S. Breznitz (Eds.), *Handbook of stress: Theoretical and clinical aspects* (pp. 270–279). New York: Free Press.

Kanner, A. D., Coyne, J. C., Schaefer, C., & Lazarus, R. S. (1981). Comparisons of two modes of stress management: Daily hassles and uplifts versus major life events. *Journal of Behavioral Medicine, 4,* 1–39.

McNair, D., Lorr, M., & Droppleman, L. (1971). *Profile of mood states.* San Diego, CA: Educational & Industrial Testing Service.

Meichenbaum, D. (1977). *Cognitive-behavior modification.* New York: Plenum Press.

Rose, S. D. (1981). How group attributes related to outcome in behavior group therapy. *Social Work Research & Abstracts, 17,* 25–29.

Rose, S. D. (1989). *Working with adults in groups.* San Francisco: Jossey-Bass.

Rose, S. D., Tolman, R. M., & Tallant, S. (1985). *Group leader's guide to stress management training.* Madison: University of Wisconsin Interpersonal Skills Training Project.

Tallant, S., Rose, S. D., & Tolman, R. M. (1989). New evidence for a multimethod group treatment approach for the management of stress. *Behavior Modification, 13*(4), 431–446.

Tolman, R. M., & Rose, S. D. (1989). Teaching clients to cope with stress: The effectiveness of structured group stress management training. *Journal of Social Service Research, 13*(2), 45–66.

Whitney, D., & Rose, S. D. (1989). The effect of process and structured content on outcome in stress management groups. *Journal of Social Service Research, 13*(2), 89–104.

Commentary

The Interface of Qualitative and Quantitative Methods in Social Work Research

Terri Combs-Orme

This commentary poses some questions about qualitative research that the author has been unable to resolve and, like Rose and Farber in Chapter 7, attempts to apply examples from the author's area of research to some of these issues.

WHAT IS QUALITATIVE RESEARCH?

One view seems to hold that qualitative and quantitative research are separate "world views," with the qualitative approach being more interested in "understanding" the human experience from the subjects' perspective, whereas quantitative research reputedly seeks to predict and explain behavior. The two purposes—understanding and prediction—are generally cast as mutually exclusive. Another view concentrates on the methods of research. Quantitative researchers use standardized measures; tightly controlled situations, whenever possible; and statistical methods. Qualitative researchers use naturalistic methods, such as participant observation; "clinical" or unstructured interviews; and case studies. Qualitative research is less constrained by previously selected hypotheses and methods and guided more by purpose.

These distinctions leave the author unclear about what, precisely, qualitative research is. However, the following are her impressions of what it is not:

1. Qualitative research is not an answer to the fact that quantitative research is biased. We quantitative researchers may not always be willing to admit it, but we know that our research is often biased, from the selection of a topic for study, to the construction and selection of measurement instruments, to the data analysis and interpretation of findings. Making the data-collection process less objective and more personal, however, does not seem likely to solve that problem. It may not make the problem any worse, but it may not necessarily make it any better.

2. Qualitative research is not the less systematic use of poorly collected quantitative data. According to the best qualitative researchers, qualitative data are collected in a precise and skilled manner, just as are quantitative data. There are correct methods and means of collecting data that are designed to improve the accuracy and validity of the data. Just as quantitative data may be unreliable and invalid and thus unusable, qualitative data may have the same problems.

3. Finally, qualitative research is not just research without numbers. Frequently, quantitative researchers think that qualitative research is simply research done by persons who do not understand and cannot use statistics. By the same token, some qualitative researchers define quantitative research only by its use of statistics, apart from a process beginning with the thoughtful conceptualization of the problem and the thorough examination of previous work in the area. Neither of these limited views is correct, but both seem to have developed because of the large amount of quantitative and qualitative research that is not done competently.

Perhaps the best way to explain the nature of the problems on each side of the quantitative-qualitative debate is to say that each side seems to believe that the incompetent, poorly done research of the other type *characterizes* that type of research. Sometimes research is poor because the data that are collected to be used quantitatively are found to be unreliable and then are used impressionistically. At other times, the data are collected naturalistically and then efforts are poorly made to apply quantitative methods of analysis. In either case, incompetence is the problem. Therefore, the next question to be posed is this: What application may qualitative research alone have for social work?

ADVANTAGES OF QUALITATIVE RESEARCH

Context

The issue of context is primary to qualitative research. "Understanding" the subject means thoroughly grasping the context in which the client operates, so that symbolic activity can be interpreted (Smith, 1986). It connotes understanding from the subject's perspective, rather than an imposition of the researcher's categories and meanings on the subject's experience. For social workers, this issue is obviously salient. In this area, qualitative research may have much to offer. For example, the birth of a premature infant who must stay for a time in a neonatal intensive care unit (NICU) constitutes a true crisis for a family. Not only must the parents endure the anxiety that their baby may die, but they also must cope with their guilt over their failure to carry the infant to term and to discharge their parental functions properly. A process of mourning occurs, similar to when a loved one dies. The field has a fairly good understanding of these processes on the basis of several research projects that have been conducted since the early 1970s. What is not so well understood is the context in which parents must operate in this situation. Sosnowitz's (1984) naturalistic observation of two NICUs provided some insights into this context:

> Intensive care units are brightly lit rooms filled with mechanized instruments emitting beeping noises and occasional alarms. The nurses and doctors hover in pairs over naked infants who are attached to machines. Wires and tubes protrude from every orifice and are taped to the infants' arms and legs. The infants are spread out on tables, with plastic boxes over their heads or enclosed entirely in incubators. The staff dress in isolation gowns, and look rushed and intense. . . . Parents are allowed on the units 24 hours a day; they sit or stand, and sometimes hover over their infants along with the staff. The infants are placed side by side, leaving little room for the people around them. Chairs are scarce, and lounges for the parents are usually nonexistent. (p. 390)

Furthermore, parents may witness the deaths of other infants as they hold their own, using special mitts constructed in the plastic hoods over their infants to avoid contact with the infants' skin. Deformed and dying infants are clearly visible around the room, as are medical personnel who are apparently impassively "going about their business."

Isolating or ignoring the context of the NICU in studies of these parents, in the absence of an understanding of this amazing context, is a hopeless task and one that carries no rewards. Yet most of the studies, by social workers and others, on parents' behavior and the interventions provided by social workers in NICUs do not mention the particulars of this context and their no doubt significant contributions to the "therapeutic process." For example, parents' grief and anxiety are measured and interventions are suggested, without any discussion of how this context may be modified to relieve the stress or how the context may be responsible for what are sometimes called "pathological grief" reactions.

Process

It is true that quantitative research is constrained in its ability to portray subjective variables, such as stress, accurately. We quantitative researchers have a number of physiological measures of stress and proxy measures of stress (such as the number of life events). But our measures of how clients perceive situations that are presumed to be "stressful" are inadequate. The same is true of "social support," a concept that is "hot" in social work now. We can measure the number of clubs and associations, nearby relatives, and telephone calls per week a client has. We are not as effective when it comes to the meaning of those events to clients.

For example, there are increasing indications that the broad class of interventions under the rubric "family support" holds great promise for improving the health and functioning of many families. The greatest limitation in the widespread use of this knowledge is an incomplete understanding of family support. Family support is not a single intervention that can be delivered at point A and measured at point B. The limitation goes beyond the fact that interventions are not adequately operationalized to the fact that many variables (family and intervention related) interact with and affect the timing and nature of the delivery of services.

Increasing cooperation between quantitative and qualitative researchers is beginning to provide answers to some of these questions (see, for example, Weiss & Jacobs, 1988), but meanwhile we are constrained in extending some thought-to-be successful interventions to other populations. Family-support programs are an example of a successful collaboration between qualitative and quantitative research: measurement design. The lack of reliable and valid measurement instruments has been one of the greatest constraints on the evaluation of social-support programs. Qualitative researchers have provided insights into some of the variables to be measured from the subjects' perspectives. Qualitative and quantitative researchers, working together, are getting closer to the accurate measurement of "family support" and its meaning *to the client.*

Thus, context and process are two areas of great concern to social work practice and social work research, in which quantitative researchers find themselves at a loss but can benefit from the contribution of qualitative research. However, qualitative research in isolation also suffers from limitations in relationship to the mission of social work research.

PROBLEMS WITH QUALITATIVE RESEARCH

One problem is that qualitative researchers reject the importance of generalizability or the representativeness of the sample. For example, the qualitative researcher who describes the NICU unit in one hospital and the parents who endure the environment of that unit does not care if the unit is similar to other units or if the parents are similar to other NICU parents. It is only the single unit that is of importance in the study. The researcher makes the point that no human experience is generalizable; everyone is unique. This attitude seems to be in direct contradiction to the purpose and mission of social work, however, as well as to the building of science.

Social reform and social progress are a large part of the legacy of social workers, if a somewhat neglected one. It is not that we social workers do not care about the pain of one NICU family, even if that family is the only one who suffers such pain. But the information on one family cannot be used to change the situation, as can statistics showing that there are thousands of such families experiencing such pain. Klaus and Kennell (1982) demonstrated the detrimental effects of the NICU on the bonding of parents and the newborns. Their work has led, in large part, to changes in NICU policies that now permit 24-hour visits by parents, parental care of their newborn on the unit, and encouragement of as much physical contact as the infant's condition permits. They made their case by thorough, painstaking work that demonstrated the broad applicability of their findings.

Guba (1987) made a similar case for the effectiveness of case studies in changing policy. "The electric effect of incisive cases on the White House is well known. Debate in Congress over authorizations or appropriations relating to handicapped children is punctuated by a steady procession of such children to testify; seeing is believing" (p. 29). Guba's observation of the White House's delight in individual cases notwithstanding, the public is unwilling to spend precious resources on social change based on single cases. Her example of the question of financing care for handicapped children is a case in point. The president had enormous sympathy for a little girl who was forced to grow up in a hospital because Medicaid would pay for the expensive equipment she needed only if it was in a hospital. His sympathy, though, led not to broad changes in Medicaid policy to permit coverage of home care services for all such children, but to a series of isolated exemptions, called "Katie Beckett waivers," named for the little girl (Shelton, Jeppson, & Johnson, 1987).

Equally important to social work's social reform agenda is the question, Does science not consist of a process of gathering data, determining how that information pertains to wider situations and how it differs, drawing tentative conclusions, and then gathering more data? In the absence of such a process of generalization, one does not engage in science but in haphazard experiences. Such random experiences may be profitable in some ways, but they do not prepare one to face new situations that are similar in some ways and dissimilar in others. And they leave one deficient to teach students.

In this regard, two famous axioms could be paraphrased: "If it can't be measured, it isn't there" (Hudson, 1978) and "If you can't measure your intervention, you can't implement it" (Gingerich, 1978). If it really is there and somehow you manage to intervene successfully, you still probably cannot replicate your success or teach anyone else how to do it.

This discussion should be followed by a caveat: This author suspects that the qualitative researcher's disdain for representative sampling and generalization is exaggerated. In actual practice, qualitative researchers move from case to cause and back again as easily as do quantitative researchers, who may miss the trees for the forest at times. Perhaps what would be most productive is a package that consists of numbers that demonstrate the extent of a problem and real cases that familiarize the power brokers with the "real people" behind the numbers.

The second problem with qualitative research as it applies to social work is that inherent in the process of context and understanding of the qualitative researcher's subjects' construction of reality is the issue of interobserver agreement. Qualitative researchers do not strive to reduce method error, although some methods are designed to assure the credibility of their data by enabling the researchers to become familiar with the context. That is, qualitative researchers assert that it is not possible to understand the subject without bringing themselves into the research process. How, then, may two researchers come to the same understanding of the subject, and how can that understanding be applied? In the absence of replicable data across observers, one cannot be sure what to do with the information or how to apply it. Again, how can this information be used to build social work knowledge and to impart that knowledge to students in such a way that they can use it in the best interests of their clients?

In some important ways, then, at least ostensibly, qualitative research in isolation seems to fall short of professional, scientific, and educational mandates, even as quantitative researchers may fall short of the social work mission to "start where the client is." It would seem that the logical suggestion would be that qualitative and quantitative researchers should work together to reduce the limitations and enhance the advantages of each. However, there are some barriers to this ideal situation that must be acknowledged.

BARRIERS TO COLLABORATION

First, social workers are not being educated to do good qualitative research. If the methods of qualitative research are specific and must be carried out with integrity to yield accurate results, then they must be taught as carefully as are research designs. Social workers should not be doing slipshod qualitative research any more than they should be doing slipshod quantitative research. Therefore, if social work is to do its own research of both types (rather than rely on other professions to do it), social work students must be trained to do so, and their education should be provided by teachers who are skilled and experienced in the type of research they teach.

Second, there are few examples of good qualitative research in the literature. There are several reasons for this situation. First, there are probably few journals that are outlets for qualitative research. At least among the major, competitive journals in the profession, there may be a bias in favor of empirical, quantitative research. Second, to the extent that funding encourages publishing (by providing resources for conducting research), qualitative research is less fundable in the current climate and thus is probably not being carried out as it would be if more funding were available.

Finally, one wonders if some qualitative researchers are not more invested in debating epistemology and the relative merits of each kind of research than they are in doing research. A debate in several of the major social work journals (for example, Mullen, 1985; Pieper, 1985, 1986a, 1986b; Thyer, 1986) centered on the potential for a new (nonpositivist) model of social work research to produce new knowledge. One issue in this debate ended with a challenge to the proponents of this "new model" to submit their research for scrutiny: "The 'proof' will lie in the 'pudding,' and I hope the pudding will be served shortly" (Hudson, 1986, p. 2). I echo this sentiment and suggest that if either qualitative or quantitative researchers have something to offer, they should simply do it, rather than waiting for the endorsement of "the other side." Ultimately, the value of any research cannot be determined until it is published and reviewed by one's peers.

REFERENCES

Gingerich, W. J. (1978). Measuring the process. Social Work, 23, 251–252.

Guba, E. G. (1987). Naturalistic evaluation. Evaluation Practice in Review, 34, 23–43.

Hudson, W. W. (1978). First axioms of treatment. Social Work, 23, 65–66.

Hudson, W. W. (1986). The proof is in the pudding [Letter to the editor]. Social Work Research & Abstracts, 22, 2.

Klaus, M. H., & Kennell, J. H. (1982). Parent-infant bonding: The impact of early separation or loss on family development (2nd ed.). St. Louis, MO: C. V. Mosby Co.

Mullen, E. J. (1985). Methodological dilemmas in social work research. Social Work Research & Abstracts, 21, 12–20.

Pieper, M. H. (1985). The future of social work research. Social Work Research & Abstracts, 21, 3–11.

Pieper, M. H. (1986a). Some common misunderstandings of the heuristic approach [Letter to the editor]. Social Work Research & Abstracts, 22(1), 2, 22.

Pieper, M. H. (1986b). The author replied [Letter to the editor]. *Social Work Research & Abstracts, 22*(2), 2.

Shelton, T. L., Jeppson, E. S., & Johnson, B. H. (1987). *Family-centered care for children with special health needs* (2nd ed.). Washington, DC: Association for the Care of Children's Health.

Smith, M. L. (1986). The whole is greater: Combining qualitative and quantitative approaches in evaluation studies. In D. D. Williams (Ed.), *Naturalistic evaluation* (pp. 37–54). San Francisco: Jossey-Bass.

Sosnowitz, B. G. (1984). Managing parents on neo-natal intensive care units. *Social Problems, 31*, 390–402.

Thyer, B. A. (1986). On pseudoscience and pseudoreasoning [Letter to the editor]. *Social Work Research & Abstracts, 22*, 2.

Weiss, H. B., & Jacobs, F. H. (1988). *Evaluating family programs.* New York: Aldine de Gruyter.

Distinguishing and Combining Qualitative and Quantitative Methods

Charles Glisson

Much of the controversy over the benefits and deficits of quantitative versus qualitative methods is fueled by the lack of specificity in discussions of the components of each method. There are two reasons for this lack of specificity. First, the terms *quantitative* and *qualitative* are applied indiscriminately to four components of the research effort: the method of gathering data, the type of data gathered, the analysis of the data, and the research design. Second, as indicated by those who actively advocate qualitative approaches, descriptions of ethnographic, grounded-theory, content analysis, and other methods that are included under qualitative approaches are not specific in presenting the technical aspects of the methodology (Kronick, 1989; Turner, 1981, 1983; Van Maanen, 1979). This commentary provides suggestions for increasing the specificity of discussions of the components of each method.

In Chapter 7, Rose and Farber characterized the type of data, one of the four research components, on the basis of the characteristics of another of the research components, the method by which the data are gathered. They described quantitative data as data that are gathered with structured scales, questionnaires, and observations and qualitative data as data that are gathered with open-ended questions and semistructured observations and interviews. Thus, the amount of structure in the data-gathering process is the distinguishing characteristic. Structure is used to describe the extent to which questions are specified, observations are focused, and categories of subjects' responses and behaviors are established before subjects are questioned or observed. Hence, structure, in this case, indicates the extent to which the researcher's attention has been directed a priori to specific characteristics and responses of subjects. Quantitative data, according to this distinction, results when the researcher is more directed, and qualitative data results when the researcher is less directed.

Rose and Farber's distinction is commonly used in the social sciences, but such a distinction misdirects the debate about the roles of quantitative and qualitative data. What is more important, the distinction contributes to confusion regarding the more general use of the terms *qualitative* and *quantitative* in describing approaches to social science research.

One problem with this distinction between quantitative and qualitative data is that it is dependent on the method used to gather the data, rather than on the characteristics of the actual data. Comparisons of various approaches to conducting research would be improved if the method of gathering data, the type of data gathered, the type of analysis applied to the data, and the research design itself were each considered and characterized separately. Separate characterizations would result in less confusion in discussions of the problems and benefits of various approaches. They also would prevent discussants from assuming generic positions when comparing qualitative and quantitative techniques and help ensure that attention would be given to the specific components of the research approach.

Quantitative data are best distinguished from qualitative data simply by the nature of the values that make up the variables of interest. According to this approach, quantitative data describe variables with values that are numbers, and qualitative data describe variables with values that are qualities. The variables age, intelligence quotient, income, years of marriage, and score on a depression scale all yield quantitative data. The variables gender, geographic location, diagnosis, attitudes about parenthood, and professional goals all provide qualitative data. The use of a particular method of gathering data does not necessarily result in the gathering of only quantitative or only qualitative data. Directive methods and nondirective methods of gathering data can provide both quantitative and qualitative data. For example, the majority of published studies in social work are directive in the method of gathering data, yet they also include both quantitative and qualitative data (Glisson, 1983, 1990).

In addition to blurring the distinction between the method of gathering data and the type of data gathered, much of the discussion about qualitative versus quantitative techniques also fails to separate the type of data from the type of analysis, partly because the terms *quantitative* and *qualitative* are used to describe both the type of data and the type of analysis that is applied to the data. For example, an analysis of variance is considered a quantitative analysis because the analysis generates numerical representations to guide conclusions. In contrast, a grounded-theory analysis is considered a qualitative analysis because the analysis generates conceptual, rather than numerical, representations to guide conclusions.

It is most important to note, however, that quantitative analyses can be applied to qualitative data and that qualitative analyses can be applied to quantitative data. For example, a variety of popular quantitative analyses, including analyses of variance, are applied to both types of data, and log-linear–based quantitative analyses are designed specifically to be applied to qualitative data. Moreover, qualitative analyses, including grounded-theory analyses, content analyses, and ethnographic analyses, are applied to both quantitative and qualitative data. An ethnographer's analysis of the implications of the number of wives in a polygamous society and the age at which an individual is considered an adult are examples of the use of quantitative data in a qualitative analysis. Thus, most researchers include what they believe are the relevant data in an analysis, regardless of whether the data have qualitative or quantitative values.

The point is that it would be helpful for social scientists to use the terms *quantitative* and *qualitative* in a more specific context. As was shown, the terms are helpful when used to describe either the type of data or the type of analytical approach, as long as the characteristics of the data and the characteristics of the analysis are considered separately. The terms are less helpful, however, in describing either the method of gathering data or the types of research designs. The terms *directive* and *nondirective* or *structured* and *nonstructured* more adequately distinguish methods of gathering data. In addition, the terms *survey*, *experimental*, *quasi-experimental*, *case study*, and *participant observation* better describe and distinguish specific research designs.

For over three decades, social scientists have advocated that researchers combine multiple methods of gathering and analyzing data within individual studies (Campbell & Fiske, 1959; Vidich & Shapiro, 1955). Although triangulation and other multimethod approaches for combining different methods and different designs to establish the convergent validity of findings have been praised, only a small proportion of social science research and little social work research have incorporated such combined approaches (Burnette, 1990; Connidis, 1983; Glisson, 1990; Jick, 1979). Social scientists are reluctant to combine methods because of the confusion over exactly how the components that constitute the methods are to be combined. A step would be made toward ending that confusion and toward increasing the number of research efforts that combine approaches if researchers would first consider and characterize separately the four research components (the method of gathering data, the type of data gathered, the type of analysis applied to the data, and the research design) and second reserve the terms *quantitative* and *qualitative* specifically for describing data and for describing analytic techniques, rather than apply them generically to complete studies or use them to describe methods of gathering data or research designs.

This is not to argue that certain analytic techniques do not lend themselves to certain methods of gathering data and to certain research designs. Grounded-theory analysis fits nicely with nondirect methods of gathering data and with participant-observation research designs. However, log-linear analyses, for instance, also can be applied to data gathered from participant-observation research designs, and grounded-theory analysis can be applied to data gathered using a survey-research design. Also, categories within each of the four research components can be combined within single studies. For example, both survey-research designs and participant-observation designs, both directive and nondirective methods of gathering data, both qualitative and quantitative data, and both quantitative and qualitative analyses can be combined within a single study. These examples of within-component and between-component combinations are not common because of the tendency of social scientists to blur the distinctions between the four components and to link conceptually certain categories of components. Although not all combinations across the four components are possible, the four research components should be kept distinct in discussions of research approaches so the benefits and deficits of specific research designs, methods of gathering data, types of data, and analytic methods can each be considered individually in relation to specific research objectives.

As a final comment, discussions of quantitative versus qualitative approaches are frequently philosophical and focus on epistemology. Philosophical issues and methodological issues, however, are each developed in separate spheres of inquiry. Therefore, it is important that the epistemological foundations of social science be discussed as philosophical issues that have implications for, but do not replace, discussions of methodology. This commentary has focused on increasing the specificity and clarity with which methodological issues are discussed. Discussions of the methodological implications of specific philosophical positions also can be enhanced by considering the four research components as separate methodological issues and by reserving the terms *quantitative* and *qualitative* for describing types of data and types of data-analytic methods.

REFERENCES

Burnette, D. (1990). *The management of chronic illness by older people living alone.* Unpublished doctoral dissertation, University of California at Berkeley.

Campbell, D. T., & Fiske, D. W. (1959). Convergent and discriminant validation by the multitrait-multimethod matrix. *Psychological Bulletin, 56,* 81–105.

Connidis, I. (1983). Integrating qualitative and quantitative methods in survey research on aging: An assessment. *Qualitative Sociology, 6,* 334–352.

Glisson, C. A. (1983, October 10). *Trends in social work research: Substantive and methodological implications for doctoral curricula.* Paper presented at the Annual Meeting of the Group for the Advancement of Doctoral Education, Tuscaloosa, AL.

Glisson, C. A. (1990). *Trends in social work research: 1977–1988.* Report prepared for the Task Force on Social Work Research, National Institute of Mental Health.

Jick, T. D. (1979). Mixing qualitative and quantitative methods: Triangulation in action. *Administrative Science Quarterly, 24,* 602–611.

Kronick, J. C. (1989, March). *Toward a formal methodology of document analysis in the interpretive tradition.* Paper presented at the meetings of the Eastern Sociological Society, Baltimore.

Turner, B. A. (1981). Some practical aspects of qualitative data analysis: One way of organizing the cognitive processes associated with the generation of grounded theory. *Quality and Quantity, 15,* 225–247.

Turner, B. A. (1983). The use of grounded theory for the qualitative analysis of organization behavior. *Journal of Management Studies, 20,* 333–348.

Van Maanen, J. (1979). Reclaiming qualitative methods for organizational research: A preface. *Administration Science Quarterly, 24,* 520–526.

Vidich, A. J., & Shapiro, G. (1955). A comparison of participant observation and survey data. *American Sociological Review, 20,* 28–33.

Synthesis

Problems and Uses of Qualitative Methodologies

Anne E. Fortune

The discussion of qualitative and quantitative research methodologies focused primarily on the participants' experiences with them: why qualitative methodologies are so rarely used in social work either alone or with quantitative methods; the value of qualitative methods to provide insights that quantitative methods do not; and when qualitative methods should be used, particularly in conjunction with quantitative methods. The definitional issues raised by Combs-Orme and Glisson—what *are* quantitative or qualitative methods?—were addressed only briefly.

QUALITATIVE VERSUS QUANTITATIVE METHODS

Glisson's attempt to distinguish four components of the research process, so that qualitative and quantitative research are no longer referred to globally, may clarify areas of mixed methodology within a single study. These four components are (1) the amount of structure in the data gathering (structured or unstructured), (2) the type of data, elsewhere called level of measurement—qualitative (nominal or categorical) or quantitative (ordinal, interval, and ratio), (3) the type of data analysis (qualitative, which results in conceptual symbols, versus quantitative, which results in numerical symbols), and (4) the design (survey, experimental, quasi-experimental, and participant observation). Research that is globally classified as qualitative or quantitative often includes mixed components: unstructured interviews, as in Rose and Farber's "quantitative" group-treatment studies, and matrix algebra to analyze social dominance patterns in a "qualitative" anthropological study. However, these distinctions between the methods do not address the epistemological issue raised by Combs-Orme: that these two types of research have different world views, with qualitative research seeking subjective understanding of human experience and quantitative research seeking prediction and explanation. These world views also include differences in the nature of what constitutes "proof" and how it is established, with quantitative methodologists using a linear conceptualization of cause and effect and qualitative methodologists stressing the context of phenomena within a whole.

These two world views, whether incompatible or not, are the substance of much of the highly charged, emotional disagreements between proponents of qualitative and of quantitative research. Perhaps purpose or world view is a fifth component of analysis—assuming it can be separated conceptually from the other components—or perhaps each study is guided by a dominant world view that circumscribes the choices among the other components. In any case, the epistemological issues must also be dealt with in any attempt to classify or explore logical differences between qualitative and quantitative research.

During the discussion, most participants continued to use the terms *qualitative* and *quantitative* in their broadest, nonspecific meanings. This synthesis also uses the generalized meaning, but will attempt to distinguish Glisson's components when possible.

UNDERUTILIZATION OF QUALITATIVE RESEARCH

Qualitative research is, in some respects, similar to the processes that good practitioners use to conceptualize, assess, and treat a client's problems. Yet it is rarely used in social work. According to Glisson's comment during the discussion, fewer than 2 percent of research articles in social work journals employ qualitative methods. Why are qualitative approaches so rarely used? The reasons for their underutilization are related to the lack of social work training, the absence of guidelines for qualitative studies, the length of studies, and the lack of reinforcement for conducting qualitative research.

Lack of Training

A primary reason for the underutilization of qualitative research is the lack of training in qualitative methods. For example, although most of the discussants had conducted some qualitative research, few had formal training in it. Their sources for procedures were texts and reports from other disciplines. They noted that written guidelines are seldom precise or directly applicable to social work situations, and opportunities to collaborate with qualitative experts are rare.

The current lack of expertise among social work researchers also inhibits the training of future researchers in qualitative methods. Few doctoral programs teach qualitative methodology. When an instructor in qualitative methodology is available, usually through junior faculty or other departments, doctoral students initially gravitate to that instructor. However, they quickly become discouraged by the quantitative culture of most doctoral programs: Their role models among the faculty conduct quantitative research, faculty members' projects from which data could be drawn are quantitative, faculty members are reluctant to sit on dissertation committees when they do not understand the methodology, and guidelines for dissertations are set up for quantitative projects. In short, with some justification, the student subculture views quantitative methodology as the most expeditious, "tried and true" vehicle for completing dissertations; consequently, few doctoral students become experienced in qualitative methods during the dissertation process.

Lack of Guidelines

A second reason for the underutilization of qualitative methods is the lack of guidelines for conducting them. Popular texts, such as Glaser and Strauss's (1967), present general principles that are difficult to translate into step-by-step rules; more recent sources, including Lofland and Lofland (1984), Miles and Huberman (1984), and Patton (1978), are more specific but contain many of the same problems. Two individuals who use the same approach to study the same phenomenon will implement it differently and will probably reach different conclusions. The process (both data gathering and data analysis) and, consequently, the results are experientially based and necessarily subjective. The data analysis takes place "inside the head," using logic and intuition that are rarely articulated clearly.

The ambiguity of guidelines has two consequences: Qualitative research is harder to do (and teach) well and is more difficult to assess for quality or confidence in the results. Because specific rules cannot guide choices, procedures must be carefully thought out and often invented. It may be difficult to select a fruitful focus and maintain it while the direction evolves during the study. Some people cannot tolerate the ambiguity and lack of structure. In larger studies, consistency among interviewers or reliability among observers is difficult to obtain. The amount of data gathered is often overwhelming, without clear-cut procedures for analyzing it. The conceptual data analyses that are typical of qualitative approaches require a skill in logic or conceptual ability that is not usually taught and, like creativity, may not be teachable.

The diffuse guidelines also hinder the assessment of the quality of a study and confidence in its results. In many qualitative approaches, it is difficult to establish reliability because data are processed in the researcher's mind as they are received; that is, data gathering and data analysis are inseparable. And, because even the best, most systematic qualitative studies reach different conclusions, validity is also difficult to establish. Unlike in quantitative research, the quality of the methodology cannot be used as a basis of confidence in the results; there are no hierarchies of procedures or "rules," such as, "A control group is better than no control and random assignment is better than existing groups." As will be discussed, these difficulties in assessing qualitative research are not insurmountable. However, qualitative researchers often aggravate the problems by omitting detailed, systematic accounts of their methodology.

Duration of Studies and Lack of Rewards

A third reason why qualitative research is underutilized in social work is its duration: Studies often take a long time, and the products tend to be book length rather than article length. Perhaps because data gathering is subjective and reliability is difficult to establish, most qualitative studies are conducted by a single investigator. Since the process is intense and time consuming, it is often spread out over time. Reports are usually lengthy because of the rich detail; the necessity to link observation and theory; and the lack of shorthand concepts, such as survey or ANOVA, to describe complex procedures. Consequently, fewer qualitative than quantitative studies are completed in a given time.

A related reason is the lack of reward for qualitative research. In the current academic climate—the source of most social work research—publication is critical. Faculty members, especially junior faculty members, who are seeking tenure feel pressured to produce many articles rapidly. Yet qualitative research–based manuscripts are often too long for articles. And even when the length of manuscripts is appropriate, journals seem reluctant to publish qualitative research, perhaps because of the editors' unfamiliarity with them, disdain for them, or caution about publishing them, given the problems in verifying their quality. Similarly, funding sources seem to prefer nonqualitative approaches. In such circumstances, many scholars choose quantitative methods, at least until they are tenured; once they have been successful in using quantitative methods, they are reluctant to change.

PROBLEMS AND SOLUTIONS

Many of the problems with qualitative methods have been alluded to: the lack of guidelines, questions about their reliability and validity, and the difficulty of replicating them. In addition, like single-subject time-series research, the generalizability of qualitative research is controversial. Some argue that each unit studied is unique—self-contained with its individual experience—so generalization to other units is not only impossible but undesirable. Others claim that every unit contains some piece of "universal truth," so that each unit's experience and each study contributes to the broader theoretical framework.

Quantitative researchers criticize and sometimes dismiss qualitative research for these problems, and the proponents of qualitative research have not helped allay suspicions by ignoring them. In extreme cases, qualitative researchers hide behind epistemology, claiming that the experiential nature of the research makes reliability checks impossible or that belief in the results depends on faith in the researcher. However, some qualitative researchers are beginning to address the problems. Lincoln and Guba (1985), for example, suggested an audit in which a second researcher would meticulously review the field notes and would evaluate the conclusions drawn from them. Reliability could be established by separating the data gathering and data analysis and having several observers view the same phenomenon. The content of interviews could be compared to assess systematic differences that are due to different interviewers.

Feedback from the respondents could be used as a check on the validity of the conclusions. In the most formal procedure, essentially an audit by those from whom the data were obtained, a random sample of participants could review the data and conclusions. In a less formal procedure, selected participants could critique the conclusions. Another check could be the response of the research community to the publication of a study, its agreement or disagreement with the conclusions. Publication would thus be considered part of a dialogue, offering hypotheses to be tested by critical professionals.

Despite the difficulties with qualitative research, it can be done well: systematic, rigorous applications can give generalizable results. Good qualitative research is as valid as is good quantitative research. Although critics compare poor qualitative research to good quantitative research, in reality, neither qualitative nor quantitative studies are usually done well in social work.

The ultimate criterion for any research is its impact: Does it "feel right" to the reader? Do people get a sense of the "truth" of the conclusions? Does it change ways of thinking? Historically, qualitative research has done as well as quantitative research in influencing thoughts and decisions. At the level of practice, Rose and Farber reported important changes in the training of leaders and in the timing of group-treatment procedures in response to qualitative data. At the level of grand theory, Freud's qualitative-based theories of psychological functioning changed both professional and popular thinking more than did the quantitative research of learning theorists. People are influenced by human experience, and quantitative research may capture it more convincingly than does quantitative research, whose truths are lost in methodological conventions and shorthand codes.

USES OF QUALITATIVE AND QUANTITATIVE RESEARCH

Ideally, a research methodology is selected on the basis of its ability to answer the research questions. A study may use several approaches to address different questions, as Rose and Farber described, or a single approach may mix components, as Glisson suggested. When do social work researchers select qualitative versus quantitative methodologies? Interrelated considerations include how much is already known about the topic, the nature of the subject matter, the ability of the methodology to capture the phenomenon, the amount of data available, and the need to validate the results.

First, most of the discussants said that they use quantitative methodologies when they know something about the phenomenon. If they can define important variables and measure them in meaningful ways, then they select quantitative methodologies, such as a structured questionnaire for data gathering or a highly controlled experiment for design. They choose qualitative methodologies when they know little or do not understand the processes, for example, the subjective feeling of receiving social support. Such a hierarchy of selection may reflect both the prejudices of the participants and the efficacy of the methodology, since good qualitative research requires an openness to phenomena that is inhibited by too much confidence in preexisting formulations.

A second consideration is the nature of the phenomena studied: Some are not amenable to quantitative measurement procedures. Qualitative methodologies may be essential to understanding cultural phenomena outside the "scientific" world view, as anthropologists and practitioners have found. Conversely, the world view that is encapsulated within quantitative measurement may not be comprehensible to those being studied. Some clients, for example, cannot rate feelings on a scale from 1 to 7 because they do not conceptualize emotions on a hierarchical linear continuum. Other phenomena, such as group processes or individuals' reactions to other people, may be too complex to be measured adequately or studied fruitfully using the linear cause-and-effect notions of quantitative methods.

A third consideration is that quantitative methodologies have not yet been developed to measure some phenomena, although they eventually will be. A quantitative iconoclast may argue that the previous two considerations are but special cases of this lack of development—that, for example, measures will be developed once knowledge is sufficient or that ostensible complexity is due to inadequate quantitative methods. Such an argument excludes the possibility of alternative truths or world views and—even if it is true—does little to further an understanding of the phenomena being studied. Some phenomena, by the nature of subjective experience, may be more amenable to qualitative methods. In any case, a pragmatic reason for using qualitative methods is the unavailability of quantitative methods.

A fourth consideration is the amount of data that are available. Several participants stated that they rely more on qualitative data when less quantitative data are available, even though qualitative data sometimes yield more important insights. This acknowledged bias—that qualitative data are useful when quantitative data do not suffice— probably reflects the expertise of most participants, rather than a deliberate devaluation of qualitative research. To put a positive interpretation on the bias, examplars of quantitative research advocate the use of qualitative research to explain what quantitative research does not.

A fifth, more egalitarian, perspective on the use of qualitative and quantitative methods is to combine them to validate a study's results (triangulation) and to understand better what the other is capturing. For example, structured quantitative measures may suggest that no change in a client took place during treatment, while unstructured interviews or participant observation may suggest that shifts in subjective experiencing occurred. A refinement may be to return the results to the study participants, as was suggested, to find explanations for the discrepancies. Perhaps the participants considered the quantitative measures frivolous or irrelevant and meaningful change lies only in the domain tapped by the qualitative measures, or perhaps treatment had different effects than were anticipated. Mixed validation applications may be particularly appropriate when there are actual or suspected discrepancies, unexpected results, or a danger of overlooking important discrepancies. Because the latter is always possible—researchers naturally favor methods in which they are competent—perhaps mixed methods should *always* be used.

REFERENCES

Glaser, B. G., & Strauss, A. L. (1967). *The discovery of grounded theory: Strategies for qualitative research.* New York: Aldine.

Lincoln, Y. S., & Guba, E. G. (1985). *Naturalistic inquiry.* Beverly Hills, CA: Sage Publications.

Lofland, J., & Lofland, L. H. (1984). *Analyzing social settings: A guide to qualitative observation and analysis* (2nd ed.). Belmont, CA: Wadsworth.

Miles, M. P., & Huberman, A. M. (1984). *Qualitative data analysis.* Beverly Hills, CA: Sage Publications.

Patton, M. Q. (1978). *Focused evaluation.* Beverly Hills, CA: Sage Publications.

Chapter 8

Modes of Practice in Developmental Research

Edwin J. Thomas

The focus of this chapter is on the modes of practice in developmental research. But first, by way of providing a context for the main discussion, a brief overview of the current scene in developmental research is presented.

OVERVIEW OF THE CURRENT SCENE

Developmental research is a relatively new approach to research that differs from conventional research methods directed toward making a contribution to knowledge of human behavior. A working definition of developmental research is that it is inquiry directed toward the analysis, design, development, and evaluation of innovations in the human services (Thomas, 1978a). These innovations consist of intervention and treatment methods at the level of direct practice, service programs and organizational structures at a broader level, and other aspects of the technical means by which the objectives of social work and social welfare are achieved. Social work, of course, consists of much more than human service technology, and it is guided by important values and humane commitments. Even so, the work of the human services is done with a human service technology. Developmental research is focused precisely on the human service technology of social work, and the newly evolved human service technology is the product of such inquiries. Further details concerning the need for developmental research and how this approach differs from conventional social science and social work research are given elsewhere (Thomas, 1978a, 1978b, 1984).

Developmental research can now be said to have arrived on the scene. Its presence, in general, however, is somewhat unobtrusive at this point inasmuch as it sometimes goes by different names (model development, social research and development, and programmatic research, among others) and often takes place under different guises, such as practice, administration, evaluation, research, or program or policy development. In any event, there is more and more of it. It is increasingly being taught, written about, funded, and carried out in one form or another by more and more researchers and practitioners in and outside social work and other areas of human service. In the past 10 years or so, there have been advances that relate to all the major aspects of developmental research—to the paradigms, concepts, methods, and techniques, as well as to such phases of developmental research as analysis, design, development, evaluation, and diffusion and adoption (Thomas, 1989). All these advances bode well for the future.

However, although considerable progress has been made, it is not yet much more than a strong beginning. Considering the larger picture, there are two sobering facts. First, the methodology of developmental research is still very much in its infancy. Aside from some early work on the utilization of knowledge and research (see, for example, Havelock, 1973; Rothman, 1974), there were few publications on developmental research in social work until about 12 years ago (see, for example, Fischer, 1978; Mullen, 1978, 1981; Reid, 1979, 1980, 1983b; Rothman, 1978, 1980; Thomas, 1978a, 1978b, 1980). There have been few publications in developmental research proper in the ensuing years, and most of what has been done has been derived from contributions made in related areas such as conventional research methods, evaluation research, assessment, and systems engineering (Thomas, 1989).

Second, developmental research is not yet widely employed to help solve problems for which that methodology would be most appropriate. Either it simply is not done or if it is carried out, the steps and phases of the developmental research process are omitted or only superficially carried out. For example, all too frequently, innovative interventions are designed in haste without proper attention to the many relevant sources of information; introduced without proper development; evaluated, often in complex experimental designs, with little or no earlier development; or adopted and implemented without having been systematically evaluated. Unfortunately, most prevailing practices related to design, development, and evaluation leave much to be desired from the point of view of development research.

Most of the many issues and unresolved problems in developmental research are new or just emerging. One issue is what the role of practice should be in developmental research. Practice can generally be centrally related to developmental research, as will be highlighted in this chapter. The modes of practice discussed here have implications for developmental research and for the future of practice in social work and related human service fields. Developmental research and related design and development approaches will be referred to for short as "D & D."

MODES OF PRACTICE

Much has been written in recent years on the relationship between practice and research, but little attention has been given expressly to the question of the role of practice in developmental research. Practice or, more generally, service is of course a major activity of social work, an important source of new helping methods, a potential focus of most D & D, and a principal beneficiary of innovations that result from D & D. Considered as a resource in D & D, practice may be said to be prevalent and abundant, but it is underutilized. That is, it is not used in D & D as much as it could be, and when it is employed, its capabilities to contribute to D & D are rarely realized sufficiently.

Conventional Practice

Conventional practice, as carried out in most service settings, is what is referred to here and need not be described in detail for anyone who is familiar with the field. Although there are important variations and complexities of practice, such differences are not the focus of this chapter. The characteristics of interest for the present purposes are the ways in which conventional practice is carried out when considered in the context of D & D. Among these characteristics are that the primary objective is service in one form or another; the clientele served are those falling within the agency's area of service; and the methods employed are regular practice methods that are consistent with the agency's procedures and practices, practice wisdom, the local state of practice, and the practitioner's model of personal practice. Other characteristics are that the monitoring of possible changes is restricted at best to the outcomes of service; possible design problems are rarely expressly worked on except occasionally and nonsystematically as an aspect of service; no methodology of developmental research is used along with the practice methods; and the results of such efforts, although occasionally innovative, are restricted in the main to possible gains in service (see Table 1 for further details).

Within the context of its main objective to provide service, practice in the conventional mode may make at least four types of contributions to D & D. These contributions are made through (1) conducting case studies and analyses of case records to learn, for example, about processes and outcomes of practice and the dynamics of clients' behavior; (2) gathering special data from practitioners and others in practice to learn, for instance, about the needs and behavior of clients and ways to change practice methods; (3) using the agency as a site within which to lodge a practice-related project with D & D implications; and (4) employing practice

Table 1. Conventional versus Developmental Practice

Area of Difference	Conventional Practice	Developmental Practice
Objective	Service	The D & D of intervention and provision of service
Cases (or events) sampled	Those within the agency's area of service	Those within the domain of D & D
Case (or event) selected	By the procedures and practices of the agency	By the criterion of developmental relevance
Area of service	Established by the purpose and function of the agency	Restricted to services that are related to the domain of D & D
Methods	Regular practice methods	Practice methods in the domain of D & D; the intervention methods or other innovations that are subject to D & D; and methods of developmental research, including developmental testing
Basis of practice	Agency regulation and practice, the state of local practice, and the practitioner's personal practice model	Relevant sources of information (such as research findings, behavior, and intervention theory); the state of the art in relation to the problems in the domain of D & D; and the intervention, model, or other innovations that are subject to D & D
Methods to evaluate the outcomes of service	Variable, generally with no systematic evaluation methodology	Evaluation methods, including time-series designs, single-system and between-group experimental designs, and experimental replication methods
Data gathered and recorded	Data on services	Data on services, the outcomes of services, and information on the D & D process and outcomes
How potential design problems are addressed	Ignoring, muddling through, trial and error	The design of interventions and developmental research in general and trial use and developmental testing in particular

(continued on next page)

Table 1. *Continued*

Area of Difference	Conventional Practice	Developmental Practice
How results are monitored and appraised	Possible monitoring of the outcomes of services	Monitoring the outcomes of services and of innovation-related outcomes in developmental testing
Outcomes	Outcomes of services (if appropriate data were gathered)	Outcomes of services and innovative interventions or models of intervention and related data

SOURCE: A revision and extension of the table presented in *Designing Interventions for the Helping Professions* (Thomas, 1984), p. 181. Adapted with permission from Sage Publications, Inc.

methods, such as treatment planning and diagnosis and assessment, in service with individuals and families, to provide information that has more general implications (such as types of clients and behavioral dynamics).

In some cases, methods of conventional practice such as these can and do result in new interventions. For example, in new areas of service, practitioners sometimes develop innovative practices and programs that are ground breaking and otherwise are ahead of current practices. (Many readers will recall that examples of such innovative practices were reported in the *Practice Digest*, formerly published by the National Association of Social Workers.) However, conventional practice generally produces innovations only incidentally and as a by-product of providing service, with the exception of using the agency as a site for a project having a D & D mission. Even so, the means by which conventional practice may make contributions to D & D are appropriate methods, as far as they go. If these methods were used in conventional practice also to achieve D & D objectives, even if the objectives were limited, the role of conventional practice in D & D could thereby be strengthened and probably without changing the primary objective or helping methods of this mode of practice.

Empirically Based Practice

With the advent of empirically based practice, research and practice have been brought together in a more intimate relationship, which makes it possible for the practitioner to use some of the methods of research and evaluation in practice (see, for example, Barlow, 1981; Barlow, Hayes, & Nelson, 1984; Berlin, 1983; Bloom, 1975, 1983; Briar,

1973, 1980; Fischer, 1978, 1981; Gambrill, 1983; Jayaratne & Levy, 1979; Marks, 1982; Mutschler, 1979; Schinke, 1983; Siegel, 1985; Thomas, 1975, 1977; Tripodi, 1983; Tripodi & Epstein, 1978, 1980; Wodarski, 1981). Work on empirically based practice has highlighted the widespread applicability in practice of measurement and quantitative and other empirically based methods (see, for example, Bloom, 1975; Bloom & Block, 1977; Blythe & Tripodi, 1989; Fischer, 1978; Fischer & Hudson, 1983; Marks, 1982; Thomas, 1975; Tripodi & Epstein, 1978, 1980), particularly of single-case experimentation (see, for example, Barlow & Hersen, 1984; Berlin, 1983; Bloom & Fischer, 1982; Fischer, 1978; Gambrill & Barth, 1980; Gingerich, 1979; Hayes, 1981; Howe, 1974; Jayaratne & Levy, 1979; Kratochwill, 1978; Nelsen, 1981; Nuehring & Pascone, 1986; Reid, 1983a; Richey, Kopp, Tolson, & Ishisaka, 1987; Stuart, 1971; Thomas, 1975, 1978c; Thyer & Curtis, 1983).

Practice carried out in the empirical mode enjoins and enables the practitioner to isolate, measure, monitor, and evaluate practice-related events more accurately than before. And, through drawing on the findings and methods of research, empirical practice emphasizes a more scientific and empirical approach to data from practice and the solution of practice problems. As many writers have indicated, empirical methods of practice promise to strengthen the scientific and empirical basis of the individual practitioner's day-to-day practice and to facilitate the making of cumulative advances in the field.

The single-case experimental methods of direct, systematic, and clinical replication have been emphasized as means by which the generality of findings may be achieved (see, for example, Barlow, Hayes, & Nelson, 1984; Bloom & Fischer, 1982). In this approach, successes can be extended and failures analyzed (see, for example, Barlow, Hayes, & Nelson, 1984; Foa & Emmelkamp, 1983) and, through what Reid and Hanrahan (1982) called "incremental experimentation," successive improvements may be made in practice methods.

Considering its role in D & D, empirically based practice contributes mainly a methodology of evaluation, particularly monitoring and single-case experimentation, that may be used in practice with a single case or cases and other systems. These aspects of evaluation are as important in D & D as they are in empirical practice because they contribute to the scientific and empirical basis of the interventions that are subject to D & D, provide an evaluation methodology for monitoring and appraising the outcomes of the interventions being developed, and yield evaluation outcomes that may be employed to help guide the D & D process.

In empirically based practice, the practitioner is also an evaluator of practice and uses practice largely as a site to try out and evaluate interventions. The author infers that most writers on empirically based practice have implied or assumed that the empirical practitioner also had a D & D function. However, generally, no reference has been made to the need for, or the details of, a methodology of designing interventions to go along with the methods of empirically based practice being proposed. Exceptions would be a few writers who have noted that methods of developmental research should accompany the use of methods of empirically based practice (see, for example, Blythe & Briar, 1985; Fischer, 1981; Reid, 1983a). Thus, as presently conceived and carried out, empirically based practice, by itself, is an insufficient model of practice for D & D. As important as the evaluation component of empirical practice is for D & D, it is limited inasmuch as there is no methodology for the design of interventions and for D & D. Practice is a rich medium and a distinctive, if not unique, source of data that can also be employed as a major tool of development.

Developmental Practice

If the considerable capabilities of practice are to be realized in facilitating the development of innovative interventions, a mode of practice is needed that has a clear D & D component. Developmental practice is suggested as an approach to practice to meet that need. Although many researchers and practitioners have engaged, at some point, in practice that has D & D objectives, little has been written to date that helps define and explicate the characteristics of this type of practice. The methodology of this mode of practice and of development is clearly just now emerging. One of the important tasks now is to identify and describe some of its important features, which is the focus of the next section. The comments in that section are an extension of the author's earlier, brief discussions of this topic (Thomas, 1984, 1985). Needless to say, further work by many others will be required to evolve a mature approach to practice that has a prominent D & D component.

CHARACTERISTICS OF DEVELOPMENTAL PRACTICE

Developmental practice is conceived as a mode of practice in which the practitioner is also a developer of interventions. Practice is a medium and a principal instrument of development, and the practitioner makes systematic use of selected methods of developmental research to achieve the D & D objectives pursued in the practice. In contrast to conventional practice, developmental practice has D & D objectives in addition to those of service; selects cases that fall within a domain of D & D by the criterion of developmental relevance; and provides service within the domain of D & D using practice methods that are appropriate to this domain, including research findings, behavior and intervention theory, state-of-the-art practice, and the intervention or model that is subject to D & D. It also gathers, monitors, and evaluates data on the outcomes of service and innovation-related results using systematic evaluation methods, including time-series and single-case experiments; addresses potential design problems and the D & D aspects of practice in general using the methods of developmental research, including developmental testing to examine such matters as the adequacy of the innovations when used on a pilot basis with clients; and, in addition to results involving service outcomes, produces innovative interventions or models of intervention along with related evaluation data. (For further details, see Table 1.)

Some Main Activities

The characteristics just indicated suggest the outlines of some of the main activities of developmental practice. These activities are the following:

Use of case-selection and sampling procedures appropriate for developmental research. At this point little is known about sampling except that it should be relevant to the developmental objective pursued at a given time. This idea is elaborated further in the following description:

> Sampling for *developmental relevance* involves selecting cases that provide opportunities for the initial design, redesign, or replicated use of interventions that fall within the domain of design established in the developmental effort. Cases involving developmental relevance are of at least two types. The first type consists of cases that present the opportunity for developmental testing of existing innovations designed earlier. Such testing may necessitate the redesign of existing innovations that are not adequate or the replication of innovations found to be adequate in testing. To obtain the best opportunities for developmental testing, cases should be selected that are likely to present design problems similar to those for which innovations have already been developed, thus providing the opportunity for applying the innovations again in the developmental testing. By continuing to sample similar cases, one increases the probability of deepening the development.
>
> In the second type of case, selection is made so that new design problems may be presented that are related to the design and to the objectives of the intervention. Here, cases are selected because they are different from those for which the innovations have already been developed. By varying the types of cases systematically from those dealt with initially, one increases the likelihood of expanding the domain of the

design and the generality of development. Sampling of both types of cases clearly enlarges the scope of development and should be carried out systematically in keeping with the strategy of development that has been adopted. (Thomas, 1985, pp. 53–54)

Among the issues that require further work are the appropriate strategies for selecting cases and the number of cases needed to achieve given D & D objectives.

Systematic implementation of the intervention, model, or other innovation. For example, if the new model or intervention were standardized, at least some prescribed assessment and intervention methods with specific conditions would be identified for carrying out the procedures. Needs for service falling outside the area of D & D would then probably be excluded, as would the use of practice methods not falling within the new program. However, allowance would probably be made for introducing possible improvements in the model or intervention. As is the case with any systematic treatment program being subjected to evaluation, practitioners must adhere to the program and examine such questions as treatment shift, the treatment integrity of the program (see, for example, Salend, 1984; Yeaton & Sechrest, 1981), and its reliability (see, for example, Billingsley, White, & Munson, 1980). These aspects of the implementation of treatment should be assessed in light of their implications for the internal and external validity of the research and evaluation outcomes being addressed—considerations that are particularly important in systematic evaluations of new programs. Thus, an important issue is how to maintain and assess the implementation of interventions at various points in D & D and to do so in light of the fact that, in many instances, changes are made along the way to improve the intervention or model.

Systematic gathering of data on the outcomes of services and D & D processes and outcomes. For example, in addition to the data gathered to monitor and evaluate practice outcomes, information could also be obtained by such means as developmental logs (see, for example, Thomas, 1984; Yaffe, 1987) or critical incidents (see, for example, Flanagan, 1954; Reid & Davis, 1987; Thomas, Bastien, Stuebe, Bronson, & Yaffe, 1987) to examine failures of implementation or outcome (see, for example, Barlow, Hayes, & Nelson, 1984; Foa & Emmelkamp, 1983) or procedural descriptiveness, including its completeness (see, for example, Thomas et al., 1987). Further work needs to be devoted to means by which the ideas and evaluations of practitioners that relate to the interventions being developed may be gathered, processed, and utilized expeditiously in the course of developmental practice.

Solving problems using D & D methods. A main source of D & D problem-solving methods and methods for designing and developing interventions and models is, of course, developmental research in general (for details on selected methods, see Mullen, 1978, 1983; Paine, Bellamy, & Wilcox, 1984; Rothman, 1980; Thomas, 1984). Clearly, methods for the phases of D & D would be particularly relevant, as would many of the emerging empirical, analytic, and practice techniques (for further details, see Thomas, 1984). However, the particular applications of such methods and techniques to developmental practice need further work, as does the exploration of new D & D methods that are relevant to developmental practice.

Testing the innovations in a development phase. As the process in the trial use by which an innovation is systematically tested, revised, or redesigned, developmental testing is critical in determining the nature and validity of the innovations that are finally derived from development. Those who have discussed development and developmental testing in some detail have implicitly or explicitly addressed these subjects as team or collective efforts involving more than one individual (see, for example, Paine, Bellamy, & Wilcox, 1984; Rothman, 1980; Thomas, 1984). In the case of developmental practice, the practitioner is also the evaluator and developer—the one who does almost everything. As such, he or she would generally be the one who defines the practice and developmental problem; carries out the practice and intervention; searches for, gathers, processes, and evaluates the potentially relevant data; and, accordingly, makes the decisions about practice and the design, carries them out, and repeats all or parts of this process until a satisfactory intervention has evolved. To the extent that developmental practice is a solitary enterprise, the practitioner could easily be locked into a subjective vicious circle that is subject to biased data, self-perpetuating conceptions, and false hypotheses without the benefit of correction.

There are at least two tasks ahead, both of which themselves are D & D activities. One is to determine what aspects of the developmental process in general may be applied in developmental practice by individuals who are working singly or as part of a team. Another task is to evolve methods, such as the use of a D & D team, to help correct the possible biases of the practitioner and to increase the objectivity of developmental testing as carried out in developmental practice.

Proceduralization of the intervention. Proceduralization is more than documentation. As applied to interventions, it has been described as "the process by which the desired activities of the helping process are described, explicated, and made into procedures that persons involved in the helping process may follow" (Thomas, 1984, p. 163). To be employed most usefully, procedures should be utilized as an ongoing product and tool. As a product, the procedure captures the details of progress made in evolving the intervention at any given point; it is then used as a tool to guide practice activity in carrying out the intervention—a process that should result in the successive refinement of the procedure when repeated (Thomas, 1984). With regard to developmental practice, the question is this: Can or should procedures be prepared by the individual practitioner for his or her own work, in addition to any practice notes prepared to record the activity of sessions? In any event, there is the issue of how often and to what degree interventions should be proceduralized to reap the benefits of employing proceduralization as both a product and a tool in the D & D process. Further work on these issues should be relevant to developmental practice and, since these are also broad issues, to D & D in general.

Some Qualifications and Skills

The qualifications of individuals who engage in developmental practice should include conventional practice skills and knowledge and additional qualities related to the D & D requirements of the practice. For example, in his field test with practitioners of selected applications of social science concepts, Rothman (1980) concluded that there were three basic qualifications of what he called "social engineers." These qualifications were conceptual thinking capability, as indicated by a familiarity and facility with theoretical writings; familiarity and skill in dealing with application situations (called practice competency); and dependability-reliability, as indicated, for example, in reporting and the completion of tasks.

In addition to these qualifications, the author suggests the following: (1) an intimate familiarity with the model, intervention, or other innovation being worked with; (2) the ability to carry out the intervention in a systematic, disciplined fashion, adhering to the program and avoiding departure from it to address problems and service issues outside the domain of D & D; (3) sound knowledge of the design and development of interventions; (4) the ability to analyze and apply one's own experience; (5) the ability to solve problems systematically; (6) skills in carrying out the constituent activities of proceduralization; (7) skills in empirically based practice; (8) the ability to see problems and possible solutions in terms not only of practice but also of D & D; and (9) dedication to the developmental mission, including a willingness, when necessary, to devote additional time and effort to the tasks of development.

Some Applications

Developmental practice would have several applications in D & D and in practice. For example, in D & D proper, it could be used as a major tool of development in projects or settings in which service otherwise was made secondary or restricted for the purpose of that project. In an established service setting, developmental practice could be employed as a distinctive mode of practice to address those aspects of service that have been identified as requiring D & D, such as designing new interventions for clients who present especially difficult problems, evolving interventions or programs in new areas, and testing new practice procedures or service programs in pilot or demonstration projects before their full-scale implementation by an agency.

SUMMARY AND CONCLUSIONS

In focusing on the issue of the role of practice in development research, this chapter presented three modes of practice —conventional practice, empirically based practice, and developmental practice—and the parts they may play in developmental research. The presentation provided the basis for two related conclusions.

The first conclusion is that practice can and should play a much larger role in D & D than it has played in the past. There are several methods by which conventional practice, as carried out routinely for the purposes of service, can produce innovative interventions. Such innovations, however, are largely incidental by-products of the provision of the service. Even so, if these methods were employed more systematically in conventional practice, the role of conventional practice in D & D could be strengthened, probably without interfering with the service.

The main contribution of empirically based practice to D & D is a methodology of evaluation, especially methods of monitoring outcomes and single-case experimentation, that may be used in practice with single-cases and other systems. Through experimental replication and incremental experimentation, empirically based practice can help contribute effective interventions in the development process. These aspects of evaluation are as important in D & D as they are in empirical practice because they help in monitoring and evaluating innovative interventions in the D & D process. Otherwise, however, empirically based practice is a limited mode of practice for D & D because it lacks an explicit methodology for the design of interventions.

The second conclusion is that D & D and developmental research in general can and should play a much more important role in practice than they have in the past. In a brief overview of the current scene in developmental research, it was indicated that despite the many advances in this still-fledgling methodology, developmental research is not yet widely followed to help solve problems for which it would be most appropriate.

Clearly, the availability of viable and usable D & D methods that were evolved for application in practice could help facilitate the wider adoption of developmental research. Developmental practice, containing the proposed D & D–related characteristics as it does, could eventually become a major vehicle for increasing the use of developmental research. Thus, developmental practice could be employed selectively in practice to address those aspects of service identified as requiring D & D, such as designing new interventions for clients who present especially difficult problems, evolving interventions or programs in new areas, and testing new practice procedures and service programs before full-scale implementation by an agency. The adoption of developmental practice and other aspects of developmental research will be enhanced by further work to make the methods more mature and ready for use.

REFERENCES

Barlow, D. H. (1981). On the relation of clinical research to clinical practice: Current issues, new directions. *Journal of Consulting and Clinical Psychology, 49*, 147–155.

Barlow, D. H., Hayes, S. C., & Nelson, R. O. (1984). *The scientist practitioner: Research and accountability in clinical and educational settings.* New York: Pergamon Press.

Barlow, D. H., & Hersen, M. (1984). *Single case experimental designs: Strategies for studying behavior change.* New York: Pergamon Press.

Berlin, S. B. (1983). Single-case evaluation: Another version. *Social Work Research & Abstracts, 19*, 3–11.

Billingsley, F., White, O. R., & Munson, R. (1980). Procedural reliability: A rationale and an example. *Behavioral Assessment, 3*, 229–243.

Bloom, M. (1975). *The paradox of helping: Introduction to the philosophy of scientific practice.* New York: John Wiley & Sons.

Bloom, M. (1983). Single system designs for preventive practitioners. *Journal of Social Service Research, 6*(3/4), 17–28.

Bloom, M., & Block, S. R. (1977). Evaluating one's own effectiveness and efficiency. *Social Work, 22*, 130–136.

Bloom, M., & Fischer, J. (1982). *Evaluating practice: Guidelines for the accountable professional.* Englewood Cliffs, NJ: Prentice-Hall.

Blythe, B. J., & Briar, S. (1985). Developing empirically based models of practice. *Social Work, 30*, 483–488.

Blythe, B. J., & Tripodi, T. (1989). *Measurement in direct social work practice.* Newbury Park, CA: Sage Publications.

Briar, S. (1973). Effective social work intervention in direct practice: Implications for education. In *Facing the challenge.* New York: Council on Social Work Education.

Briar, S. (1980). Toward the integration of practice and research. In D. Fanshel (Ed.), *Future of social work research* (pp. 31–37). Washington, DC: National Association of Social Workers, Inc.

Fischer, J. (1978). *Effective casework practice: An eclectic approach.* New York: McGraw-Hill.

Fischer, J. (1981). The revolution in social work. *Social Work, 26,* 199–207.

Fischer, J., & Hudson, W. W. (1983). Measurement of client problems for improved practice. In A. Rosenblatt & D. Waldfogel (Eds.), *Handbook of clinical social work* (pp. 673–694). San Francisco: Jossey-Bass.

Flanagan, J. C. (1954). The critical incident technique. *Psychological Bulletin, 51,* 327–358.

Foa, E. B., & Emmelkamp, P. M. (1983). *Failures in behavior therapy.* New York: John Wiley & Sons.

Gambrill, E. D. (1983). *Casework: A competency-based approach.* Englewood Cliffs, NJ: Prentice-Hall

Gambrill, E. D., & Barth, R. P. (1980). Single-case study designs revisited. *Social Work Research & Abstracts, 16,* 15–20.

Gingerich, W. J. (1979). Procedure for evaluating clinical practice. *Health and Social Work, 4,* 104–130.

Havelock, R. G. (1973). *Planning for innovations through dissemination and utilization of knowledge.* Ann Arbor: Institute for Social Research, University of Michigan.

Hayes, S. C. (1981). Single-case experimental design and empirical clinical practice. *Journal of Consulting and Clinical Psychology, 49,* 193–212.

Howe, M. W. (1974). Casework self-evaluation: A single subject approach. *Social Service Review, 48,* 1–24.

Jayaratne, S., & Levy, R. (1979). *Empirical clinical practice.* New York: Columbia University Press.

Kratochwill, J. R. (1978). Foundations of time-series research. In J. R. Kratochwill (Ed.), *Single-subject research: Strategies for evaluating change.* New York: Academic Press.

Marks, I. M. (1982). Toward an empirical practice: Behavioral psychotherapy in the 1980s. *Behavioral Therapy, 13,* 63–82.

Mullen, E. J. (1978). The construction of personal models for effective practice: A method for utilizing research findings to guide social interventions. *Journal of Social Service Research, 2,* 332–337.

Mullen, E. J. (1981). Development of personal intervention models. In R. M. Grinnell (Ed.), *Social work research and evaluation* (606–632). Itasca, IL: F. E. Peacock.

Mullen, E. J. (1983). Personal practice models. In A. Rosenblatt & D. Waldfogel (Eds.), *Handbook of clinical social work* (pp. 623–650). San Francisco: Jossey-Bass.

Mutschler, E. (1979). Using single-case evaluation procedures in a family and children's service agency: Integration of practice and research. *Journal of Social Service Research, 3,* 115–134.

Nelsen, J. C. (1981). Issues in single-subject research for nonbehaviorists. *Social Work Research & Abstracts, 17,* 31–37.

Nuehring, E. M., & Pascone, A. B. (1986). Single-subject evaluation: A tool for quality assurance. *Social Work, 31*, 359–365.

Paine, S. C., Bellamy, G. T., & Wilcox, B. (1984). *Human services that work: From innovation to standard practice.* Baltimore, MD: Paul H. Brooks.

Reid, W. J. (1979). The model development dissertation. *Journal of Social Service Research, 3*, 215–225.

Reid, W. J. (1980). Research strategies for improving individualized services. In D. Fanshel (Ed.), *Future of social work research* (pp. 38–52). Washington, DC: National Association of Social Workers.

Reid, W. J. (1983a). Developing intervention methods through experimental designs. In A. Rosenblatt & D. Waldfogel (Eds.), *Handbook of clinical social work* (pp. 650–673). San Francisco: Jossey-Bass.

Reid, W. J. (1983b). Research developments. In S. Briar (Ed.), *1983–84 supplement to the encyclopedia of social work* (17th ed.). New York: National Association of Social Workers.

Reid, W. J., & Davis, I. P. (1987). Qualitative methods in single-case research. In N. Gottlieb, H. A. Ishisaka, J. Kopp, C. A. Richey, & E. R. Tolson (Eds.), *Perspectives on direct practice evaluation* (pp. 56–74). Seattle: University of Washington School of Social Work.

Reid, W. J., & Hanrahan, P. (1982). Recent evaluations of social work: Grounds for optimism. *Social Work, 27*, 328–340.

Richey, C. A., Kopp, J., Tolson, E. R., & Ishisaka, H. A. (1987). Practice evaluation in diverse settings. In N. Gottlieb, H. A. Ishisaka, J. Kopp, & E. R. Tolson (Eds.), *Perspectives on direct practice evaluation* (pp. 153–170). Seattle: University of Washington School of Social Work.

Rothman, J. (1974). *Planning and organizing for social change: Action principles from social science research.* New York: Columbia University Press.

Rothman, J. (1978). Conversion and design in the research utilization process. *Journal of Social Service Research, 2*, 117–131.

Rothman, J. (1980). *Social R & D: Research and development in the human services.* Englewood Cliffs, NJ: Prentice Hall.

Salend, S. J. (1984). Therapy outcome research: Threats to treatment integrity. *Behavior Modification, 8*, 211–222.

Schinke, S. P. (1983). Data-based practice. In A. Rosenblatt & D. Waldfogel (Eds.), *Handbook of clinical social work* (pp. 1077–1095). San Francisco: Jossey-Bass.

Siegel, D. H. (1985). Effective teaching of empirically based practice. *Social Work Research & Abstracts, 21*, 40–48.

Stuart, R. B. (1971). Research in social work: Social casework and social group work. In J. B. Turner (Ed.-in-chief), *Encyclopedia of social work* (17th ed., pp. 1106–1122). New York: National Association of Social Workers.

Thomas, E. J. (1975). Uses of research methods in interpersonal practice. In N. A. Polansky (Ed.), *Social work research: Methods for the helping professions* (pp. 254–284).

Thomas, E. J. (1977). The BESDAS model of effective practice. *Social Work Research & Abstracts, 13*, 12–17.

Thomas, E. J. (1978a). Generating innovation in social work: The paradigm of developmental research. *Journal of Social Service Research, 2*, 95–116.

Thomas, E. J. (1978b). Mousetraps, developmental research, and social work education. *Social Service Review, 52,* 468–483.

Thomas, E. J. (1978c). Research and service in single-case experimentation: Conflicts and choices. *Social Work Research & Abstracts, 14,* 20–31.

Thomas, E. J. (1980). Beyond knowledge utilization in generating human service technology. In D. Fanshel (Ed.), *Future of social work research* (pp. 91–104). Washington, DC: National Association of Social Workers.

Thomas, E. J. (1984). *Designing interventions for the helping professions.* Beverly Hills, CA: Sage Publications.

Thomas, E. J. (1985). The validity of design and development and related concepts in developmental research. *Social Work Research & Abstracts, 21,* 50–55.

Thomas, E. J. (1989). Advances in developmental research. *Social Service Review, 63,* 578–598.

Thomas, E. J., Bastien, J., Stuebe, D. R., Bronson, D. E., & Yaffe, J. (1987). Assessing procedural descriptions: Rationale and illustrative study. *Behavioral Assessment, 9,* 43–56.

Thyer, B. A., & Curtis, G. C. (1983). The repeated pre test–post test single-subject experiment: A new design for empirical clinical practice. *Journal of Behavior Therapy & Experimental Psychiatry, 14,* 311–315.

Tripodi, T. (1983). *Evaluative research for social workers.* Englewood Cliffs, NJ: Prentice Hall.

Tripodi, T., & Epstein, I. (1978). Incorporating knowledge of research methodology into social work practice. *Journal of Social Service Research, 2,* 65–79.

Tripodi, T., & Epstein, I. (1980). *Research techniques for clinical social workers.* New York: Columbia University Press.

Wodarski, J. S. (1981). *The role of research in clinical practice: A practical approach for the human services.* Baltimore, MD: University Park Press.

Yaffe, J. (1987). *The developmental log: A method of assisting in the development of innovations.* Unpublished manuscript.

Yeaton, W. H., & Sechrest, L. (1981). Critical dimensions in the choice and maintenance of successful treatments: Strength, integrity and effectiveness. *Journal of Consulting and Clinical Psychology, 49,* 156–168.

Commentary

Developmental Research: Model or Method?

Shirley Jenkins

It is rare in social work to have the opportunity to examine a paradigm, or conceptual framework, put forth by an investigator and then to return to it 10 years later to see how it has worked out. In his 1978 article, "Generating Innovation in Social Work," Thomas put forth a creative challenge to social work researchers who had been content to borrow from the methods of the behavioral sciences and to add in incremental fashion to knowledge of human behavior and intervention outcomes. His challenge was to generate a new technology of intervention, indeed, to develop the total concept of social engineering in social work. Such a technology would utilize a range of basic information from diverse sources beyond those of the behavioral sciences, in which the developmental researcher would incorporate both innovation and evaluation. The technology, or technical means to achieve objectives, includes a range of types, such as physical frameworks, intervention methods, service systems, and social policy. Why, then, not develop a research approach to encompass person, process, and environment? This approach would be a uniquely social work intervention and would truly reflect the social work task. Thomas stated that new methods are needed for developmental research, some of which he referred to, including the study of the phases of research utilization, selection criteria in research utilization, models for retrieving data from the literature, the formulation of models for action, and the evaluation of social problems. Analysis, development, and evaluation constitute the developmental research model. In 1978, Thomas said, "Much work needs to be done" (p. 97).

Ten years later, in his 1988 paper for the conference (Chapter 8), Thomas focused on one aspect of the projected model: modes of practice for developmental research. He stated that developmental research has not been widely employed in the past decade and that it is either not done or not properly done.

When one focuses on practice modalities, the distinction between conventional and empirically based practice seems clear and easy to document. Thomas's presentation of developmental practice, however, raised more questions than answers. It asked the reader to consider the practitioner who "does almost everything"—"defines the practice and developmental problem; carries out the practice and intervention; searches for, gathers, processes, and evaluates the potentially relevant data; and, accordingly, makes the decisions about practice and the design, carries them out, and repeats all or parts of the process until a satisfactory intervention has been evolved." The dangers of a "subjective vicious circle" were noted, and steps to reduce bias were introduced. The problems, however, may be more basic than the control of bias and raise four questions about the conceptual approach.

First, with regard to developmental research, is it a model or a method? A paradigm that describes the concept and sets forth the process, including the interactions, is not of the same conceptual order as a method, which describes how to proceed.

Among the many definitions of *model* in the dictionary are these: "a type or design of product; a description or analogy used to help visualize something . . . that cannot be directly observed [and] a system of postulates, data, and inferences. . . . " *Method*, on the other hand, is defined as "a systematic procedure, technique, or mode of inquiry employed by or proper to a particular discipline or art [and] . . . a discipline that deals with the principles and techniques of scientific inquiry" (*Webster's Ninth New Collegiate Dictionary*, 1985, pp. 762 and 747, respectively). Given these definitions, is empirical research not a method and is developmental research not a model? Does each phase in the developmental process not require a method unique to its character, and why are the old-fashioned criteria of reliability, validity, and tested knowledge not still appropriate? Although a model of innovative intervention is of great importance, the history of research has shown that there is often a long lag between findings and interventions—as witness the lag between Klineberg's (1935) work on the intelligence quotients of minority children and the work of J. McVicker Hunt, Martin Deutsch, and others that led to Head Start (Zigler & Anderson, 1979). Furthermore, there have been unsuccessful attempts to combine innovation with evaluation. For example, the action-research model of the 1950s, in which outcome was consistently fed back into the hopper and methods and goals then altered, had many problems, mainly because the process was like standing on shifting sand.

Is the issue confused when the research label is put on some of the implementation processes that may go all the way from trial and error to political negotiation? Those scholars who have sought general theories have often faltered, stumbling on the block that what explains everything often explains nothing. In fact, social work is a field fraught with conflicts and contradictions, with various agendas for practitioners, administrators, clients, and bureaucrats. Social work technology is less like the product of engineering skills than like the best possible fit of conflicting goals and interests.

Comer (1988) reported on an enterprise—the Social Factor—that seems to be appropriate to the developmental model. Comer, a psychiatrist at Yale University, conducted a project in two low-income black elementary schools in New Haven. As Comer stated, "I was totally unprepared for what happened the first day the students arrived. All hell broke loose" (p. 27). From then to the day, five years later, when he opened the envelope containing the test scores in mathematics and reading and "jumped for joy and danced around my office" (p. 31), Comer documented the process of what seems to fit Thomas's model: innovation, intervention, practice, evaluation, and more innovation. It was a process involving many methods. Along the way, there were conflicts over theories among practitioners and between administrators and clients.

This discussion of process leads to a second question, one raised by Thomas in Chapter 8 and by Reid (1987): What are the limits of developmental research and the problems of subjectivity in self-evaluation? Without the goal, at the least, of a quasi-experimental design, are we social workers not in danger of applying a Good Housekeeping stamp of approval to our clients?

The third question has to do with the state of the art. How sure are we of the validity of our interventions? Few interventions have been tested with rigor; the multiplicity of variables complicates the process. There are growing concerns about the reliability and generalizability of the single-subject approach. In developing new methods, we cannot afford to trivialize the task of knowledge building or lose validity and reliability in the grand design.

The last question relates to a goal often put forth in the profession: the pious hope of relating research more closely to practice. In the literature on developmental research, not only is the process increasingly complex, but the burden of implementing the complicated tasks falls to the practitioners. These paragon practitioners would need conceptual thinking capability, practice competency, and dependability and reliability. The practitioners who could undertake the social engineering tasks represent a fraction of an elite group in the profession. Thus, the final question is this: Will the implementation of Thomas's paradigm further isolate researchers from the real world of practice and thus promote an idea that assumes more importance than the reality of the field?

REFERENCES

Comer, J. (1988, August 7). The social factor. *New York Times*, Sec. 4A, pp. 27, 28, 30, 31.

Klineberg, O. (1935). *Negro intelligence and selective migration.* New York: Columbia University Press.

Reid, W. J. (1987). Research in social work. In A. Minahan (Ed.-in-chief), *Encyclopedia of social work* (18th ed., Vol. 2, pp. 474–487). Silver Spring, MD: National Association of Social Workers.

Thomas, E. J. (1978). Generating innovation in social work: The paradigm of developmental research. *Journal of Social Service Research, 2,* 95–116.

Webster's ninth new collegiate dictionary. (1985). Springfield, IL: Merriam-Webster.

Zigler, E., & Anderson, K. (1979). An idea whose time had come: The intellectual and political climate for Head Start. In E. Zigler & J. Valentine (Eds.), *Project Head Start: A legacy of the war on poverty* (pp. 3–19). New York: Free Press.

Commentary

Modes of Research for the Development of Interventions

Jack Rothman

This commentary on Chapter 8 addresses the issue of the modes of developmental research for practice. Before this subject is discussed, however, it is necessary to clarify the domain of inquiry. Developmental research is part of a broader category of research endeavor that aims explicitly to create tested, reliable instrumentalities of practice. The area includes social research and development (R & D) (Rothman, 1980), experimental social innovation (Fairweather, 1967), behavioral community assessment (Matthews & Fawcett, 1985), educational R & D (Baker & Schultz, 1971), and similar efforts. Thomas and this author have begun to use the term intervention *design and development* (D & D) as a way of roughly identifying and grouping these various currents that have a core of common purposes and methods.

Specifically, this commentary focuses on the developmental phase of D & D, during which a proposed formulation of an intervention is field-tested to examine its feasibility (piloting), pattern of implementation (operationalization), and effect (evaluation). Little has been written about variances within the developmental process; rather, this process is treated in a global fashion. Indeed, the developmental process has been largely ignored in social research. What follows are four suggested approaches to development, with examples drawn primarily from the author's work. The approaches are not mutually exclusive, and combinations can and do occur.

PROCEDURALIZATION

Proceduralization entails delineating the sequential steps and behaviors in which the practitioner engages when carrying out a given intervention design. It involves the discrete phased operationalization of a design concept, which, because it is a cognitive statement, always contains some degree of vagueness or uncertainty about its implementation in the real world. To the degree that social work achieves a reasonable level of technology in its repertoire of practice methods, the proceduralization of intervention approaches is necessary. Conceptually, what is involved is an engineering function: articulating how something works and endeavoring to make it work.

Thomas, Bastien, Stuebe, Bronson, and Yaffe (1987) used the term *procedural descriptiveness* to signify the adequacy of proceduralization for a given intervention. Procedural adequacy involves such matters as the completeness of the intervention (the inclusiveness of the steps from the beginning to the end) and its specificity (the sufficiency of detail in carrying out the various steps). The authors provided an example by way of their assessment of the procedure for the assessment and modification of behavior in open settings. This procedure consisted of 16 steps, from intake and making an inventory of the problems to termination and follow-up. A critical-incident technique was used to examine the application of this formulation when carried out in practice. A critical incident referred to occasions when a practitioner departed from the prescribed format of the intervention, which suggested that there was a defect in the design that needed to be adjusted. This technique allows a basic procedure to be progressively more attuned to the environment of the practice task.

The author and his colleagues (Rothman, Erlich, & Teresa, 1976) approached this issue by using the phrase *pattern of implementation* in their work on a demonstration project, the Community Intervention Project. One of their observations was that alternative procedural patterns may exist for carrying out the same basic design. For example, when a partialization (or demonstration project) strategy for diffusing an innovation in service is applied, a common arrangement is to allow for the direct flow of the innovation from the demonstration site (partial segment) to the full target system. However, in some instances, the demonstration must first have an impact on a key decision-making unit, such as the board of directors of an agency or the city council, which has the authority to provide legitimation or funding before the flow can take place. This arrangement involves a pass-through or indirect procedural pattern.

There is also the issue of the optimal degree of detail of the proceduralization, a matter that affects the extent to which the discretion of the practitioner enhances the outcome. In the demonstration project just mentioned, a procedure was designed for increasing participation in organizations and communities through the strategy of offering relevant benefits. Five broad steps were set forth to constitute a procedure. In a more recent project dealing with case management in the field of mental health, 15 functions were delineated, and a more intricate model of implementation was devised (Rothman, 1988).The complexity of the phenomena being addressed, as well as the desirability of the practitioner's discretion, which includes professional capability, may have implications for the character of procedural descriptiveness. An additional issue is whether reinvention in application should be viewed as a detrimental or favorable phenomenon. In any case, the usefulness of proceduralization as a developmental modality should be obvious.

FACILITATING AND LIMITING FACTORS

In any practice situation, a variety of factors help or impede an intervention. Lewin's (1947) force-field theory offers a basic conceptual tool for analyzing this phenomenon (see also Jenkins, 1961). In the development of an intervention design, it is useful to delineate carefully the facilitating and limiting factors that impinge on implementation. In this way, a practitioner can be prepared to emphasize the facilitators and avoid or neutralize the sources of limitation.

In the work of the author and his colleagues, some 20 practitioners, through systematic recording in logs, made note of all such factors that they encountered in carrying out a common intervention design. Accordingly, it was possible cumulatively to identify a wide range of positive and negative forces that affected the implementation of that practice strategy. The categories for such recording included these:

• personal (the practitioner): knowledge, skills, training, experiences, and so forth

• the agency: administrative support, facilities, links with other organizations, attitudes of the staff, and the like

• clients: interest, attitudes toward the agency, relationship to the practitioner, and so on

• community: participation in the agency, support of the agency, and support of the clients, among others.

Through such data, helpful guides for practice can be devised. The author and his colleagues employed checklists as a way of helping practitioners put the information to use. In addition to mapping the force-field context for a given intervention, more generalized data across different interventions can be accumulated on a comparative basis, allowing for broader theoretical contributions. For example, when the author and his colleagues aggregated data from four different interventions, they found that practitioners consistently rated the personal factor as the most facilitating and the organizational factor as the most limiting for the conduct of practice. Whether conceived in this broader way or focused on a particular intervention, force-field analysis offers potential as a developmental tool.

IDENTIFYING CRITICAL ELEMENTS IN IMPLEMENTATION

One of the functions of development is to spot areas of implementation that need special attention or particular action. The partialization strategy described earlier is an example. One of the first tasks in its implementation is to identify a relevant subpart of a larger community or organization, so an initial small-scale demonstration of an innovative program or service can be mounted. As practitioners in the demonstration project carried out this design, they indicated the critical importance of choosing the right demonstration site in partializing, and they identified four operational criteria for doing so (Rothman & Lubben, 1989). These criteria were as follows:

- Access: Choose a partial entity in which there is receptivity and where entry can be smooth
- Success: Try for a site that has a high potential for attaining the goal, since the remainder of the implementation is predicted on the initial success.
- Linkage: Check for the degree of current or potential interaction and exchange between the partial and ultimate target groups, because information about a successful implementation needs to be communicated effectively.
- Acceptance: Seek an initial setting that has adequate acceptance in the larger entity so the successful demonstration is given credence.

It may be difficult to predict what the critical elements may be in implementing an innovative practice. This uncertainty suggests the value of including this modality as an approach within development research. It also underlines more generally the importance of development itself as a means of testing and refining a practice concept or theory before one encourages its widespread utilization in the field.

SPECIFYING THE MECHANICS OF IMPLEMENTATION

The implementation of any design entails a multiplicity of decisions about what may be called the "mechanics" of practice. These decisions include the optimal number of members for group therapy; the number of sessions that should be planned to deal with a given presenting problem; the time that should be spent on different practice functions (such as assessment or follow-up); and the kinds of collateral contacts that should be made with schools, welfare agencies, and families. Attention to such variables is another means of mapping the contours of the practice situation and allows the user of the product of development to anticipate and make plans regarding his or her behavior during the intervention on

the basis of the careful codification of the experiences of other practitioners. In this way, the use of documented norms, rather than trial and
error, may become more characteristic of practice.

In the Community Intervention Project, the practitioners kept careful
records of the number of community agencies they contacted each week,
the types of agencies that they contacted (public or private informal
associations), the number of individuals they contacted, and the types of
individuals they contacted (governmental officials, board members,
agency staff, supervisors, and so on). They also noted reasons for each of
these contacts.

As a further aid to the developmental process, the author and his
colleagues analyzed the data separately for these intervention cases when
the level of attainment of the intended objectives was high. These separate
analyses allowed for the calculation of the means and the range for cases
of ostensibly successful implementation. Thus, the parameters and central tendencies of the mechanisms of implementation of cases of previous
successful practice were produced as an output of development and a
guide to effective intervention.

PRACTICE IN A DEVELOPMENTAL CONTEXT

Development incorporates practice as an intrinsic feature. What is field
tested, essentially, is an *intervention design put into practice*. However, methods
that are used as tools in developmental research can be adapted to be used as
tools of intervention by all practitioners in their regular work roles.

Proceduralization suggests the need to attend carefully and inquiringly
to the sequential steps that are required to carry out a practice initiative.
Force-field analysis alerts the practitioner to a conscious noting of the
facilitating and limiting factors that he or she may encounter in pursuing the
objectives of service. Many practitioners already do these things intuitively;
a developmental perspective is conducive to more rigorous application.
Other contributions of the developmental perspective to practice involve
pinpointing critical elements in carrying out an intervention concept and
systematically mapping the mechanics of practice. Although such actions as
aids to practice do not result in generalizations that can be disseminated in
the field, they offer practitioners a more rigorous means of analyzing and
adjusting their approaches to intervention.

Certain methods, formerly associated exclusively with the use of
research, including single-subject design, psychometric assessment, and
program evaluation, are beginning to be used as tools of practice. To this
list, as Thomas demonstrated, it now seems propitious to add research
methods employed in the development of interventions.

REFERENCES

Baker, R. L., & Schultz, R. E. (1971). *Instructional product development.* New York: Van Nostrand Reinhold.

Fairweather, G. W. (1967). *Methods for experimental social innovation.* New York: John Wiley & Sons.

Jenkins, D. H. (1961). Force field analysis applied to a school situation. In W. G. Bennis, K. D. Benne, & R. Chin (Eds.), *The planning of change* (pp. 238–244). New York: Holt, Rinehart & Winston.

Lewin, K. (1947). Group decision and social change. In T. M. Hartley & E. L. Hartley (Eds.), *Readings in social psychology.* New York: Holt, Rinehart & Winston.

Matthews, R. M., & Fawcett, S. B. (1985). Assisting in the job search: A behavioral assessment and training strategy. *Journal of Rehabilitation, 51*(2), 31–35.

Rothman, J. (1980). *Social R & D: Research and development in the human services.* Englewood Cliffs, NJ: Prentice-Hall.

Rothman, J. (1988). *An empirically based model of case management: Results of a field study.* Los Angeles: Center for Child and Family Policy Studies, School of Social Work, University of California at Los Angeles.

Rothman, J., Erlich, J. L., & Teresa, J. G. (1976). *Promoting innovation and change in organizations and communities: A planning manual.* New York: John Wiley & Sons.

Rothman, J., & Lubben, J. (1989). The partialization strategy: An empirical reformulation of demonstration project planning. *Social Work, 34,* 45–60.

Thomas, E. J., Bastien, J., Stuebe, D. R., Bronson, D., & Yaffe, J. (1987). Assessing procedural descriptiveness: Rationale and illustrative study. *Behavioral Assessment, 9,* 43–56.

The Contribution of Developmental Research

Ronald W. Toseland

In Chapter 8, Thomas drew attention to a much-neglected aspect of developmental research. He distinguished between practice performed for the purpose of developmental research and practice conducted for other purposes. In addition, he described the major elements of developmental practice, providing guidelines that help to clarify and make more specific this step in the process of developmental research.

Jenkins and Rothman and the workshop participants acknowledged the important contributions of Thomas's work to the evolution of a paradigm of developmental research. They also raised a variety of questions that stimulated a lively discussion of the issues involved in implementing developmental research in field settings.

Jenkins raised the issue of whether developmental research is a model or a method. She suggested that if it is a model with distinct processes, then many different methods could be used appropriately to implement it. In her view, the choice of the methods to be used when conducting developmental research would depend on the phase in the developmental research process and the requirements of the specific situation.

Thomas argued that the developmental-research-and-practice method is not intended to be a substitute for other methods. Rather, it should be considered a distinct methodology with an important role to play in designing and developing interventions. Thomas indicated that more effort needs to be placed on conducting developmental research, but because they have different objectives, developmental research should not be seen as a replacement for conventional research or conventional practice.

Both Thomas and Rothman pointed to the important role that design and development (D & D) has played in American industry. Both lamented the fact that the developmental research model has not been more widely adopted in social work. Both reiterated their long-held beliefs that the wider adoption of the developmental research paradigm would result in new and improved strategies for intervening with clients who need specific social services.

Several participants in the workshop raised questions about the procedures to be used when conducting developmental research. Jenkins wondered whether the developmental model would include trial and error and other less rigorous research processes. Rothman discussed aspects of developmental research procedures by suggesting several other elements, including methods for developing prototypical interventions, the proceduralization and operationalization of prototypical interventions, careful and systematic consideration of facilitative and hindering factors in implementing newly designed interventions, and attention to the mechanics of implementation. These comments were helpful because they stimulated a discussion about the differences between practice in a developmental context and conventional practice.

The reliability and validity of interventions that were developed through the application of research-and-development (R & D) processes were also discussed. Jenkins pointed out that methodological rigor may be sacrificed in developmental research. Both Thomas and Rothman indicated that rigor is important but that rigor in a D & D context may be different from rigor in an experimental-design context. Developmental research may require a distinct set of methodologies that is uniquely suited to the objectives of the D & D of interventions. The workshop participants agreed that an important challenge for the future is to develop, clarify, and test methodologies for each step of the developmental research process.

Several participants also raised the issue of practical barriers. Responding to Thomas's statement that developmental research has not been widely adopted in the past decade, one participant mentioned that little consideration has been given to the barriers that are encountered when one conducts developmental research or to the incentives and resources that would be necessary for developmental research to take place more widely. For example, few funding bodies or administrators of social service agencies set aside resources for developmental research. The high demand for service, budgetary constraints, and the lack of interest in the risky, long-term payoffs of R & D all contribute to the problem. Another participant pointed out that social service agencies often find it difficult to implement the kind of systematic, long-term research processes that are required when a developmental research project is undertaken. Others wondered whether enough social work practitioners had the skills necessary to conduct developmental research. Despite these impediments, all the participants recognized the potential contribution that additional developmental research could make to the D & D of more effective social work interventions.

Although differences of opinion about what constitutes developmental research and practice were not fully resolved during the discussion, it was clear that Thomas's efforts to separate conventional practice from developmental practice had helped clarify the nature of the issues and heighten awareness and consideration of the essential elements of practice within an R & D framework.

Part 3

Utilization of Research

Chapter 9

Research Utilization: The Substructure of Belief

Stuart A. Kirk

> The essential lesson to be learned has nothing to do with the relative validity of the facts underlying the argument; it is the argument itself that is the education.
>
> —Thomas (1983, p. 149)

Social work is a practicing profession; its knowledge base is to be used. Its knowledge, derived from many sources, strives for scientific and professional respectability. The development, testing, and modification of that knowledge through standard procedures of scientific inquiry are among the hallmarks of a modern profession. The use of research by practitioners is viewed as an important part of this process.

In the 1960s, the profession developed serious concerns about its knowledge base, the validity of the assumptions made about interpersonal intervention, and the effectiveness of the services that were delivered. These concerns were congruent with a political climate in which many institutions were being critically examined. Were mental hospitals and prisons really engaged in rehabilitation? How well were schools educating students? Were welfare programs helping families to move out of poverty? Were the civil rights of members of racial minorities adequately protected? Were women offered the career opportunities and encouragements that men enjoyed? It was a time of profound self-examination for institutions and professions.

In January 1973, the month of Richard Nixon's second inauguration as president, Scott Briar, then editor-in-chief of *Social Work,* predicted a difficult future for the profession (Briar, 1973). Citing John Ehrlichman, Nixon's adviser for domestic affairs, who had made unflattering comments about social workers needing honest work, Briar wrote an editorial calling for social work to prove its worth in what he dubbed the "Age of Accountability." The lead article in that issue of *Social Work* was Fischer's (1973) infamous query "Is Casework Effective?"

The purpose of this chapter is to examine one facet of the profession's internal self-scrutiny that developed into a concern about "research utilization" among direct-service practitioners. This topic has been the source of considerable ferment for the past 25 years. There is now a sizable literature, and research utilization has been the focus of special conferences and at least a dozen studies.

This chapter revisits how this topic emerged and was defined in social work, retracing the trail for signs that went unnoticed and pathways not taken. The point of departure for this review is a return to the beginning to examine some of the earliest studies about the utilization of research in social work and to determine with hindsight how they may illuminate the present circumstances. Three articles published over 20 years ago provide the site for this review.

SYMBOLS AND SUBSTANCE

If one reviews the literature on the utilization of research in social work, looking carefully at the footnotes, one finds that an early citation is to Eaton's (1962) "Symbolic and Substantive Evaluative Research"; this citation became an obligatory footnote in nearly all subsequent publications. The questions Eaton asked and the data he presented constituted a new line of inquiry for social work. No one before had asked practitioners about their attitudes toward research or how they might use it or how important they thought it was for themselves or their agencies. While opening a new territory for exploration, Eaton left a cleared path that others would follow.

It is noteworthy that this seminal piece virtually is not discussed or analyzed in any detail in the text of later works, but is relegated to the status of a footnote. Eaton's contribution has taken on a symbolic function in the professional literature, a critical one that shaped subsequent discussions. For that reason, a careful analysis both of what it says and of how it says it will provide insight into the literature on the use of research in social work.

The article, a report of a study, presented findings from a survey of 282 social workers in the Veterans Administration (VA) and a similar survey of nearly all the 4,000 employees of the California Department of Corrections. The respondents were asked to react to hypothetical situations regarding what they thought their agency should do if it received a sizable amount of unrestricted new funds and how they would interpret and communicate to others several hypothetical research findings. Nine tables displayed the percentages of responses to items on the questionnaires. The data were presented simply and were easy to read; no cross-tabulations, bivariate correlations, or tests of significance were reported.

Eaton asked the VA social workers the following: "If your agency received a ten thousand dollar annually renewable gift, what would be your priority for its use?" The most frequent first priority (of 41 percent of the respondents) was to raise starting salaries to recruit more qualified caseworkers. The second most frequently cited priority (by 35 percent) was to "support work on a research project regarded as important by the agency" (p. 424). When asked what they would do if they had the freedom to devote a day a week to some professional activity, the VA social workers responded that their first choice would be to "do research." Their answers to several other questions expressed orientations that were supportive of research. Among personnel in the California Department of Corrections, research was also high on the list of priorities.

In addition, 159 mental health professionals in the California Department of Corrections were presented with two brief research summaries, one offering encouraging findings and the other offering discouraging ones. They were asked to check only one recommendation about how they would publicize the findings. Their most frequent response to both summaries was to reexamine and continue the study to get more information. Their next-most-frequent responses were to publish it in a reputable journal and to issue the report to newspapers. Although there appeared to be a slight tendency to publicize the encouraging findings more than the discouraging ones, Eaton did not indicate if the differences were statistically significant. Virtually no one recommended that the findings not be released.

The VA social workers were asked to indicate, for each of the four brief research findings, whether they would agree with, be doubtful about, or disagree with communicating the "facts" through each of five verbal and five written channels of communication. Eighty-six percent agreed that they would "report facts orally to [their] immediate supervisor," 76 percent would "keep this fact to [themselves] until someone asks about it," almost half would "report the facts orally to a special staff meeting of social workers, staff physicians and nurses," one in five would "tell fellow workers [they] can trust," and 15 percent would "informally tell [a] hospital administrator." In relation to written communication, one-third would report the facts in writing to their supervisors and one-third agreed that the facts should be included in the next monthly administrative report. Relatively few (16 percent) suggested publication in a journal, and almost no one suggested submission to a patients' newspaper or to the press.

Where Eaton went with these data could not be inferred easily from the data themselves. In fact, those data could have been used to claim that social workers are supportive of research. But Eaton had a different destination in mind, and he pursued it vigorously and without doubt. His article's influence comes not primarily from his data, which were seldom cited, but from his rhetoric, which offered an interpretation of it. It is his interpretive rhetoric that constitutes the "message" of the article, a message that echoes throughout the subsequent literature on the utilization of research.

One theme of his presentation was the purity of evaluative research as science. The thesis of the article appeared in the second paragraph as a conclusion: "Research has two very different functions for organizations: a *symbolic* function and a *substantive* one" (p. 422). And Eaton left little doubt about the preferred kind of research. It was the "pure" one, the one innocent of biases or social constraints; the other kind was tainted and received only ritualistic avowal in committee meetings.

Eaton claimed further that scientists pursue their work in an open-minded, even-handed, and objective way (p. 426) and stated that findings from this dispassionate inquiry should be widely shared. He stressed the need for unhampered, open communication among scientists, distinguishing such communication from the secretive tendencies of business and governmental organizations (p. 438).

A major element of the article was a description of the difficulty that pure science encounters with practitioners in large social service agencies. In the opening sentence of the abstract of the article, Eaton pinpointed the problem as the contradiction between the avowed objectives of research and the acceptance of its findings by clinicians (p. 421). He further claimed that a favorable climate for research can be maintained only when research does not threaten those in power; therefore, organizations have a preference for symbolic, rather than substantive, research (p. 422).

These assertions have the ring of what is now conventional wisdom: Organizations control information for their own advantage. The point is not that these are unreasonable observations, but that this theme saturated the article, from its opening to its closing sentences, and did so even though the data did not present such a clear uncontested picture. Furthermore, precious little research was cited to support his bold assertions.

Another important theme of the article is that the fears of practitioners about their bosses and their place in the agency lead to the corruption of science and the suppression of knowledge. Eaton worked this theme from beginning to end in clear language. He began the assault with an astonishing statement—made without example, evidence, or citation—that in the professions, many of the findings of the more gifted practitioners are never written up or are filed away as being inconclusive because of organizational concern for disturbing the status quo (p. 422). From this assertion about the lost or suppressed works of the best and the brightest, he moved quickly (and with liberty) through the "findings" to conclude that practitioners have reason to react personally to data from evaluative research because the findings may raise questions about their competence (p. 427). Research, he claimed, is a personal threat to practitioners. Only the strong and those with a "secure self-image" can handle it (p. 427).

With his beliefs firmly in hand, he went to great lengths to interpret his data as supporting the view that practitioners were reluctant to interpret research findings, particularly negative ones, and were unwilling to communicate them. Thus, he interpreted the respondents according a high priority to research as merely symbolic; the respondents were not really interested in substance. In reviewing the data about the respondents' readiness to communicate, he argued that silence and ambivalence predominated (pp. 432–433), even though 86 percent of the social workers were willing to report research data to their immediate supervisors (p. 434), an appropriate reporting channel. With written communication, he saw only great reluctance. Although granting that it is plausible that verbal communications within organizations may be the conventional way to share information, which is what organizational research suggests, he jumped immediately into the morally loaded language of censorship, claiming that "academically trained members of professions exhibited self-censorship attitudes even when research findings had favorable implications" (p. 436).

Eaton had an argument to make, and he made it. His thesis was presented boldly in the introduction, not as a hypothesis, but as the conclusion. The point is not that he grossly misinterpreted his data, but that the data were largely irrelevant to the thrust of the article. It was the powerful rhetoric, not the results of the surveys, that made the article influential and that appeared to affect the shape of subsequent work.

RESEARCHER VERSUS PRACTITIONER

The 1960s produced a watershed of new social programs. They also ushered in an age in which serious and systematic efforts were made to evaluate them. Evaluation research, the attempt to use research methodology to assess the process and effectiveness of interventions, came of age. In 1967, *Social Work* published one of the first reports of these evaluative efforts to appear in a social work periodical. "Researcher Versus Practitioner: Problems in Social Action Research" (Aronson & Sherwood, 1967) described the efforts of two sociologists to evaluate antidelinquency demonstration programs in New York City. The authors' purpose was to persuade readers of the central importance of evaluation and to describe problems that they encountered in doing it. The article contained no footnotes or citations to pertinent literature.

The article pointed out that evaluative research was being required increasingly by funding agencies, in this case by the Ford Foundation and the President's Committee on Juvenile Delinquency and Youth Crime. It indicated that a fortune was about to be spent on a variety of programs on delinquency and poverty and that without evaluation, no one would know which funds were well spent and which were wasted (p. 90).

The authors educated the readers about the rational procedures that should guide the development of a demonstration project: setting objectives, specifying how the objectives are to be achieved, and conducting an evaluation to determine whether the objectives were reached (p. 90). Their important message was that for there to be an evaluation, there must be a program that is conceptualized and specified in a way that appears rational to the researcher. The authors presented evaluation as technically easy, as long as the program planners and implementers do their job. The bulk of their article, as suggested by its title, was a description of how practitioners, by impeding the knowledge-development enterprise, make life frustrating for researchers.

Using rhetoric and anecdote, Aronson and Sherwood presented the practitioners they dealt with as small-minded. The researchers were frustrated by the practitioners' "preoccupation with the components of programs without reference to their objectives or to the connections between those components and the kinds of changes the program was intended to produce" (p. 91). This preoccupation, they said, is illogical. They could barely get the practitioners to specify goals (p. 91). The researchers complained that they had to do the conceptual work for the practitioners.

The authors described the designers of the program as reluctant theorists and the providers of service as slow learners. The latter "frequently did not understand the necessity for the comparison group," "did not always keep to the requirements for maintaining equivalent groups," would not complete records, and sometimes would be reluctant to provide clients' names (pp. 92–93). The practitioners were also fearful that the research would be used against them (p. 92).

Difficulties were not limited to the research procedures themselves. The practitioners frequently would not implement the interventions according to plan: "Almost every social action program . . . was changed by the practitioners almost as soon as the program began" (p. 93). Moreover, the authors recognized that a successful program often meant something different to the practitioners than to the researchers. In commenting on this situation in relation to a summer-camp program, they presented a condescending example of how a camp director *knew* that his program was a success because he could see its achievements "in the smiling faces of the campers," whereas the researcher did not doubt that the boys smiled frequently at the camp, but the frequency of smiling was not how the outcome variables were operationalized (p. 94). Using anecdotes from their experience, the authors continually contrasted the rational requirements of scientific evaluation with the cautious, well-meaning, but narrow-minded preoccupation of practitioners.

These were the early days of evaluation research, when researchers expected that rational decisions about social policy would be natural outgrowths of social experimentation. Social science research methodologies would be taken from the laboratory and applied directly to real-life social action demonstration projects. The practical and conceptual limits of experimental group designs were still not appreciated, nor were the intricacies of the work of practitioners. Consequently, the difficulties of evaluation research were placed at the feet of unwilling social workers who were providing services, but not advancing science.

THE PRACTITIONER'S VIEW OF RESEARCH

Concern about impediments to the advancement of practice knowledge came not only from sociologists, but from the heart of the profession. The 1960s witnessed the beginning of a profound reassessment of social casework and its role and effectiveness. The reassessment was cogently framed by Briar (1968a, 1968b) in two influential articles in which he challenged the profession to return to the historical conception of casework as broader than therapy and to examine carefully its effectiveness and its use of emerging knowledge, particularly from the growing body of research on psychotherapy and sociobehavioral interventions. This latter plea served as a preface to what Fischer (1981) would describe a decade later as "The Revolution in Social Work," a movement to integrate social work practice and empirical research.

But in 1968, the shape of the problem, as well as its nature, was still to be defined. The first direct study of the interface of research and practice was reported by Rosenblatt (1968) in an influential study that appeared in a special issue of *Social Work*, of which Briar was editor-in-chief. It was the first study of the use of research by practitioners that was conducted by a social worker. Since then, many others have built on this work.

Rosenblatt's data were from 308 practitioners in the New York City area who completed a questionnaire. The respondents were asked first to think of a recently completed case in which they had encountered some difficulty in deciding on a treatment plan and then to indicate which listed activities they would engage in before arriving at a decision, what they would do if they had more time, the value of different sources of help, the importance of different experiences that might have improved their practice, and which master's degree courses they found most helpful. The responses to these queries were reported separately and simply, by rank order of what sources of help were valued more. The author concluded that in each area, research was rated the least used or the least useful activity (p. 56).

Although he avoided the hyperbolic rhetoric of the Eaton study and the heavy reliance on anecdotes used by Aronson and Sherwood, Rosenblatt's article is important because of the careful way in which the subject was made significant and interpreted. It built on the concerns that had been so influentially articulated by Briar, especially the need for social workers to develop and pay attention to an empirically derived knowledge base. In his opening two sentences, Rosenblatt stated the case for the importance of the use of research in the profession: Social work research must be used to be of value (p. 53); if it is not used, it is purposeless. Equally important, if it is not used by practitioners, researchers lose purpose. If what social work researchers have to say is not heard, or, worse, is not taken seriously and used, then the research enterprise is futile. The nature of the dependence of researchers on practitioners, discussed in a patronizing way by Aronson and Sherwood, was not, and subsequently has not been, fully explored. Instead, the relationship of research to practice was pursued (as it was by Eaton and Aronson and Sherwood) with a twist that subtly protected researchers by laying the blame on others.

Finding that practitioners do not sufficiently value research, Rosenblatt offered three possible explanations. First, those who enter social work, through self-selection and the preference of admissions committees of graduate schools, do not have a scientific bent. Second, clinicians do not find research findings especially valuable in solving practice problems. However, Rosenblatt barely discussed these two possibilities.

The third explanation, described in 11 paragraphs, is obviously the one that Rosenblatt wished the reader to take the most seriously. It was presented as reasoned speculation. The explanation, skillfully presented, echoed Eaton's: Practitioners are unscientific in their thinking, protective of the status quo, and threatened by researchers. Researchers, on the other hand, are the good soldiers of progress and light, championing objectivity and logic with a fervor worthy of moral crusaders.

While recognizing that the roles of researchers and clinicians should be complementary, Rosenblatt argued that the ideal relationship breaks down in reality. Practitioners find protection in fuzzy thinking that cannot be tested, although its consequence is that the profession is kept from progressing while it is tossed to and fro by fashion and fad.

Although he stated that the profession is impeded, over the long range, by the obstacles to progress placed by clinicians, Rosenblatt offered a sympathetic view of their predicament. Practitioners must retain faith in their approach to remain helpful to clients. To adopt the skeptical perspective of the researcher would make them less effective. Moreover, the researcher turns the table on practitioners, making them, instead of their clients, the object of study. Becoming the object of study is likely to "disturb" the practitioners, making them "uncomfortable and awkward." Even with the tacit promise from the researcher of improving knowledge in the future, practitioners recognize that this is a "promissory note to improve practice, which does not fall due until some indefinite future time" (p. 58).

Rosenblatt concluded that for the sake of the profession, practitioners "need to make a long-range commitment to research," even though there may be few immediate payoffs. Clinicians should be altruistic for the benefit of researchers and the profession. He continued: "As part of that commitment they accept the need to support research, to co-operate with researchers, and to pay attention to research findings. They, not the researchers, will decide what to use and how it will be used" (p. 59). He proposed an arranged marriage between practice and research in the hope that if they began to live together, love would follow. But his article, like those by Eaton and Aronson and Sherwood, suggests that he had less faith that the old-world custom would result in love than in unpleasant intercourse.

THEMES FROM THE 1960s: THE SUBSTRUCTURE OF BELIEF

These three influential articles were products of their time, thoughtful attempts to address vaguely felt problems about the interface of science and practice in social work. They are important articles, not only because they were among the first, but also because they each went deliberately beyond their data in an attempt to provide an analysis of the problem. In doing so, they were also more revealing. The articles are worth examining because they are succinct statements of a perspective that was and, equally important, is still shared by many researchers and scholars in social work. They speak not only in the voice of their authors, but in a voice of a generation of social work researchers.

Although each study probed a different aspect of the research-practice interface and in a different way, all three share a common perspective. This perspective constitutes the substructure of belief about the utilization of research in social work. The perspective, culled from both their explicit language and latent messages, can be described by what it conveys and what it omits. Three dominant themes emerge in the perspective.

The first theme concerns *the role of science and scientists.* In each article, science and scientific research are presented as being of enormous value to the profession and to society. Science is the engine of progress, the bringer of light into a world of darkness, the carrier of reason into the realm of superstition. Scientists, that is, researchers, are disinterested observers of practice whose motives are innocent, whose methods are refined, and whose hearts are pure. They want nothing more than to improve the world through the careful study of practice. Rationality and objectivity are the melodies of the researcher's song. It is a song not sung well or with gusto by practitioners.

Omitted from their portraits of research is any suggestion that researchers' motivations may extend beyond the good and worthy; that scientists are not strangers to aggrandizement or status seeking; that the research process itself can be subjective, sometimes fatally so; or that researchers may have a personal, as well as a professional, stake in persuading practitioners to value their (the researchers') work. There is little recognition of the limits of scientific technology and scant awareness that what researchers have labored to produce may not be particularly usable. These omissions, indeed these other sensitivities, emerged only later as the products of a critical self-consciousness among social researchers.

A second theme concerns *the impediments to science that are present in the world of practice.* Science has a rough time in that world. The forces of corruption are everywhere, setting traps for the naive researcher. In each article, science is depicted as struggling with the forces of organizational banality. Social agencies are described as barely tolerant hosts of scientific work, providing temporary accommodations for the guest researchers, eager for them to depart, and concerned that the transients will leave wet towels on the floor—a mess for the permanent residents. Researchers are warned that agency administrators are interested only in findings that support the status quo or that place their agencies in a favorable light. Thus, the administrators may misinterpret, misuse, censor, or ignore the research findings. In sum, it is difficult to do science in the noisy world of practice; it is much easier to do it in the quiet laboratory among fellow researchers with sympathetic views.

There is little recognition in these articles that applied research makes new demands on researchers and their enterprise, as well as on the organizations in which it takes place. Evaluative research is more complex to implement than is laboratory science. The complexities are greater because less is controllable. The methods of study are more cumbersome, the data are more difficult to gather and less certain, and the statistical inferences are shakier. The fault lies, perhaps, not only in the politics of organizations, but in the realities of practice in a turbulent world. There is also little acknowledgment that within the sacred halls of science, tolerance for the unconventional has its limits, that discoveries often elicit hostility or defensiveness, and that researchers themselves have no special immunity to bias.

The third theme that emerges revolves around *the practitioner as wimp*. Practitioners are easily threatened. Even mild-mannered, slow-moving researchers with hearts of gold make them flinch. Practitioners are self-serving and self-protective and lack the power of intellect to be brave about research. So they subvert research projects; use excuses about the confidentiality of clients and about commitments to service to be unco-operative, censor, or ignore unflattering findings; and, in general, are covert enemies of science. They *say* they are fans of research, but look at what they do. Moreover, they are not among the brightest undergradu-ates. The bright ones go to graduate schools in other fields, leaving social work schools and agencies with the remnants. And the leftovers do not appreciate the importance of what researchers do as scientists. Practi-tioners are simply too human and mortal. Progress demands the dedi-cation of the farsighted, the selfless, and the brave.

There is not much in the literature of the 1960s about the practitioner as a dedicated pragmatist or the researcher as an unrealistic idealist. Practitioners may have had reason not to abandon their clients to march in the scientific parade. Sound knowledge about effective social inter-vention was, in fact, skimpy. The research technology to study the world of actual practice was not yet well developed. Journal articles that re-ported the results of research were, and sometimes are, unreadable or trivial, and frequently both. Many research articles are devoid of practical applications. Practitioners, therefore, may have sound reasons for ignoring researchers; at times their doing so may represent good judgment.

STUDIES FROM THE 1970s AND 1980s

Studies on the use of research in social work since those by Eaton, Aronson and Sherwood, and Rosenblatt have mined fairly narrow veins. And, tellingly, all the digging has been done by academics; not a single article on the subject has been written by a full-time practitioner. More research has been done on social workers' views and uses of research. Other studies have examined how social work students were taught and what they thought. And many attempts have been made to integrate the roles of researcher and practitioner and the technologies of science and practice. These efforts have also been studied. Across this literature are the footprints of the themes of the 1960s.

Studies of Practitioners

In 1979, citing his and his colleagues' earlier survey of practitioners (Kirk & Fischer, 1976; Kirk, Osmalov, & Fischer, 1976) and those of Eaton, of Rosenblatt, and of Casselman (1972), this author summarized the conventional wisdom of the day about social workers' orientation to research:

> They profess a high regard for research, but they don't like to study research; they seldom use research studies in their professional work or to improve their skills; their professional reading is not research oriented; they are not likely to conduct research after leaving school; and they have considerable difficulty accepting research with negative findings. (Kirk, 1979, p. 9)

These conclusions came from surveys of practitioners who were asked such questions as whether they did research, used it directly in solving practice problems, had found their research courses helpful, and so forth. These conclusions were buttressed by two small-scale studies that seemed to indicate that social workers could not accurately recognize common statistical symbols (Weed & Greenwald, 1973; Witkin, Edleson, & Lindsey, 1980). Another study suggested that practitioners had less favorable views about the importance and usefulness of research than did graduate students in social work (Rosen & Mutschler, 1982). In total, the surveys of practitioners continued to paint a bleak picture of the status of research in the profession.

Studies of Students

The presumed sad state of affairs led to an intensive study of social work students, sponsored by the Council on Social Work Education (CSWE). Surveys of bachelor's, master's, and doctoral degree students of social work at 15 universities found some good news:

> In sum, several preliminary findings were consistent with the general expectations of faculty and students. The higher the educational level, the more research courses completed. The more research courses completed, the more important and useful research was thought to be. The higher the educational level and the more research courses completed, the more research knowledge acquired. (Kirk & Rosenblatt, 1981, p. 37)

Learning about research was not necessarily an enjoyed or easy experience for students (Kirk & Rosenblatt, 1977). Nevertheless, the students' attitudes appeared to be reasonably positive, although Rosen and Mutschler (1982) suggested that these positive attitudes could be the result of obtaining socially desirable responses from students while they are in school.

Ideal of the Practitioner-Scientist

The most attention-getting idea that emerged in the 1970s as a proposed solution to the gaps between researchers and practitioners and between methods of research and methods of practice was to merge the roles of scientist and practitioner, grounding the merger in the developing methodologies of single-case evaluation. A technological fix was proposed before there was an adequate understanding of the complexity or nature of the problems. Books and articles about this approach began pouring forth and a short time later, studies appeared about these new efforts.

Studies of the teaching of integrated methods. After neglecting the research curriculum in MSW programs for some years, schools of social work began to add new content on single-subject designs to courses or to revamp more dramatically how they taught students about the role of research in practice. A CSWE publication in 1980 described how different schools were attempting to come to terms with these new ideas about the integration of research and practice in education (Weinbach & Rubin, 1980). Thoughtful studies of these teaching innovations were published in journals (Barth, 1984; Siegel, 1983, 1984). Clearly, the hope was that the barriers between researchers and practitioners, evident from previous surveys and so eloquently framed by the 1960s, would be ameliorated by new educational formats that introduced students to the world of single-subject designs.

Since they were committed to empirical approaches to practice, it was predictable that this new generation of clinical researchers would turn their empirical gaze at their own effectiveness as teachers of the new technology. Much as caseworkers had when studies showed their efforts to be demonstrably ineffective, they flinched.

The first to do so was Welsh (1983), after interviewing his former students who had taken a special course on single-subject designs. None of the students who had taken the course was using single-subject research a year after graduation. Welsh, continuing the practice from the 1960s, pointed a finger at agencies and their administrators who did not provide the environmental conditions needed to encourage research among practitioners.

Gingerich (1984) also surveyed his former students of single-subject research. Using a mailed questionnaire, 119 of his 231 students who had graduated and were in direct-service positions responded. Forty percent of the respondents indicated that they had used at least one single-case evaluation technique since graduation. Gingerich properly noted that asking one's former students if they are using the material you labored so hard to teach them and that you so clearly valued may affect which students choose to respond and what they say. The extent of these potential biases is unknown, but probably not insubstantial.

A follow-up study of the University of Washington's innovative attempt to teach an integrated practice and research course produced similar results, beginning with a 50 percent response to a questionnaire mailed to alumni (Richey, Blythe, & Berlin, 1987). Although the responses indicated various degrees of use of some of the components of practice-evaluation techniques, only 11 percent of the respondents who had undergone this specialized education reported that they conducted single-subject or group research studies in their current practice.

Studies of the training of practitioners. Studies have also been conducted on the effectiveness of training for current practitioners. In a study, impressive in its intensity and thoroughness, six practitioners in a family agency were given special intensive training (and college credit) in evaluation procedures in biweekly meetings with the project director (Mutschler, 1979, 1984). Moreover, the agency administrators and board of directors were supportive of the project. The practitioners were randomly assigned cases on which they would use their newly learned evaluation techniques. Data analysis and other supports came from the university. The practitioners and clients were studied during the project and surveyed four months afterward. At follow-up, it was found that only three of the 15 evaluation procedures were being used by a majority of the six workers. Of the 90 possible instances of use (6 workers x 15 procedures = 90), 48 were used during the implementation phase of the project, and only 22 were used four months later (Mutschler, 1984). The gulf between the aspirations of clinical researchers and the realities of practice persists.

NEW PERSPECTIVES

Even if a chasm of belief and behavior continues to exist between researchers and practitioners, the substructure of belief from the 1960s may be fading. New perspectives on the interface of knowledge, technology, and practice are clearly needed and may be on the horizon. One fruitful avenue for inquiry may be to explore the nature of knowledge that is useful to practitioners. Perhaps progress could be made if we researchers could gain a better understanding of how information and knowledge are obtained, developed, valued, and used by practitioners (Ashford, 1987).

For researchers, this avenue begins where the client (that is, the practitioner) is. We researchers know less about this subject than we think, and our ignorance impedes the collaboration of researchers and practitioners. Qualitative studies involving the observation of and in-depth interviews with clinical practitioners may be an important way to begin.

Additional headway may be made if we stop assuming that practitioners are or should be researchers. As many have observed, there are parallels between the problem-solving activities of practitioners and researchers, and there are habits of mind that should be encouraged among both. Nevertheless, the immediate goals, motivations, expected rewards, and roles of practitioners and researchers are not completely congruent. When researchers overlook these differences, both parties expect to be disappointed. For example, research technologies that are helpful to scholars may not be equally useful to clinicians. Handing practitioners a finely crafted single-subject design may be like giving a carpenter a large computerized hammer; it may have its proper uses, but who wants to carry it up on the roof? We will have to wait a few years to see if the latest technological innovations, such as expert systems and computerized client data-management systems, will be more successfully transported into the world of practice. Nevertheless, we are beginning to develop a greater sensitivity to the problems of implementing innovations (Robinson, Bronson, & Blythe, 1988).

The interface between knowledge and practice is being approached from other directions as well. Rothman (1980) borrowed from the research and development (R & D) process in industry to develop models of how available knowledge can be retrieved and converted into usable applications. He proposed using an empirical knowledge base to design, develop, and refine strategies for service and then to disseminate these "products" among practitioners. In providing a comprehensive model of the links between knowledge and application, he shifted the burden of responsibility from practitioners to the developers and the object of utilization from a research report to a refined service model.

Similarly, Thomas (1978) (and some other notable clinical researchers, such as Rose and Farber [see Chapter 7] and Reid and Smith [1989]) has been using a different form of developmental research to produce usable models of service. These attempts are not based on an industrial R & D model, but they share with social R & D the objective of modifying the way in which clinical scholars use scientific methods to develop models of service. Rather than produce research for the consumption of practitioners, developmental researchers generate intervention procedures for use in the social services environment. These various approaches are not without problems (Reid, 1987). For instance, the implementation of models of service or procedures has complexities that may rival those of the utilization of research. The importance of these new directions, however, is that they are efforts to analyze and modify the nature of the clinical research enterprise so that its products are more likely to meet a felt need among practitioners. Notably absent, for the most part, is the latent hostility toward practitioners and the practice environment that marked the literature of the 1960s.

Will a friendly revisit to the literature on the use of research help contemporary researchers find a path through the terrain ahead? It may. The visit suggests that we researchers should not see science and scientists as so pure or practitioners as the enemies of research utilization, should not view the world of practice merely as a research swamp, and should recognize that clinical research is different from but equal to laboratory science. The old views, whatever their merit at the time or their validity today, should not distort our vision or slow our progress. We now know much more about the problems of applied and evaluative research and the vagaries of utilization. The "use" of research is not as simple as it seemed to be 25 years ago, nor is "research" or "knowledge" or "practice." We have learned a great deal since the 1960s, and what we have learned suggests that we should display great modesty in the face of what we still do not know.

REFERENCES

Aronson, S. H., & Sherwood, C. C. (1967). Researcher versus practitioner: Problems in social action research. *Social Work, 12*, 89–96.

Ashford, J. B. (1987). *A framework for analyzing knowledge utilization in social work practice.* Unpublished manuscript, Arizona State University, Tempe.

Barth, R. P. (1984). Professional self-change projects: Bridging the clinical-research and classroom-agency gaps. *Journal of Education for Social Work, 20*, 13–19.

Briar, S. (1968a). The casework predicament. *Social Work, 13*, 5–11.

Briar, S. (1968b). The current crisis in social casework. In *Social Work Practice, 1967* (pp. 19–33). Columbus, OH: National Conference on Social Welfare.

Briar, S. (1973). The age of accountability [editorial]. *Social Work, 18*, 2.

Casselman, B. (1972). On the practitioner's orientation toward research. *Smith College Studies in Social Work, 42*, 211–233.

Eaton, J. L. (1962). Symbolic and substantive evaluative research. *Administrative Science Quarterly, 6*, 421–442.

Fischer, J. (1973). Is casework effective? A review. *Social Work, 18*, 5–20.

Fischer, J. (1981). The revolution in social work. *Social Work, 26*, 199–207.

Gingerich, W. J. (1984). Generalizing single-case evaluation from classroom to practice. *Journal of Education for Social Work, 20*, 74–82.

Kirk, S. A. (1979). Understanding research utilization in social work. In A. Rubin & A. Rosenblatt (Eds.), *Sourcebook on research utilization* (pp. 3–15). New York: Council on Social Work Education.

Kirk, S. A., & Fischer, J. (1976). Do social workers understand research? *Journal of Education for Social Work, 12,* 63–70.

Kirk, S. A., Osmalov, M. J., & Fischer, J. (1976). Social workers' involvement in research. *Social Work, 21,* 121–124.

Kirk, S. A., & Rosenblatt, A. (1977). *Barriers to students' utilization of research.* Paper presented at the Annual Program Meeting, Council on Social Work Education, Phoenix, AZ.

Kirk, S. A., & Rosenblatt, A. (1981). Research knowledge and orientation among social work students. In S. Briar, H. Weissman, & A. Rubin (Eds.), *Research utilization in social work education* (pp. 29–39). New York: Council on Social Work Education.

Mutschler, E. (1979). Using single-case evaluation procedures in a family and children's service agency: Integration of practice and research. *Journal of Social Service Research, 3,* 115–134.

Mutschler, E. (1984). Evaluating practice: A study of research utilization by practitioners. *Social Work, 29,* 332–337.

Reid, W. J. (1987). Evaluating an intervention in developmental research. *Journal of Social Service Research, 11,* 17–39.

Reid, W. J., & Smith, A. D. (1989). *Research in social work* (2nd ed.). New York: Columbia University Press.

Richey, C. A., Blythe, B. J., & Berlin, S. B. (1987). Do social workers evaluate their practice? *Social Work Research & Abstracts, 23,* 14–20.

Robinson, E. A. R., Bronson, D., & Blythe, B. J. (1988). An analysis of the implementation of single-case evaluation by practitioners. *Social Service Review, 62,* 285–301.

Rosen, A., & Mutschler, E. (1982). Social work students' and practitioners' orientation to research. *Journal of Education for Social Work, 18,* 62–68.

Rosenblatt, A. (1968). The practitioner's use and evaluation of research. *Social Work, 13,* 53–59.

Rothman, J. (1980). *Social R & D: Research and development in the human services.* Englewood Cliffs, NJ: Prentice-Hall.

Siegel, D. H. (1983). Can research and practice be integrated in social work education. *Journal of Education for Social Work, 19,* 12–19.

Siegel, D. H. (1984). Defining empirically based practice. *Social Work, 29,* 325–331.

Thomas, E. J. (1978). Generating innovation in social work: The paradigm of developmental research. *Journal of Social Service Research, 2,* 95–116.

Thomas, L. (1983). Humanities and science. In *Late night thoughts on listening to Mahler's Ninth Symphony.* Toronto, Ont., Canada: Bantam Books.

Weed, P., & Greenwald, S. R. (1973). The mystics of statistics. *Social Work, 18,* 113–115.

Weinbach, R. W., & Rubin, A. (Eds.). (1980). *Teaching social work research: Alternative programs and strategies.* New York: Council on Social Work Education.

Welsh, G. J. (1983). Will graduates use single-subject designs to evaluate their casework practice? *Journal of Education for Social Work, 19*, 42–47.

Witkin, S. L., Edleson, J. L., & Lindsey, D. (1980). Social workers and statistics: Preparation, attitudes, and knowledge. *Journal of Social Service Research, 3*, 313–322.

Commentary

What Is the Utilization Agenda?

Jesse E. Gordon

Chapter 9, by Kirk, exemplifies the curiosity that informs a search for understanding and is a well-presented communication of where that curiosity and search have led. Kirk's comments remind me of a story of three elderly women, intently rocking in their chairs on the porch of their retirement hotel. After a while, one of the women uttered a long sigh; the others ceased their rocking for a moment and then slowly resumed. After another while, "*oy, veh is mir*" broke from the lips of the second of the women. Again the rocking ceased for a long moment and then slowly resumed. After some more minutes of silent rocking, the third woman said somewhat plaintively, if not accusingly, "I thought we agreed not to talk about our children."

That could have been a story of three social work researchers whose punchline would be, "I thought we agreed not to talk about practitioners." The lament about practitioners' nonuse of research is connected with the stance of the early utilization theorists toward practitioners, as Kirk described. It is the stance of parents toward their children who seem so obdurate in the face of parental guidance and wisdom. And as later theorists have come to appreciate, such a stance works no better with practitioners than it does with children.

In "Dissection of the Psychical Personality," Freud (1933) claimed that children's superegos—their standards and expectations for themselves and sense of obligations to others—are derived not from what their parents do, but from their parents' superegos, which were derived from the parents' parents. Freud explained that parents try to display and model for their children not a fair picture of themselves, but an idealized picture of what they *should* be like, that is, the picture instilled as superego by their own parents. Thus, in Freud's view, the standards children acquire are more closely connected to their grandparents' than to their parents'.

Freud's idea leads to the question, Do we proponents of the utilization of research indeed practice in our own lives what we preach to practitioners? For example, at a pool party, a colleague of mine who teaches behavior modification courses and who has written extensively on behavioral methods noticed that his exuberant daughter was getting overly excited. He then went to her and warned her that she had better calm down and cut out the running around. So much for the controlled application of positively reinforcing stimuli.

But perhaps this example is too trivial. No doubt, were her behavior a serious problem, he might have followed a behavioral paradigm more formally. A less trivial example is this: Despite the enormous body of research on the selection of mates, marital compatibility, and predictors of successful marriages, no one in the social sciences selects his or her mate after a careful review of the literature (and perhaps a meta-analysis). Why not? Is the research irrelevant? Is the situation too trivial? In our support of the principle of research utilization, are we researchers missing something? I suggest that we are and, furthermore, that another issue is involved.

THE REAL GOAL

Freud's exegesis on the conservatism of the superego—that it does not change much in one generation—was actually an indirect dig at one of his many apostates. Freud saw that Adler's apostasy was connected with the doctrinaire Marxism with which Adler explained the sexual oppression of the times—an oppression that would be overcome when the proletariat came to power (Roazen, 1975).

The Marxist doctrine that Freud was so anxious to repudiate is embodied in the phrase "being precedes consciousness" (Marx, 1970, p. 263), which means that where one stands in relation to the economic and social structure determines how and what one thinks and believes. If the proponents of research utilization do not do much of it themselves, though they urge it on others, perhaps utilization is not their real goal. It may be a tactic in another game: the game of power, in which members of the academy whose consciousness is shaped by their organizational setting seek to assert influence and power over the rival world of practice, as these two cultures compete for dominance, prestige, self-justification, grants, and salaries. Invoking the empiricist standards of our mentors as we educate our young may illustrate precisely the Marxist dictum that Freud was arguing against. Thus, considerable anxiety has been expressed about the fate of the American Psychological Association, now that its practitioner members have predominated over its academic members, who had controlled the association since its inception. The game is competition; the goal, power; and the tactic, research utilization in the service of accountability.

In developing this tactic, researchers invented a "need" of practitioners for the practical knowledge products of the research enterprise, based in universities, as if understanding phenomena is not an adequate human good in its own right. Thus, we researchers claim that society will not support research that does not have a commercial payoff and thereby join the critics of centers of intellectual life in agreeing, by implication, that the only justification for the creation of knowledge and understanding is the pragmatic consequences for efficient production.

That "need" we invented is based on the demand for accountability. But where does that demand come from? Accountability to agencies and to society is not a felt need of practitioners. It is only sporadically and unconvincingly a need for agency administrators, planners, and policymakers. But as uncountable studies have shown, such planners and policymakers themselves are seldom guided by empirical research. When planners and policymakers invoke accountability (a Congressional committee rarely asks to see the results of its appropriations, and then it does so mainly to justify a budgetary cut or an increase), it is more likely their tactic in a political game.

When power is the aim, it is no wonder that the principle of research utilization turns out to refer mainly to evaluation research. Evaluation research increases the demand for academic researchers, provides funds for grants and contracts, and explicitly places researchers in a position of power over the practitioners whose work is evaluated and in a favored position with policymakers and granting agencies. Our consciousness of an imperative to utilize research thus seems to be a function of the academic locales and values of our contexts.

But when we appeal to practitioners' need to be accountable for what they do, we are often barking up the wrong tree, and our barks are among the worst and most ineffective forms of influence. They are really threats. Surely, we researchers have learned something about aversive stimuli, though that is another realm of knowledge that we do not utilize in our work.

ADDRESSING PRACTITIONERS' REAL NEEDS

Perhaps practitioners do not use information gained from research because we researchers are addressing our wishful need for practitioners to be accountable rather than practitioners' real needs. If we examine what it is about social workers—our potential customers—that we could appeal to, we would ask the following: What do they like about their work? What do they want to maximize in their lives? What conception of themselves do they want to affirm and enhance? We researchers do not use research on marriage and marital satisfaction to choose our spouses because compared to the importance of the pursuit of a satisfying sense of ourselves, the *t*-test and a probability figure have little persuasive power. Practitioners are similarly influenced by their conceptions of themselves and the values they wish to maximize.

One suggestion, then, stimulated by Kirk's analysis is that we researchers become better consumers and utilizers of research. The theories and knowledge derived from studies of consumer satisfaction and job satisfaction could guide us in engineering and marketing research-based knowledge so practitioners will accept it. No business owner would accept the excuse from a failed salesman that "I sold them, but they didn't buy." The fault is not in the customer; it may be in the selling of the product.

THE FINAL IRONY

One last thought sparked by Kirk's chapter: Why do we researchers believe that the value of our work lies only in its pragmatic consequences? We undervalue ourselves when we do not recognize that, for many, curiosity and the wish to understand are sufficient reasons and justifications for research. And that idea suggests a final irony: If we were to accept our curiosity and wish to understand as being intrinsically valid, we might not only turn out less trivial, funding-source-driven research, but we might, at last, find a common ground with practitioners. Practitioners have a strong drive to know and understand their clients and to understand what is going on in their treatment relationships. They are perpetually taking seminars, participating in continuing case conferences, sharing experiences, and taking and paying for supervision from those who can help them to new understandings. When empirical social work knowledge and empirically based intervention methods help to gratify practitioners' need to understand, the knowledge and methods may be more readily consumed because they will enable practitioners to do the parts of their jobs that they like and enjoy the most. Using single-case design to evaluate practice is an exercise in sadomasochism; as a means of providing additional information about the client system and about what is happening in treatment, that is, as an aid to understanding, it can be as fascinating as any good social history or set of process notes.

Like Kirk, I think there is hope for the knowledge-utilization enterprise, and that hope lies in a strengthened alliance between practitioners and researchers—an alliance of mutually complementary competencies. Such an alliance would replace the antagonistic, challenging, competitive dominant/submissive relationship of the academy versus the profession and the research-versus-practice mentality animated by the quest for power. In 1919, Kurt Lewin dreamed of an alliance between farmers and research psychologists in which they would work together to design a better hoe (Morrow, 1969). That alliance has not yet been formed; clearly, it is not an easy rapprochement. Similarly, we find it difficult to move beyond the history of our relationship with practitioners. As Loewald (1960) noted, we must lay to rest these ghosts that walk about and haunt us, converting them from agitated and agitating spirits of the past into mere ancestors. If we can give up the stance of hostile critic of the very audience whose favor we wish to earn, we could abandon the power game, give up the absurdity of attacking our natural allies in fratricidal rivalry, and recognize the commonalities among us: curiosity, commitment to our work, and the human wish to fulfill a conception of ourselves as caring and competent.

REFERENCES

Freud, S. (1933). Dissection of the psychical personality. Lecture 31 in S. Freud, *New introductory lectures in psychoanalysis*. New York: W. W. Norton.

Loewald, H (1960). On the therapeutic action of psychoanalysis. *International Journal of Psychoanalysis, 41*, 16–33.

Marx, K. (1970). *A contribution to the critique of political economy*. New York: International Publishers.

Morrow, A. (1969). *The practical theorist*. New York: Basic Books.

Roazen, P. (1975). *Freud and his followers*. New York: Alfred A. Knopf.

Commentary

Making Research Usable

Robert F. Schilling

Kirk's careful abstraction and analysis of the seminal contributions to the area of research utilization provided a useful developmental perspective. It is well to recall that the field of research utilization has a history of only 25 years. Kirk's critical analysis of Eaton's benchmark article reminds one that it is never too late to scrutinize influential contributions. Journal editors state that they favor contributions that stir controversy; if an author presents original data in so doing, all the better. Regardless of whether the data presented are derivational or original, authors of controversial articles must be prepared for others to find fault with their methods or interpretations (see, for example, Blenkner, Jahn, & Wasser, 1964).

As a researcher who has carried out numerous agency-based projects, the author winced when reading Kirk's assessment of Aronson and Sherwood's (1967) article on problems in social action research. How many of us have returned from frustrating forays into service agencies, complaining that practitioners cannot see beyond their daily tasks and that administrators are not open to research? However, is it really fair to expect social workers to be enthusiastic about activities that are not likely to yield immediate payoffs for their work with clients and that will surely take up much of their time?

The different perspectives of practitioners and researchers may hinge in part on their adherence to, respectively, faith and skepticism (Bloom, 1975; Schilling, Schinke, & Gilchrist, 1985). A degree of faith is desirable. Most people would prefer to be helped by a worker who believes in the efficacy of his or her intervention, and few, including researchers, would opt for a worker who was skeptical about the efficacy of the helping process in general. Nearly two decades ago, Briar and Miller (1971) observed that the scientist's paradigm of hypothesis-experiment is analogous to the social casework formula of study, diagnosis, and treatment. Unfortunately, studies of practitioners' beliefs and behavior offer little evidence that the analogy has much application in the realm of current practice (Rosen & Mutschler, 1982; Schilling, Schinke, & Gilchrist, 1985).

Kirk's summary of the themes of the literature on research utilization from the 1960s gives one pause. As with many new agendas, the promise of research utilization extended far beyond what turned out to be possible. Numerous studies have demonstrated that social workers do not use published research to guide and improve their practice and that even among those who were trained in the scientist-practitioner model, few use empirical methods in their practice (Richey, Blythe, & Berlin, 1987).

It is worth noting that medicine, for all its scientific claims, struggles with the same problem in ways that are not so different from those with which social work struggles. For instance, studies have repeatedly found that the advice of physicians is a powerful determinant in patients' decisions to quit smoking, yet physicians tend to discount their own influence to do so and hence spend little time trying to get patients to stop smoking (Anda, Remington, Gironda, & Davis, 1987; Ockene, 1987). This example from medicine is presented because it is thought that the biomedical field offers clear guidelines that physicians then follow. Although medicine can claim much more precise indicators of outcome and specifies relatively clear treatment protocols, many areas of medical practice are guided, or misguided, by convention and custom as much as by empiricism.

Kirk suggested that social workers may hardly be expected to base their practice on the literature when the literature rarely offers clearly delineated recommendations for intervention, such as the latest empirically derived strategy for handling psychotic episodes. Hence, researchers would do well to consider the extent to which the literature *does* inform practice before they criticize workers for not consulting it when they have a difficult client.

Kirk offered several sensible suggestions that might help the profession move along the path of research utilization. Certainly, developmental research and packaged intervention models have much to offer and have not yet been exploited fully. Kirk emphasized that researchers would do well to try to understand the challenges, reinforcers, and interests of practitioners. Beyond such understanding, this author offers the following suggestions:

1. The professional literature has proved to be a poor vehicle for transmitting research findings to social workers. Yet, researchers know, from their experiences as teachers, workshop leaders, and conference planners, that practitioners are keen on developing their skills. Researchers could, following a design-and-development approach, develop testable, replicable workshop formats that would bring packaged interventions to workers (Thomas, 1978, 1987). In such workshops, practitioners would learn of areas in which there is a consensus about what constitutes

optimal practice, receive feasible protocols for assessing such problems, and learn how to make decisions about treatment options (Stein & Rzepnicki, 1984). They might practice carrying out such actions using role play, computer software, or paper-and-pencil aids.

2. Students are rarely exposed to research utilization in the field, even when schools of social work imbue them with the importance of drawing on theory and research in their practice. Given the findings on social workers' use of research, it is known that fieldwork instructors in agencies do not model this kind of activity. Thus, if we researchers are serious about helping new practitioners learn to utilize research findings, we must help field agencies institute such procedures.

3. Administrators should be involved in issues related to research utilization. They need to know about the latest findings from research to upgrade workers' skills; to develop, fund, and administer services that incorporate acceptable and, ideally, optimal protocols of practice; and to demonstrate to regulators, courts, and others that their agency's practices are current and based on sound theory, research, and evaluation.

4. We should begin in areas that we are more certain about and that can be readily translated into intervention packages. For example, there is considerable evidence that attention deficit disorders are often organic, that medication is usually helpful, that behavior management strategies may be useful, and that diet is not likely to be a contributing factor (Pelham et al., 1990; Vyse & Rapport, 1989). Similarly, emerging data suggest that strategies for the management of anger may be useful in work with family violence (Schilling, 1990; Schinke, Schilling, Barth, Gilchrist, & Maxwell, 1986; Whiteman, Fanshel, & Grundy, 1987).

5. Packaged interventions need not overly restrict workers. For instance, relapse prevention strategies (Marlatt & Gordon, 1985) could be adopted within various agencies with different treatment philosophies, because relapse remains *the* major concern in any addiction treatment setting. In Mullen's (1983) view, personal models of practice consider information from a range of sources, including experience, theory, and research, and emphasize personal accountability.

6. The *process* of intervention should not be neglected in research utilization. Some of the most replicated and accepted research on practice is in this area (Beutler, Crago, & Arizmendi, 1986). Moreover, it is known that if the process (the practitioner's style, for example) is not attended to, then the "active," or more frequently specified, elements of the intervention will be poorly received by the client (Orlinski & Howard, 1986).

Central to Kirk's remarks is the notion that research utilization may be viewed as a relative, not an absolute, concept. Even the staunchest advocates of empiricism recognize that all research that is useful to social work has some methodological flaws and that the most rigorous research often has little application. Social workers who have been trained in the empiricist tradition rightfully hold that the scientific method generates knowledge that cannot be obtained through other kinds of inquiry. But as a group, social work researchers must do more to render such knowledge useful to practitioners.

REFERENCES

Anda, R. F., Remington, P. L., Sienko, D. G., & Davis, R. M. (1987). Are physicians advising smokers to quit? The patient's perspective. *Journal of the American Medical Association, 257,* 1916–1919.

Aronson, S. H., & Sherwood, C. C. (1967). Research versus practitioner: Problems in social action research. *Social Work, 12,* 89–96.

Beutler, L. E., Crago, M., & Arizmendi, T. G. (1986). Therapist variables in psychotherapy process and outcome. In S. I. Garfield & A. E. Bergin (Eds.), *Handbook of psychotherapy and behavior change* (3rd ed., pp. 257–311). New York: John Wiley & Sons.

Blenkner, M., Jahn, J., & Wasser, E. (1964). *Serving the aging: An experiment in social work and public health nursing.* New York: Institute of Welfare Research, Community Service Society of New York.

Bloom, M. (1975). *The paradox of helping: Introduction to the philosophy of scientific practice.* New York: John Wiley & Sons.

Briar, S., & Miller, H. (1971). *Problems and issues in social casework.* New York: Columbia University Press.

Marlatt, G. A., & Gordon, J. R. (1985). *Relapse prevention.* New York: Guilford Press.

Mullen, E. J. (1983). Personal practice models. In A. Rosenblatt & D. Waldfogel (Eds.), *Handbook of clinical social work.* San Francisco: Jossey-Bass.

Ockene, J. K. (1987). Smoking intervention: The expanding role of the physician. *American Journal of Public Health, 77,* 782–789.

Orlinski, D. E., & Howard, K. I. (1986). Process outcome in psychotherapy. In S. L. Garfield & A. E. Bergin (Eds.), *Handbook of psychotherapy and behavior change: An empirical analysis* (3rd ed., pp. 311–381). New York: John Wiley & Sons.

Pelham, W. E., McBurnett, K., Harper, G. W., Milich, R., Murphy, D. A., Clinton, J., & Thiele, C. (1990). Methylphenidate and baseball playing in ADHD children: Who's on first? *Journal of Consulting and Clinical Psychology, 58,* 130–133.

Richey, C. A., Blythe, B. J., & Berlin, S. B. (1987). Do social workers evaluate their practice? *Social Work Research & Abstracts, 23,* 14–20.

Rosen, A., & Mutschler, E. (1982). Social work students' and practitioners' orientation to research. *Journal of Education for Social Work, 18,* 62–68.

Schilling, R. F. (1990). Perpetrators of child physical abuse. In R. T. Amerman & M. Hersen (Eds.), *Treatment of family violence: A sourcebook* (pp. 243–265). New York: John Wiley & Sons.

Schilling, R. F., Schinke, S. P., & Gilchrist, L. D. (1985). Utilization of social work research: Reaching the practitioner. *Social Work, 30,* 527–529.

Schinke, S. P., Schilling, R. F., Barth, R. P., Gilchrist, L. D., & Maxwell, J. S. (1986). Stress-management intervention to prevent family violence. *Journal of Family Violence, 1,* 13–26.

Stein, T. J., & Rzepnicki, T. L. (1984). *Decision making in child welfare services.* Boston: Kluwer-Nijhoff.

Thomas, E. J. (1978). Generating innovation in social work: The paradigm of developmental research. *Journal of Social Service Research, 2,* 95–116.

Thomas, E. J. (1987). Assessing procedural descriptiveness: Rationale and illustrative study. *Behavioral Assessment,* 43–56.

Vyse, S. A., & Rapport, M. D. (1989). The effects of methylphenidate on learning in children with ADHD: The stimulus equivalence paradigm. *Journal of Consulting and Clinical Psychology, 57,* 425–435.

Whiteman, M., Fanshel, D., & Grundy, J. F. (1987). Cognitive-behavioral interventions aimed at anger of parents at risk of child abuse. *Social Work, 32,* 469–474.

Commentary

Opening the Door to Knowledge Utilization

Craig Winston LeCroy

Although much has been written in the field of research utilization, most has been rhetoric and has not been critically reviewed with regard to its conceptualization and methodology. In addition, studies on research utilization actually limit the understanding of the complexities involved in integrating research with practice.

This limitation has resulted primarily from the manner in which the studies have operationally defined research utilization (LeCroy, Ashford, & Macht, 1989). Researchers' understanding of practitioners' limited use of research is based on the observation that practitioners do not read research articles on a weekly basis. However, this is not a conceptually adequate definition of research utilization. In fact, there is little information about what constitutes a knowledge-based, research-utilizing social worker on which to evaluate the field's progress in stimulating practitioners to use research findings. Contrary to the conclusion that is so often found in the literature, not utilizing research by failing to read research studies does not point to the demise of the scientific base of social work (LeCroy, Ashford, & Macht, 1989).

Several studies have suggested that the utilization of research in social work has important conceptual and methodological difficulties. For example, Larsen (1980) stated that "studies limited to a single indicator of utilization, and one which is action-based, measure one narrow dimension and may be expected to miss conceptual utilization entirely" (p. 429). Thus, Caplan (1977) noted that when studies defined research utilization only as the direct influence of research findings on programs or decisions, they found that research was rarely used. However, when the concept of utilization was extended to include the consideration of research-based concepts and generalizations in formulating questions, setting goals, and planning activities, the use of research was found to be common. It is important to recognize that practitioners' decisions may be influenced by knowledge that is generated by research and filters down to them. Indeed, they may make knowledge-based decisions but may not remember the source of their information or distinguish when they are relying on means for decision making that would not be considered knowledge based.

The utilization of knowledge, rather than of research, should be the focus of the profession. Kirk touched on this issue briefly in Chapter 9, when he suggested that the literature on utilization has paid little attention to the limits of scientific technology. Indeed, the limits of technical rationality must be addressed if the profession is to confront seriously the issues involved in making social work more knowledge based. Schon (1983) would argue that social work is one of the professions that suffer from "shifting, ambiguous ends and from unstable institutional contexts of practice, and are therefore unable to develop a base of systematic, scientific professional knowledge" (p. 23). He posited a critical question for social work: "If applied science consists in cumulative, empirical knowledge about the means best suited to chosen ends, how can a profession ground itself in science when its ends are confused and unstable?" (p. 23).

A broader conception of knowledge is needed to understand knowledge-based practice. Referring only to scientific research as usable knowledge creates the perception of a gap between practice and research that may not necessarily exist. Clearly, it appears that social work will not obtain a scientific conclusiveness outside "ordinary knowledge" (Emmert, 1985). If it is recognized that there is a continuum of knowledge that is available for informing practice, then the strain between research and practice is weakened.

The philosophical bias toward technical rationality has limited the use of knowledge in practice. The result has been an emphasis on the research and development (R & D) model, which suggests that research leads to application. However, an alternative view is that utilization depends on the identification of a problem for which research is to be applied. The current ideology of social work research is biased toward innovation, not toward solutions to action-oriented problems. The goal of the R & D model is to translate scientific evidence into a usable form, rather than to use scientific evidence to solve instrumental concerns. The unfortunate consequence is that the predominant model of utilization may be an inappropriate approach to enhancing the use of scientific evidence in decision making. The alternative is to focus on a user orientation that is more relevant to the practitioner. Thus, the goal is to move a problem to information instead of moving the information to the problem and therefore make it easier to achieve an instrumental end (see Ashford & LeCroy, 1988).

To understand and enhance the utilization of research, one must understand how social workers use knowledge. As Kirk found, most of the studies he reviewed came to the disheartening conclusion that social workers fail to use research to inform their practice. How can this conclusion be explained? Of the three explanations that Rosenblatt (1968) put forth, the one he addressed the least is the most plausible: "Clinicians do not find research findings especially valuable in solving practice problems" (p. 56). A more recent study by DeMartini and Whitbeck (1986) confirmed this conclusion. DeMartini and Whitbeck found that on-the-job training and personal experience were the most frequent sources of knowledge that social workers used for decision making, whereas books and journals were among the least frequently used sources.

What can account for the fact that experiential knowledge is relied on most in a profession that would like to claim a scientific knowledge base? Experiential sources of knowledge are relied on because the information that practitioners need is instrumental rather than scientific. Practitioners have a different end view from scientists—one that may not necessitate an optimal solution. Such practical ends are easily satisfied by experiential forms of knowledge. The result is that practitioners achieve their ends without the need to engage in systematic modes of inquiry or consultation with scientific research.

Boyd and Menlo (1984) suggested that practitioners seek different levels of knowledge by asking three different types of questions: tactic-seeking questions, strategy-seeking questions, and knowledge-seeking questions. According to this framework, the underutilization of research is due to the way in which social workers typically state their problems—in a tactic-seeking manner.

With tactic-seeking questions, practitioners ask for tactics to address their immediate concerns about their clients. One example of a tactic-seeking question is the following: "What can I do to increase the participation from Mr. Jones in our family sessions?" (Ashford & LeCroy, 1988). Because the action to be carried out has an immediate end in view, there is no reason for the practitioner to look to research-based information. The solution to a tactical problem can be found in experiential sources of knowledge.

With strategy-seeking questions, practitioners shift their focus to general concerns about their clients. An example of a strategy-seeking question is, "What can a social worker do to increase the participation of family members in counseling sessions?" (Ashford & LeCroy, 1988). This question represents a higher level of abstraction because it seeks a solution to a general situation or problem.

A knowledge-seeking question attempts to ascertain whether scientific information exists that could be used to resolve a specified problem, not what information or procedures could be incorporated into a plan of action (Boyd & Menlo, 1984). This level of discourse attempts to establish a relationship among variables. For example, the practitioner may ask, "What factors are likely to increase the participation of family members in counseling sessions?" (Ashford & LeCroy, 1988).

This form of discourse is rarely used by practitioners, however. Since such demands are rarely made in social work, it is understandable why practitioners often fail to use research-based evidence in their decision-making activities.

The problem-solving perspective presented here is a vastly different view of how the utilization of research may be understood and enhanced. If the profession could develop an epistemology of practice in which problem solving would be a major research endeavor of practitioners, the present concern about the nonuse of scientific information would be mitigated because uncertain practice situations could be linked to opportunities to apply the scientific method. Thus, the door to knowledge utilization would be opened, and social workers could move a step closer to improving their practice.

REFERENCES

Ashford, J. B., & LeCroy, C. W. (1988). *Problem solving in social work practice: A user approach to knowledge utilization.* Unpublished manuscript.

Boyd, R. D., & Menlo, A. (1984). Solving problems of practice in education. *Knowledge: Creation, Diffusion, Utilization, 6,* 59–74.

Caplan, N. (1977). A minimal set of conditions necessary for the utilization of social science knowledge in policy formation at the national level. In C. Weiss (Ed.), *Using social research in public policy making.* Lexington, MA: Lexington Books.

DeMartini, J. R., & Whitbeck, L. B. (1986). Knowledge use as knowledge creation. *Knowledge: Creation, Diffusion, Utilization, 7,* 383–396.

Emmert, M. A. (1985). Ordinary knowledge and policy science. *Knowledge: Creation, Diffusion, Utilization, 7,* 97–112.

Larsen, J. K. (1980). Research utilization: What is it? *Knowledge, Creation and Utilization, 1,* 429.

LeCroy, C. W., Ashford, J. B., & Macht, M. W. (1989). A framework for analyzing knowledge utilization in social work practice. *Journal of Sociology and Social Welfare, 16,* 3–17.

Rosenblatt, A. (1968). The practitioner's use and evaluation of research. *Social Work, 13,* 53–59.

Schon, D. A. (1983). *The reflective practitioner: How professionals think in action.* New York: Basic Books.

Synthesis

Research Utilization: Reflections on the Rhetoric

André Ivanoff

Kirk's presentation in Chapter 9 invites reflections on the rhetoric used in the literature on the utilization of research in social work practice. In that chapter, Kirk discussed three rhetorical themes that emerged from the early literature in this area—the superiority of the intent and methods of science and scientists; the impediments to science posed by the world of practice; and the practitioner as a moral, intellectual, and rational wimp. He also described the more recent model of the practitioner-scientist as the technological fix of the research utilization movement. Kirk recommended that researchers expand their information about practitioners' use of knowledge, stop assuming that practitioners should be researchers, and pay greater attention to the models of research and development and developmental research as sources of innovations in services.

The responses to Kirk's chapter addressed one or more of the rhetorical themes, but, in general, agreed with Kirk's conclusion: Research is not being used in practice. Kirk provided reason to doubt that research utilization is even a viable goal. Gordon argued that evaluation researchers are motivated by the struggle for power and supremacy in the profession and that the condescending and domineering attitudes of researchers toward practitioners make rapprochement difficult.

LeCroy contended that research utilization is based on narrow conceptions of the direct influence of research on practitioners. He suggested that "knowledge utilization," which incorporates information from multiple sources, rather than research utilization, which relies on research evidence, should be the focus. Schilling noted that an understanding of the interests and perspectives of practitioners is not enough and that researchers must examine the methods and means used to transfer information from research to practice.

THREE PRIORITIES

The philosophical and pragmatic issues involved in education for research utilization commanded the most attention. Three overlapping priorities emerged from the discussion: to identify obstacles to the use of research, to strengthen the emphasis in social work education on the importance of evidence in direct practice, and to increase practitioners' awareness of the importance of research.

Identification of Obstacles

In surveys of practitioners and students, research utilization is defined as reading research articles in journals, conducting research, and using research to solve problems in practice. Alternatively, the inability to recognize statistical symbols is cited as evidence of the nonuse of research.

Do reading articles on research and conducting practice evaluations constitute research utilization? Should conducting practice evaluation be distinguished from using the products of others' research? Should practitioners' attitudes and conceptual orientations be measured, or is actual utilization the only proper indicator? Despite all their criticisms of the current definitions of research utilization, the presenters offered disappointingly little in the way of constructive suggestions about how to resolve the various definitional dilemmas.

LeCroy's definition of research utilization is so broad that it may be more a hindrance than a solution. LeCroy argued for the study of knowledge utilization, rather than research utilization, when "knowledge" is meant to include all forms of evidence and belief, not just research evidence. The value of LeCroy's approach is its potential to produce a more complete view of practice and to determine the influences of more commonly used sources of knowledge, such as personal experience and on-the-job training. Some participants were excited that this approach might lead to practitioners having some input into the shaping of research questions and methods and to the possibility that if practitioners are involved in deciding the questions for study, they may be more likely to use the results of the research in practice. Others were pleased because knowledge utilization may increase the transfer of research information to practitioners by targeting the most useful types of information and avenues of presentation.

Although the study of the development and utilization of knowledge is a worthwhile activity that may result in dramatic changes in professional education, it does not immediately address the issue of research utilization whose goal is to transfer information from its original state to an applied situation. The danger of mixing research utilization with knowledge utilization is that research utilization may lose its identity as an underdeveloped source of information for increasing the effectiveness of practice. Research findings, particularly those from studies of social work clients, are a particularly important source of information.

Another obstacle is the field's ignoring the progress made by research utilization, which, over the past 30 years, has radically changed social work practice. The examination of research evidence has led to the development of paradigms not only for conducting studies but also for evaluating the products of research. Criticisms of social work research like Fischer's (1973) had a shattering effect on the field, which learned that it needed to rethink the paradigms used for evaluating the effects of intervention, as well as the intervention paradigms themselves. Kirk and Kutchins's (1988) and Kutchins and Kirk's (1986, 1988) work on the *Diagnostic and Statistical Manual of Mental Disorders (Third Edition)* (American Psychiatric Association, 1980) may have a similar influence, calling into question major assumptions that guide assessment and intervention.

Training

Is it possible to move students from asking practice questions that are based only on experiential knowledge to those based on more abstract knowledge? Methods that teach students to apply whole theories to individual cases may discourage the consideration of evidence and facts. They do not teach the consideration of inferences or encourage the conceptualization of alternatives. It may be a mistake to think that there is a difference between the science of practice and research or in the way practitioners and researchers think. We need to look closely at what we educators do to develop students' thinking and curiosity.

In the discussion, models that are used to train students to work with children were cited as an example. Scott Briar noted that in training for work with children, social work students are taught that they should apply various theories of child development. This teaching continues, despite the fact that current research has linked few of these theories to effective practice with children. Such training may be based more on ideology than on the reality of practice. Unfortunately, students carry the ideology with them and continue to practice from that perspective, not questioning its true utility if they are not taught the openness of a scientific perspective. It is not that students lack curiosity, but that educational methods do not cultivate their curiosity.

These training issues raised more general questions as well. Why are social work researchers and educators not more concerned with how the products of research get to consumers? Is the problem one of dissemination, rather than of utilization? Should the task be to focus on providing research information to practitioners in ways in which they regularly acquire new information, rather than in academically convenient formats?

Increasing Dissemination and Utilization

Among the pragmatic considerations for improving research utilization is the need to identify the conditions that are necessary for stimulating curiosity. Educators struggle between teaching students to be competent and teaching them to be critical. The scarcity of studies on empirically based practice that could directly inform practice and demonstrate reflective questioning within practice contributes to this problem.

The suggestions offered to ameliorate this problem incorporate the arguments of Gordon, LeCroy, and Schilling: (1) use available methods and techniques, as Schilling recommended; (2) increase researchers' understanding of practitioners' thinking, as LeCroy argued; and (3) stand outside the research-education world view to explore practitioners' perceptions, values, and interests, as Gordon suggested. All these actions are necessary to identify more appropriate and effective means of communication. How do practitioners think about practice problems? How do they regard themselves as problem solvers? What are the primary values that guide the practitioner's search for new information? What motivates practitioners to be curious and accept new information? The actions that follow the examination of these issues must be constructive and collaborative. It is particularly important that practitioners regard them as constructive, not as condescending.

Expecting individual practitioners to collect, synthesize, and translate research into practice is unrealistic. Rather, educators and others who are concerned with providing research information to practitioners should take on the role of "information agent." Information agents would be formally responsible for gathering, synthesizing, and disseminating information on practice through such avenues as workshops.

THE FUTURE OF RHETORIC

If the function of rhetoric is to persuade, the earlier rhetoric of research utilization failed. It did not inspire practitioners to read, use, or conduct more research. It did not stop researchers from conducting agency-based research (Blythe, 1989). Nor did it convince the Council on Social Work Education's (CSWE) Commission on Accreditation or clients

(Campbell, 1988) that the application of practice evaluation principles does not enhance the conduct of practice.

The rhetoric has had an impact, however. It appears to have stimulated some proponents to question the original goal of research utilization: to improve practice and practice knowledge through the use of systematically based, empirical information. The persistent overreification of the roles of practitioner and researcher is one indication of its impact. Weary-sounding comments throughout the discussion reflected many years of frustrated attempts to work against the rhetoric. Expert practitioners were described as being more likely to "give up hypotheses" than were researchers. Published research was accused of espousing a narrow "party" line. Research in agencies was described as not popular and not permitted (it is not clear whether this restriction extended to practice evaluation activities), and the lack of competition in providing social work services was cited as an indicator of the low demand for accountability by both funders and consumers. Researchers were accused of engaging in semantic power struggles by attempting to make practitioners adopt the language of research.

There was general agreement that the earlier rhetoric of research utilization did not serve researchers or practitioners well. Many participants also noted that the field has moved beyond that rhetoric in the past decade. For example, Fraser, Lewis, and Norman's (1989) survey of graduate social work programs found that over 80 percent of the respondents agreed either "quite a lot" or "completely" with CSWE's (1988) requirement that students be prepared to evaluate their own practice. There is evidence of efforts by agency staffs to initiate clinical research activities (Durkin, 1988; Grasso, Epstein, & Tripodi, 1988) that are apparently independent of the efforts of educators or encouragement from the literature (Blythe, 1989). Earlier, more rigid definitions of what constitutes empirical clinical practice and the application of evaluation principles have been adapted to meet the exigencies of agency practice (Blythe & Tripodi, 1989). Changing information technologies that provide feedback to practitioners and avenues for communication create possibilities for research utilization that cannot be measured by the number of journal articles a practitioner reads (Bronson & Blythe, 1987; Schilling, Schinke, & Gilchrist, 1985).

REFERENCES

American Psychiatric Association. (1980). *Diagnostic and statistical manual of mental disorders* (3rd ed.). Washington, DC: Author.

Blythe, B. J. (1989, May). *Evolution and future development of clinical research utilization in agency settings.* Paper presented at the conference, Research Utilization: A Decade of Practice, Detroit.

Blythe, B. J., & Tripodi, T. (1989). *Measurement in direct social work practice: Guidelines for practitioners.* Newbury Park, CA: Sage Publications.

Bronson, D., & Blythe, B. J. (1987). Computer support for single-case evaluation of practice. *Social Work Research & Abstracts, 23*(3), 10–13.

Campbell, J. A. (1988). Client acceptance of single-system evaluation procedures. *Social Work Research & Abstracts, 24,* 21–22.

Council on Social Work Education. (1988). *Handbook of accreditation standards and procedures.* Washington, DC: Author.

Durkin, R. (1988). The Sage Hill behavior rating system: Some of its clinical, administrative, and research uses. *Journal of Child Care,* 19–29.

Fischer, J. (1973). Is casework effective? A review. *Social Work, 18,* 5–20.

Fraser, M. W., Lewis, R. E., & Norman, J. L. (1989, March). *Research education in M.S.W. programs: Four competing perspectives.* Paper presented at the Annual Program Meeting, Council on Social Work Education, Chicago.

Grasso, A. J., Epstein, I., & Tripodi, T. (1988). Agency-based research utilization in a residential child care setting. *Administration in Social Work, 12,* 61–80.

Kirk, S. A., & Kutchins, H. (1988). Deliberate misdiagnosis in mental health practice. *Social Service Review, 62,* 225–237.

Kutchins, H., & Kirk, S. A. (1986). The reliability of DSM-III: A critical review. *Social Work Research & Abstracts, 22,* 3–12.

Kutchins, H., & Kirk, S. A. (1988). The business of diagnosis: DSM-III and clinical social work. *Social Work, 33,* 215–220.

Schilling, R. F., Schinke, S. P., & Gilchrist, L. D. (1985). Utilization of social work research: Reaching the practitioner. *Social Work, 30,* 527–529.

Chapter 10

Clinical Significance: Problems and New Developments

Srinika Jayaratne

Researchers make a clear distinction between "statistical significance" or "experimental significance" and "clinical importance" or "applied significance" (Gingerich, 1985; Rankin & Marsh, 1985). It is the latter that is typically equated with "clinical significance." For example, Barlow, Hayes, and Nelson (1984) noted that "a statistically significant result can be very trivial indeed and be very far from the usual meaning of the word significant" (p. 28). They went on to argue that clinical significance deals with individual well-being, whereas statistical significance says nothing about the individual; Bloom and Fischer (1982) stated that "one can have practical (that is, clinical) significance but not statistical significance and vice versa" (p. 397). Hersen and Barlow (1976) claimed that "if treatment effects are not obvious, a fortiori, their clinical value probably has not been demonstrated. This condition is not rectified by assessing statistical significance" (p. 311). And, according to Jacobson, Follette, and Revenstorf (1984) "a change in therapy is clinically significant when the client moves from the dysfunctional to the functional range during the course of therapy on whatever variable is being used to measure the clinical problem" (p. 340).

Despite the concerted effort to distinguish clinical significance from its statistical counterpart, Nietzel, Russell, Hemmings, and Gretter (1987) pointed out that the "empirical literature does not exist that would establish the clinical significance of treatment effects with the same confidence routinely accorded to their statistical significance" (p. 156). In fact, as Jacobson, Follette, and Revenstorf (1984) stated, "there is little consensus as to what clinical significance is, except the universal agreement that it is not merely statistical significance" (p. 338).

The foregoing comments by researchers establish a functional difference between statistical significance and clinical significance, an approach to which the author is in full agreement. If statistics has a place in the measurement of clinical significance, it is at best secondary. In defining clinical significance, the goal should be to assess the relative progress of a specific client system during treatment or as a result of some intervention. Whether the same treatment of a different client system by the same therapist in the same context results in a similar change is a different issue. The two should not be tied together a priori for the purposes of establishing clinical significance. Clinical significance, therefore, should stand apart from statistics, since as Jacobson, Follette, and Revenstorf (1984) correctly pointed out, "clinical significance is conceptually independent of psychometric considerations" (p. 498). This position on the nature of significance does not preclude the use of statistics. It does, however, limit the role of statistics to a subsidiary status.

DEFINITIONS

In examining the clinical research literature, it is difficult to come up with definitions of *clinical,* which appears less frequently than *treatment* and *intervention.* Consider the following examples. Hoch (1965), in trying to define the process of treatment, argued that "treatment behavior is everything the patient does in the treatment situation" (p. 69). This perspective ignores the behavior of the therapist. Erikson (1977), in describing the evidence provided in the psychotherapeutic encounter, noted that "this will consist of my reporting to you what a patient said to me, how he behaved in doing so and what I, in turn, thought and did" (p. 138). In contrast to the first definition, this definition sees the clinical situation as truly interactive. Thomas (1984) defined an intervention as "a planned intrusion into the life or environment of an individual, couple, family, or other target unit that is intended to bring about beneficial changes for the individuals or others involved" (p. 29). This definition recognizes, at least implicitly, that treatment is a possible independent variable and thus brings the concept closer to a research perspective.

Although Thomas's definition of *clinical* appears to be relatively congruent with that of other researchers, the pragmatic determination of clinical significance may cross the boundaries of the traditionally defined treatment environment—that of the worker and client system. A worker may use not only his or her observations and those of the client system in determining clinical significance, but also information from "significant" others in the client system's environment—family members, employers, coworkers, or friends. Similarly, clients may judge their clinical progress not only through self-assessment and evaluation, but also through observations of others' responses to their behaviors. What is of import to these others may also be of clinical import to the worker and the client. In other words, the parameters included in the attribution of clinical significance by these others may play a critical role in the attribution of clinical success by the practitioner and the client.

In light of these issues, the author proposes the following definition as a basis for the discussion in the remainder of this chapter: *Clinical significance is the perception of an important change in an attribute or behavior in oneself or another as a result of treatment*. This definition of clinical significance relates the importance of change to perception and is similar to that proposed by Hayes and Haas (1988), who contended that significance is "the practical importance of behavioral improvement" (p. 189). The inclusion of perception in the definition allows for individual differences in levels of perceived significance, as well as differences in expectancy. Two individuals who observe the same behavior may expect different levels of change, and once some change has occurred, they may judge the level of significance of the change differently. As is argued later, the meaning of significance is unalterably tied to individual expectancy and perception, so to understand significance, one must pay attention to individual attributional processes. And when one pays attention to attributions, one is paying attention to the process of determining clinical significance. Therefore, the study of clinically significant outcomes must occur in conjunction with the study of the process of determining clinical significance.

THE ROLE OF ATTRIBUTION

Attribution theory is predicated on the assumption that people search for the meaning of events around them. This search is an active process—whether the consequences of the events are positive or negative—if the events are of importance to that individual. In other words, people try to interpret the meaning of events through the attributional processes of explanation and prediction.

Although explanation and prediction have not been core elements in the definition of clinical significance, it is indeed arguable that the judgment of significance carries with it a sense of expectancy with regard to future behavior. For example, if a practitioner indicates that there has been a significant change in the self-deprecatory statements made by a client, it is likely that the practitioner assumes that this change will be maintained at least for some time and hence is predicting the client's future behavior. It is not likely that a practitioner would judge a change to be significant if he or she believed the change to be temporary. If the practitioner believes that an important change has been achieved, but is uncertain about its long-term maintenance, then it is likely that he or she will lower or moderate the level of significance attributed to this change. Furthermore, it is probable that the practitioner's perceptions of this client's behavior in other domains will be influenced by this perception (something similar to autocorrelation in a statistical sense). Thus, an attributional analysis would allow researchers to examine why an event or behavior is deemed to be significant or important by a given individual at a given point. The question of whether this behavior or event will be maintained in the future at the attained level of significance is an empirical question—one that should be incorporated into the analysis of clinical significance.

The components of the process of the construct are determined by the constituent elements of attribution theory. If one were to present this process in the form of a model, it would be as follows:

Action + intention + disposition = clinical significance

The reporting of clinical significance is a function of the observed action, the intentions attached to that action, and the allocation of a dispositional source to that action by the observer making the report. Although action, intention, and disposition are proposed as the constituent elements included in the determination of clinical significance, their relative contribution remains an empirical question. In other words, do intention and disposition, for example, have equal weights in the explanation of a given clinical situation? The weights would probably shift, depending on particular person-situation configurations. Whether these weights would remain constant over different cases for the same reporter is a difficult but important empirical question. To understand better the nature of clinical significance in a given situation, one must assess the existence and degree of each of these components of clinical significance. The failure to do so would be analogous to measuring clinical outcome without paying attention to the clinical process. Therefore, the author proposes that the measurement of the process of clinical significance be distinguished from the measurement of outcome in clinical significance.

COMPONENTS OF CLINICAL SIGNIFICANCE

Observation of Actions

In a practice situation, a clinician constantly assesses and evaluates what he or she perceives and takes action accordingly. Similarly, the client acts in accordance with what he or she perceives to be the demands made of him or her by the worker and others in the environment. These interactions, in a general sense, constitute what is termed the *process* of intervention. Since the interactions are inevitably tied to the achievement of some explicit or implicit goals of treatment, they would be intimately tied to the evaluation of change. Thus, even if questions that pertain to the process of intervention are not asked, the determination of clinical significance would be strongly correlated with them. Yet, as Kazdin (1986) noted, "measures related to client reactions to treatment as well as factors reflecting the administration of treatment" (p. 102) are not part of the typical measurement of clinical significance.

Attribution theory clearly points out that the participation in these interactions, as well as the perceptions of these interactions, is an active process. The theory also argues that the interactions that are cognitively processed by anyone in the situation are a function of a variety of personal needs, biases, and other factors. The extent to which there is a better fit between the perceived needs and biases of the client and the activities and presentations of the worker should result in the greater likelihood of achieving significant clinical change (see, for example, Abramowitz, Berger, & Weary, 1982; Bordin, 1979). In fact, several researchers have concluded that lack of congruence in client/worker expectations contributes significantly toward dropout from treatment (Baekeland & Lundwall, 1975; Borghi, 1968; Fischer, 1978). Therefore, since the determination of clinical significance is inherently tied to the perception of the process of intervention, the assessment of the significance of the process (hereafter called "process significance") must be an inherent component of the measurement of clinical significance. *Process significance* is defined as the degree to which an individual's expectations of treatment are congruent with the activities that occur within the context of treatment.

Judgment of Intention

In a practice situation, the social worker's assessment and evaluation of the client's actions would be mediated by his or her judgment about the intentions of the client. So, for example, clients who do not comply with their workers' requests may be labeled "uncooperative" or "resistant," whereas those who do comply may be labeled "cooperative" and "motivated." These simple labels illustrate that similar assessments would be made in relation to all other aspects of a client's behavior. Since such assessments are judgments or perceptions of intention, they will affect the worker's view of the probability that the client will attain his or her goal or resolve his or her problem and, hence, the worker's judgment of clinical significance. The client, in turn, may perceive that the therapist's action is based on a "lack of understanding" or "inexperience," for example, and, therefore may consider the therapist's suggestions and behavior to be incongruent with his or her expectations. Thus, both parties will bring their attributional biases to bear in assessing the nature and process of treatment. The result may be differential expectations regarding the potential for achieving clinically significant change.

If one's intentions and one's perceptions of another's intentions affect the way one makes judgments, and attribution theory says they do, then the determination of intention must become a part of the process of determining clinical significance. In other words, the significance of intention should be a component in the assessment of clinical significance. The *significance of intention* is defined as the degree to which an individual accepts specified goals as being congruent with his or her expectations regarding the outcome of treatment.

Dispositional Attribution

Dispositional attribution in the clinical situation may determine in many ways the nature of the interventions selected, as well as the goals of treatment. An external causal attribution may dictate that the client's environment is in need of change, whereas an internal attribution may dictate that the client's behaviors and cognitions are in need of change. In addition, there will be situations in which both the internal and external dimensions are viable targets of intervention. The potential for successful intervention in such situations may vary, depending on the client's perception of his or her control of the situation. The determination of control may be of particular importance, given the relationship between perceptions of control and motivation (Pomerleau & Rodin, 1986; Wortman, 1975) and the finding that "greater feelings of control have been shown to enhance satisfaction and performance in a variety of situations" (Pomerleau & Rodin, 1986, p. 499). Thus, an attempt must be made to determine the dispositional significance for a given case. *Dispositional significance* is defined as the degree of control that an individual is perceived to have in a given situation. In the research context, it may include the perceptions of the client, the worker, and possibly significant others.

In summary, the separate measurement of these elements is necessary to understand the process of determining clinical significance. They are the core elements that individual practitioners and their clients, as well as significant others, may utilize, but not necessarily express, when they assess the nature of change that has occurred. By gaining a better understanding of these elements, researchers will get a better handle on what is meant by clinical significance.

THE CLINICAL SIGNIFICANCE OF OUTCOME

As was noted earlier, there is no consensus about the meaning of clinical significance. However, the numerous suggestions were well articulated by Gingerich (1985). In stark contrast to the foregoing discussion, all these definitions emphasize the outcome component of clinical significance. The following are some of the more prominent methods that have been proposed for determining the clinical significance of outcome.

Social Comparison

In a social comparison, the level of functioning of a peer or a peer group with no problems is compared to the level of functioning of a client or group of clients (Kazdin, 1977). Jacobson, Follette, and Revenstorf (1984) proposed that clinical significance is achieved only when a client moves from a dysfunctional range to a functional range on some criterion variable during the course of treatment. Thus, for example, the truancy rates of boys displaying academic problems with those who are performing adequately in school could be compared.

This procedure assumes, of course, that data on such a comparative group are available and uses group normative data, thereby ignoring significant changes within individuals. On the other hand, each individual is judged on whether he or she falls within the parameters of the normative group. Neither the worker nor the client is actively involved in determining whether clinical significance has been achieved. Thus, the level of the goal to be achieved is abstract (albeit predetermined) and is independent of a particular client, worker, or significant other. Gingerich (1985) considered social comparison to be "the most rigorous and objective assessment of applied significance" (p. 716).

It is questionable, however, whether such a procedure would make any sense with a severely disturbed population or an individual who cannot achieve "normality" for whatever reason. Thus, an individual who shows an obviously dramatic change on some scale but still does not fall within the normative category would, by definition, have to be judged as not having achieved significant change. In addition, the assumption of normality has some problems with respect to values and cultural biases, which may be easily overlooked with this procedure.

Goal-Attainment Scaling

In goal-attainment scaling, the worker identifies a series of expected outcome levels (goals) for an individual client. The levels range from the worst possible to the best possible anticipated outcomes (Kiresuk & Lund, 1978). This procedure was not designed to determine clinical significance. Its use for this purpose was suggested by Gingerich (1985) on the basis that "a goal or standard of adequate performance is established before treatment. . . . If the goal is achieved, the client change has attained a level of applied significance" (p. 700).

Although this argument is appealing because of its very simplicity, this procedure is typically based on the worker's judgment alone. Involvement of the client is typically not a part of goal-specification process (although nothing inherent in the procedure would prevent its inclusion), and the goals reflect the perceptions of the worker. Furthermore, the anticipated level of goal attainment is tied to an expected outcome six weeks from the date of completion of the scale. This latter criterion raises a variety of questions about worker's expectations and perceptions of control, long-term goals, and so on.

Mutual Goal Attainment

This method is different from goal-attainment scaling in that it involves the specification of agreed-upon goals by the worker and the client and it does not establish a series of possible outcomes. Thus, it resembles a contract-based approach to treatment. As Gingerich (1985) pointed out, "assuming that a realistic goal has been set for the client . . . one simply notes whether the client's performance has reached the desired goal" (p. 696).

This method assumes that such a goal can be set "honestly," that is, without the worker's coercion or the imposition of power as occurs when a set of goals for a child is proposed by parents and supported by the worker or when goals are set according to legal guidelines and judicial requirements. When coercion and power are used, mutual agreement on goals is a result of obligation, rather than choice, and the concept of mutuality is simply a figment of the imagination. Furthermore, this method pays little attention to what significant others may have to say about such goals. Clearly, it could benefit considerably from the involvement of others in the specification process and by acceptance of the possibility that there are likely to be divergent and even contradictory goals.

Subjective Comparison

In this method, which was suggested by Kazdin (1977), "qualified individuals" who know the client make judgments about the improvement of the client. By qualified individuals is meant significant others whose lives will be affected by the client or whose behaviors could affect the life of the client. These assessments are based on personal observations with no regard to any explicitly stated group or comparative norm.

Since these are perceptual measures, there is bound to be a divergence of perspectives among the observers, which Kazdin saw as a problem, owing to concerns about reliability and validity. This procedure, by design, does not constrain the observer by the provision of a strict definition. Rather, the format may be similar to that used in the measurement of global indicators in the assessment of quality of life or quality of work (see, for example, Andrews & Withey, 1976).

CRITIQUE

Of the procedures just discussed, the one that has gained the most prominence is social comparison, proposed by Jacobson and his colleagues (Jacobson, Follette, & Revenstorf, 1984; Jacobson & Revenstorf, 1988). Although this approach has much appeal, there are two major problems with it. First, its proponents argue that it is far better to have a normative "cutoff point" with regard to clinical success. The author finds this a difficult proposition for many of the reasons stated earlier. In addition, experiences with cutoff points with such nonclinical indicators as the Graduate Record Examination, the Scholastic Aptitude Test, and intelligence quotient have been far from successful. The clinical arena presents a much more difficult challenge in this respect. This proposition, therefore, has some serious negative implications from both an experiential and a cultural perspective.

Second, Jacobson and Revenstorf's (1988) statement that "most consumers, when they enter psychotherapy, expect to be as normal as their functional counterparts by the time therapy has ended" (p. 134) places the definition of normality on the consumer. It is not clear what role the definitions of normality proposed by the practitioner play in this situation and how the standardized normative data fit in. One could visualize a situation in which a worker showed percentile graphs and normative ranges to a client to convince the client that there was clinical success, while the client sat there still depressed. In other words, although the perceptions of the client are important, it is also important to determine the reasons for these perceptions (attributions) and to ensure that these attributions then play a role in building a better definition of clinical significance.

In general, it is difficult to disagree with any one or a combination of these approaches to the measurement of outcome in clinical significance, but it is easy to find fault with them. Although all make good sense for given problems and situations, they all present problems in other contexts.

In addition, of course, other equally good procedures have probably been left out of this presentation. For example, pretest-posttest comparison is a simple and widely employed strategy to determine clinical significance. However, it requires the use of statistical tests; therefore, given the author's emphasis on clinical as opposed to statistical significance, it is not a primary option. One obvious question emerges when one examines these procedures: Do they have to be mutually exclusive? Although the answer may be no, and the desired method may be one of multifactorial measurement, the practicality of such a complex measurement strategy remains to be seen. A research agenda that explores these possibilities as options, alternatives, and correlates would be valuable.

FURTHER ISSUES

Given the discussion and some of the implicit assumptions in the procedures cited, some additional issues are presented here. These issues are presented as caveats, since they are necessary elements in the determination of the outcome component of clinical significance.

Multiple sources of information are necessary. In a "real" clinical situation, many individuals will be affected by any change in a client system. These individuals, who are typically called "significant others," must be a part of the process of determining clinical significance. Although the ratings of individuals tend to be unstable, combining them in some way may result in increasing the overall stability of the estimates (Beutler & Hamblin, 1986). Therefore, the inclusion of significant others as a source of information in a study of clinical significance study is a requirement.

Disagreement is a reality of practice. Although it may be highly desirable from an objective empirical position to have mutually agreed-upon goals—that is, goals on which the worker, the client, and possibly significant others agree—the probability of achieving them is remote. It is important to note, for example, that disagreement on goals does not necessarily mean that the goals are contradictory goals; they may simply indicate different levels of attainment. When there is such disagreement, recognizing it and assessing it may result in a clearer picture of clinical significance than attempting to monitor a consensus goal. Thus, this lack of consensus should be treated as a reality of practice and a viable research issue, rather than as a clinical setback or a research conundrum. In fact, some may even argue that the lack of consensus is a clinical problem and that the achievement of consensus is a clinical goal. Therefore, one should not only expect different parties to have different goals, but one should also attempt systematically to gather information on the perceptions of change in the client, as well as changes in the worker's perceptions as a function of the client's change. Thus, the attainment of clinical significance does not necessarily produce a unitary figure, but rather a composite picture.

The attainment of goals is a transient process. Much of the research on clinical significance tends to discuss goals or changes as having a finite end. It is likely, however, that as treatment progresses, not only goals but the desired levels for the achievement of goals may change. These changes are likely to occur when the client acquires further skills and knowledge and the attributional processes in which an individual engages change. Therefore, it is desirable to view clinical significance as a process of changing criteria and systematically to assess the degree to which each of these criteria are being achieved. To some extent, this strategy implies a flexible approach to the measurement of the significance of outcome—a strategy that may be more amenable to time-series data

Global measures of change may not be as bad as they sound. Global ratings have been condemned for overestimating the amount of change (see, for example, Garfield, Praeger, & Bergin, 1971). On the other hand, studies have clearly demonstrated that both specific and general measures of outcome contribute to general ratings (see, for example, Cartwright, Kirtner, & Fiske, 1963; Green, Gleser, Stone, & Siefert, 1975), and an extensive methodology on global ratings of satisfaction is emerging in the areas of life satisfaction, job satisfaction, consumer satisfaction, and health-outcome satisfaction. How applicable these models will be in the mental health arena and how they will contribute to the determination of clinical significance remains to be seen. To eliminate such strategies from the process perfunctorily would be unfortunate. Therefore, global ratings of change that are obtained from multiple sources should be encouraged.

CONCLUSION

In discussing the attributional factors related to the determination of clinical significance, I proposed a model that takes into consideration both the process factors that lead to the *determination* of clinical significance and outcome factors that may lead to the *reporting* of clinical significance. The model, as proposed here, would allow for individual variation and perceptual differences and would not rely on a consensus definition of a goal or outcome criterion. Undoubtedly, this kind of approach would result in some major problems and issues in measurement. But, like most other problems, they could probably be resolved. Instead of accepting clinical significance as a given, we should treat it as a dependent variable in research—at least until we can agree on what it is.

Some Additional Questions

Should the determination of clinical significance occur only after the passage of time? The tendency has been to talk about clinical significance at the point of termination of treatment. This question does not encompass those interventions that seem to have a lag before change occurs (although it well may). Rather, the question is related more to the idea that a "real" clinical change would be something that is expected to have some lasting effect. One could think of a set of concepts—similar to those proposed by Rosen and Proctor (1981) and Greenberg (1986) for distinguishing among ultimate outcomes, instrumental outcomes, and intermediate outcomes— that could help in this endeavor.

Should the determination of social desirability be an inherent part of clinical significance? Practitioners engage in an array of activities to maximize the probability that they are getting reasonably accurate information from their clients. The purpose is simply to deliver the best possible service. Clearly, clients' willingness to divulge information about themselves and others could be affected by social desirability—even under the best clinical circumstances. Although much of the discussion of social desirability centers on responses to self-report inventories and much of the clinical information is gathered via interviews, social desirability could be an equally important element in verbal self-reports. In fact, Strosahl, Linehan, and Chiles (1984) reported, in relation to suicidal situations, that "prediction accuracy is enhanced by including social desirability assessment, particularly among psychiatric patients" (p. 449). Given multiple sources of information, one could predict considerable variance in goals and attributions. Some or all these goals and attributions could be influenced by social desirability. Given a willingness to accept individual differences in perceptions and attributions, would the determination of social desirability contribute to the attainment of some degree of consensus among goals?

Should clinical significance be determined independently by statistical means in addition to subjective assessments? Several authors have proposed the computation of explained variance and effect sizes for determining clinical significance (see, for example, Hays, 1963; Hudson, Thyer, & Stocks, 1985). Since these computations occur after the fact, this information may have little impact on the immediate processes of treatment (although such data could be used to achieve administrative and organizational changes). Furthermore, statistics could help in the decision, although many clinicians and an increasing number of researchers are skeptical. As Stevens (1968) asked, "Can no one recognize a decisive result without a significance test?" (p. 883).

Clearly, there is no simple solution to the determination of clinical significance. Emphasizing the outcome aspects of clinical significance results in a lack of understanding of the rationale behind the decision. It provides a half-truth. Emphasizing the process aspects of clinical significance leads researchers in no particular direction regarding useful measures of outcome in clinical significance. An equal emphasis on both process and outcome will, this author believes, provide better answers.

REFERENCES

Abramowitz, S. I., Berger, A., & Weary, G. (1982). Similarity between clinician and client: Its influences on the helping relationship. In T. A. Wills (Ed.), *Basic processes in helping relationships* (pp. 357–379). New York: Academic Press.

Andrews, F. M., & Withey, S. B. (1976). *Social indicators of well-being.* New York: Plenum Press.

Baekeland, F., & Lundwall, L. (1975). Dropping out of treatment: A critical review. *Psychological Bulletin, 82,* 738–783.

Barlow, D. H., Hayes, S. C., & Nelson, R. O. (1984). *The scientist-practitioner: Research and accountability in clinical and educational settings.* New York: Pergamon Press.

Beutler, L. E., & Hamblin, D. L. (1986). Individualized outcome measures of internal change: Methodological considerations. *Journal of Consulting and Clinical Psychology, 54,* 48–53.

Bloom, M., & Fischer, J. (1982). *Evaluating practice: Guidelines for the accountable professional.* Englewood Cliffs, NJ: Prentice-Hall.

Bordin, E. S. (1979). The generalizability of the psychodynamic concept of working alliance. *Psychotherapy: Theory, Research & Practice, 16,* 252–260.

Borghi, J. (1968). Premature termination of psychotherapy and patient-therapist expectations. *American Journal of Psychotherapy, 22,* 460–473.

Cartwright, D. S., Kirtner, W. L., & Fiske, D. W. (1963). Method factors associated with changes in psychotherapy. *Journal of Consulting and Clinical Psychology, 66,* 164–175.

Erikson, E. H. (1977). The nature of clinical evidence. In S. J. Morse, & R. I. Watson (Eds.), *Psychotherapies: A comparative casebook* (pp. 138–148). New York: Holt, Rinehart & Winston.

Fischer, J. (1978). *Effective casework practice: An eclectic approach.* New York: McGraw-Hill.

Garfield, S. L., Praeger, R. A., & Bergin, A. E. (1971). Evaluation of outcome in psychotherapy. *Journal of Consulting and Clinical Psychology, 37,* 307–313.

Gingerich, W. J. (1985). Significance testing in single-case research. In A. Rosenblatt & D. Waldfogel (Eds.), *Handbook of clinical social work* (pp. 694–720). San Francisco: Jossey-Bass.

Green, B. C., Gleser, G. C., Stone, W. N., & Siefert, R. F. (1975). Relationships among diverse measures of psychotherapy outcomes. *Journal of Consulting and Clinical Psychology, 43,* 689–699.

Greenberg, L. S. (1986). Change process research. *Journal of Consulting and Clinical Psychology, 54*, 4–9.

Hayes, S. C., & Haas, J. R. (1988). A reevaluation of the concept of clinical significance: Goals, methods, and methodology. *Behavioral Assessment, 10*, 189–196.

Hays, W. L. (1963). *Statistics for psychologists.* New York: Holt, Rinehart, & Winston.

Hersen, M., & Barlow, D. H. (1976). *Single case experimental designs: Strategies for studying behavior change.* New York: Pergamon.

Hoch, P. H. (1965). Short-term versus long-term therapy. In L. R. Wolberg (Ed.), *Short-term psychotherapy* (pp. 51–66). New York: Grune & Stratton.

Hudson, W. W., Thyer, B. A., & Stocks, J. T. (1985). Assessing the importance of experimental outcomes. *Journal of Social Service Research, 8*, 87–98.

Jacobson, N. S., Follette, W. C., & Revenstorf, D. (1984). Psychotherapy outcome research: Methods for reporting variability and evaluating clinical significance. *Behavior Therapy, 15*, 336–352.

Jacobson, N. S., & Revenstorf, D. (1988). Statistics for assessing the clinical significance of psychotherapy techniques: Issues, problems, and new developments. *Behavioral Assessment, 10*, 133–145.

Kazdin, A. E. (1977). Assessing the clinical and applied importance of behavior change through social validation. *Behavior Modification, 1*, 427–452.

Kazdin, A. E. (1986). Comparative outcome studies of psychotherapy: Methodological issues and strategies. *Journal of Consulting and Clinical Psychology, 54*, 95–105.

Kiresuk, T. J., & Lund, S. H. (1978). Goal attainment scaling. In C. C. Attkisson, W. A. Hargreaves, M. J. Horowitz, & J. E. Sorenson (Eds.), *Evaluation of human service programs* (pp. 341–370). New York: Academic Press.

Nietzel, M. T., Russell, R. L., Hemmings, K. A., & Gretter, M. L. (1987). Clinical significance of psychotherapy for unipolar depression: A meta-analytical approach to social comparison. *Journal of Consulting and Clinical Psychology, 55*, 156–161.

Pomerleau, O. R., & Rodin, J. (1986). Behavioral medicine and health psychology. In S. L. Garfield & A. E. Bergin (Eds.), *Handbook of behavior change* (3rd ed., pp. 483–522). New York: John Wiley & Sons.

Rankin, E. D., & Marsh, J. C. (1985). Effects of missing data on the statistical analysis of clinical time-series data. *Social Work Research & Abstracts, 21*, 13–16.

Rosen, A., & Proctor, E. (1981). Distinctions between treatment outcomes and their implications for treatment. *Journal of Consulting and Clinical Psychology, 49*, 418–425.

Stevens, S. S. (1968). Measurement, statistics, and the schemapiric view. *Science, 161*, 849–856.

Strosahl, K. D., Linehan, M. M., & Chiles, J. A. (1984). Will the real social desirability please stand up? Hopelessness, depression, social desirability, and the prediction of suicidal behavior. *Journal of Consulting and Clinical Psychology, 52*, 449–457.

Thomas, E. J. (1984). *Designing interventions for the helping professions.* Beverly Hills, CA: Sage Publications.

Wortman, P. M. (1983). Evaluation research: A methodological perspective. *Annual Review of Psychology, 34,* 223–260.

Attribution Theory and Clinical Significance: Further Issues

Tony Tripodi

In responding to Jayaratne's provocative chapter on clinical significance, this commentary first poses a brief example of a client with multiple goals. This example is used as an illustrative context for considering this author's perceptions of Jayaratne's contributions, some comments on his conclusions, and problems not addressed.

EXAMPLE

Suppose the goals of treatment for an adolescent boy in a public school are to increase his expression of anger with peers, decrease his depression, increase his completion of homework and grades, and maintain his school-attendance pattern.

After five treatment contacts over a period of one month, the boy does not perceive that he expresses anger to peers. The worker, however, believes that the boy's behavior is more provocative. In fact, a peer not only perceives the boy's behavior as more aggressive, but gets in a fight with him. This fight leads to the boy's suspension from school for one week, during which time he does not do any homework. He feels good; he thinks he won the fight, has gained status among his peers, and is less depressed. His mother, however, thinks he is more depressed because of her observation that he spends more time alone in his room, watching television.

Two weeks later, the boy is attending class and tries out for the football team, but is not doing any homework. The worker perceives that the boy is responding to treatment, noting that he is not depressed, as measured by the latest version of a rapid assessment instrument on depression. The boy's mother thinks he is worse, since he is less interested in doing homework. The boy thinks his treatment, which is required, is a waste of time and not helpful to him.

CONTRIBUTIONS

• Using attribution theory, *Jayaratne offers a model that can serve as a frame of reference for studying clinical significance as a perception of judgment.* This model incorporates parameters of process and outcome in proposing research that may contribute to the psychology of interpersonal perception. In relation to the example, changes in each dependent variable and the attributed importance of those changes by the worker, mother, client, and peer could be studied. Increased expression of anger might be regarded as a criterion that could be predicted by components of the model, such as the client's expectancy of perceived changes in his verbal expressions. For each dependent variable, a multidimensional model might be hypothesized, for example, in which process and expectancy variables would be combined in various mathematical modeling procedures for the purpose of prediction. Of course, the procedures for identifying such predictors might be laborious and cumbersome; that is, as Jayaratne indicated, measurement would be difficult.

• *The construct of clinical significance is separated from that of statistical significance.* This statement means that one could discuss significant changes by referring to criteria other than statistical change. Subjective judgments that were deemed important could be used to decide on changes observed in the network of worker-client system interactions. Depending on the objectives of the worker, the failure to attend school might be regarded as clinically significant, even though it is socially undesirable. Graphic analysis, predetermined levels of change, and posttherapeutic perceptions of change could be employed as long as their importance was attributed to such change.

• *The importance of perspectives by persons other than the worker are emphasized.* In the example, it is obvious that there can be congruence or disparity among the perceptions of the mother, the worker, the client, and the peer.

• *It is emphasized that the magnitude of change may vary over different points in time.* The client in the example may be perceived as making progress, not changing, or deteriorating as a function of when measurements are taken.

COMMENTS ON CONCLUSIONS

• Jayaratne concluded that although it is difficult to define, clinical significance should be treated as a dependent variable, with multidimensional models constructed to explain and predict it. If the dependent variable is difficult to specify and may be defined subjectively as different by researchers, workers, clients, and significant others, it would seem that the number of hypothetical models developed would be unlimited; that is, many dependent variables might be regarded as clinically significant for one client, as well as for multiple sets of clients. An alternative research stance would be to work on operational definitions of clinical judgment until there is more agreement; otherwise, one might seek to define alternate concepts that are relatively more tractable.

• Not only are the dependent variables of clinical significance elusive, but so are the presumed explanatory variables, such as expectancies of goals and of treatment outcomes. Obviously, expectancies can change throughout the treatment process. The worker's assertions of subjective probabilities about the client's expression of anger and feelings of depression can change from interview to interview, for example. The specification of these components would be difficult, particularly if a worker is seeking to make judgments of clinical significance during treatment. A methodological problem that would need to be solved is when measurements of predictor variables should be taken. More than likely, one would first have to study the natural history of the variables that are identified and measured.

• In the literature referred to by Jayaratne, the constructs of practical significance and clinical significance have been employed to examine the meaning of statistical significance and to illustrate that statistically significant changes may or may not be clinically important. One may argue that the construct of clinical significance is not necessary if not used in this manner, particularly if the construct adds more noise to the process of judgment. A less abstract concept is that of "important change," which is necessary for clinicians to understand when they make decisions about termination or the referral of clients. Whether one studies clinical significance or "important change," the problems of establishing definitions and criteria that Jayaratne and others have indicated will remain.

• By emphasizing "perception" in his definition of clinical significance, Jayaratne stressed the phenomenological aspects of judgments of clinical significance. Of course, defining clinical significance in this way makes for a better fit with attributional theory. However, what becomes critical is how perceptions are valued and how those values are to be weighted in the perceptual process. Moreover, behavioral change and perceptions of behavioral change are not necessarily congruent. Hence, the client in the example may not perceive changes in his own behavior, as was noted by his lack of perception of expressed anger toward peers. The potential problem is that Jayaratne's definition may not necessarily include behavioral changes in clients. A researcher, for example, may measure and perceive changes, but the researcher may not be regarded as a worker, client, peer, or significant other.

PROBLEMS NOT ADDRESSED

• Much of the discussion of clinical significance focuses on the objectives of change. It is obvious that there are many treatment objectives that are centered on maintenance, the prevention of new problems, and the avoidance of relapse. *Hence, discussions of clinical significance also should focus on "no change goals."* For example, one goal for the client in the example was to maintain his pattern of school attendance; since his pattern changed at one month, his behavior indicated the lack of goal attainment. One may argue that "no change goals" are merely the obverse of "change goals" and that the way to observe whether "no change goals" are maintained is to study "change variables" over specified periods to observe whether negative or clinically undesirable changes occur.

• Although Jayaratne discussed the inclusion of different perspectives, he did not indicate how it should be accomplished. Clinical judgments are multidimensional, consisting of different judges, different variables, and different measurement times. How are these various components of outcomes to be aggregated? Or should they be combined? For the client in the example, does one talk about a separate clinical significance for the expression of anger, school attendance, depression, and other variables, distinctly for the worker, the client, the mother, and the peer? Or does one make a composite rating? The basic problem is that the multidimensional aspects of combined models, assignments of weights, and so forth are ignored. Consider this example: Suppose the client is less depressed, but is doing worse in school, and that change is regarded as clinically significant by the worker, but not by the client, and only partially by the mother. What is clinically significant? If it is a matter of subjective perceptions, are all perceptions equally valued? These and many other questions can be raised about the multidimensional aspects of clinical significance.

• The outcome strategies presented by Jayaratne and others in the literature from which he cited were focused on a priori sets of goals, norms, and values. *It is possible, such as in the evaluation of programs, that many benefits of treatment cannot be known in advance and that there may be a posteriori observations that result in positive or negative unanticipated outcomes?* In the example provided, the boy may have strengthened a relationship with his father because of his football activities, which, in turn, may have resulted in more positive familial interactions. Is this information not clinically significant because there were no previously stated goals and expectations?

In sum, Jayaratne's article is interesting and original. Whether his proposals for research will clarify the construct of clinical significance remains to be seen. Nevertheless, his chapter stimulates thought and, it is hoped, will lead to fruitful discussions by researchers and practitioners.

The Use of Decision Theory to Explicate the Process of Clinical Decision Making

Rona L. Levy

In Chapter 10, Jayaratne takes an important step forward in explicating the process of determining clinical significance by moving it into the realm of social psychological theory. Social psychological theory provides an extensive database of research that can be used directly and can provide a model for further research in the area of clinical significance. The specific area that Jayaratne discussed is attribution theory.

From the clinician's perspective, Jayaratne described the process of intervention as one in which "a clinician [first] constantly assesses and evaluates what he or she perceives and [second] takes action accordingly." Thus, he addressed the assessment and evaluation of perception. I propose the addition of another social psychological theory that has its own database—specifically, decision theory—to explicate the second part of his description, the action-taking component.

Elsewhere (Levy, 1978), I discussed the use of decision theory to study the process of clinical decision making during assessment and throughout treatment. The basic reasons for using decision theory are twofold. First, most of the information received during the clinical process is "compromised" in the sense that the validity and reliability of these data may be called into question. As Mahoney (1978) stated, "Let us . . . dismiss the notion of an ideal experiment and instead devote our attention to the continuum of fallible effort along which all experiments must fall" (p. 660). What is true for experiments is even more true for clinical activities. Second, there are a number of choice points throughout the clinical interaction in which the decision process is most evident. The first point usually is when an assessment strategy is chosen. Given the options available with a particular case, a therapist must choose assessment strategies that are practical in light of that case and that will yield useful data. A subsequent choice point is when an intervention strategy is selected. This decision is made on the basis of, among other things, knowledge; personal experience; and, again, feasibility. The goal in this decision is to choose an intervention that will enhance the client's chances of meeting some selected criterion. A third important decision point in single-subject designs is when to alter phases. The decision to change from a nonintervention (baseline) phase to intervention may be the result of the clinician's determination that he or she has an accurate assessment of preintervention levels of behavior. This decision also may be affected by the determination that, whatever the baseline level, the client is not at the clinical criterion level and the clinician feels pressured to begin treatment. Further decision points need not be explicated, since they are obvious.

The basic model for studying this decision-making process is the area in decision theory called *weighted utility* (Dawes & Corrigan, 1974). The position of this model is that the decision-making process may be described as one in which the decision maker weighs the pros and cons of alternative choices and then makes a choice that will maximize the potential benefits.

In the clinical situation, the clinician would need to be specific regarding the quality of each source of data and the recommendations indicated by each source for continuing in one direction or another. For example, in considering what to do after receiving a wife's report of a change in her husband's level of anger, one would give a numeric weighting to the quality (the validity) of the spouse report data and determine separately how much the change in the reported data indicates continuing in a particular direction. Further information on applying this model in a clinical situation may be found in Levy (1978).

Thus, attribution theory, as described by Jayaratne, would be useful in explaining the process by which the clinician assesses and evaluates where the client is and why the client may be at this state. Decision theory would then further elucidate the process of choosing what is to be done next.

As Jayaratne pointed out, the use of attribution theory allows one to answer such interesting questions as the weight given to the action versus intention versus disposition in the determination of clinical significance. A model expanded to include decision theory would allow one to find better answers to such questions as these: When and why is treatment terminated? How are the client's perceptions of clinical significance related to the clinician's actions? What are the content and criterion validities of the way clinicians decide how and even whether to continue treatment?

The only question I had in reading Jayaratne's chapter concerns the distinction between judgment of intention and dispositional attribution. I believe this point could be explicated further.

REFERENCES

Dawes, R. M., & Corrigan, B. (1974). Linear models in decision-making. *Psychological Bulletin, 81,* 95–106.

Levy, R. L. (1978). *Clinical conclusions from compromised data sources: The use of subjective expected utility.* Paper presented at the 12th Annual Meeting of the Association for the Advancement of Behavior Therapy, Chicago.

Mahoney, M. J. (1978). Experimental models and outcome evaluation. *Journal of Consulting and Clinical Psychology, 46,* 660–672.

Synthesis

Clinical Significance as Process and Outcome

John G. Orme

The concept of clinical significance grew, in part, out of dissatisfaction with the use of statistical significance as a criterion by which to judge the effects of intervention. Clinical significance is an alternative, and some would argue a conceptually distinct, criterion. However, the concept of clinical significance is still much in its formative stages.

In Chapter 10, Jayaratne made an important distinction between the *process* by which a judgment of clinical significance is reached and the *outcome* of this process. He noted that previous conceptualizations of clinical significance focused exclusively on the determination of outcome and that emphasizing clinical significance as the outcome of some unknown process may not be informative. Following from this conceptualization, Jayaratne argued that it would be useful to conceptualize clinical significance as a multidimensional dependent variable and to model the process by which judgments of clinical significance are reached. He proposed attribution theory as a theoretical model to explain this process. Levy, in response to Jayaratne, proposed an additional but complementary theoretical model: decision theory.

The empirical examination of the process by which judgments of clinical significance are reached would require the reliable and valid measurement of the construct of clinical significance. The valid measurement of clinical significance is a formidable task. There is no consensus even on the essential features of the conceptual definition of clinical significance, as Jayaratne noted, which makes the construct difficult to operationally define and measure. For example, Jayaratne defined clinical significance as "the perception of an important change in an attribute or behavior in oneself or another." Tripodi noted that Jayaratne's emphasis on *perceptions* of change does not necessarily include behavioral change. One may even question whether clinical significance should be conceptualized in terms of change, because change seemingly does not include the objectives of intervention that are focused on prevention and maintenance, as Tripodi stated. Finally, consensus does not exist even on the term "clinical significance," with Jayaratne, Tripodi, and some of the discussants preferring the term "importance."

The multidimensional nature of clinical significance and the disagreement over its conceptual definition have led to multiple methods for operationally defining it, and Jayaratne provided a brief overview of these methods. Each method involves the comparison of a client's functioning and some explicit or implicit criterion and a determination of whether a discrepancy exists between a client's functioning and some criterion. For example, a client's functioning may be compared with (1) the average functioning of a peer group with no problems ("social comparison"), (2) some implicit criterion determined subjectively by the client or significant others ("subjective comparison"), or (3) intervention goals set by the social worker, the client, or both. Other criteria also could be suggested, such as a comparison with a peer group that exhibits exemplary behavior, a comparison with expectations from theories of development of psychopathology, or a comparison with certain cultural norms or values.

As Jayaratne noted, the criterion or standard used in each of the methods of operationally defining clinical significance is in some way incomplete and deficient. Also, each individual method fails to incorporate all the dimensions of the construct of clinical significance or contains dimensions that are irrelevant. It is not surprising that no single method provides a completely valid indicator of clinical significance; it is generally recognized that multiple methods are necessary for the valid measurement of most constructs and certainly for one as complex as this. It is not the use of multiple methods per se that is important, however; the multiple methods must encompass all the dimensions relevant to the construct and must exclude dimensions that are irrelevant to the construct (the presentation of socially desirable responses, for example). Of course, the adequate conceptual definition is a prerequisite to determining whether the operations used to measure a construct are adequate.

Although the use of multiple methods to measure clinical significance may lead to a more valid measurement of this construct, the results of multiple methods rarely are in complete agreement. Jayaratne noted in the discussion following the presentations that little evidence exists concerning the comparability of different methods. Such disagreement creates problems for social work practitioners who require information about clinical significance to make decisions about the initiation and continuation of interventions. Jayaratne, for example, emphasized the importance of eliciting perceptions of clinical significance from multiple participants who are knowledgeable about a particular client or client system (such as the client, the social worker, significant others), and he noted that the failure to include multiple sources of information may lead to inconclusive statements about clinical significance. A consensus on clinical significance may be reached more easily on some problems than on others (for instance, physical abuse versus self-esteem), but disagreements among respondents probably are more the rule than the exception, as Jayaratne stated. As Tripodi and Levy suggested, it would be useful to formulate decision rules for practitioners, especially in cases in which different respondents or methods disagree. These rules may involve assigning different values or weights to judgments made by different respondents or methods.

Assuming the valid measurement of clinical significance using multiple indicators, theoretical models could be proposed and tested that attempt to explain the process leading to individual differences in perceptions of clinical significance. Jayaratne argued that attribution theory provides such a theoretical model. He included as the components of this model the observation of action, the determination of the intent of the action (for example, was it purposeful?), and the allocation of a disposition for the action (whether the action was motivated by internal or external considerations). For a given action, individual differences in the attribution of intentions and dispositions are hypothesized to result in individual differences in perceptions of clinical significance. In addition, attributions and, consequently, perceptions of clinical significance may change over time, necessitating the inclusion of time as an important factor in the model. Other factors also may be included in a model to explain the process by which perceptions of clinical significance are formed, such as the need to present socially desirable responses (which presumably contaminate judgments of clinical significance) and expectations of change, as Jayaratne suggested, or still other factors, such as individual differences in background characteristics, perceptions of costs and benefits, or personal and social values.

The issue of the role of personal values in making judgments of clinical significance recurred throughout the discussion of clinical significance. For example, Walter W. Hudson noted that problems do not exist in the abstract; someone must define them as such, and these definitions can be based on different value systems. Also, as was noted, Tripodi, Jayaratne, and others suggested that decisions about the importance of an outcome are at the core of clinical significance. Presumably something is not important in the abstract; rather, it is important to someone or some group for some reason. Although the inclusion of values in models attempting to explain the process by which judgments of clinical significance are reached may be useful, an interesting question raised by Anne Fortune was whether "hard science" methods are most appropriate at this time for the examination of the role of values in judgments of clinical significance.

There are still numerous unresolved problems regarding the measurement of clinical significance, as Tripodi and others so aptly illustrated. Also, the field is just beginning to articulate the processes by which judgments of clinical significance are reached. Indeed, Jayaratne's argument that it is important to understand the process by which clinical judgments are made is an important contribution to the continuing conceptualization of clinical significance. In addition, the theoretical models proposed by Jayaratne and Levy provide valuable suggestions for better understanding this process. The articulation and critical appraisal of the parameters of clinical significance presented in these articles should lead to improved procedures for understanding and determining clinical significance and, hence, improved decisions about practice and outcomes for clients.

Chapter 11

Problems and Issues in Meta-Analysis

Joel Fischer

What responsibilities do social workers have when new tools or technologies became available? The possibilities range from uncritical and total adoption of the new technology to uncritical and total rejection of the new technology. Somewhere in between lies the critical evaluation and assessment of the potential of the new technology and adoption or adaptation of those components that can withstand careful scrutiny and that appear to offer benefits for some aspects of the social work enterprise. With the advent of the methods of meta-analysis, social work has the perfect opportunity to engage in the process of careful and critical evaluation of a new technology that may have important implications for the field.

Meta-analysis is actually a generic term for a number of different methods of reviewing the empirical literature or synthesizing data. It is distinct from primary analysis (the original analysis of data in a study) and secondary analysis (reanalysis of data from a given study using better statistical procedures or answering new questions). The term *meta-analysis* (or analysis of analyses) was coined by Glass (1976) to refer to a method of statistically analyzing the findings of a number of empirical studies. Since 1976, the method developed by Glass has been refined and modified by Glass and others; in addition, a number of other "meta-analytic" methods have been developed. It is in this broader sense, then, of any method of aggregating and statistically analyzing the findings of several studies, that the term *meta-analysis* is used in this chapter.

Meta-analysis arose, in part, from dissatisfaction with the traditional, narrative review of research, which is the most common form of research review in social work (see, for example, Fischer, 1973; 1976; Maas, 1966, 1971, 1978; Mullen, Dumpson et al., 1972; Reid & Hanrahan, 1982; Rubin, 1985; Wood, 1978). In a traditional narrative review, the reviewer assembles a group of studies on a particular topic and attempts to organize a series of possibly diverse outcomes to produce a reasonably consistent overall conclusion. Although this organization may use some quantitative methods (such as totaling the number of positive outcomes and comparing the total with the number of negative outcomes, sometimes called the "box score" approach), the narrative review, to distinguish it from meta-analysis, does not attempt to aggregate findings statistically across studies to yield a standardized numerical estimate of the magnitude of the independent variable or effect size (ES). Thus, narrative reviews have been criticized as subjective (having few if any formal rules), scientifically unsound (ignoring good statistical practices), and inefficient in extracting useful information (especially when numerous studies are being reviewed) (Light & Pillemer, 1982).

In the past 10 years, meta-analysis has practically been a growth industry unto itself, especially in the fields of education and psychology, which are of special relevance to social work because of their emphasis on the meta-analysis of clinical or therapeutic services. The basic methodology has been developed and debated in dozens of books and articles (Glass, McGaw, & Smith, 1981; Green & Hall, 1984; Hedges & Olkin, 1985; Hunter, Schmidt, & Jackson, 1982; *Journal of Consulting and Clinical Psychology*, 1983; Light, 1983a; Michelson, 1985; Rosenthal, 1984; Walberg & Haertel, 1980).

At the same time, many substantive areas in the social and behavioral sciences and human services have been evaluated through meta-analytic techniques; by 1983, over 300 meta-analyses had been conducted (Kulik, 1984, cited in Bangert-Drowns, 1986), and many more have been done since then. In the 1980s, some topics of meta-analysis included psychotherapy in general (Smith, Glass, & Miller, 1980), psychotherapy versus placebos (Prioleau, Murdock, & Brody, 1983), cognitive therapy versus systematic desensitization (Berman, Miller, & Massman, 1985), family therapy (Hazelrigg, Cooper, & Borduin, 1987), psychotherapy with children (Casey & Berman, 1985), effects of professional versus nonprofessional training (Berman & Norton, 1985), deinstitutionalization in mental health (Straw, 1983), preventive health care for children (Shadish, 1982), psychotherapy versus drug therapy (Steinbrueck, Maxwell, & Howard, 1983), sex roles and mental health (Bassoff & Glass, 1982), and cognitive coping strategies (Mullen & Suls, 1982). In addition, there were numerous reviews of specific disorders and specific treatments (Shapiro, 1985) and, in education, dozens of examples, ranging from curriculum and instruction to programmatic research investigations of such issues as the effects of home environment, peer influences, and socioeconomic status on academic achievement (Walberg & Haertel, 1980).

Despite the hundreds of meta-analyses in related fields, only a few articles on meta-analysis in social work could be located. These articles included Videka-Sherman's (1985, 1988) report on the effectiveness of practice, Tobler's (1986) report on adolescent drug prevention programs, two reviews of meta-analysis (Nurius, 1984; Nurius & Yeaton, 1987), and two interesting and creative applications of meta-analysis to single-system designs (Corcoran, 1985; Gingerich, 1984). It is not clear why social work has been so slow to adopt meta-analytic procedures, although two possibilities include a paucity of studies on which to perform meta-analysis and the profession's traditional reluctance to explore and adapt new technologies.

Nevertheless, since the profession uses a pluralistic knowledge base, a continuing awareness of new developments in knowledge as they occur is obviously required. This awareness should be combined with evaluations of the relevance of the developments to social work, which, in turn, require awareness of tools that can aid social workers in making decisions about new knowledge. With allegiance to the scientific method as a superordinate value in social work and the use of empirical- or research-related criteria for the selection of knowledge as one way of operationalizing that allegiance, it would appear that any new tool that may be of value in the objective assessment of the empirical status of a given body of knowledge—as meta-analysis purportedly is—would be a potential candidate for utilization by social workers.

Thus, the recent origins of meta-analysis and social work's slowness to examine it present an excellent opportunity for we social work researchers to evaluate and possibly disseminate this knowledge to the field before our approach to the assessment of empirical research becomes outdated. The potential benefits of meta-analysis for social work—to help social work researchers evaluate our efforts and the efforts of others in related disciplines to avoid unsound or irrational adaptation of their work—appear too great to wait much longer.

To further that goal, then, this chapter evaluates both the potential of meta-analysis for social work and the problems associated with its use. The following section presents a brief overview of several methods of meta-analysis. It is followed by a critique of those methods—the problems and issues—and the final section, which offers some conclusions about the utility of meta-analysis and its potential value to the field, compared to and possibly combined with more traditional approaches to the integration of research.

META-ANALYTIC METHODS

Several approaches to meta-analysis have been developed since the mid-1970s, and many of them overlap in that they combine either significance levels or ESs or both. When combined across studies, the significance-level approach provides information about whether the results for the set of studies likely was due to chance, while the ES-size approach examines the magnitude of the effect (how meaningful it is) across studies.

Since the major purpose of this chapter is to critique meta-analytic methods, it is not necessary to present an in-depth review of each approach, especially since the references provided earlier cover all the approaches in great detail. However, a brief overview is presented here, using the categories developed by Bangert-Drowns (1986) to describe five basic methods of meta-analysis.

The first method, developed by Glass (1976), is, by far, the best known and most commonly used. As do all approaches, this method transforms the outcomes of each study into a common metric, which allows results to be compared across studies and outcome measures. This transformation is done by computing an ES by subtracting the mean of the control group from the mean of the experimental group and then dividing that by the standard deviation of the control group:

$$ES = \frac{\overline{X}_E - \overline{X}_C}{S_C}$$

This formula allows the use of a Z-table to compare the mean difference between the two groups in standard deviation units. The Glass approach develops an ES for each outcome measure in a study.

The second method is called "study effect meta-analysis" (SEM) by Bangert-Drowns (1986). Developed by Mansfield and Busse (1977), SEM is similar to the Glass method except that ESs related to each dependent variable are combined. SEM also appears to be more rigorous than Glass's approach in that it excludes studies with weak internal validity.

The third method is the combined probability method developed by Rosenthal (1976, 1978, 1983; Rosenthal & Rubin, 1982a, 1982b, 1986). Though continuously evolving, Rosenthal's approach basically uses Stouffer's Z, a sum of individual Z-scores. A one-tailed probability level for each study is calculated, and its corresponding standard normal deviate, or Z, is listed. The Z-scores are then summed across studies (average Zs are used if there is more than one outcome measure in a study) and divided by the square root of the number of studies to produce an overall Z score. The overall Z score reflects the overall probability that the combined results of the studies could have occurred by chance.

The fourth method is data pooling with a test of homogeneity (Hedges, 1982a, 1982b; Hedges & Olkin, 1985). This method also routinely uses an ES similar to Glass's method, the one exception being that the denominator in the equation is the pooled standard deviation, rather than the standard deviation of the control group (sometimes called Cohen's d). The distinguishing characteristic of this method is the test for homogeneity of ESs, H, which represents the variability among study outcomes as the sum of squared differences between each ES and the weighted ES. The H is distributed as a chi-square that, when not significant, suggests that the data are homogeneous; thus, ESs can be pooled across studies and a mean ES tested statistically. If H is significant, the data are seen as heterogeneous, suggesting they should not be pooled and that possible moderator variables should be tested individually using ESs associated with each variable.

The last method is called data pooling with sampling error correction (Hunter & Schmidt, 1978; Hunter, Schmidt, & Jackson, 1982). This approach focuses on measures of variation, sampling error, and mediating variables. It develops an ES for each study and then calculates the sum of squared differences between each ES and the estimated population effect, which is then weighted by proportional sample sizes. Next, the variation due to sampling error is subtracted from the total variation. If this subtraction removes roughly 75 percent of the overall variation, it is assumed that the ESs are homogeneous and that mediating variables need not be examined. If the variation is still large, mediating variables are examined to see if they have any impact on outcome.

Benefits of Meta-Analysis

As can be inferred from the preceding discussion, numerous potential benefits can accrue to both social work research and practice from the use of meta-analysis. Some of these benefits are as follows:

• Meta-analysis efficiently summarizes large bodies of literature. With the huge outpouring of research in the social and behavioral sciences and the helping professions, it is difficult to develop a traditional, narrative review that succinctly and cogently summarizes those data. Meta-analysis is designed to integrate scores of study outcomes and processes in a manageable format.

• Meta-analysis is able to develop a common metric for transforming disparate data from a number of different studies into a format for easy comparison.

• Meta-analysis adds to the potential rigor and objectification of research reviews by providing quantitative, rigorous analyses of outcomes. These analyses can overcome the more subjective analyses of traditional, narrative reviews. Furthermore, meta-analysis can increase statistical power by combining results from several studies into a single analysis.

• Meta-analysis can examine relationships and trends that are too subtle to be otherwise located (Green & Hall, 1984). The statistical analysis of the data across studies allows the meta-analyst to discover what factors, substantive or methodological, may be associated with various outcomes.

• Meta-analysis not only allows general, overall conclusions to be reached about a body of research, it also permits the study of "interactions" among studies, testing hypotheses that individual studies and traditional reviews cannot, such as the effect of different theoretical orientations on a range of outcomes.

• Because of its focus on the quantification of variables, meta-analysis pressures researchers, theoreticians, and practitioners to conceptualize more sharply and to examine the empirical evaluation of interventions more critically (Fiske, 1983). By requiring the clear specification of variables, the ordered classification of various categories (types of problems of clients or of treatments, for example), and the clear explication in the primary research report, meta-analysis focuses attention on the continuing problems of vagueness and obtuse reporting in the social and behavioral sciences and human services.

• Meta-analysis can point to specific gaps in the literature, thereby leading to the selection of more focused and meaningful new directions for research.

• Meta-analysis can contribute to the quality of subsequent research by highlighting criteria for good-quality research and by illustrating research methods that appear to have been most successful in earlier investigations.

These benefits are far from trivial and constitute major advances in the art and science of reviewing research. However, they are based on an important assumption: that meta-analysis will be applied "properly" and in error-free ways so that conclusions are untainted by inappropriate assumptions or methodological flaws in the meta-analysis itself. This assumption is not always correct.

PROBLEMS AND ISSUES

The many potential contributions of meta-analysis to research reviewing and the newness of the meta-analysis enterprise make it crucial that potential problems in the implementation of meta-analysis are openly debated. Open debates can lead to a clearer evaluation of the prospects of the utilization of one or more of the meta-analytic methods by social workers.

Unfortunately, a plethora of problems is associated with meta-analysis. These problems range from questions about the basic assumptions of meta-analysis to issues regarding the statistical properties of some of the computations involved in meta-analysis. This section describes a number of them. Each of the problems does not necessarily apply to all the methods just outlined. Therefore, when possible, these distinctions will be pointed out.

Much of the literature cited earlier discusses the problems of meta-analysis; indeed, the number of problems or potential problems is large enough to prohibit the exhaustive presentation of them here. Thus, this section consists essentially of a summary of some of the major problems. More detailed critiques appear in Glass, McGaw, and Smith (1981); Green and Hall (1984); Hunter, Schmidt, and Jackson (1982); *Journal of Consulting and Clinical Psychology* (1983); Light (1983a); Michelson (1985); Rosenthal (1984); Searles (1985); Strube, Gardner, and Hartmann (1985); Strube and Hartmann (1982, 1983); Wilson (1985); Wilson and Rachman (1983); and Wortman (1983). Since many of these criticisms have been debated back and forth in the literature—with the debate often rising (or lowering) to the level of invective—no attempt will be made to present every minute aspect of all sides of each debate. Instead, the purpose here simply is to establish the range of possible problems that could impede a meta-analytic review.

The problems are grouped into three categories for discussion: (1) the selection of studies for review, (2) meta-analytic statistics, and (3) interpretation of the results of meta-analysis. The purpose of such a categorization is partly for convenience and partly heuristic. The categorization allows the grouping of issues with some conceptual similarities, although certainly some overlap exists among the categories. Thus, it is less than definitive but somewhat more than arbitrary.

Selection of Studies for Review

Several issues are included in this category. They are combining divergent studies, the methodological quality of the primary research, sampling bias caused by unpublished studies, the effects of deficient reporting, and other limitations imposed by the primary studies.

Combining divergent studies. Although the main purpose of meta-analysis is to synthesize results from a number of different studies, it has been criticized as being inappropriate conceptually or methodologically. Called the "apples and oranges" problem, this criticism cuts to the heart of meta-analysis, arguing, at the most basic level, that it makes no sense to integrate the findings of different studies (Glass, McGaw, & Smith, 1981).

Broken down into its components, this problem involves issues regarding (1) combining studies of divergent methodological adequacy (because of its significance, this problem will be discussed in a separate section), (2) combining different independent variables, and (3) combining different dependent variables.

The issue of combining independent variables is one of construct validity in that the question can be raised that when more than one independent variable (say, theoretical orientation) is examined in a single meta-analysis, it could obscure differences among subcategories (Presby, 1978). For example, Smith, Glass, and Miller (1980) examined 18 (19 including the placebo) types of therapy; this examination was made even more problematic by collapsing the types into superclasses of therapies called behavioral, verbal, and developmental. Thus, the question of whether such categories represent true, underlying constructs may blur distinctions and diminish the practical and theoretical relevance of such an analysis. Similarly, the constraints on external validity would be considerable. In other words, of what importance is it that the average ES for verbal therapies is .85 and for developmental therapies is .42?

Perhaps, as Glass, McGaw, and Smith (1981) suggested, the answer to these questions lies in the purpose of the reviewer. If the reviewer wishes to make broad, global statements about the effectiveness of some set of interventions as a way of informing policy decisions or even simply wishes to summarize a body of literature in a global fashion, then the issue of construct validity can be assessed against the purpose of the reviewer and the hypotheses developed to establish the validity of the categories selected. In addition, subsequent analyses can be conducted in which the overall ES is broken down into ESs related to the specific categories.

The main dangers of this approach are that such global answers to problems could lead to an unwarranted laxity and decreased motivation for critical thinking by practitioners in a field of study if they hear that, overall, some global intervention, such as psychotherapy, is effective. It is all too easy to attempt inappropriately to transfer such global conclusions to one's specific approach to practice. Furthermore, such broad conceptualizations could lead to the development of poorly formulated hypotheses in future research in which a range of independent variables is targeted for analysis. Thus, questions that are particularly relevant to particular groups of problems or clients may be overlooked.

The second part of this problem, combining different dependent variables, has been dealt with in two major ways. The first is to use a separate ES for each outcome measure (as in Glass's approach) and the second is to combine or pool related outcome measures. The consequences of this decision are significant. If one calculates an ES for each outcome measure, then it is difficult to interpret the combined effect of all the outcome measures. What would be measured if the conclusion of a meta-analysis of 565 separate ESs (one for each outcome measure) was that therapy X produces an overall ES of 1.29 on ———? It would be difficult to know just what was being affected.

Indeed, a study by Burns (1981, cited in Bangert-Drowns, 1986) showed that some individual studies can seriously distort the overall meta-analysis when an ES is calculated for each measure. Burns found a total of 413 ESs from 33 studies, but the range of ESs per study was from 1 to 120. Thus, a given study that uses several outcome measures can exert an undue influence on the overall meta-analysis by virtue of the number of measures it uses.

This use of studies with numerous outcome measures contributes to what may be called the problem of "inflated n's." Since a single study can be overrepresented because of its many outcome measures, it can affect the external validity of a meta-analysis. That is, it is difficult to know what the target population is, because the sample is so distorted.

To make this problem even more complicated, since the mean ES is used (average of all the ESs in a review), and the mean is affected by extreme scores, a study that contributes disproportionately large or small ESs also can distort the results. Thus, 10 large ESs from one study can produce an overall moderate ES when averaged with 10 low ESs from 10 studies. Such analyses would give a false impression of moderate effectiveness when, in fact, in this example, only one study showed effectiveness and 10 did not. Similarly, the use of a separate ES for each outcome measure violates the statistical principle of the assumption of independence, thereby producing possibly unreliable results (this problem is discussed in more detail elsewhere in this section).

On the other hand, averaging different measures into a single ES also presents problems (Wilson, 1985). Since difference measures often respond differentially to the same treatment, pooling the measures may distort or destroy such differential effects. Thus, the failure to attend to the conceptual relevance of individual measures produces possibly meaningless averages.

In a similar vein, Paul (1985) illustrated how averaging measures into a single ES can destroy important differences and thus create problems of interpretation, as well as of calculation. Using data from an earlier study (Paul, 1966), he demonstrated that the mean ES, which indicated the advantage of systematic desensitization over placebo treatment on two key scales, was .45, but the mean of all measures was .04.

When one considers pooling ESs, one possibility is to examine the pooled effects in comparison with the studies with the best designs that are included in the sample. If the results appear to diverge substantially, perhaps pooling is not the best choice. Similarly, if the range of measures and effects is diverse, pooling is not recommended. One also can determine whether pooling is appropriate by using the procedures recommended by Hedges and Olkin (1985) for testing sets of ESs for homogeneity.

The choices between using separate ESs for each measure or pooling measures may leave you feeling "damned if you do and damned if you don't." However, the reality of such constraints must be addressed so the rationale for choosing a method can be evaluated.

Methodological quality of primary research. One of the most serious problems in meta-analysis is the issue of limitations caused by variations in the methodological adequacy of the primary studies. That is, the inclusion of primary studies with methodological flaws can produce meta-analytic conclusions that also are flawed—in other words, "garbage in, garbage out." This is such a crucial problem that many of the critiques of meta-analysis cited earlier spent considerable time attempting to deal with it (see also Erwin, 1984).

Two major issues in this regard are defining quality and deciding what to do about studies of varying quality (Strube, Gardner, & Hartmann, 1985). The first issue is more or less subjective. That is, one may define a high-quality study as any study that used random assignment and a control group. Someone else may argue that those two conditions are insufficient without the addition of a placebo group. Others may argue that the "lower limit" of quality would include rigorous (say, matched but not randomly assigned) quasi-experiments. Of course, even if the most rigorous standards are applied (random assignment with control and placebo groups), it is obvious that implementation of the design could pose numerous other problems, such as the measurement or provision of treatments at different intervals, which opens up the design to several other threats to internal validity; differential mortality; nonintegrity of treatment (the lack of comparability among the practitioners' implementation of treatments); differential times of exposure to treatments or placebos; differential levels of enthusiasm, warmth, empathy, or other interpersonal skills among practitioners; and so on. The flaws that could result from these problems range from mild to severe and could result in any number of threats to the internal validity of a study. It also is clear that different reviewers will have different criteria and that few will spend the time and energy to analyze the primary studies that are required to ferret out all these possible flaws, any of which could seriously affect the conclusions of a meta-analysis.

Be that as it may, the next decision a meta-analyst has to make is what to do about these variations in quality. Two general decisions have been made in the literature on meta-analysis: (1) to exclude studies with methodological deficiencies and (2) to code these studies and analyze the impact of the quality of studies on the overall outcome.

The first approach—to exclude studies of poor quality—is best represented by the SEM method, which attempts to be as rigorous as possible in the criteria for including studies. Unfortunately, although methodological inadequacies, such as no random assignment or control or placebo group, can be easily detected and although studies that do not have these flaws can be excluded, it is virtually impossible to find a meta-analysis that has been thorough enough to rule out studies that contain some of the other flaws just described. Furthermore, ruling out some studies that appear methodologically inferior (at least to a particular reviewer) could lead to the omission of important information that will affect the overall conclusion of the review because, among other reasons, methodological flaws do not necessarily invalidate a study's conclusions; they only diminish the confidence one can have in the conclusions.

The second approach, coding the quality of studies and examining the impact of quality on outcome through a regression model, is exemplified by Glass's approach. Recognizing that internal validity can affect a study's findings, Glass, McGaw, and Smith (1981) argued that internal validity is an empirical issue and that meta-analysis can handle the problem by analyzing the effect of threats to internal validity on ES. Thus, the reviewer may code studies as high, medium, or low on internal validity and then examine the level of quality as an independent variable. Indeed, Glass, McGaw, and Smith (1981, p. 221) contended that this method supports the conclusion that "many weak studies can add up to a strong conclusion."

Can a coding such as Glass's really handle the issue? First, such a coding system is likely to be as subjective as the criteria for including studies that was discussed earlier, so it may not reliably (or validly) capture the range of threats to internal validity. Second, such a system is a global and indirect way of dealing with the variety of specific threats to internal validity and, as such, cannot properly eliminate such threats. Third, an overabundance of studies with methodological flaws in a given sample of studies (as is likely to be the case in many areas of research) will not provide an adequate basis for comparing studies of different levels of quality. Fourth, the results of such an analysis reveal only whether there is a difference among studies whose methodological adequacy varies; it does not even address whether the reported results in a study are valid. And finally, it is likely that no amount of massaging of the data can turn a deficient database into a useful meta-analytic conclusion.

In all, whatever approach the meta-analyst chooses in this area is likely to produce problems. One possibility is to attempt to use rigorous criteria of inclusion and then to code them for minor methodological inadequacies to determine their impact on ES. It also would be possible to do a separate meta-analysis of the excluded studies to examine their impact on outcome. Whatever the meta-analyst decides to do, he or she should make the criteria clear and explicit and thoroughly describe the method of analyzing the research. The bottom line, though, is that the field of meta-analysis has yet to demonstrate convincingly methods of analysis that can overcome basic limitations in the database of primary studies.

Sampling bias caused by unpublished or undiscovered studies. A key limitation in conducting any research review (meta-analysis or otherwise) is that studies in the review may or may not (but probably not) be representative of all the studies conducted in a given area. The potential lack of representativeness is a result of two problems: (1) the reviewer may not have done an adequate job in finding all the published research, and (2) there is a potentially huge body of research on any given topic that was conducted but never published. The latter problem has been dubbed the "file drawer problem" (Rosenthal, 1979) in that many studies that were never published were said to be tucked away in file drawers. Overall, this potential sample bias could operate in two ways: the magnitude of effects and significance levels may not be representative, and the direction of effects may not be representative (Strube, Gardner, & Hartmann, 1985).

The first problem—not discovering the total number of published studies—may be illustrated by Smith, Glass, and Miller's (1980) report, which claimed that "all controlled studies of the effectiveness of any form of psychotherapy formed the population of interest for this project" (p. 55). Although the authors placed some minimal limitations on their definitions (p. 57), a subsequent analysis found that possibly hundreds of controlled studies that were available at the time and that met the reviewers' definition were omitted (Searles, 1985).

The second problem—unpublished studies—is a function, at least in part, of well-established evidence that publications are biased toward the reporting of statistically significant findings and may discriminate against studies that use new methods or that include novel theoretical variables (Strube, Gardner, & Hartmann, 1985). These biases are so severe that they may cause meta-analysis to exclude studies that have not reached statistical significance from most meta-analyses and thus to skew the sample and hence the results. The exclusion of such studies may be one reason why the results of so many meta-analyses are positive, or positively biased (discussed later).

Some attempts have been made to deal with this problem. Rosenthal (1979) developed the "fail-safe *N*," which calculates the number of hypothetical no-effect studies that are needed to make an overall significant p nonsignificant for use in the meta-analytic method of combining probabilities. Orwin (1983) developed a similar procedure for use in the analysis of ES. Both these procedures are a step forward, but neither is a substitute for an exhaustive search that produces all published and unpublished work. Such a search is difficult and time consuming, but if it is not done, any given meta-analysis is likely to be reporting the results of a biased sample and is, therefore, biased in its conclusions.

Effects of deficient reporting. One of the key steps in meta-analysis is the coding of the characteristics of studies so that the meta-analysis itself can be conducted. The success of this coding depends on three variables: the customary reporting practices of the research area being integrated, the individual differences among the researchers in the area of study (Orwin & Cordray, 1985), and the training (or effectiveness) of the coders. All these problems become exaggerated when the primary information needed is missing or incomplete and is either estimated or transformed.

Orwin and Cordray (1985) investigated part of this problem by examining just two sources of information that could influence the quality of reporting: interrater reliabilities and confidence judgments. Their study showed that both reliabilities and confidence judgments varied greatly across individual coding items and studies. Their reanalysis, which incorporated reliability corrections and confidence judgments, concluded that "deficient reporting injects considerable noise into meta-analytic data which can lead to spurious conclusions regarding causes of effect sizes, adequacy of models, and related matters" (p. 144). In other words, just two of several potential sources of deficient reporting could seriously affect the overall conclusions of a meta-analysis. To counter the effects of deficient recording, Orwin and Cordray suggested that meta-analysts take the reliability of coders more seriously, rate the quality of data and incorporate that information into analyses, and consider alternate sources of information, such as contacting the original investigators.

Although any or all these methods may be helpful, the extent to which they can and will be implemented by meta-analysts is unknown. Yet, such coding problems are at the heart of a successful meta-analysis. Indeed, the training of coders for meta-analysis and the extent to which such phenomena as "observer drift" occur in meta-analytic reviews typically are not reported. If this lack of reporting also means it was not attended to with special care, then the problems for the actual statistical analysis of data in a meta-analysis could be tremendous.

Other limitations imposed by primary studies. A number of other factors related to the primary studies can impose restrictions or lead to variations in the interpretation of meta-analysis. Strube, Gardner, and Hartmann (1985) summarized these factors as limitations that are due to the psychometric, methodological, and theoretical characteristics of the original studies.

Psychometric factors include such problems as measurement error (a concern specifically addressed by Hunter, Smith, & Jackson, 1982, in their data-pooling-with-sampling-error-correction approach) and the validity of measurement. Variations in the reliability or validity or both of variables in the primary studies can produce corresponding variations and result in confused interpretations in the meta-analysis.

Methodological factors (other than quality, which was discussed previously) include variations among studies in the goals of the primary researcher, the type of design (between-subject versus within-subject or experimental versus correlational), types of comparison conditions, nature of the control, and method of data analysis. These differences are bound to have an influence on the meta-analysis and can be significant contributors to variability in the outcome of a meta-analysis.

Theoretical factors—the theories that were used to inform the research—also can have an effect on meta-analysis. A theory typically guides a researcher's selection of variables, both independent and dependent. Thus, a wide range of variables could have been omitted from a substantial portion of the primary research, which would impose potentially serious limitations on what could be concluded from that research.

The point is that the final calculation and interpretation of a meta-analysis is not necessarily guided by the actual importance of the intervention (Strube, Gardner, & Hartmann, 1985). Although some of the other variables discussed here may be treated as artifacts and statistically analyzed (as in Hunter, Schmidt, & Jackson's 1982 approach to meta-analysis), the fact that so many of them are in operation imposes considerable constraints on what can be determined by a meta-analysis, especially of a broad range of psychometrically, methodologically, and theoretically different studies.

Meta-Analytic Statistics

The problems reviewed in this section address the calculation of ES, the nonindependence of data, the potential positive bias in meta-analysis, and the use of aggregated versus unaggregated data.

Calculation of ES. The most commonly recommended procedures for estimating ES are Δ (Glass, McGaw, & Smith, 1981) and d (Cohen, 1977). Which procedure yields the best estimate? Meta-analysts do not agree on this question. The basic difference is that Δ uses the standard deviation of the control group to scale the differences between group means, while d uses the pooled standard deviation. Glass, McGaw, and Smith (1981) argued that the standard deviation of the control group is the best choice because it has the advantage of assigning equal ESs to equal means, since pooling could lead to different standardized values of identical mean differences in a study in which several treatments are compared to a control, because sample standard deviations for different treatment groups will be different. Also, the computations for Δ are clear and easily calculated.

On the other hand, Hedges (1981, 1982a) contended that the pooled standard deviation is a more precise estimate because the assumption of the homogeneity of variances for *populations* is reasonable, especially since the use of two groups per experiment with equal population variances is typical in meta-analysis (Hedges & Olkin, 1985). Hedges (1981) also obtained a distribution for Δ showing that it is positively biased, he developed a correction factor (K) that, when multiplied by the ES, d produces an unbiased ES. However, this correction factor is most important for smaller samples, so when the sample size exceeds 10, the ESs with and without K virtually are identical (Hedges, 1982a).

If studies largely use such correlational procedures as r, the correlations can be used as the direct measure of ES. And, of course, t and F values can be readily transformed into r, though they also can be transformed into the other measures of ES. Similarly, Green and Hall (1984) suggested that when outcome measures (such as the Stanford-Binet measure of intelligence) are clearly identifiable and comparable across studies, one can use them directly, rather than resort to an ES such as Δ or d.

A more serious complication that arises from this problem is that the use of different methods to calculate ES on the same set of data results in vastly different findings. On one set of measures, Paul (1985) calculated ESs that ranged from 1.93 to 3.06, depending on whether pooled standard deviations or the standard deviation of the control group was used and on whether the data were posttest only, pre–post change data, or improvement scores. This may be one factor that accounts for the increasingly common phenomenon of divergent results of different meta-analyses applied to the same studies (Searles, 1985); moreover, it leads, at best, to serious questions of over- or underinterpretation, depending solely on the meta-analytic method used.

With regard to the dispute between the use of Δ and d, it appears as though d with the correction factor K for small samples is viewed by many meta-analysts outside the Glass "camp" as the best estimate of ES. Again, however, there is still substantial disagreement among meta-analysts on this issue. Since Δ and d essentially are similar, the choice of which estimate of ES to use—at least until further statistical analyses and proofs are available and become widely accepted—may depend more on the personal preferences of the individual meta-analysts and the type of estimates he or she wishes to discuss then on precise statistical theory.

Nonindependence of data. Meta-analysis typically is carried out on large data sets that derive multiple results from the same study. Such analyses can produce the problem of the nonindependence of data, throwing in jeopardy the reliability of estimates and raising serious questions about use of statistics, such as parametric statistics, that assume independence. Landman and Dawes (1982) described five possible sources of nonindependence: (1) nonindependent samples across studies, (2) multiple measurements of the same subjects across time, (3) the use of several measures with the same subjects, (4) the nonindependence of scores in a single outcome measure (such as the use of a global outcome plus several subsets of items that make up the global measure), and (5) the nonindependence of studies (say, multiple experiments) within a given article.

Glass, McGaw, and Smith (1981) recognized that the problem of nonindependence is particularly difficult to resolve. A number of solutions have been suggested, ranging from Tukey's jackknife procedure (Mosteller & Tukey, 1968), to averaging ESs or significance levels to produce one per study (though this obscures within-study analyses), to simply ignoring the problem. In actual practice, the latter "solution," ignoring the problem, is by far the most frequently used. Apart from simply ignoring the problem, none of the proposed solutions adequately deals with all the problems of nonindependence.

These problems can be immense. Glass, McGaw, and Smith (1981) showed that after nonindependence was taken into account, a confidence interval ranged from .002 to .371, whereas when independence was assumed, a confidence interval ranged from −.10 to +.50, a difference of well over 300 percent.

Thus, nonindependence continues to be a serious problem for meta-analysis. Indeed, the expected lack of reliability from the inappropriate use of statistics that assume independence could be one of the factors responsible for the frequently discrepant findings of different meta-analyses on the same body of research. Meta-analysts will have to develop statistical procedures to deal more readily with this problem or, at least, as Strube, Gardner, and Hartmann (1985) suggested, warn readers of the possible distortions in their conclusions.

Positive bias. Meta-analyses may be positively biased. Across the wide range of meta-analytic reviews, especially in the area of psychotherapy, a vast majority of reviews have found positive effects. This situation is especially striking when those results are compared with more traditional, narrative reviews of similar research (Green & Hall, 1984).

This issue was particularly illuminated by Cooper and Rosenthal's (1980) study in which graduate students and faculty members were randomly assigned to two methods of research review: traditional (narrative) and statistical (meta-analysis). Each group summarized the same seven studies on a single hypothesis. In essence, the meta-analytic reviewers found significantly more support for the hypothesis and estimated a significantly larger magnitude of effect than did the traditional reviewers. Those conclusions were upheld across academic status and gender.

One possible reason for the existence of positive bias in meta-analysis lies in the construction of the meta-analytic statistics on ES, such as Δ and d. It is easy to demonstrate how positive bias occurs: Any difference between the experimental and control groups in which the experimental group mean is larger than the control group mean will yield a positive ES, even when the statistics in the primary analysis show that difference to be nonsignificant. When the standard deviation is relatively small, the magnitude of the ES can be great. For example, a nonsignificant mean difference of .5 between the experimental and control groups with a control group standard deviation of .25 would yield an ES of 2.0 using Glass's Δ. Thus, any sample of null studies is likely to produce a substantial number of positive ESs.

This situation is somewhat analogous to the power of conventional statistics in that, with everything else being equal, the larger the difference between the means and the smaller the variability, the greater the ES (although even a large standard deviation will produce a positive, albeit relatively small, ES when the experimental group mean is larger than the control group mean). The basic issue here, though, is that when the statistics in the primary analysis show the difference to be nonsignificant and thereby likely to be due to chance, and the ES statistics show a positive ES, this built-in positive bias in calculating the ES (of what value is a positive ES when it may be due to chance?) typically leads to similarly inflated and possibly spurious meta-analytic conclusions.

This process is further complicated by the practice of combining several ESs. As Green and Hall (1984) pointed out, a string of weak or conflicting results that a traditional reviewer may discount may add up to a credible pattern for the meta-analytic reviewer. This process operates somewhat like the nonparametric sign test in that a number of positive but nonsignificant findings could add up to an overall significant effect.

In addition to these reasons, the positive bias in meta-analysis— especially in comparison to traditional narrative reviews—could, of course, be a result of any of the problems reviewed in this section, acting alone or in interaction with the others to inflate the real relationship among the variables studied. But to the extent that such positive bias exists in meta-analysis, it obviously could influence a field's perception of the strength of findings in that field and thus undermine support for future research. A complacency factor could set in. In addition, such bias may seriously undercut the major raison d'être for meta-analysis: that it produces more objective results than traditional narrative reviews. Thus, the jury is still out on that issue.

Aggregated versus unaggregated data. One incurs serious problems in aggregating data from individual studies when one tries to draw conclusions about unaggregated phenomena. Stated another way, the aggregation of individual data to determine relationships at the group level can lead to error—or, at least, to different conclusions—partly because there could be differences in error variance (discrepancies between individual and group covariation) when group data are used. Indeed, the use of aggregate data has been shown to produce a number of hazards, even in an individual study (Borgatta & Jackson, 1980). Hunter, Schmidt, and Jackson (1982) addressed the problems of variation, including sampling error, in their method of data pooling with sampling error correction, but this problem was not exactly their focus, at least as it is conceptualized here.

An example from a different area may illuminate this issue. In examining the relationship between leadership and commitment in a number of organizations, Glisson (1986) found that when individual responses were the unit of analysis, the relationship was positive, but when individual responses were aggregated and group data were analyzed, the relationship was negative. This discrepancy probably was caused by greater within-group variation than between-group variation; that is, the characteristics of the individual have more influence on individual responses than do the characteristics of the group. The question for meta-analysis is this: Are similar systematic—or even unsystematic—changes introduced when one moves from analyzing a single study to aggregating the results of those individual studies?

Interpretation of the Results of Meta-Analysis

The final problems to be discussed are the interpretation of ES and issues regarding causality in meta-analysis.

Interpretation of ES. Since ES, such as Δ or d, is so crucial to most meta-analyses, it may seem surprising that there is no real consensus about how to interpret the meaning of ES, especially when only one overall ES is reported and there is no test of statistical significance. Thus, while there is a consensus about the conclusion than an ES of .25 means that the typical client in the experimental group exceeded the score of 59 percent of the clients in the control group, the meaning beyond that is unclear. Of course, many meta-analysts would be comfortable in stopping with that demonstration. Others, though, may wonder just how meaningful an ES of .25 (or .10 or .97) actually is.

Cohen (1962) suggested some rough guidelines for interpreting ESs as small, medium, or large; his rules of thumb were that a .2 ES was small, a .5 ES was medium, and a .8 ES was large. These suggestions were supported by Light (1983b).

Glass, McGaw, and Smith (1981) disagreed with this reasoning and proposed a more individualized interpretation. Thus, they argued that some ESs are meaningful without being compared to anything else (such as a zero ES), but that others can be interpreted by comparing them with known and familiar effects, such as the effects of well-known interventions. They further contended that as experience accumulates, particular magnitudes of ES will gain meaning by reference to what is typical in similar circumstances. Thus, if a certain drug is known consistently to produce ESs of .50 on standardized measures, then a new drug that consistently produces ESs of 1.00 is particularly meaningful.

The essence of this argument is that there is no inherent value to an ES of any given size because every ES must be validated in the context of what is typical, what is expected, and what is desired. Unfortunately, this argument begs the question and seems to undermine the elaborate statistical calculations that form the basis of ES. In other words, why go through all the complicated procedures if, when one finally calculates an ES, the final interpretation is subjective? This situation may even negate the benefits of meta-analysis over more traditional, narrative reviews.

It is perhaps too obvious an issue to wonder what should be done when there are no commonly accepted standard or typical bases, such as the ESs collected over time from several reviews of the same phenomenon. Indeed, it is as likely that the results of different independent meta-analyses of the same material could yield discrepant overall results (see, for example, Smith, Glass, & Miller, 1980, versus Andrews & Harvey, 1981, versus Landman & Dawes, 1982).

The issue becomes even more complicated when ESs within a single study are compared. Some authors routinely use parametric statistics, such as ANOVA, to compare mean differences between two or more ESs for statistical significance. Others, especially the Glass group, essentially use nonstatistical comparisons. The use of nonstatistical comparisons leads to several problems, such as the use of qualifiers like *relatively* larger

(ES), *about* equally effective, *somewhat* smaller (ES), and so on, whose meaning the reader must interpret (see, for instance, Smith, Glass, & Miller, 1980). It also can lead to different interpretations of similar ESs within the same study. Thus, Smith, Glass, and Miller (1980) defined the ES of .98 (standard error [S.E.] of .05) for behavior therapy as "clearly superior" (p. 98) to the ES of .85 (S.E. of .04) for verbal therapies. But in other places in the same study, they interpreted the same or even larger differences in ES as *not* being different. Thus, an ES of .69 (S.E. of .05) for psychodynamic therapy with neurotics was considered to be "the same magnitude of effect" (p. 90) as an ES of .90 (S.E. of .16) for psychodynamic therapy with psychotics. In both cases, they also violated their "rule" that "a mean difference equal to two standard errors was used as a guideline for interpreting nonrandom differences between two effects" (p. 90). Such discrepant interpretations appear throughout this study.

The BESD table developed by Rosenthal and Rubin (1982c) is one attempt to standardize the interpretation of ESs, and it is, indeed, useful. But it, too, falls short of judging the real or perhaps more accurately, statistical, significance of any given ES.

The whole issue is made even more complicated by the fact that the same ES can be interpreted in a number of different ways. As Strube, Gardner, and Hartmann (1985) pointed out, a d of 1.0 can be interpreted in several ways: (1) the treated group has a mean outcome exceeding an untreated group by one standard deviation, (2) the treatment accounts for 20 percent of the variance in outcome, (3) 84.1 percent of the treated subjects can be expected to exceed the average untreated subject on the outcome measure (U_3), and (4) treatment increases the success rate for subjects by 44.7 percent (BESD). Since all these descriptions really reflect the same underlying effect, it is crucial that meta-analysts not attempt to inflate or deflate their results according to their own biases by selecting a particular ES estimate. At the least, such a variety of interpretations can contribute to the confusion of readers who are trying to understand the complications of a meta-analysis. In all, then, this crucial issue of the substantive interpretation of ES must be addressed and clarified in subsequent research on and refinement of meta-analysis.

Issues regarding causality. Meta-analysts typically misinterpret their work, claiming that it is able to establish causal relationships among variables. This claim simply is not correct. As Cooper (1982) suggested, a review contains two different sources of evidence about the relationships among variables. The first is from the individual studies in which the researchers manipulated the independent variable in experiments to examine causality. The second is from the review itself, in which the meta-analyst uses a variety of statistical methods to look for associations among variables.

The essence of the problem is the manipulation of variables. The only way to establish causality is to manipulate independent variables systematically to establish their relationship to dependent variables. Even if a meta-analytic review is based on rigorous experiments, since it does not systematically manipulate variables or order them temporally, there is no basis for inferring which characteristics of the studies that were reviewed actually caused different outcomes. In other words, even a large ES or significant combined probability does not provide conclusive evidence of *why* such results were obtained. A whole range of other variables that simply cannot be eliminated are potential alternative explanations for most results of meta-analyses.

THE PROMISE

Although the discussion of the problems of meta-analysis far exceeded the discussion of the benefits of meta-analysis, the point is not that the problems so outweigh the benefits that meta-analysis can be ignored. Rather, the issue is that many of these problems place limitations on what can be expected from meta-analysis at this stage in its development. Furthermore, one hopes that the categorization of problems in such a manner will lead to a research agenda—for example, the development and refinement of appropriate meta-analytic statistical procedures—that is designed to address them in some way. Indeed, it is the assumption that some of those problems will be addressed successfully that allows the promise of meta-analysis to be elaborated on here. Thus, this section discusses some of the implications and potential contributions of meta-analysis for social work that have not yet been addressed in this chapter.

Narrative Review versus Meta-Analysis: The Debate

At the heart of any type of research review are the logic, rigor, and training of the reviewer. There simply is no substitute for these qualities, whether the review is a traditional, narrative one or a meta-analysis. The success of the review depends on the extent to which the reviewer is aware of and adequately deals with problems in his or her method of review.

These principles can be viewed as bridging the gap between the somewhat arbitrarily constructed "camps" of the advocates of narrative reviews and those of meta-analyses. Indeed, Cook and Leviton (1980) and Leviton and Cook (1981) noted a number of factors that make a harsh distinction between these methods seem unnecessary. These factors include the fact that all literature reviews are based on both qualitative judgments and quantitative techniques; that there are no inherent weaknesses in traditional reviews; that many criticisms of narrative reviews were aimed at the poor practices of reviewers, rather than at any inherent methodological problems; and that both meta-analytic and narrative reviews can provide important and even complementary information.

As if to second these ideas, Light and Pillemer (1982), who are supporters of meta-analysis, argued that qualitative information is as important as quantitative information for explaining conflicting and puzzling outcomes. They discussed six ways in which qualitative information is essential for literature reviews. They also described three broad strategies for combining different types of information in a review: quantifying descriptive reports, presenting quantitative outcomes narratively, and allying statistical and descriptive evidence while maintaining the integrity of each. Their main point was that reviews that are organized to utilize both types of information will ultimately maximize knowledge about the complexities of evaluating programs.

Slavin's (1986) work on "best-evidence synthesis" (BES) is an interesting development along these lines. BES combines the quantification of ESs and the systematic, exhaustive selection of the best meta-analyses with attention to methodological and substantive issues and individual studies characterizing the best narrative reviews. Rigorous criteria for inclusion are at the heart of BES, so it focuses on the studies in a substantive area that have the best internal and external validity using clearly specified criteria for inclusion. Data on ES are used to complement the thorough discussion of the literature being reviewed. Thus, the literature-synthesis section may seem like the analogous section in a narrative review with the addition of a table describing the characteristics of the studies and the ESs. Basically, the ES is a point of departure for the critical discussion and evaluation of the literature.

In essence, then, the "debate" over meta-analyses versus narrative reviews may be illusory, akin to debates among adherents of competing theoretical orientations in clinical practice. The goal of research reviewing is to make possible the best judgments about what problems, treated by what methods, informed by what theory, affecting what clients, in what situations, will be best. Strategies for handling such questions through the review process could then involve the following:

• The use of only a narrative review. A narrative review alone may be used when the number of primary studies is small, say under 20, or when the outcomes are clearly in the same direction, which renders quantitative aggregation less necessary.

• The use of a meta-analysis alone. A meta-analysis may be used alone when the number of primary studies is large (more than 20), when the results are not consistently in one direction, and perhaps when a combination of methods, including the calculation of ES, combined probabilities (both with "fail-safe" procedures), testing for heterogeneity, and sampling error corrections were used.

• A combination of methods, along the lines suggested by Light and Pillemer (1982) or Slavin (1986), could be used.

The basic point of this discussion is that review methods should be utilized in the same way primary research methods are used. That is, one first develops a research question and then selects a method of analysis that appears to be the best for that particular question.

Meta-Analysis and Social Policy

Meta-analysis can have a particular impact on social policy, in large part because the results of a meta-analysis can be easily communicated to nonprofessional policymakers, especially when they are in an early stage of policy analysis and are evaluating different policy options.

Kiesler (1985) discussed several contributions that meta-analysis could make to the formulation of policies. He suggested that meta-analysis could be useful in providing a preliminary, overall look at a potential policy problem; examining the effects of interventions across a broad array of problems (from health and mental health to child welfare); and focusing attention on the lack of studies in areas for which answers are needed to formulate policies.

Kiesler (1985) also identified problems that may affect the use of meta-analysis for developing policies. When added to the problems reviewed in the previous section, these problems span the full range, from questions about statistics to oversimplifying and overgeneralizing conclusions ("psychotherapy is effective"). Yet, the use of meta-analysis for the formulation of policies is an interesting and relatively unexplored arena.

Nurius (1984) also made some interesting suggestions for using meta-analysis to inform this and other areas of practice. She emphasized the importance of translating research findings (meta-analytic or otherwise) into understandable form and providing generalizations to be converted into guidelines for action. She noted that meta-analytic methods and findings can be incorporated into existing research-utilization frameworks in social work, such as social research and development (Rothman, 1980a, 1980b) or the developmental research paradigm of Thomas (1978, 1984). Not only could meta-analysis be useful in the context of knowledge development within these systems (by aggregating and analyzing the data), but the research-utilization systems provide a series of steps and

procedures for transforming meta-analytic results into practice principles and then disseminating them to the professional audience.

Single-System Designs

One of the least explored areas for the use of meta-analytic procedures is that of single-system or single-case designs (Bloom, Orme, &
Fischer, in press). Such applications in social work have been described by
Gingerich (1984) and Corcoran (1985) and in clinical psychology by
Hartmann and Gardner (1982, cited in Strube, Gardner, & Hartmann,
1985). Meta-analytic procedures have potential for both the analysis of
outcomes in a study (a perennial problem in single-system designs) and
for the aggregation and evaluation of data across single-system designs.

Unfortunately, the characteristics of some complex single-system
designs, such as the alternating treatment design, pose still unresolved
problems about how the within-phase standard deviation should be
determined. Of even more concern is that the data in a substantial portion
of single-system designs are autocorrelated and thus nonindependent,
thereby, once again, imposing limitations on the statistics that can be used
when the assumption of independence is violated.

In addition to the use of parametric statistics, as was described here,
Hartmann and Gardner (1982, cited in Strube, Gardner, & Hartmann,
1985) discussed the possibilities of using nonparametric statistics, such as
the sign test and log-linear techniques, to analyze data from single-system
designs. Although they assume independence, nonparametric statistics
may be useful when precise parametric information is not available or
cannot be estimated with confidence. It is even possible to estimate ESs
from nonparametric statistics (Glass, McGaw, & Smith, 1981; Strube,
Gardner, & Hartmann, 1985).

A number of problems still need to be resolved in the application of
meta-analysis to single-system designs, including the different procedures
and interpretations that may be necessary for analyzing one study (within-
subject) versus aggregating the results of several studies (between-subject)
(see Strube, Gardner, & Hartmann, 1985). Nevertheless, as a new technology applied to what also is a relatively new technology, the integration
of meta-analysis with single-system designs may have an interesting
future.

THE FUTURE OF META-ANALYSIS

As with any development in research or in practice, the future of
meta-analysis depends on the ways its advocates can develop and refine

the methodology to overcome reasonable criticisms of its applications. If the past 10 years provide any hint about the next 10 years, those refinements and developments are on the horizon. The fast pace of new developments in meta-analysis over the past 10 years, then, augurs well for the future.

It is likely that meta-analysis is not a fad, although it may be some time before it is uniformly accepted as a legitimate contribution to research in the social and behavioral sciences. But since the potential benefits of meta-analysis can be seen as crucial to the ongoing success of social work, it is hoped that the viability of meta-analysis will be enhanced, rather than only challenged, because what meta-analysis attempts to do is develop an empirical base that can be used to inform practice. Again, the primary mandate generated from adherence to the scientific method as an orienting value of social work is to inform practice, and the research review is a key way to cumulate, interpret, and disseminate knowledge about effective interventions and other major domains of practice. The results of rigorous research reviews, in other words, make a central contribution to the empirical base of practice and, ultimately, to the evaluation and establishment of the effectiveness of social work. Whether meta-analysis will be the major contributor in that effort or just one of several contributors remains to be seen. But, at the least, it can generate a great deal of renewed interest in the research review process per se. If that alone is its contribution, meta-analysis will be evaluated by future generations of social workers as worthy, indeed.

REFERENCES

Andrews, G., & Harvey, R. (1981). Does psychotherapy benefit neurotic patients? *Archives of General Psychotherapy, 38,* 1203–1208.

Bangert-Drowns, R. L. (1986). Review of developments in meta-analytic methods. *Psychological Bulletin, 99,* 388–399.

Bassoff, E. S., & Glass, G. V. (1982). The relationship between sex roles and mental health: A meta-analysis of twenty-six studies. *Counseling Psychologist, 10,* 105–112.

Berman, J. S., Miller, C. R., & Massman, P. J. (1985). Cognitive therapy versus systematic desensitization: Is one treatment superior? *Psychological Bulletin, 97,* 451–461.

Berman, J. S., & Norton, H. C. (1985). Does professional training make a therapist more effective? *Psychological Bulletin, 98,* 401–407.

Bloom, M., Orme, J. G., & Fischer, J. (in press). *Evaluating practice: Guidelines for the accountable professional* (2nd ed.). New York: Free Press.

Borgatta, E. F., & Jackson, D. J. (Eds.). (1980). *Aggregate data: Analysis and interpretation.* Beverly Hills, CA: Sage Publications.

Casey, R. J., & Berman, J. S. (1985). The outcome of psychotherapy with children. *Psychological Bulletin, 98*, 388–400.

Cohen, J. (1962). The statistical power of abnormal-social psychological research: A review. *Journal of Abnormal and Social Psychology, 65*, 145–153.

Cohen, J. (1977). *Statistical power analysis for the behavioral sciences*. New York: Academic Press.

Cook, T. D., & Leviton, L. C. (1980). Reviewing the literature: A comparison of traditional methods with meta-analysis. *Journal of Personality, 48*, 449–472.

Cooper, H. M. (1982). Scientific guidelines for conducting integrative reviews. *Review of Educational Research, 52*, 291–302.

Cooper, H. M., & Rosenthal, R. (1980). Statistical versus traditional procedures for summarizing research findings. *Psychological Bulletin, 87*, 422–449.

Corcoran, K. J. (1985). Aggregating the idiographic data of single-subject research. *Social Work Research & Abstracts, 21*, 9–12.

Erwin, E. (1984). Establishing causal connections: Meta-analysis and psychotherapy. *Midwest Studies in Philosophy, 9*, 421–436.

Fischer, J. (1973). Is casework effective? A review. *Social Work, 18*, 5–20.

Fischer, J. (1976). *The effectiveness of social casework*. Springfield, IL: Charles C Thomas.

Fiske, D. W. (1983). The meta-analytic revolution in outcome research. *Journal of Consulting and Clinical Psychology, 51*, 65–70.

Gingerich, W. J. (1984). Meta-analysis of applied time-series data. *Journal of Applied Behavior Analysis, 20*, 71–79.

Glass, G. V. (1976). Primary, secondary, and meta-analysis of research. *Educational Researcher, 5*, 3–8.

Glass, G. V., McGaw, B., & Smith, M. L. (1981). *Meta-analysis in social research*. Beverly Hills, CA: Sage Publications.

Glisson, C. A. (1986). The group versus the individual as the unit of analysis in small group research. *Social Work with Groups, 7*, 15–30.

Green, B. F., & Hall, J. A. (1984). Quantitative methods for literature reviews. *Annual Review of Psychology, 35*, 37–53.

Hazelrigg, M. D., Cooper, H. M., & Borduin, C. M. (1987). Evaluating the effectiveness of family therapies: An integrative review and analysis. *Psychological Bulletin, 101*, 428–442.

Hedges, L. V. (1981). Distribution theory for Glass's estimates of effect size and related estimators. *Journal of Educational Statistics, 6*, 107–128.

Hedges, L. V. (1982a). Estimation of effect size from a series of independent experiments. *Psychological Bulletin, 92*, 490–499.

Hedges, L. V. (1982b). Fitting categorical models to effect sizes from a series of experiments. *Journal of Educational Statistics, 7*, 119–137.

Hedges, L. V., & Olkin, I. (1985). *Statistical methods for meta-analysis*. New York: Academic Press.

Hunter, J. E., & Schmidt, F. L. (1978). Differential and single-group validity of employment tests by race: A critical analysis of three recent studies. *Journal of Applied Psychology, 63*, 1–11.

Hunter, J. E., Schmidt, F. L., & Jackson, G. B. (1982). *Meta-analysis: Cumulating research findings across studies.* Beverly Hills, CA: Sage Publications.

Journal of Consulting and Clinical Psychology (1983), *5*(1), whole issue.

Kiesler, C. A. (1985). Meta-analysis, clinical psychology, and social policy. *Clinical Psychology Review, 5,* 3–12.

Landman, J., & Dawes, R. M. (1982). Psychotherapy outcome. *American Psychologist, 37,* 504–516.

Leviton, L. C., & Cook, T. D. (1981). What differentiates meta-analysis from other forms of reviews? *Journal of Personality, 49,* 231–236.

Light, R. J. (Ed.). (1983a). *Evaluation studies review annual, Vol. 8.* Beverly Hills, CA: Sage Publications.

Light, R. J. (1983b). Introduction. In R. J. Light (Ed.), *Evaluation studies review annual, Vol. 8* (pp. 13–23). Beverly Hills, CA: Sage Publications.

Light, R. J., & Pillemer, D. B. (1982). Numbers and narrative: Combining their strengths in research reviews. *Harvard Educational Review, 52,* 1–26.

Maas, H. J. (Ed.). (1966). *Five fields of social service: Reviews of research.* New York: National Association of Social Workers.

Maas, H. J. (Ed.). (1971). *Research in the social services: A five-year review.* New York: National Association of Social Workers.

Maas, H. J. (Ed.). (1978). *Social service research: Reviews of studies.* Washington, DC: National Association of Social Workers.

Mansfield, R. S., & Busse, T. V. (1977). Meta-analysis of research: A rejoinder to Glass. *Educational Researcher, 6, 3.*

Michelson, L. (Ed.). (1985). Meta-analysis and clinical psychology. *Clinical Psychology Review, 5,* 1–89.

Mosteller, F. M., & Tukey, J. W. (1968). Data analysis, including statistics. In G. Lindsey & F. Aronson (Eds.), *Handbook of social psychology.* Reading, MA: Addison-Wesley.

Mullen, E. J., Dumpson, J. R., et al. (Eds.). (1972). *Evaluation of social intervention.* San Francisco: Jossey-Bass.

Mullen, E. J., & Suls, J. (1982). The effectiveness of attention and rejection as coping styles: A meta-analysis of temporal differences. *Journal of Psychosomatic Research, 26,* 43–49.

Nurius, P. S. (1984). Utility of data synthesis for social work. *Social Work Research & Abstracts, 20,* 23–32.

Nurius, P. S., & Yeaton, W. H. (1987). Research synthesis reviews: An illustrated critique of "hidden" judgments, choices and compromises. *Clinical Psychology Review, 7,* 695–714.

Orwin, R. G. (1983). A fail-safe N for effect size. *Journal of Educational Statistics, 8,* 157–159.

Orwin, R. G., & Cordray, D. S. (1985). Effects of deficient reporting on meta-analysis: A conceptual framework and reanalysis. *Psychological Bulletin, 97,* 134–147.

Paul, G. L. (1966). *Insight versus desensitization in psychotherapy.* Stanford, CA: Stanford University Press.

Paul, G. L. (1985). Can pregnancy be a placebo effect? Terminology, designs, and conclusions in the study of psychosocial and pharmacological treatments of behavioral disorders. In L. White, B. Tursky, & G. Schwartz (Eds.), *Placebo: Clinical phenomenon and new insights* (pp. 137–163). New York: Guilford Press.

Presby, S. (1978). Overly broad categories obscure important differences between therapies. *American Psychologist, 33*, 514–515.

Prioleau, L., Murdock, M., & Brody, N. (1983). An analysis of psychotherapy versus placebo studies. *Behavioral and Brain Sciences, 6*, 275–310.

Reid, W. J., & Hanrahan, P. (1982). Recent evaluations of social work: Grounds for optimism. *Social Work, 27*, 328–340.

Rosenthal, R. (1976). Interpersonal expectancy effects: A follow-up. In R. Rosenthal, *Experimental effects in behavioral research* (pp. 440–471). New York: Irvington.

Rosenthal, R. (1978). Combining results of independent studies. *Psychological Bulletin, 92*, 500–504.

Rosenthal, R. (1979). The file drawer problem and tolerance for null results. *Psychological Bulletin, 86*, 638–641.

Rosenthal, R. (1983). Assessing the statistical and social importance of the effects of psychotherapy. *Journal of Consulting and Clinical Psychology, 51*, 4–13.

Rosenthal, R. (1984). *Meta-analytic procedures for social research.* Beverly Hills, CA: Sage Publications.

Rosenthal, R., & Rubin, D. B. (1982a). Comparing effect sizes of independent studies. *Psychological Bulletin, 92*, 500–504.

Rosenthal, R., & Rubin, D. B. (1982b). Further meta-analytic procedures for assessing cognitive differences. *Journal of Educational Psychology, 74*, 708–712.

Rosenthal, R., & Rubin, D. B. (1982c). A simple, general purpose display of magnitude of experimental effect. *Journal of Educational Psychology, 74*, 166–169.

Rosenthal, R., & Rubin, D. B. (1986). Meta-analytic procedures for combining studies with multiple effect sizes. *Psychological Bulletin, 99*, 400–406.

Rothman, J. (1980a). *Social R & D: Research and development in the human services.* Englewood Cliffs, NJ: Prentice-Hall.

Rothman, J. (1980b). *Using research in organizations: A guide to successful application.* Beverly Hills, CA: Sage Publications.

Rubin, A. (1985). Practice effectiveness: More grounds for optimism. *Social Work, 30*, 469–476.

Searles, J. S. (1985). A methodological and empirical critique of psychotherapy outcome meta-analysis. *Behaviour Research and Therapy, 23*, 453–463.

Shadish, W. R. (1982). A review and critique of controlled studies of the effectiveness of preventive child health care. *Health Policy Quarterly, 2*, 24–52.

Shapiro, D. A. (1985). Recent applications of meta-analysis in clinical research. *Clinical Psychology Review, 5*, 13–34.

Slavin, R. W. (1986). Best-evidence synthesis: An alternative to meta-analytic and traditional reviews. *Educational Researcher, 15*, 5–11.

Smith, M. L., Glass, G. V., & Miller, T. I. (1980). *The benefits of psychotherapy.* Baltimore, MD: Johns Hopkins University Press.

Steinbrueck, S. M., Maxwell, S. E., & Howard, G. S. (1983). A meta-analysis of psychotherapy and drug therapy in the treatment of unipolar depression with adults. *Journal of Consulting and Clinical Psychology, 51*, 856–863.

Straw, R. B. (1983). Deinstitutionalization in mental health: A meta-analysis. In R. J. Light (Ed.), *Evaluation studies review annual, Vol. 8* (pp. 253–278). Beverly Hills, CA: Sage Publications.

Strube, M. J., Gardner, W., & Hartmann, D. P. (1985). Limitations, liabilities, and obstacles in reviews of the literature: The current status of meta-analysis. *Clinical Psychology Review, 5*, 63–78.

Strube, M. J., & Hartmann, D. P. (1982). A critical appraisal of meta-analysis. *British Journal of Clinical Psychology, 21*, 129–139.

Strube, M. J., & Hartmann, D. P. (1982). Meta-analysis: Techniques, applications, and functions. *Journal of Consulting and Clinical Psychology, 51*, 14–27.

Thomas, E. J. (1978). Generating innovation in social work: The paradigm of developmental research. *Journal of Social Service Research, 2*, 95–116.

Thomas, E. J. (1984). *Designing interventions for the helping professions* Beverly Hills, CA: Sage Publications.

Tobler, N. S. (1986). Meta-analysis of 143 adolescent drug prevention programs: Quantitative outcome results of program participants compared to a control or comparison group. *Journal of Drug Issues, 4*, 537–567.

Videka-Sherman, L. (1985). *Harriett M. Bartlett practice effectiveness project.* Silver Spring, MD: National Association of Social Workers.

Videka-Sherman, L. (1988). Meta-analysis of research on social work practice in mental health. *Social Work, 33*, 325–338.

Walberg, H. J., & Haertel, E. H. (Eds.). (1980). Research integration: The state of the art. *Evaluation in Education, 4* [whole issue].

Wilson, G. T. (1985). Limitations of meta-analysis in the evaluation of the effects of psychological therapy. *Clinical Psychology Review, 5*, 35–47.

Wilson, G. T., & Rachman, S. (1983). Meta-analysis and the evaluation of psychotherapy outcome: Limitations and liabilities. *Journal of Consulting and Clinical Psychology, 51*, 54–64.

Wood, K. (1978). Casework effectiveness: A new look at the research evidence. *Social Work, 23*, 437–458.

Wortman, C. B. (1983). Evaluation research: A methodological perspective. *Annual Review of Psychology, 34*, 223–260.

Commentary

Meta-Analysis: A User's Perspective

Lynn Videka-Sherman

In Chapter 11, Fischer presented a balanced picture of many of the strengths and weaknesses of meta-analytic approaches. This commentary addresses some of the points he raised and adds others from the perspective of a researcher who has applied meta-analysis in several reviews of the effectiveness of social work practice.

AN ALTERNATIVE VIEW

Many of Fischer's criticisms of meta-analysis are potential problems in any form of literature review, not only in meta-analysis. One example is the often-discussed "apples-and-oranges" problem, that dissimilar studies are combined in meta-analysis reviews and therefore yield meaningless information about the effects being studied. The apples-and-oranges problem is not restricted to meta-analysis. Fischer's (1973) qualitative review of the effectiveness of casework mixed widely varying studies of social work intervention with different groups of clients. One could certainly question the meaningfulness of including interventions with the frail elderly and preteenagers who were at risk of becoming juvenile delinquents in the same review. The point is that the decision concerning the definition of the population of studies to be reviewed is a conceptual decision that is central to the quality of any literature review; it is not unique to meta-analysis. Defining the population of studies to be reviewed is often a difficult decision, since conceptual frameworks for setting inclusion criteria are often fuzzy. Is it meaningful to talk of a unitary approach to social work practice? One could generate an extensive debate on that topic alone. Fischer and others have implied that it is somehow a potential problem associated with meta-analysis. It is a potential problem, but it is not unique to meta-analysis.

Certain problems have been erroneously associated only with meta-analysis because of an important strength of the method: the explicitness with which all decisions must be made in conducting it. Because of the systematic and quantitative nature of meta-analysis, many decisions that are made on an ad hoc basis and that are not even identified as decisions in traditional qualitative reviews of research are explicated in a meta-analytic review. Such decisions involve criteria for the inclusion of studies, how to consider outcomes reported on multiple measures, how to combine findings in different directions, and many other issues. There are no "right" answers for many of the decisions to be made, whatever literature review method one uses. Meta-analysis offers a distinct advantage in improving the quality of discourse about the findings of a set of studies on a particular question because it makes explicit many of the decisions that must be made in conducting any kind of literature review.

Some meta-analytic methods are criticized because they allow for the inclusion of studies whose research designs vary in methodological rigor. There is a logical error in this argument. As Hedges and Olkin (1985) noted, a range in the quality of designs does not by itself doom the validity and value of the results of a meta-analysis. If there is a range of methodological flaws in the studies being reviewed and some strong studies are included, one can use the meta-analysis to detect findings that are robust across different methodologies. A flawed methodology does not necessarily mean that incorrect results were found; it simply means that one can be less confident that the independent variable, rather than other uncontrolled factors, produced the detected result.

Furthermore, in a meta-analysis of studies in which the quality of the methods varies, the reviewer can empirically examine the effects of the flaws and biases of designs on the direction and nature of the findings. Meta-analysis cannot overcome systematic flaws or biases in the entire set of studies, however. For example, meta-analysis cannot detect the results of convenience sampling, which characterizes much of the outcome research on social work intervention.

SOME ADDITIONAL PROBLEMS

There are a few problems that one confronts when conducting a meta-analysis that Fischer did not mention. Among them is the inconsistency of the information presented in original research reports. For instance, as this author (see, for example, Videka-Sherman, 1988) found, research reports contain little information about clients or practitioners, which makes it difficult to understand how client and practitioner factors contribute to the effectiveness of intervention. Another problem is the unevenness and incompleteness with which outcome data are reported. In 26 percent of the studies in the mental health outcome study this author (Videka-Sherman, 1988) reported, crucial information was missing about design factors (such as the rate of attrition of subjects from the study or

evidence about the validity or reliability of measures or sampling procedures); information was also sometimes incomplete for outcome data.
Likewise, the majority of original research reports reviewed for the
Harriett M. Bartlett Practice Effectiveness Project (Videka-Sherman, 1985,
1986) were missing one or more of the following pieces of information: the
variability of data on the outcome measures (standard deviations or
standard errors), sample sizes that take into account experimental mortality, and exact probability values when test statistics were not reported.

Another problem is the lack of an agreed-upon methodology for
calculating effect sizes (ESs) for widely varying presentations of original
data even when sufficient data exist. In most meta-analyses to date,
reviewers have had to construct code books to compute ESs. Although
Glass, McGaw, and Smith's (1981) compilation of suggested formulas for
computing ESs is the most complete of all the reviews to date, those
researchers' methods did not include much detail on the use of nonparametric statistics or more complex designs, such as repeated measures
designs. Since the technology for meta-analysis is still in an early stage of
development, one may expect to see more work on developing computation algorithms for a greater variety of research designs and types of
data.

As Fischer noted in Chapter 11, some of the assumptions made in
meta-analyses are tenuous. The key statistical assumption regarding the
computation of ESs (that the distribution of individual scores on the
outcome measure is normal) is refutable in many situations in which
research reviewers would like to use meta-analysis. The techniques that
have been developed for computing nonparametric ESs require access to
original data, which is often impossible to gain and would require
enormous additional efforts for even a small set of studies. The extra effort
notwithstanding, the idea of using multiple sets of original data to
conduct more rigorous meta-analyses is an interesting one that would
contribute much to the advancement of quantitative methods of reviewing
the research literature.

RECOMMENDATIONS

Journals should set criteria for minimum necessary data to be presented in a research report. These criteria should include a clear description
of the research design, sufficient data to allow a secondary analysis
(accurate n's for each cell in the design, measures of central tendency or
distributions, measures of variability, and exact test statistics when
statistical tests are made). Journals also should require that information
on the research design is reported fully and accurately, including sampling

procedures, methods of assignments to experimental conditions, and the validity and reliability of the measures used in the study. This author endorses Schuerman's (1988) suggestion that the offices of journals should become archives of copies of the original data of studies for the purposes of secondary analyses. Although the expense of doing so would be enormous, so would the return in advancing knowledge for social work practice research.

Should social workers use meta-analysis as a tool for research reviews? Yes. Meta-analysis is a systematic approach to reviewing findings across studies in an efficient manner. It will become even more useful as the number of studies of social work practice grows.

Should meta-analysis be the sole method of reviews of social work research, replacing all qualitative research reviews? No. The development of knowledge in social work should be viewed as a dialectical process that should be informed by a variety of approaches. For that matter, research reviews in any form cannot be the sole method of developing knowledge in a field. Campbell's (1987) idea that knowledge development is an evolutionary process in any field is a useful one. We should not be looking for the approach to building knowledge for practice, but, rather, for enduring ideas that are robust when viewed through different lenses and from different perspectives.

REFERENCES

Campbell, D. T. (1987). Guidelines for monitoring the scientific competence of preventive intervention research centers: An exercise in the sociology of scientific validity. *Knowledge: Creation, Diffusion, Utilization, 8,* 389–430.

Fischer, J. (1973). Is casework effective? A review. *Social Work, 18,* 5–20.

Glass, G. V., McGaw, B., & Smith, M. L. (1981). *Meta-analysis in social research.* Beverly Hills, CA: Sage Publications.

Hedges, L. V., & Olkin, I. (1985). *Statistical methods for meta-analysis.* New York: Academic Press.

Schuerman, J. R. (1988). Editorial. *Social Services Review, 62,* 351–352.

Videka-Sherman, L. (1985). *Harriett M. Bartlett practice effectiveness project.* Silver Spring, MD: National Association of Social Workers.

Videka-Sherman, L. (1986). *Studies of research on social work practice: A bibliography.* Silver Spring, MD: National Association of Social Workers.

Videka-Sherman, L. (1988). Meta-analysis of research on social work practice in mental health. *Social Work, 33,* 325–338.

Commentary

Meta-Analysis: A Heuristic Tool for Social Work Training

Paula Nurius

Chapter 11, by Fischer, is a welcome addition to the literature on data synthesis in general and meta-analysis in particular because, despite the surge of attention to the topic in allied fields, the social work literature has been surprisingly quiet about it. At least two areas of emphasis characterize the meta-analysis literature to date. One, of course, has involved applications of meta-analysis. The second has focused on the analytic and methodological features of meta-analysis, both pro and con. Within this area, a steady stream of revisions and alternatives has emerged as the technique has been iteratively studied, employed, and refined.

This commentary discusses the potential utility and limitations of meta-analysis as a galvanizing force for the review process and as an aid to the social work educator.

Fischer's conclusion captures an organizing theme for these comments: "At the least, [meta-analysis] can generate a great deal of renewed interest in the research review process per se. If that alone is its contribution, meta-analysis will be evaluated by future generations of social workers as worthy, indeed." As with many innovations going through their shakedown period, meta-analysis offers some useful means to ends and secondary payoffs in addition to the original goal for which it was designed. One of the strengths of Fischer's article is the balanced and constructively critical analysis he brought to bear on the premise, problems, and promise of data-synthesis methods. Fischer pointed out that the process of explicit, systematic, critical scrutiny is consistent with the tenets of scientific inquiry that social work has historically embraced but has not yet become adept at. Moreover, as he emphasized, what will ultimately determine the utility (or lack thereof) of meta-analysis for social work is *how* it is used.

HEURISTIC POSSIBILITIES FOR EDUCATORS

A principal use of meta-analysis is to develop knowledge through consolidation of disparate findings and the addressing of a broader net of questions than any single study could accomplish. For educators who are committed to promoting empiricism in clinical practice, two additional, more heuristic applications also are of interest: the promotion of both critical consumership and clear thinking—that is, the development of the skills and habits of systematic inquiry as a component of professional judgment.

One way in which meta-analytic methods may be used in training is to highlight and make explicit the tasks of sampling/selecting from, reviewing, analyzing, synthesizing, and interpreting *any* body of knowledge, including the narrative literature, as well as other professional sources (such as clinical supervision and an individual's and others' experiences), in addition to empirical outcome studies. The larger and more complex the input "pool" becomes, the more prone one becomes to use heuristic shortcuts, such as the reliance on the most salient information, the information that confirms one's perspective or expectation, or the information that is most charismatically or authoritatively asserted. Under such clouded and complex circumstances, review and synthesis methods—both qualitative and quantitative— become critically important.

A second way in which meta-analysis may be used in training is to help bring home the fact that the synthesis of any data or information is essentially a *conceptual*, substantively grounded task. Fischer pointed out that although it objectifies the review process to a considerable extent, meta-analysis is nonetheless rife with decision points that require subjective judgments, choices, and compromises. This situation is by no means unique to meta-analysis. Rather, these dilemmas and choice points exist in *any* review or synthesis. Quantitative methods merely make them more evident and explicit.

This explication and the need to take a position in print on how one contended with hard decisions (such as one's rationale for certain criteria for sampling and inclusion of studies) can understandably generate discomfort and a sense of vulnerability to criticism. In more traditional narrative reviews, the numerous judgments, choices, and so forth are far less apparent to the reviewer or to the consumer.

EXAMPLES OF APPLICATIONS

A few years ago, this author conducted a meta-analysis partly to get a better working sense of the method. The experience was so tedious, frustrating, and time consuming that she has not undertaken another such project. Nevertheless, the effort was worthwhile with respect to the substantive questions. Moreover, several secondary payoffs have proved invaluable.

One payoff is that the author has routinely incorporated *parts* or aspects of meta-analysis into her reviews and has come to expect that her students will do so as well. This approach of selecting those aspects of a methodology that most directly translate into sustainable habits is consistent with findings regarding the continued use of case evaluation methods following initial exposure. That is, students do transfer parts of the model to their everyday practice, typically those they view as most relevant and pragmatically manageable.

A second payoff has been the utility of abbreviated training in meta-analysis as a more intuitive mechanism for bringing home such points as validity, reliability, representativeness, and generalizability. For example, the issues involved in deciding which studies to select include inclusion and exclusion criteria, validity with respect to the identified problem or intervention, and obtaining a representative sample. The issues involved in how to deal with various types of findings facilitate an examination of which types of findings are appropriate for which kinds of research questions, the costs and benefits of different techniques for transforming and aggregating data, and the constraints and qualifications of these decisions for analyzing and interpreting outcomes.

Meta-analysis has been useful in making it painfully obvious that during any type of information synthesis, one either is making *implicit* judgments and choices (on some level drawing on some source of referents) regarding the many decisions Fischer illustrated or is *not* attending to them and is likely finding what one has been looking for, with all the dangers that implies. In short, meta-analysis has been useful in rendering a number of basic yet critical scientific principles more consumable and understandable to students, in augmenting the sense of the utility of the skills needed to synthesize information that are more likely to result in valid and reliable judgments and outcomes, and in illustrating the intimate links between scientific methods and the conceptual or substantive domain that is relevant to the question at hand.

One essential task in promoting empiricism in clinical practice is to shape students' skills in reasoning and making inferences and judgments along systematic, empirically oriented lines. A central task of students is to obtain, examine, and synthesize information—in one fashion or another—from a variety of sources. In addition to their value as aids to a quantitative review of the findings of studies reported in the literature, meta-analytic methods are intriguing springboards for the broader educational and socialization of students.

Synthesis

Meta-Analysis in Social Work

William Nugent

This synthesis of the major points and issues covered in the session on meta-analysis summarizes the important advantages of using meta-analysis and the problems and limitations associated with this methodology. It then considers meta-analysis as a metaphor for the educator and ends with a discussion of future directions for the use of meta-analysis in social work.

META-ANALYSIS: THE PROMISE

One purpose of empirical clinical practice is to accumulate research knowledge for practitioners (Barlow, Hayes, & Nelson, 1984). To do so requires the analysis of a large body of research results at some point. Through such an analysis, important information can be extracted from the large body of research and distilled for easy consumption. In the past, the narrative review filled this purpose. Meta-analysis is, in a sense, this same process, albeit in a more objective (in the sense of being replicable) manner: Studies are combined, statistics are computed, and the results are used to describe and summarize the results of a large number of research studies. Meta-analysis is a quantitative approach to the research review and can add to the rigor of this process. Its greatest contribution is, perhaps, that it can help explicate the review process and, if it is done appropriately, reduce bias.

A particularly salient advantage of meta-analysis is the use of statistics that create a common metric for aggregating and synthesizing studies that use *different* dependent variables. This feature enables the reviewer to make meaningful quantitative statements about the effects of treatment variables at the level of an aggregation of research studies. It is important to realize that, for the most part, the statistics employed in meta-analysis are *not* used to test statistical hypotheses. For example, the statistic Δ, or d, is used primarily as a descriptor. In meta-analysis, the reviewer is looking for the *replication of effect*, as opposed to hypothesis testing in the statistical sense.

META-ANALYSIS: THE PROBLEMS

Although meta-analysis may be a great methodological innovation, it is not without problems. Given the potential impact that meta-analytic studies may have (and, indeed, have already had) on practitioners and policymakers, the limitations of meta-analysis need to be well understood and, if possible, rectified. In Chapter 11, Fischer detailed many of the critical limitations of meta-analytic techniques. In a sense, these limitations are no different from those facing the qualitative reviewer of research. Furthermore, many of Fischer's criticisms of meta-analysis are directed toward the application of meta-analytic techniques, not to the methodology per se.

Fischer cited several serious limitations: A single study can greatly influence the results of a meta-analysis through the manner in which the studies are combined; the use of different statistics on the same set of data can produce different results; and the methodological rigor of the component studies making up the aggregation can affect the results. Fischer noted that there seem to be two critical assumptions and limitations inherent in the use of meta-analysis: that its methods are properly used and that the methods themselves are valid and reliable. He stated that all these concerns, together with the relative newness of meta-analysis, combine to raise serious questions about the validity of meta-analytic results.

The most salient limitation of meta-analysis may be that any meta-analysis can never supercede the limits of the methodological quality of its component studies. In carrying out any meta-analysis, a crucial question is whether "less-than-methodologically-robust" studies should be included. If studies are excluded on these grounds, few will remain for inclusion; few social work studies are without methodological flaws. Furthermore, flawed studies do not mean that the results are wrong—just that threats to internal validity cannot be ruled out on purely methodological grounds. It seems crucial that reviewers should be clear about the criteria they use in deciding which studies to include or exclude from a meta-analysis.

Locating studies for inclusion also is a problem, a difficulty to which those who had done meta-analyses strongly testified. Incredible resources are particularly necessary to locate unpublished studies. Such efforts may or may not be worth the expenditure of such resources. Yet, a meta-analysis will only be as representative of research in any area as is the sample of studies that are included.

Some claimed that meta-analyses may be positively biased—that is, may tend to enhance or inflate any evidence of treatment effects. The sometimes contradictory results of traditional narrative reviews and meta-analyses were cited as evidence of this bias. However, others argued that meta-analyses may not be positively biased but that traditional narrative reviews may tend to be negatively biased, that is, they tend to underestimate treatment effects. This issue seems to be unresolved at this time.

Fischer viewed all these problems as being serious enough to recommend that, at this time, meta-analysis should be used only as a rough guide to integrating and summarizing the results of research. Others thought that such a recommendation was too strong. The clear and explicit presentation of exactly how any given meta-analysis is carried out can go a long way toward rectifying many of the concerns that Fischer voiced.

META-ANALYSIS: METAPHOR FOR EDUCATION

Some, notably Nurius, discussed whether educators should use meta-analysis with their social work students. Regardless of how meta-analysis is used for reviewing aggregations of research studies, it can, at the least, be used to stimulate interest. It can serve a valuable heuristic and teaching function. The meta-analytic approach may be used as a metaphor for the education of future social work researchers. It can be a means of showing that there is a great need for more informed analytic thinking in research, as opposed to ideological evaluation and commitment. It also can illustrate the need for the clear and explicit reporting of decisions made in research by researchers.

These observations are especially salient when viewed in light of the many concerns about the limitations of meta-analytic techniques. The final determination of the value of meta-analysis will be how it is used, which, in turn, will depend, to a great extent, on how students are trained by social work educators.

META-ANALYSIS: FUTURE DIRECTIONS

A number of thoughts were expressed about the future approaches that social workers may take regarding meta-analysis. Some of these thoughts were directed toward the editors of journals. Given that the crucial raw material of meta-analyses are, in general, journal articles, some attention should be paid to the quality of articles that are accepted for publication. Articles that are published should include summary statistics, such as means, standard deviations, and group sizes, that are needed for a meta-analysis. Several participants noted that many published articles *lack* these statistics—a limitation that necessarily precludes them from being included in a meta-analysis. Some thought also should be given to the publication of results in which statistically significant findings are *not* obtained. These ideas also imply that researchers should take responsibility of keeping the data they accumulate intact for several years in case some future researcher may want to include the data in a meta-analysis. The creation of a "central clearinghouse" in which research data are accumulated over time and stored for future researchers also should be considered.

Researchers need to report more clearly and in greater detail the exact methods they use in their research. In this way the methodological rigor of studies included in a meta-analysis can be upgraded. Researchers need to report such information as sample statistics; demographic data on subjects and practitioners, as well as other client and practitioner variables; and detailed information on sampling frames. In a sense, the researchers who conducted the original studies carry a large part of the responsibility for the quality of meta-analyses; these researchers are making the "raw material" for meta-analytic studies.

Fischer claimed that the key issue in the future of meta-analysis in social work is whether the problems noted earlier (and in his chapter) are insurmountable. At this point, he stated, the answer is, "We don't know." He suggested that meta-analytic techniques should be used as a rough guide and be integrated with the traditional narrative review. It should be noted that both meta-analysis and the traditional narrative review contain potential limitations and biases.

Finally, meta-analytic techniques need further research and development. As was noted in the session, little is known about the meta-analytic techniques that are required for aggregating single-subject data. Much the same can be said for procedures that are necessary for aggregating single-subject data from group studies. These are areas in which fruitful research and development work could be done.

CONCLUSION

The most general conclusion about meta-analysis in social work that one could draw from the session might be said to focus not on meta-analysis but on social work researchers. Meta-analysis is no more than a tool, much like a hammer or an automobile. As such, it is inherently neither bad nor good and, like all tools, has limitations. Properly used, a tool can provide its user with useful results or outcomes. Improperly used, any tool can cause harm and undesirable outcomes. Ultimately, the usefulness of meta-analysis rests in the hands of social work researchers—both present and future.

REFERENCE

Barlow, D. H., Hayes, S. C., & Nelson, R. O. (1984). *The scientist-practitioner: Research and accountability in clinical and educational settings.* New York: Pergamon Press.

Part 4
Epistemology for Clinical Social Work

Chapter 12

Symposium 2: On the Epistemology of Social Work Practice Knowledge
(with Apologies to Plato's Symposium)

Martin Bloom

Social work has never valued or seriously engaged in the examination of its assumptions about research. —Heineman-Pieper (1985, p. 8)

But then, if I am right [in his argument in the Allegory of the Cave], certain professors [of social work] must be wrong when they say that they can put a knowledge into the soul which was not there before, like sight into blind eyes. —Plato, *The Republic*, Book VII

I do not say that we can here and now give definitive answers to all these ancient questions, but I do say that a method has been discovered by which, as in science, we can make successive approximations to the truth, in which each new stage results from an improvement, not a rejection, of what has gone before. —Russell (1945, pp. 835–836)

OK, so I got my A in my theory class and an A in research. What am I supposed to do now with my client who will be coming to my office in the next hour?—A student of the author

I believe that I am prepared with an answer, wrote Plato at the beginning of *The Symposium*, some 2,500 years ago. Let me speculate how a Symposium on Knowledge might have been written.

Just the other day, a friend asked about the speeches in praise of Knowledge, which were delivered by Socrates, Aristophanes, and the others at Agathon's supper. These speeches were delivered some time ago, and so you will have to excuse the infirmities of memory. Let me begin at the beginning and endeavor to give you the most worthy remembrances of things past.

Phaedrus began with the observation that what a strange thing it is that other aspects of social work practice and research are honored with long and worthy monographs, whereas the topic of knowledge about Knowledge (so epistemology may be briefly defined) has no encomiast among all the scientists, philosophers, religionists, and lay people who otherwise strongly assert that they have the unimpeachable knowledge, albeit contradictory to all the others. The mere possession of "knowledge" appears to be self-confirming to its possessor; having an epistemology seems addictive. This makes discussions about Knowledge disputatious, and discussions about epistemologies vitriolic.

Then Phaedrus presented his empiricist view of epistemology:

> When I think about the origin, nature, and extent of knowledge, it appears certain to me that the mind is, initially, like a blank tablet. From whence does it obtain its ideas? In one word, from Experience, both from the five senses and from reflections about what these senses provide.

If something, like a client's problem, exists, it exists in some manner open to our experience of it. If it exists, then it can be described in experiential terms and measured. If we cannot measure the client's problem, then it does not exist and cannot be treated as such. We can, of course, "treat" people's perceptions of their "problems," such as when we try to convince the paranoid who is out walking the streets of some major metropolis that no one is out to get him (in particular). Reality is something that has to be seen to be believed. As with any basic idea, there may be many other components affixed to it, but, mused Phaedrus, this is enough to get the symposium going—even if not everyone believes that the ultimate answer has already been presented.

This, or something like it, was the speech of Phaedrus. The next one of import was by Pausanias, the rationalist, who said that he felt that Phaedrus had not set the argument in the right form. I think, therefore, I am going to reverse the emphasis, he said, because clearly and distinctly, believing something makes it so. The hard reality is this: Ideas, as processes within the mind, shape one's experience of experience, select what is to be considered, and interpret it according to one's values, vested interests, and prior knowledge. Reality is something that has to be believed to be seen. Pausanias continued: Knowledge, of course, is vital to any rational problem-solving process, as Helen of Chicago (whose books launched a thousand social work students) affirmed some time ago. Ask and you will be told; speculate and you will infer new combinations of ideas beyond the ken of your client. But beyond all else, follow the logical psychological process of solving problems. People have irrational ideas that cause them to feel unhappy; the task of the therapist is to change these irrational beliefs to rational ones by logical disputing so their humors are once again in balance.

Aristophanes was supposed to speak next, but he had the hiccough and so Eryximachus, the physician (reconciler of opposites, in the original Greek), spoke, saying that Pausanias made a fair beginning but a lame ending. It is true, he stated, as Phaedrus said, that the outer reality (things in themselves) causes one's sensations and experiences, but that outer reality is, in itself, unknowable. The sensations get "known" by the actions of one's mental apparatus that organizes them in preexisting mental categories of space, time, causation, and so on or linguistic deep structures. Thus, an inevitable combination of the cognitive (mental structures) and the behavioral (experiential) leads to the most efficacious resolution of the two earlier epistemological statements. Therapists must present experience to their clients by telling them this or that fact of life, but they must see to it that this experiential knowledge is embedded in their clients' own cognitive apparatus so that they, as individuals, may use the information expeditiously.

Aristophanes, having recovered from the hiccough, amused the gathering with his history of the knowledge of Knowledge, as a way of explaining its current forms and predicaments. The original nature of Knowledge was not as it is now, all fragmented and disparate, he noted. Rather, it was Whole, each component interlocked with every other in logical and meaningful ways. But terrible was the might of this primordial Knowledge, and it was obstreperous, as intellectuals are apt to be, so the gods feared for their very positions of power in the universe. The dean of the gods came up with a plan that would humble the pride and improve the manners of Knowledge. This plan involved dividing Knowledge into parts, categories, fields of study, academic disciplines—each with enough substance to make ends meet and appear autonomous. But, in fact, each part needed all the others to become Whole and meaningful again.

Thus, saith Aristophanes, Systems Theory was created, whose intellectual nature is such that the components are always looking for their "other half" but, because of the nature of things, rarely find a good fit. In a more somber tone, Aristophanes noted that the gods still keep an eye on academe and if even these humble components get too powerful, they may again be split and become like beings "hopping about on a single leg." The crowd nodded to one another on the wisdom of Aristophanes' meaning, even if his words missed their mark: Reductionism into atomistic pieces loses a major component of Knowledge, namely, the interrelationship of parts.

Agathon spoke next, offering this Heuristic homily to epistemology: In any situation, events occur that each observer may interpret as he or she wishes; there is no inherently superior perspective on reality. Each has his or her own values and biases, and when you push either empiricism or rationality to its limits, there is no difference. Thus, there is no superior method by which one comes to know reality. The workings of sophisticated procedures that seek to find statistically significant results not only divert attention from what is important in Human Affairs, which is facing and pragmatically resolving the significant issues of everyday life, but also idealize artificialities in the place of substance. To play on the words of the poet, One man's Mead is another man's Parsons.

Science, observed Agathon, is both the process of discovery and a confirmation of hypotheses for which different types of logical or psychological approaches may be necessary. So, at different times, scientists and scientific practitioners need to be objective, as well as subjective, about concepts and observables; they need to be concerned with predicting prospective events, as well as explaining past events. The use (by scientific practitioners) of the knowledge that other people have experienced requires some abstract language to relate the old to the new situations accurately. One person's hot experience rapidly cools in the hands of another without abstraction. Agathon noted that there are two different, mutually exclusive, paths to the future. It is important to describe both of them because one, the Pseudoscience that has captivated social work for the past 30 years, is better known, while the other, named the Heuristic Approach, can be understood as *not* being like the epistemology of Pseudoscience.

First, Agathon mentioned the fiction of empirical data promulgated by the Pseudoscientists—that there is something out there that our senses or our instruments register in a quantitative way and thus confer to it an empirical status. According to people who hold the Heuristic perspective, only indirect effects are observed, and these are interpreted by beliefs, expectations, language, and culture, among other things. Thus, any one source of knowledge, such as yardsticks measuring table tops or projective tests, or therapists' empathic sensitivities, has no ontological superiority over other sources.

Another fiction maintained by Pseudoscientists is that there are objective researchers who may recognize their values, but who can elect to keep themselves from influencing the choices made during the entire scientific process. Pseudoscientists also believe that scientists can select some portion of reality to study, as in the context-limited laboratory or in a controlled field experiment, that will provide meaningful information in other messy and complex situations. The Heuristic view is that values cannot be effectively isolated in any scientific enterprise and that sterile laboratory findings or overcontrolled field studies provide little guidance for workers in the real world. Generalizations that do emerge from such research "decay" over time.

Other fictions held by Pseudoscientists abound, such as the prejudice that practitioners are unreliable observers of reality, that statistical significance is the goal of research (even in social work), and that scientists always select the right problems to solve. The Heuristic position opposes these fictions and finds one aspect particularly pernicious, that we practitioners are committing professional suicide by conspiring to co-operate with society's gatekeepers regarding accountability, since we will never be able to offer objective, valid, reliable confirmations of anything we do.

At long last, Socrates spoke, although he tried to excuse himself from the obligation, saying that he had assumed each speaker was to speak the truth about epistemology, rather than to praise and promote his or her own conception of it. As Phaedrus hinted, the truth about epistemology is paradoxical, since one would need an epistemological platform from which to make true statements about epistemology, but one needs an epistemology to build that platform. So, instead of claiming any knowledge about Knowledge, Socrates said he would merely relate a story that was told to him years ago by a wise woman, Diotima. Because he did not wish to offend anyone present, he would take both sides in his dialogue, rather than ask questions of others—his usual method of discourse.

DIOTIMA: Have you noticed, Socrates, that all the epistemologists you and your colleagues have discussed have been men? And do you have any inkling that a male perspective permeates the definitions and constructions of epistemology?

SOCRATES: Why no, Diotima, I never noticed, nor do I see any way in which something as abstract as epistemology could be biased by being formulated by men. I strongly feel that epistemology, as the basic assumptions of our science and the helping professions, is made of sterner stuff.

DIOTIMA: Then tell me, Socrates, What is contained in your Knowledge about knowing?

SOCRATES: That is easily stated: There are beliefs and feelings of various sizes and shapes.

DIOTIMA: Feelings?

SOCRATES: You know, affections, passions, and the like. Oh, I know what you are going to ask next: Are all feelings known or are some unconscious and unknown in the ordinary sense of the word?

DIOTIMA: Why, yes, I was going to ask something of the sort. How do you answer your own question, Socrates?

SOCRATES: Some have said that these unconscious feelings—an interesting oxymoron, by the way—exist and cause us complex problems, but
I hold that feelings are simply things secretly known or forgotten and that
all remembrances of things past can be resurrected, but with too much
effort and with too little effect (although the therapist may be paid well for
the effort). Rather, go for the here-and-now behaviors, which, of course,
including feelings, as well as thoughts and actions, and have done with it.

DIOTIMA: Bravo, Socrates, spoken like a true and mortal man. But I care
more for these feelings, known or unknown, because they appear to me
to be just as much an experience of reality as are abstract ideas or beliefs.
Moreover, feelings are portions of human affairs about which we must
take some responsibility, since we know we can affect them, for better or
for worse. Now, feelings may never rise to the ethereal heights of abstractions for your gentlemen. But they remain fundamental building
blocks of everyday life, which abstract philosophy and science must
account for, whether or not they fit neatly.

Indeed, the helping professional may use this form of knowing, an
intuition or an empathy born of "understanding" a client, largely by
imagining himself or herself in the client's position. Thus, the helping
professional may not need abstract knowledge of the general situation
as much as strong, direct knowledge of the specific situation that guides
the helper to help the client help himself or herself. This combination of
abstract knowledge and particular information enables the scientific
practitioner to help in specific steps that can be corrected by feedback
from objective evaluation. Single-system designs are especially useful
here because they provide some approximate rigor that science so
highly values to the immediate situation, which the practitioner so
desperately needs.

SOCRATES: Ah, but wait a moment, Diotima. Abstract knowledge of
general situations is useful exactly because it can be applied, by artful
steps of connecting the particular instance to the class named in the
abstraction. Then, using the power of the logical mapping (theory), one
gains conceptual and pragmatic leverage over some portion of the real
world. Through such stratagems as these, Americans have placed a man
on the moon, although it must be admitted that our city streets are clogged
with homeless people.

DIOTIMA: Your example, Socrates, proves my point, that a scientific
practitioner is the ultimate goal of an applied epistemology. The scientific
practitioner has to be concerned with both abstract knowledge and
responsible knowledge, with collective norms and with particular values,
with general problem-solving skills and with creative applications. But
values themselves, don't you see, are statements of caring and

responsibility—the states of affairs that you and I prefer in this social context and time. What the male epistemology has neglected to include is the affective dimension of knowledge and, in so doing, has once again glorified the abstract over the existential.

SOCRATES: But Diotima, what if the helper and client differ on their values of desired outcomes? What higher platform can they appeal to to resolve this relativism your perspective leads to?

DIOTIMA: There is no question that each will differ from the other on values, which is why we have to continue to talk about feelings as a continuing part not only of solving problems, but, what is equally important, of promoting solutions of new desired states of affairs. In so doing, we clarify what options are probable and encourage the client to select the most desired from among them. This may be a solution to the difference between what is and what ought to be. We in applied science cannot ever separate values from knowledge and action.

SOCRATES: Well, Diotima, I see what you are saying about this gender bias in epistemology, but it seems to be merely one of the many issues facing us.

Socrates went on to list several dozen other fine points of epistemology, which might better be presented in Symposium 3. Upon hearing this list, Diotima said that Socrates had perhaps not fully comprehended her point about affective understanding. Socrates persisted, seeking clarification of her point. She replied that her earlier comments were the lesser mysteries of Knowledge, into which even Socrates could enter, but that she did not know whether he could attain the greater and more hidden ones that are the crown of these lesser ones and to which if he pursued them in a right spirit, the lesser ones would lead. Ever patient in the face of obtuseness, she continued assertively:

DIOTIMA: He who would understand Knowledge must begin in infancy with sensory (sensory-motor) experiences that give some understanding of the world in its own terms. Then, there begins a long series of intellectual experiences that move from the concrete single experience to the abstract and general knowledge. At the same time, there is a parallel growth of affective knowledge, first of oneself, then of others, and then of other persons and ideas or things in general. Knowledge, Socrates, is synergistic; add to it, and it adds more. The person with sensory, rational, and affective knowledge is ready to begin another series of experiences, with other people and things, but also with Nature itself. The knowledge possessed by the community of persons exceeds its individual members, beyond this time and this place. Ultimately, as one understands the knowledge of his or her individual self, and the shared experiences of others, past and present, then one recognizes that the experience of information and one's participation in that process are all that there is in life, each being part of it, each contributing to it.

For the scientific practitioner, this intellectual process amounts to a kind of social epistemological contract in which individuals surrender (agree) to common assumptions about the nature of Knowledge, and work within these assumptions. In return, the scientific practitioner benefits from the cumulative growth of what is known. Such practitioners have to be trained to observe scientifically, that is, with intersubjective agreement among other, similarly trained workers, which is how communications of individual practice wisdom are standardized. However, as with any contact, a practitioner always has the option to make a creative leap, to break out of the paradigm into one that is more effective for resolving experienced problems or for defining new questions. The scientific practitioner is at once part of the Many, but remains One. This dynamic tension is what spurs whatever his or her contributions are to the world.

SOCRATES: Such were the words of Diotima, and I am persuaded of their truth. Being persuaded of their truth, I try to persuade others.

Just then, there was a great knocking at the door, and the voice of Alcibiades was heard resounding in the halls. Though clearly stoned, Alcibiades did manage some further observations on the person of Socrates, which need not concern us here. Talking went on deep into the night, and one by one, all fell asleep, save Socrates who rose and went on his daily activities. . . .

REFERENCES

Allman, L. R. (1982). The aesthetic preference: Overcoming the pragmatic error. *Family Process, 21*, 43–56.

Anderson, H., & Goolishian, H. A. (1988). Human systems as linguistic systems: Preliminary and evolving ideas about the implications for clinical theory. *Family Process, 27*, 371–393.

Bloom, M. (1975). *The paradox of helping: Introduction to the philosophy of scientific practice.* New York: John Wiley & Sons.

Chafetz, J. S. (1988). *Feminist sociology: An overview of contemporary theories.* Itasca, IL: F. E. Peacock Publishers.

Dell, P. F. (1982). Beyond homeostasis: Toward a concept of coherence. *Family Process, 21*, 21–41.

Dunn, W., Mitroff, I., & Deutsch, S. J. (1981). The obsolescence of evaluation research. *Evaluation and Program Planning, 4*, 207–218.

Fischer, J. (1981). The social work revolution. *Social Work, 26*, 199–207.

Fischer, J. (in press). Whither the revolution. *Journal of Social Service Research.*

Geisman, L., & Wood, K. M. (1982). Evaluating practice: Science as faith. *Social Casework, 63*, 266–271.

Gurman, A. S., Kniskern, D. P., & Pinsof, W. M. (1986). Research on the process and outcome of marital and family therapy. In S. Garfield & A. Bergin (Eds.), *Handbook of psychotherapy and behavior change* (3rd ed.). New York: John Wiley & Sons.

Heineman-Pieper, M. (1985). The future of social work research. *Social Work Research & Abstracts, 21,* 3–11.

Heineman-Pieper, M. (1986). Some common misunderstandings of the heuristic approach [Letter to the editor]. *Social Work Research & Abstracts, 22,* 2, 22.

Hoffman, L. (1990). Constructing realities: An art of lenses. *Family Process, 29,* 1–12.

Hudson, W. W. (1978). First axioms of treatment. *Social Work, 21,* 65–66.

Hudson, W. W. (1982). Scientific imperatives in social work research and practice. *Social Service Review, 56,* 246–258.

Kaplan, A. (1964). *The conduct of inquiry: Methodology for behavioral science.* Scranton, PA: Chandler.

Keeney, B. P., & Sprenkle, D. H. (1982). Ecosystemic epistemology: Critical implications for the aesthetics and pragmatics of family therapy. *Family Process, 21,* 1–19.

Kuhn, T. S. (1970). *The structure of scientific revolution* (2nd ed.). Chicago: University of Chicago Press.

Mahoney, M. J. (1985). Academic clinical psychology: The quest for a richer harvest. In R. A. Kasschau, L. P. Rehm, & L. P. Ullmann (Eds.), *Psychology research, public policy, and practice: Toward a productive partnership.* New York: Praeger Publishers.

Mitroff, I. I. (1973). Systems, inquiry, and the meanings of falsification. *Philosophy of Science, 40,* 255–276.

Mitroff, I. I., & Pondy, L. R. (1974). On the organization of inquiry: A comparison of some radically different approaches to policy analysis. *Public Administration Review, 5,* 471–479.

Mullen, E. J. (1985). Methodological dilemmas in social work research. *Social Work Research & Abstracts, 21,* 12–20.

Peile, C. (1988). Research paradigms in social work: From stalemate to creative synthesis. *Social Service Review, 62,* 1–19.

Popper, K. R. (1959). *The logic of scientific discovery.* New York: Harper Torchbooks.

Rodwell, M. K. (1987). Naturalistic inquiry: An alternative model for social work assessment. *Social Service Review, 61,* 231–246.

Roman, P. (1982). In search of truth: The evasiveness of reality and the permanence of beauty. *International Social Science Review, 35,* 82–93.

Russell, B. (1945). *A history of western philosophy.* New York: Simon & Schuster.

White, L. A. (1938). Science is sciencing. *Philosophy of Science, 5,* 360–389.

Wood, K. M. (1988). *Epistemological issues in the development of social work practice knowledge.* Paper presented at the conference, Empiricism in Clinical Practice: Present and Future. Great Barrington, MA.

Zukav, G. (1979). *The dancing Wu Li masters: An overview of the new physics.* New York: William Morrow.

Commentary

Bloom on Bloom: A Follow-up

Martin Bloom

I found Bloom's article (Chapter 12), presumably written for a contemporary audience of scholars, researchers, and practitioners in social work, to be baffling, to say the least. The article contains no central theoretical frame of reference, no distinctive research methodology, and no data. It appears to contain a nonrandom survey from one ethnic minority involving a small sample ($N = 6$) regarding their views on the nature of knowledge, an extraordinarily vague and diffuse topic that provides neither principles of social work practice nor answers for qualifying examinations. To his credit, the author confesses the limitations of recalled information, although this confession did not seem to prevent his presentation of long quotations.

What was Bloom trying to say? Because I have been obliged to read every word he has ever written, I find that I have developed a certain facility in understanding the twists and turns of his logic. However, Chapter 12 has more than its share of twists and turns. Yet, upon careful rereading and reflection, I believe that I have discovered what might have been the major points of the article and the major implications for social work practice. First, the major points.

MAJOR POINTS

As you may have observed, Bloom subtly identified each speaker with a label—for example, "Phaedrus presented his empiricist view of epistemology"—suggesting that Phaedrus was merely the spokesperson for the empirical position in epistemology. And, if you were to read the background references for Chapter 12, you would note in his cryptic writing style the memorable phrases of memorable writers on epistemology of the ancient and modern worlds—the empiricist, the rationalist, the combined empiricist-rationalist as reconciler of opposites (cognitive behaviorists), and those taking the heuristic approach, which is essentially an antipositivist epistemology that must eschew, on principle, a clear and concrete statement of its principles. The discussion by Aristophanes is not merely a humorous interlude; it is a systems analysis of the universality of knowledge, which makes a great deal of sense, but, of course, does not get us far.

I gather that Bloom made his point through the doppelganger effect of having Socrates report Diotima's remarks, although this is not clear in the text. (Bloom refused to confirm or deny this inference.) Ms. Diotima appeared to be saying that even epistemology may be a gender-biased enterprise, while Mr. Socrates (here made to play Every Man, the Fool) fell into every conceivable trap to illustrate her point.

MAJOR IMPLICATIONS

Major implications for social work practice: The most difficult part of the article occurred at the end when Diotima first described the developmental view on epistemology—including both cognitive and affective development—and then connected this view to social work practice through the notion of a social epistemological contract. To make any sense of this passage, one has to connect several other pieces from Diotima's last speeches. In connecting thoughts and feelings as intrinsically part of the helping enterprise, Diotima was seeking a way to be both the "scientist" and the "artist" (practitioner.)

Her solution was to combine the client's values and goals with the practitioner's theories and skills, as they are monitored and evaluated in practice using single-system designs. So, the "scientific practitioner" is someone who has agreed to some social epistemological contract, agreed, that is, to some view of reality—empirical, rational, heuristic, or whatever—to get on with the business of helping scientifically and artistically through evaluated practice. There are many ways to help, and we do not have definitive answers on which is best for what condition in what situation. The best we have is to be rigorous in understanding what we are doing with and to clients and to face these value-laden facts with openness and humility, if we are ever to reach the goal of effective and humane practice.

This reminds me of my favorite definition of science: Science is the art of having absolute faith in the probabilities that emerge from applying relatively unclear concepts to relatively complex events according to relatively vague hypotheses. This definition may have little to do with Chapter 12 or this commentary, but we all need something to which we give passionate commitment, so I thought I would offer this definition as my concluding thought.

Commentary

Penetrating the Veil of Appearance in Empirical Clinical Practice

José B. Ashford

In Chapter 12, Bloom used a genre that is rooted in the tradition of a Platonic dialogue to review the range of epistemological issues in the practice of social work. His choice of a dialogue, rather than of a mono-logue, discourse, or a treatise, should not be characterized solely as an artful literary device. It also has considerable significance for evaluating the rationality of his arguments. In fact, students of Platonic dialogues (Rosen, 1968) maintain that one cannot penetrate the irony of a dialogue and understand its significance if one overlooks its dramatic function. The dramatic function of this dialogue appears, at first glance, to be an apology for an empiricist epistemology. After further scrutiny, however, it seems that the conversation between Socrates and Diotima reveals the ultimate issues that Bloom wished the reader to examine.

Bloom seemed to be questioning the skepticism of feminist relativism and to assert a view of science that is similar to Campbell's (1987) notion of a mutually reinforcing scientific community. That is, he used Diotima's conversation with Socrates to articulate questions that dispute the putative male bias in empirical clinical practice. Furthermore, he used the statements in their conversation to subject his conceptions of a scientific practitioner and an "epistemological contract" to counterarguments that are consistent with the dialectic method used by Plato. It is important to note, however, that Diotima's statements in Symposium 2, as in Plato's Symposium, probably represent a thinly constructed disguise for Bloom's views. This observation regarding the dramatic function of Diotima's statements is derived from Platonic criticism (Rosen, 1968). If it is accurate, then Bloom's dialogue does not conform to the standards typically associated with true Platonic irony. In a true Platonic irony, Bloom's views on epistemology would have to conflict with the traditions and arguments of his peers (Ivanoff, Robinson, & Blythe, 1987) in empirical clinical practice.

Since Bloom's ultimate questions are not dramatically at odds with current epistemological disputations in social work, this commentary identifies a number of issues that take seriously Locke's (1894) position on the extent to which knowledge is limited by sensory experience. Moreover, it reopens Hume's (1902) devastating critique of naive empiricism (Maxwell, 1975) by examining the problem of induction in empirical clinical practice. Since the scientific practitioner relies heavily on inductive inferences, these comments will focus on counterarguments derived from the knowledge issue that Weimer (1976) termed the "justification of induction." And last, this commentary seeks clarification of why empiricism, instead of pragmatism, is the foundation theory for a movement in social work that strongly emphasizes the evaluation of practice.

KNOWLEDGE AND THE LIMITS OF EMPIRICAL DATA

A major irony that should not be overlooked in Bloom's article is his use of a Platonic or a rationalistic style of argument at a conference on empiricism in clinical practice. This stylistic approach is ironic primarily because Plato is generally characterized as an idealist philosopher who was highly suspicious of knowledge derived from sensory experience. Unlike most empiricists, Plato assumed that the visible or the observable world can present to the mind only objects that result in beliefs or opinions. He also argued in his divided-line thesis that one acquires knowledge by having the mind move from the lowest levels of reality (things) to the highest levels (forms or mathematical objects). In fact, he cautioned, in his theory of forms and in his allegory of the cave, not to mistake the sensory experience associated with appearances with that of true reality.

A number of modern philosophers of science (Mahoney, 1976; Maxwell, 1975; Weimer, 1975) have offered similar caveats regarding the limits of knowledge derived from empirical data. Many of these philosophers have argued convincingly that some views of science tend to overemphasize the role played by empirical data in the creation of knowledge. Mahoney devoted significant attention to challenging conventional views in science that support the supremacy of data as the primary source of knowledge. He argued that any approach to knowledge that has data as its foundation must not ignore the conceptual nature of knowledge. In fact, he reasserted a version of science that accepts relativism and the mutability or changeability of facts.

Although many empiricists may concede that "scientific data always presupposes some form of conceptualization" (Mahoney, 1976, p. 133), it is Mahoney's view that they do not recognize that this concession has serious implications for empiricist theories of knowledge. If empiricists concede that events or facts receive their meaning from conceptual perspectives, then facts are relative to the concepts or assumptions of the observer. The upshot of such a situation is a view of science in which the primary source of knowledge is theory or concepts, not scientific data. This is not to suggest that Diotima and other empiricists in Bloom's dialogue ignore this realization, but that they have merely minimized its implications. With similar concerns in mind, Mahoney (1976) stated: "The admission of factual mutability destroys the notion that science progresses by data accumulation. Data are not the firm building blocks of knowledge. In at least one sense, they are the products of theory—not its parents" (p. 133).

The important role that Mahoney attributed to concepts, frameworks, and categorizations of information in the development of knowledge is an issue that is receiving minimal attention in social work. It is not clear in Bloom's dialogue whether participants at his banquet on epistemology, or, for that matter, in the profession of social work, consider this an important issue that warrants further scrutiny. This lack of clarity is especially surprising in view of the position taken by NASW's initial Commission on Practice in the "Working Definition of Social Work Practice" (Subcommittee on the Working Definition, 1958). This commission attempted to shift the profession's conceptualization of practice from an emphasis on method to an emphasis on knowledge. In particular, it devoted substantial attention to identifying barriers in the thinking of social workers that delayed the profession's growth and development (Bartlett, 1970). It identified "such barriers as a mistrust of the deductive approach and resistance to frames of reference . . . as particularly salient obstacles to overcome" (Ashford & LeCroy, 1988, p. 1). Similar obstacles also are evident in the empirical clinical practice movement.

It is implied in the scientific practitioner movement that social work is a profession that ought to be guided by method rather than by knowledge. As a consequence, minimal attention is devoted to issues of knowledge that surround the framing or classification of problems. In fact, virtually no attention is directed toward these ends in many professional papers in social work whose explicit purpose is to clarify the key components of empirical clinical practice. Furthermore, few scholars in the empirical clinical practice movement, with the exception of Gambrill (1983), recognize the significant role of critical reasoning or logical processes in practice. The attention that Gambrill devotes to improving the thinking skills of practitioners is most illustrative of a view of science that does not ignore that validated methods of practice can be applied illogically or irrationally. In essence, clinical reasoning processes are issues that warrant equal time with those of measurement and validity, since logic is as important a source of knowledge as are empirical data.

To some extent, the current preoccupation in social work with "applying practice methods with empirically validated effectiveness" (Ivanoff, Robinson, & Blythe, 1987, p. 418) is due to what Lindblom (1987) referred to as an excessive concern with the issues of validity and verification. In his critique of Campbell's (1987) guidelines for optimizing scientific validity, Lindblom (1987) raised several issues that challenge the worship of the fetishism of validity in the applied social sciences:

> The pursuit in the social sciences of a degree of validity even roughly comparable to that achieved in the natural sciences is, for most propositions that might be so pursued, foolish in the same way that attempting to fly without mechanical aids is foolish. . . . Because we cannot widely achieve a very high degree of validity, much of our efforts as social scientists ought to go in other directions. . . . Might then appropriateness of conceptualization rival validity as a goal for social sciences? (pp. 512–516)

Lindblom's suggestion that it is inappropriate for applied scientists to devote inordinate attention to the pursuit of rigorous degrees of validity, in a social world plagued by extreme complexity and by high uncertainty, has definite support in the social work literature. Helen of Chicago (Perlman, 1957), who is given cursory attention in Bloom's dialogue, subscribes to a pragmatist epistemology of social work that rejects a profession that pursues fixed or validated solutions to clients' problems. In her problem-solving or pragmatic method, knowledge is best conceived as an activity that is dependent on processes of reflection that are not unlike Schon's (1983) thesis on "reflection-in-action" discussed in Chapter 13. In a pragmatist conceptualization of practice, "knowledge is defined as any activity that results in consequences that resolve problems in living" (LeCroy, Ashford, & Macht, 1989, p. 11). Furthermore, in conceptualizations of practice that are rooted in a pragmatist epistemology, it is assumed that "social workers should not take for granted that what 'works' in one situation (which is considered truth in the philosophy of pragmatism) will also 'work' in other situations" (Lecroy, Ashford, & Macht, 1989, p. 11).

Although some aspects of pragmatic conceptualizations of practice are still prevalent in social work, pragmatism's views regarding validated knowledge have been repudiated by some scientific practitioners without any clear justification. Many empirical clinical practitioners accept the feasibility of achieving validated knowledge but rationalize the use of single-systems technology by means of pragmatic principles of evaluation. That is, their justification for using single-systems technology may be to evaluate the consequences of their pragmatic practices, rather than to develop empirical generalizations or what Socrates referred to in

Bloom's dialogue as abstract knowledge. If this is the case, are they also conceding that data generated from single-subject research cannot be characterized as generalizable knowledge?

JUSTIFICATIONISM AND INDUCTION

Perhaps this author's concerns about the foundation theory under-lying the scientific practitioner movement in social work are due, in part, to fear that empirical clinical practitioners are accepting on faith the logical status of knowledge derived from inductive inference. "Inductive inference is taken by almost everyone to be the method by which science operates; and if it is the method of science, then it must be a rational source of knowledge" (Weimer, 1975, p. 430). However, as Mahoney (1976) pointed out, J. F. Fries demonstrated in 1828 that

> logical relations such as probability refer only to propositions and that
> propositions can only be derived from other propositions, not from facts.
> Data can never necessitate an assertion or generalization and without this
> necessary interrelationship there can be no logical inference. (p. 136)

If this is a prevalent view in the philosophy of science, then an important question that should not be ignored is this: Why has empirical or scientific data remained the primary authority appealed to by empiricists in making their claims about knowledge?

Moreover, one should not continue to overlook the inherent irra-tionalities attributed to empiricism by nonjustificationist philosophers (Bartley, 1962, 1964; Weimer, 1975). It is the position of most non-justificationists that the major problem with empiricists' claims about knowledge is their acceptance of a justificationist conception of knowl-edge. The justificationist theory of knowledge assumes that the identifi-cation of knowledge cannot occur without proof or authority. However, as Bartley (1962) and Mahoney (1976) pointed out, this approach to knowledge is inherently irrational primarily because it appeals to the authoritarian structure of traditional epistemology. "Our conventional approaches to knowledge have always invoked some form of ultimate epistemological authority—sense data, logic, revelation or whatever. However, the authority of this authority is always taken on faith" (Mahoney, 1976, p. 140). In fact, Popper (1959, 1963) identified how the failures of justificationism in contemporary empiricism have contributed to considerable irrationality (Weimer, 1975). "No wonder that contem-porary empiricists are the best representatives of existentialist despair and dread—by the consistent application of their own criteria of rational-ity, they have shown that their trust in empiricism was not justified—and have retreated to a faith in empiricism rather than a defense of it" (Weimer, 1975, p. 436).

REFERENCES

Ashford, J. B., & LeCroy, C. W. (1988). *Problem solving in social work practice: A user approach to knowledge utilization.* Manuscript submitted for publication.

Bartlett, H. M. (1970). *The common base of social work practice.* New York: National Association of Social Workers.

Bartley, W. W. (1962). *Retreat to commitment.* New York: Alfred A. Knopf.

Bartley, W. W. (1964). Rationality versus the theory of rationality. In M. Bunge (Ed.), *The critical approach to science and philosophy* (pp. 3–31). New York: Free Press.

Campbell, D. T. (1987). Guidelines for monitoring the scientific competence of preventive intervention research centers. An exercise in the sociology of scientific validity. *Knowledge: Creation, Diffusion, Utilization, 8,* 389–430.

Gambrill, E. D. (1983). *Casework: A competency-based approach.* Englewood Cliffs, NJ: Prentice-Hall.

Hume, D. (1902). *Enquiry concerning the human understanding.* Oxford, England: Clarendon Press.

Ivanoff, A., Robinson, A. R., & Blythe, B, J, (1987) Empirical clinical practice from a feminist perspective. *Social Work, 32,* 417–423.

LeCroy, C. W., Ashford, J. B., & Macht, M. W. (1989). A framework for analyzing knowledge utilization in social work practice. *Journal of Social Welfare, 16,* 3–17.

Lindblom, C. (1987). Alternatives to validity. *Knowledge: Creation, Diffusion, Utilization, 8,* 509–520.

Locke, J. (1894). *Essay concerning human understanding.* New York: Dover Publications.

Mahoney, M. J. (1976). *Scientist as subject: The psychological imperative.* Cambridge, MA: Ballinger.

Maxwell, G. (1975). Induction and empiricism: A bayesian-frequentist alternative. In G. Maxwell & R. M. Anderson (Ed.), *Minnesota studies in the philosophy of science* (pp. 106–165). Minneapolis: University of Minnesota Press.

Perlman, H. H. (1957). *Social casework: A problem-solving process.* Chicago: University of Chicago Press.

Popper, K. R. (1959). *The logic of scientific discovery.* New York: Basic Books.

Popper, K. R. (1963). *Conjectures and refutations.* New York: Harper & Bros.

Rosen, S. (1968). *Plato's symposium.* New Haven: Yale University Press.

Schon, D. A. (1983). *The reflective practitioner: How professionals think in action.* New York: Basic Books.

Subcommittee on the Working Definition of Social Work Practice for the Commission on Social Work Practice. (1958). Working definition of social work practice. *Social Work, 3*(3), 5–8.

Weimer, W. (1975). The psychology of inference and expectation: Some preliminary remarks. In G. Maxwell & R. M. Anderson (Ed.), *Minnesota studies in the philosophy of science* (pp. 430–486). Minneapolis: University of Minnesota Press.

Weimer, W. (1976). *Psychology and the conceptual foundations of science.* Hillsdale, NJ: Lawrence Erlbaum Associates.

Commentary

Thoughts on the Epistemology of Social Work Practice Knowledge

Cheryl A. Richey

The dialogue format of Chapter 12 coaxed the reader to ponder the myriad issues, questions, and paradoxes that surround the topic of knowledge in social work practice. Two specific questions that it raised are these:

1. What is the problem? Why is epistemology an important issue for social work educators, researchers, and practitioners to consider?

2. How may social workers better address or correct these problems, assuming that the problems exist and can be identified? More personally, how may a consideration of epistemological issues help one do a better job as an educator, mentor, researcher, colleague, and practitioner?

WHAT IS THE PROBLEM?

While reading the dialogue, the author was struck with the ever-expanding number of possible epistemological conflicts among the speakers as each one stepped forward to elucidate yet another viewpoint and supporting argument. Several of the speeches echoed past discussions with students of their explicitly stated (or implicitly inferred) attitudes about empirically based practice. Conflict or lack of accord between individual epistemological orientations is, no doubt, common and, in itself, may not be a problem. In fact, differences in cognitive styles or world views may enhance many intellectual, artistic, and interpersonal endeavors. However, as a social work educator, the author has become increasingly aware of how discordance in epistemological positions among students and faculty, students and field instructors, and faculty and field instructors can limit the transmission and acquisition of information and, subsequently, the integration or assimilation of knowledge with decisions about practice and practitioners' behaviors. Consequently, despite efforts to train, convince, persuade, or convert, conflicts in personal epistemologies or ways of knowing can diminish understanding and learning among everyone in the educational enterprise. In short, the problem is one of the eroded influence of educators to shape prospective social work professionals to become not only empirically minded, but committed to public social service, disadvantaged clients, and social change. Several examples of epistemological conflicts in social work education come readily to mind. These examples will be presented after the clarification of how personal epistemologies can differ.

Differences in Personal Epistemologies

The various epistemological orientations often appear to be defined in terms of two polarities, the subjective perspective and the objective perspective. The subjective knower is said to understand a phenomenon through close, intimate contact with it, by either directly experiencing it or empathically connecting with others' personal experiences (Belenky, Clinchy, Goldberger, & Tarule, 1986). The subjectivist is keenly self-aware and carefully attentive to the inner voices of emotion and intuition that guide what is accepted as truth. The objectivist or "procedural" knower, on the other hand, listens attentively to the voice of reason and achieves knowledge through detached observation, careful description, measurement, and critical thinking (Belenky, Clinchy, Goldberger, & Tarule, 1986).

It is likely that few personal epistemologies reflect completely either a subjective or objective orientation. More realistically, they may be placed along a continuum between these two dimensions. Thus, the following examples of epistemological discord reflect positions along this subjective-objective gradient.

Conflicts in Personal Epistemologies

One conflict is the discordance between the epistemological orientation of social work educators, which is notably more toward the objective end of the continuum, and that of some students, which is decidedly closer to the subjective pole. An extreme subjective orientation would be communicated by such statements as, "All I need to know is ultimately inside of me" and "My gut never fails to show me the truth; I just need to tune into it and listen."

For the past several years, the author has asked first-year master of social work students at the beginning of their educational unit, a cluster of sequenced and integrated practice and research courses, to rate their degree or level of endorsement of 12 components of competency-based social work practice, as discussed by Gambrill (1983) and Hepworth and

Larsen (1986). These components include an emphasis on the client's strengths, attention to person-situation factors, and monitoring progress. The component that has consistently received the lowest relative scores has been "supporting one's decisions and judgments with evidence." Although the reasons for this rating have not been systematically collected, the finding suggests that a fair number of students are not keen on backing up or defending something "known" with objective data. The author is not familiar with any large-scale study of the epistemological orientations of social work students, but guesses that a sizable percentage of them fall close to the subjective end of the continuum. Two surveys related to this hypothesis. Coan's (1979) study of 866 psychologists found a relationship between subjective orientation and class, religion, and ethnic minority status. Coan concluded that the more subjectively oriented professionals seemed to have experienced some lack of accord with mainstream American society. A more recent study of 135 women from diverse backgrounds reported that the largest percentage of respondents (almost half) fell into one of five possible epistemological categories, that of subjective knowing (Belenky, Clinchy, Goldberger, & Tarule, 1986). Although percentage distributions among the other four classifications were not explicated, the two categories that incorporated more objective strategies for knowing received relatively modest endorsements by the respondents. Furthermore, the subjective knowers were distributed across class, ethnic, age, and educational boundaries.

The lack of accord between the epistemological orientation of some educators and students is troubling for several reasons. First, there is evidence that personal epistemologies change little as a result of course work in college (Unger, Draper, & Pendergrass, 1986). Thus, some subjective knowers may well remain largely untouched by efforts to encourage them to embrace the scientific method and adopt it in practice. Second, the failure of educators to "convert" these students may not be immediately detected, since some subjective knowers, like chameleons, use the rational or analytic voice in academic situations, but follow their inner voice in other contexts (Belenky, Clinchy, Goldberger, & Tarule, 1986). Perhaps another explanation for the erosion of practice-evaluation activity by social workers after graduation (see Richey, Blythe, & Berlin, 1987) is a shift or return to a more subjective epistemological orientation.

Another example of epistemological conflict in social work education is the objectively oriented student paired with a more subjectively oriented practicum supervisor. Although the supervisor may be a treasure trove of clinical wisdom, she or he may be unable to describe decisions and actions or explain the rationale for choices in ways that are received and assimilated by a student who only understands the voice and language of reasons. The supervisor may be able to demonstrate good clinical practice ("Watch what I do"), but the student may be unable to learn by empathic observation alone. One consequence of such an epistemological mismatch would likely be incomplete transfer of valuable practice knowledge, values, and skills to the social work trainee. The supervisor also would likely experience diminished returns from the student in the form of the intellectual stimulation and emotional rapport and support that can result from successful mentor-protégé relationships (Richey, Gambrill, & Blythe, 1988).

RESOLVING EPISTEMOLOGICAL CONFLICTS

The author's thoughts about possible remedies for epistemological discord reflect a desire to connect objective and subjective orientations—to forge a rapprochement between what appear to be categorically distinct and mutually exclusive styles of knowing. This position seems to be similar to that voiced by Diotima in Chapter 12, who spoke in favor of including values and feelings with scientific procedures for developing abstract knowledge and solutions to problems.

In service of this rapprochement, it may be helpful to reconceptualize objectivity and subjectivity, not as polar ends of single continuum, but as two independent constellations. The concept of androgyny is a useful model (Bem, 1974). For example, instead of being either masculine or feminine, a person of either sex can be androgynous, that is, highly "masculine" (instrumental) *and* highly "feminine" (expressive).

Fluency in Two "Languages"

Conceptualizing the constructs of objective and subjective as independent allows the development of a 2 x 2 table and four profiles based on the level (high–low) of each dimension. It is conceivable that an individual could be "high" or skillful in both subjective and objective epistemological modes. This individual, a "connected" knower, is able to think, perceive, and speak in both the language of reason and the language of personal experience. The connected knower utilizes procedures of scientific inquiry and is attentive to his or her reactions and perceptions and those of others (Belenky, Clinchy, Goldberger, & Tarule, 1986).

The educator's goal with students for whom objectivism is a second language is not to weaken or eliminate their "mother tongue," but to expand their understanding and use of another language that can clarify and enhance what is known. To do so, objectively oriented academics must become fluent in the language of personal experience to facilitate genuine dialogue and "passionate" learning (Belenky, Clinchy, Goldberger, & Tarule, 1986). One method for achieving this goal may be connected teaching. Belenky and her colleagues suggested that one characteristic of connected teaching is intimacy among students and the instructor, which facilitates mutual disclosure and vicarious experiencing.

Communicating the Insider's Perspective

Learning among subjective knowers may be facilitated if they can understand and empathize with the personal experience of others. For example, the instructor or supervisor could verbalize, perhaps with a think-aloud procedure, the cognitive processes involved in a clinical decision. This act of personal disclosure or transparency is, no doubt, difficult, but the payoffs may be worthwhile if it assists students in making their tacit knowledge explicit and thus facilitating their more active participation in learning.

One strategy for portraying the insider's perspective is to assign readings that convey to the relatively unafflicted the private worlds of the suffering. The readings that the author has used have included a collection of personal, gripping accounts of the experience of depression (Rippere & Williams, 1985) and a poem of a young woman who eventually succeeded in killing herself. These readings, which make heavy use of metaphor, apparently speak to students with a power unmatched by their course texts or the *Diagnostic and Statistical Manual of Mental Disorders, Third Edition* (American Psychiatric Association, 1980). The use of metaphor may be a particularly effective means of establishing rapport, challenging existing beliefs and perceptions, and conveying new concepts (see Barker, 1985; Marlatt & Fromme, 1987).

Making Written Material More Enticing

Making written material more enticing was one recommendation for enhancing research activity among practitioners expressed by Gambrill (1987). Certainly professional writing must remain descriptive and verifiable. Yet, a brief account of the internal decision-making processes as they unfolded or an allegorical sketch of an otherwise complex series of actions and reactions could greatly enhance understanding among subjective learners who might otherwise remain untouched by the standard manuscript.

The writings of Lopez are one model of how objective and subjective language can be integrated to achieve a more complete phenomenology. In his collection of essays *Crossing Open Ground*, Lopez (1988) recounted various personal experiences, including "A Reflection on White Geese," a story of the annual migration of geese through northern California. The essay begins with a careful description of the geographic location; the size, plumage, and mating behavior of geese; and other pertinent historical and scientific information. In addition to this objective chronicle, Lopez shares with the reader how he personally experienced the geese:

> I remember watching a large flock rise one morning from a plowed field about a mile distance. I had been watching clouds, the soft, buoyant, wind-blown edges of immaculate cumulus. The birds rose against much darker clouds to the east. There was something vaguely ominous in this appari-tion, as if the earth had opened and poured them forth, like a wind, a blizzard, which unfurled across the horizon above the dark soil, becoming wider and higher in the sky than my field of vision could encompass, great swirling currents of birds in a rattling of wings, one fluid recurved sweep of 10,000 passing through the open spaces in another, counterflying flock, while beyond them lattice after lattice passed like sliding walls, until in the whole sky you lost your depth of field, and felt as though you were looking up from the floor of the ocean through shoals of fish. (p. 32)

Such prose is probably well beyond what most professionals who have been trained in scholarly writing could ever hope to create. Yet, it seems worthwhile to attempt to instill some degree of vividness or emotion into the professional literature, which, after all, should be addressing issues that are worthy of passion.

REFERENCES

American Psychiatric Association. (1980). *Diagnostic and statistical manual of mental disorders* (3rd ed.). Washington, DC: Author.

Barker, P. (1985). *Using metaphors in psychotherapy.* New York: Brunner/Mazel.

Belenky, M. F., Clinchy, B. M., Goldberger, N. R., & Tarule, J. M. (1986). *Women's ways of knowing.* New York: Basic Books.

Bem, S. L. (1974). The measurement of psychological androgyny. *Journal of Consulting and Clinical Psychology, 42,* 155–162.

Coan, R. W. (1979). *Psychologists: Personal and theoretical pathways.* New York: Irvington.

Gambrill, E. D. (1983). *Casework: A competency-based approach.* Englewood Cliffs, NJ: Prentice-Hall.

Gambrill, E. D. (1987). The state of the art in practice evaluation. In N. Gottlieb, H. A. Ishisaka, J. Kopp, C. A. Richey, & E. R. Tolson (Eds.), *Perspectives on direct practice evaluation* (pp. 2–20). Seattle: Center for Social Welfare Re-search.

Hepworth, D. H., & Larsen, J. A. (1986). *Direct social work practice: Theory and skills.* Chicago: Dorsey Press.

Lopez, B. (1988). *Crossing open ground*. New York: Charles Scribner's Sons.

Marlatt, G. A., & Fromme, K. (1987). Metaphors for addiction. *Journal of Drug Issues, 17,* 9–28.

Richey, C. A., Blythe, B. J., & Berlin, S. B. (1987). Do social workers evaluate their practice? *Social Work Research & Abstracts, 23,* 14–20.

Richey, C. A., Gambrill, E. D., & Blythe, B. J. (1988). Mentor relationships among women in academe. *Affilia: Journal of Women and Social Work, 3,* 34–47.

Rippere, V., & Williams, R. (1985). *Wounded healers: Mental health workers' experiences of depression*. New York: John Wiley & Sons.

Unger, R. K., Draper, R. D., & Pendergrass, M. L. (1986). Personal epistemology and personal experience. *Journal of Social Issues, 42,* 67–79.

Commentary

Epistemological and Semantic Traps

Roberta Wells Imre

This commentary on Bloom's paper focuses on several issues that seem to be basic to our problems of dealing with epistemological matters in social work. My reactions combine emotions and rationality, illustrating the important point that this combination is the way we as human beings, social workers or not, respond to ideas. Rationality and other intellectual processes discipline our feelings, but our feelings inform our intellects about what needs or requires thinking about. It is often our emotional valuing that calls our intellects into action. One reason why we are not always aware of this process is that it is so easy to get caught in semantic traps of our own making. This has something to do with the ways human beings necessarily use the resources of their culture in their thinking. Most of us have been brought up in Western intellectual traditions that by now, often without our awareness, have become an integral part of the way we think. Reading Greek philosophy is difficult at best, but trying to think as they thought in that historical period and cultural setting leaves us open to the temptation of attributing to them ways of thinking that were really born in our time and place. This commentary addresses some of these modern semantic traps.

Gender issues represent one of these problems. There seems to be a tradition in our culture, as well as in others, to believe that male and female thinking are profoundly different—in fact, categorically separate—and we tend to ascribe certain characteristics to each. For example, rational, objective, analytic, scientific thought is believed to be masculine, and emotionality (concern with feelings) and subjectivism (the "bleeding heart" syndrome) are considered to be feminine. Since a higher value has been placed on what is deemed to be masculine, it is not surprising that throughout history, it frequently has been difficult for women to be heard. Feminist thought has begun to show us the ways in which what are deemed to be feminine perspectives not only have been undervalued, but frequently have not come to our attention at all. It often requires overcoming cultural conditioning to perceive and then to assert what in fact has always been there, albeit for the most part unseen and unacknowledged.

What is considered to be feminine tends not to be regarded as intellectual and may even be referred to pejoratively as "effeminate" when it appears in a man. It is about time that we recognize and accept without apology that being fully human means both thinking and feeling and that neither sex has a corner on either of these human capacities. Whatever tendency, perhaps gender related, we have to favor one side or the other, we all have whole brains, including both right and left sides.

Another semantic trap in social work is found in Gordon's (1965) historic paper in which he described knowledge and values as separate categories. The problem with this view of knowledge and value as a dichotomy (a view that has been shared by other disciplines in our culture) is that it blinds us to the ways in which valuing and knowing are integrated in human thought.

If we look at the issue of values defined as preferences (for example, what we think "ought to be" as clearly different from "what is," that is, facts), it is apparent that preferences tend to be very personal and subject to idiosyncratic whim. There is no particular basis for considering my preferences to be any better than those of others, even though we are all capable of insisting on our own perspectives, either indirectly by denigrating the views of those who disagree or, more directly, by coming to verbal blows over our differences. On the other hand, if we share the same preferences, then we are apt to be sure we are right and to see it as "intersubjective confirmation," forgetting or simply not crediting at all the views of others who may not agree. In social work, we tend to require of students that they accept what we have designated to be our professional preferences, but we also emphasize that they must be prepared to accept their clients even when the clients' ideas are different. We then tend to abandon students to their own resources for understanding how this can work in practice. We act as if we can know what is good (valuable), but we are hung up on that word "preferences," which is supposed to be separate from knowledge.

It is helpful to scrap our usual definitions and look at the problem somewhat differently by changing our vocabulary and using the more philosophical terms of "good" or "goods" or even goodness. If we look at what we believe to be the nature of the good in social work, we can perhaps find a better defense of our values and see more clearly the ways in which knowing and valuing are not in fact separate categories in human experience. Hopefully we can observe that rationality is not limited to science and that in real life, which is the stuff of social work, rationality is not often, if ever, confined to intellectual ideas uncontaminated by feelings.

In *Whose Justice? Which Rationality?* the philosopher Alasdair MacIntyre (1988) refers to the fact that different traditions have different views of justice and of what counts as rationality in the particular context at issue. Now that, surely, is a revolutionary idea for social workers to consider as we struggle with the knowledge-value problem. MacIntyre notes that philosophical perspectives on these matters originate in the minds of scholars whose thinking is both conditioned by, and responsive to, their particular historical and cultural times, including the relevant traditions. Arguments, and the definitions on which they are based, arise within these traditions and cannot be understood correctly apart from these contexts. In light of this perspective, the meaning of rationality is not limited to the particular scientific empiricist tradition on which arguments within social work have usually depended.

Leaving aside the issue of relativism and the search for universal principles, it is safe to say that the traditions from which most of us come provide us with resources to reason about and research the nature of the good in social work. Such an approach extends our concept of research beyond the empirical techniques we have tended to associate with anything considered to be "real" research. (The importance of broadening our perspectives is well illustrated by the response of one doctoral student to a discussion of my dissertation, which was a form of philosophical research, when he queried incredulously: "You mean you didn't have any *data?*")

There is much work to be done here, and it involves putting empirical research into a perspective where it can be seen as one kind of research. Such a view might make it possible to see more readily how valuing and knowing, thinking and feeling, do and should occur together. Such a perspective allows room for a clearer identification of the goods involved in social work practice, including how these goods enter what we believe constitutes knowledge in our profession.

For example, recent feminist thought calls attention to some crucial ideas that have been minimized, if not actively denigrated, in much social work thinking, especially in research. Gilligan (1982) and others, including Belenky, Clinchy, Goldberger, and Tarule (1986), have suggested that it is not only feelings that are important, but also the idea that feelings are intimately connected to human relationships, which in turn motivate us to be responsive to others. It is relationships with our families and others that teach us to be sensitive to human need and hurt and to want to do something about it. For some time now some of us have been calling attention to the importance of caring as an essential good in social work (Imre, 1982). It is responsiveness to the pain of others that spurs most social workers to mobilize intellectual resources for understanding both the role of caring in human lives and the social conditions that foster or prevent caring relationships. The example that most readily comes to mind is that moral outrage at seeing children living on the streets or in welfare hotels should become an important part of research into such conditions and what is needed to alleviate them. As reported by Boffey (1988) in the *New York Times,* this perspective was shared by a majority of the members of the Study Commission of the Academy of Sciences regarding their report to Congress on homelessness and health needs (Institute of Medicine, 1988). This group issued a supplementary statement to the report expressing their "anger and dismay" at the conditions they found and their concern that the report did not reflect these feelings.

If research is to help us in practice to be able to respond to people with appropriate care, it seems necessary to jettison the dichotomy of knowledge and value and its often latent hierarchical connotation of rationality and emotionality, and to accept that for human beings to be responsive to each other, both rationality and emotionality must occur together. Chasing the chimera of emotionally antiseptic research designed to discover "facts" or "what is" will not help much in this task. We have a better chance of understanding and improving practice if we can free ourselves from these limiting definitions.

Cassell's (1977) description of what it is like to engage in interdisciplinary studies is relevant here. He notes how perspectives in any discipline (and social work is no exception) become solidified in paradigmatic structures in which our emotional and cognitive investment gives us a sense of security. He says, "People do not hold white-knuckle tight to their frames of reference out of pure reason but because to give up a frame of reference is extremely unsettling" (p. 357).

We seem to be holding "white-knuckle tight" to our neat definitions of knowledge and value, feminine and masculine, rationality and emotionality, when the way out is to be found by letting go of this paradigmatic structure. What will be lost in terms of security will be more than compensated for by the possibility of new insights and perceptions about how we can know what is essentially good in social work practice and how through research we might find ways to make it better.

Blasphemous as it may sound, I do not want to be a "scientific practitioner," and I do not "desperately need" rigor of a kind that only scientific researchers can provide. Insofar as possible, I do want to be a responsive, caring human being, able to use myself in a disciplined, professional way for the benefit of other human beings who happen to have problems. Not incidentally, I suspect that this is what most people hope to find when seeing a social worker. And it is also, I believe, what we should teach students to try to be. In order to be and to develop this kind of social worker, it is necessary to feel, imagine, and think in an intelligent, disciplined fashion, all at the same time—which most of us find to be rigorous. We will only be able to understand more clearly how we can do this, and how we might do it better, if we scrap some of our definitions. Such a vocabulary change could open the way for us to see and thus more fully credit the valuing in our knowing and the feeling in our thinking, all of which occur in the midst of practicing social work, which presumably is what empirical researchers in our profession want to study.

REFERENCES

Belenky, M. F., Clinchy, B. M., Goldberger, N. R., & Tarule, J. M. (1986). *Women's ways of knowing*. New York: Basic Books.

Boffey, P. M. (1988, September 20). Homeless plight angers scientists. *New York Times*, pp. A1, B10.

Cassell, E. J. (1977). How does interdisciplinary work get done? In H. T. Englehart, Jr. & D. Callahan (Eds.), *Knowledge, value and belief* (pp. 355–361). Hastings-on-Hudson, NY: The Hastings Center.

Gilligan, C. (1982). *In a different voice: Psychological theory and women's development*. Cambridge, MA: Harvard University Press.

Gordon, W. E. (1965). Knowledge and value: Their distinction and relationship in clarifying social work practice. *Social Work, 10,* 32–35.

Imre, R. W. (1982). *Knowing and caring: Philosophical issues in social work*. Lanham, MD: University Press of America.

Institute of Medicine. (1988). *Homelessness, health, and human needs*. Washington, DC: National Academy Press.

MacIntyre, A. (1988). *Whose justice? Which rationality?* Notre Dame, IN: University of Notre Dame Press.

Synthesis

The Epistemology of Social Work

Jane F. Gilgun

In the discussion of Chapter 12 by Bloom, there seemed to be a consensus that empiricism always implies an epistemology—that each empirical practitioner has a personal epistemology that may or may not be articulated. The practitioner not only may not articulate his or her world view, but also may not be aware of its nature. World view would encompass how the practitioner views clients, the nature of his or her interaction with clients, the nature of practice, the nature of change, and the nature of measurement. A major difficulty with empirical practice, therefore, lies in understanding the individual epistemology of the practitioner, which is not only personal, but often idiosyncratic and unarticulated. To communicate with others about practice, practitioners need to make their underlying assumptions as clear as possible.

Another aspect of epistemology is the match of the practitioner's epistemology with that of the client. If the client system's and practitioner's world views are different, the intervention is likely to be stymied. To develop effective interventions, then the practitioner must not only discover his or her own epistemology, but must understand the epistemology of the client system.

We social workers do have scientific knowledge to help us develop interventions, although this knowledge does not preclude our understanding the personal epistemologies that may be at work. Scientific knowledge and personal epistemologies work together to help us form hypotheses about the client system. Ideally, practitioners test individual hypotheses continually throughout their work with clients and do not wait until the end to test some overarching hypothesis. Rather than looking for one big test of effectiveness, practice consists of a series of small interventions that are meant to test hypotheses. This process can lead to change. How to test hypotheses continually has not been clearly articulated in the practice literature, but it needs to be.

Practice also involves both induction and deduction. The practitioner relies on previous knowledge, which leads to a deductive approach, and continually tests hypotheses to move toward a higher level of abstraction, which is the overarching hypothesis. The continual modification of hypotheses is characteristic of induction.

With regard to induction, deduction, and epistemologies, the use of validated procedures or interventions requires that these procedures are tailored to the individual situation. Thus, no amount of validated, scientific knowledge is truly useful unless practitioners are able to take it and apply it effectively on the idiographic level. Practice, after all, is an idiographic process. It is difficult to take validated procedures and fit them effectively into another particular practice situation. Practitioners need training to do so.

Practitioners need knowledge of the systems into which they intervene as well as knowledge of interventions. Edith Abbott (cited in Marsh, 1983) warned long ago about the danger of practice disintegrating into a "headless machine." Practice can do so if client systems are not well understood and if practitioners are trained to "plow right in" to the systems with little understanding of them.

Some participants said they would rather not be scientific practitioners if scientific practice means the mindless and heartless application of validated procedures into systems that practitioners have not been trained to assess. Others pointed out that the opposite is just as dangerous—that is, intervention on the basis of "gut feelings" with no thought about what has been shown to work in similar situations. What appeared to be emerging was a consensus that scientific practice consists of the application of knowledge from both assessment and intervention, the ability to tailor this knowledge to individual cases, and the ability to test hypotheses. The scientific practitioner, then, uses validated knowledge, tailors it to individual cases, assesses the impact of each intervention, and is aware of the personal epistemologies at work. The scientific practitioner is open to self-correction in the face of facts that contradict hypotheses, and many sources of knowledge lead to self-correction.

Most participants appeared to agree that social work has an enormous task in that its mission is to solve some intransigent social problems—a mission that is comparable to that of finding a cure for cancer. Furthermore, we social workers are under a lot of pressure to provide some solutions to these problems. A practitioner who is aware of personal epistemologies, who is knowledgeable about assessment and intervention, and who can test hypotheses and evaluate the outcome of individual interventions is in a position to work toward the solutions.

REFERENCE

Marsh, J. C. (1983). Research and innovation in social work practice: Avoiding the headless machine. *Social Service Review, 57*(4), 582–598.

Chapter 13

Epistemological Issues in the Development of Social Work Practice Knowledge

Katherine M. Wood

Much has been written over the years about epistemological issues in the development of social work practice knowledge—what kind of knowledge is needed, in what areas, from what sources it should come, what methods should be used to obtain it, who should be responsible for gathering it, and how it should be used once it is acquired. Some issues seem to have generated a fair degree of consensus, while others have generated considerable disagreement but little mutual enlightenment or resolution. When there are disputes, the lines are drawn not only between researchers and practitioners, but also among different camps of researchers and, to a lesser extent, among practitioners. The proponents of the opposing camps have succeeded in converting few by their rhetoric; rather, the arguments seem only to harden the respective positions.

Some level of resolution of the issues is crucial to social work's intellectual and professional integrity and further development. It is also important for the profession's political survival, since social workers deal with others in several sociopolitical contexts who are or could become hostile to the profession and are not reassured by their observations of the intellectual confusion in the profession. These others include politicians and bureaucrats, who are in control of the funding in areas of practice in which social work increasingly must compete with other professions for legitimation, community acceptance, and scarce resources, and academics in other disciplines, who are impatient not only with social work's in-house arguing but with any divergence from the traditional epistemological stance of academe.

RESEARCH VERSUS PRACTICE, OR RIGOR VERSUS RELEVANCE

Use of Research by Practitioners

Although some practitioners hold that social work practice is and should be based on organized practice wisdom, rather than on a systematic body of scientific knowledge (see, for example, Austin, 1976; Strean, 1978), most practitioners probably would agree, at least in principle, that the development of the knowledge base of the profession is imperative. They would probably also prefer that this base consist as much as possible of validated and specifically focused knowledge about their clients' problems and what constitutes good practice, not the fuzzily defined and highly speculative conceptualizations that still constitute too large a proportion of their "knowledge" base.

Furthermore, practitioners attend to research findings when they perceive the findings to be *relevant* to their practice concerns. For example, in a study of a sample of National Association of Social Workers members in New Jersey, this author (Wood, 1977) compared the attitudes toward research that practitioners espoused with the practitioners' knowledge of specific research findings on various aspects of casework and group work practice. All the studies with which the practitioners were presented had been published in major social work journals that were easily accessible to the practitioners. However, few of the practitioners could identify specific studies (of which there were relatively few at that time), which led to the conclusion that the practitioners had not read the articles or, if they had, had quickly forgotten what the studies had found. This conclusion was in line with the equally dismal findings of Rosenblatt (1968) and Kirk and Fischer (1976) that practitioners "rarely find research studies helpful in practice" (Kirk & Fischer, p. 69). But the author's study produced another nugget: The practitioners in her survey *did* know about some specific findings of practice research, which had "trickled down" to them somehow, even though they had not read the research reports. For example, few knew that William Reid and Ann Shyne were the authors of the 1969 seminal study of planned short-term versus open-ended treatment, and it seemed apparent that they had never read *Brief and Extended Casework*, the book that reported on the study. But they did know that short-term intervention "won" in the experimental study.

Selection of Areas of Study

Of course, there have since been research studies that practitioners have perceived to be equally relevant to practice, but there also have been many studies that have been only peripherally relevant to practitioners' concerns. The perusal of research articles or the topics of doctoral dissertations leads to the impression that researchers sometimes choose a research question because it fits a particular (usually quantitative) research methodology, not because of its substantive importance. One doctoral student, in a moment of honesty, confided that she could get her degree by doing research on a "Mickey Mouse" topic, as long as the study contained many sophisticated statistical analyses.

As Geismar and this author proposed (Geismar & Wood, 1982), the question, "Which research methodology is the best for the profession?" makes no sense. The methodology used in a study cannot stand apart from the issue or question under investigation. A commonsense practice principle has long been that the practitioner, together with the client system, must define the problem *before* selecting a strategy of intervention and that the strategy must then match the problem; it cannot be chosen on the basis of the practitioner's pet theory. Although the same principle should surely apply to research, a number of writers (see, for example, Brennan, 1973; Guzzetta, 1980, cited in Karger, 1983; Karger, 1983; Vigilante, 1974) have observed that social work has granted to the quantitative methodology that is preferred by the natural and social sciences (although social science is beginning to turn to other approaches) a position of exaltation that is not warranted. The research question is then chosen to fit the methodology, and the result may well be a "Mickey Mouse" study of little substantive importance.

The Positivist Paradigm

The predominant paradigm in the definition of knowledge building by the university, by many social work researchers (the majority of whom are university based), and in many social work research courses is the descendant of the logical positivism of the earlier years of this century. The positivist philosophy rests on several philosophical assumptions:

> An ontological assumption of a single, tangible reality "out there" that can be broken apart into pieces capable of being studied independently; the whole is simply the sum of the parts.
>
> An epistemological assumption about the possibility of separation of the observer from the observed—the knower from the known.
>
> An assumption of the temporal and contextual independence of observations, so that what is true at one time and place may, under appropriate circumstances (such as sampling), also be true at another time and place.
>
> An assumption of linear causality; there are no effects without causes and no causes without effects.

An axiological assumption of value freedom, that is, that the methodology guarantees that the results of an inquiry are essentially free from the
influence of any value system (bias). (Lincoln & Guba, 1985, p. 28)

Relevance versus Rigor

For certain kinds of questions concerning our knowledge base for
practice, these assumptions may be good enough (meaning heuristically
valuable albeit not "true" in any sense of ultimate truth) to guide the
inquiry. Indeed, enormous progress in science has resulted from the
employment of this paradigm. But because the paradigm emphasizes
operationalism, it ignores meanings and implications and involves what
Mishler (1979) called "context stripping." If the question has to do with
understanding meanings, implications, and contexts, then the paradigm
and its resulting research approaches prove inadequate to the task.
Furthermore, the aim of the positivist paradigm is rigor, but although it
is sometimes possible to achieve rigor and relevance simultaneously (as
was accomplished by Reid & Shyne, 1969), it is usually difficult to do so,
and diminished relevance may be the price that must be paid for rigor.

Practitioners must also deal with the rigor versus relevance dilemma:

In the varied topography of professional practice, there is a high, hard
ground where practitioners can make effective use of research-based
theory and technique, and there is a swampy lowland where situations are
confusing "messes" incapable of technical solution. The difficulty is that
the problems of the high ground, however great their technical interest, are
often relatively unimportant to clients or to the larger society, while in the
swamp are the problems of greatest human concern. . . .

There are those who choose the swampy lowlands. They deliberately
involve themselves in messy but crucially important problems and, when
asked to describe their methods of inquiry, they speak of experience, trial
and error, intuition, and muddling through.

Other professionals opt for the high ground. Hungry for technical rigor,
devoted to an image of solid professional competence, or fearful of entering a world in which they feel they do not know what they are doing, they
choose to confine themselves to a narrowly technical practice. (Schon, 1983,
pp. 42–43)

When a choice must be made between rigor and relevance, most researchers choose the high ground, and most practitioners opt for the much-
more-difficult-to-traverse swamp.

It is more comfortable for the members of any profession or discipline
to hold to one paradigm or philosophy and to feel the security of like-
mindedness in their referent group. It is less comfortable to allow that
there may be different ways of looking at things and that one perspective

is not necessarily better or more "true" than another—only more or less appropriate and heuristically worthwhile for seeking answers to specific knowledge questions. Physicists seem to be able to juggle the existence within their field of several perspectives. Thus, many of the propositions of Newtonian mechanics, well established through extensive experimental research, are still valid today for many applications. But the Newtonian paradigm was not found useful for understanding systems of atomic and subatomic dimensions, so in these areas it has been replaced by quantum physics, whereas for systems moving near the speed of light or in enormous gravitational fields, Einstein's perspective has been more fruitful. In writing on the "epistemology of family therapy," Keeney (1982) suggested that although "Newtonian epistemology is concerned with knowing the nature of billiard balls and the forces that operate on them," the systems perspective of family therapy is more interested in the interactional system that comprises all the balls on the billiard table. The new perspective "jumps from the paradigm of things to the paradigm of pattern" (p. 154).

Knowledge questions that are of importance to social work practice sometimes involve a better understanding of the equivalent of individual billiard balls, and it may even be that in certain circumstances, the entire billiard game can be best understood by looking at the behavior of individual balls as they collide with each other. Some kinds of statistical analysis permit this kind of examination. But social work is the practice profession that deals with contexts, more so than any other helping profession; if the research findings are based on context stripping, to that degree will their utility to practice be compromised. This is one of several reasons that practitioners find it hard to use research: Practitioners are interested in three-dimensional contexts, while researchers seem to depict a two-dimensional practice process that practitioners think of as unreal. Experimental group-comparison research reports on group aggregates, but practitioners deal with clients who are each, in Erikson's (1959) term, "a universe of one" and who may or may not be like the clients who responded to the experimental intervention. Furthermore, such research rarely examines within-group differences, specifically the differentiation between the group that benefited from the experimental intervention and the group that did not. Practitioners are equally interested in the kinds of clients who did not benefit and why they did not.

Within the community of social work researchers, there has been increasing criticism of the logical positivist model as *the* paradigm for scientific activity in social work (see, for example, Brennan, 1973; Heineman, 1981; Imre, 1984; Ruckdeschel & Farris, 1981; Vigilante, 1974). Some of these writers appear to be recommending that the traditional logical-positivist perspective should be scrapped. This model and the types of research methodology it generates, however, still have a useful place in social work for studying certain kinds of restricted knowledge questions. The point is that although the logical-positivist model should continue to be seen as one of the *necessary* approaches to knowledge building, it is, in itself, not *sufficient*. The enormous list of questions to which social workers need answers concerning clients and their problems, as well as social work practice, is too broad ranging for any one perspective to be applicable to all.

An analogy may be drawn to the situation of practice. Not every client can be fitted into the Procrustean bed of any one practice theory—cognitive-behavioral theory, family systems theory, ego psychology, or whatever. Some of the propositions and practice principles of these "theories" have received more empirical validation than have others, and the degree of empirical validation a given theory enjoys should indeed be one of the criteria the practitioner utilizes in deciding which theoretical lens to employ in a particular case. But another, perhaps more important, criterion is whether a specific theory seems to "fit" the client and the facts of the case; that is, the practitioner may make a judgment that, given the demands of this case, relevance is more important than rigor.

Researchers like to look at billiard balls as if each could be isolated and studied separately, while practitioners are more interested in the pattern described by all the balls in motion, their interaction with each other, with the cue, and with the person who is manipulating the cue. Both perspectives are valuable, depending on what you want to know. If you want to understand the billiard ball in situation, that is, in interaction with its context, the systemic perspective of the practitioner makes sense. If you are interested in understanding why a particular billiard ball wobbles and does not roll true, the positivistic perspective of most researchers is more appropriate because understanding the interaction among the balls will not necessarily lead to the discovery that the "dysfunctional" ball is defective in some way.

The competence of practitioners, it may be hypothesized, is related, in part, to the ability of practitioners to be polyocular—to have a variety of lenses through which to view their cases and the clinical judgment necessary to select the conceptual lens that fits best the data of the case. Indeed, in a given case—or even in one interview in a case—the competent practitioner may be utilizing several different descriptive and prescriptive theories in rapid succession or even simultaneously. If practitioners can manage such pluralism and can deal with the contradictions and ambiguities involved, researchers may likewise be expected to use more than one perspective in their knowledge-building efforts.

Reaching Practitioners

Part of the tension between researchers and practitioners in social work seems to be attributable to the different philosophical paradigms from which they operate. That is, there are sharp differences between their cosmologies, ontologies, epistemologies, axiologies, and other beliefs relevant to developing an integrated world view. Thus, researchers and practitioners frequently talk *at* each other, rather than to each other, because each is incorrectly assuming that a shared meaning exists.

In addition, practitioners believe that researchers talk down and lecture to them. They react with resentment and stubbornness when they are told that, as Rosenblatt (1968) stated, they *must* "accept the need to support research, to cooperate with researchers, and to pay attention to research findings," especially when this demand is represented as an arranged or forced marriage and they are assured that "once the vows are pronounced and the two partners begin to live together, then love will follow." In this proposal, it is clear who should dominate and who should be subjugated—an unequal arrangement that is not likely to lead to marital bliss. Although Rosenblatt went on to say that practitioners, not researchers, "will decide what to use [of research findings] and how [they] will be used" (p. 59), this remark is stating the obvious and is not sufficiently mollifying to neutralize the practitioners' view that the researcher's philosophy and belief system are being imposed on them and that they are not being given the courtesy of being listened to. Practitioners have always decided and will continue to decide which products of research they will attend to. In doing so, they apply their own criteria that emerge from their different paradigmatic perspectives. The relevance of research findings to their practice and the avoidance of context stripping are two of their principal criteria. Practitioners indeed have final control over the results of research, in that they have the power to use them or ignore them. Passive resistance is a powerful strategy; practitioners are still not showing up at the church where the forced marriage is to be solemnized.

Again, the idea that the typical practitioner is uninterested in research is an inaccurate canard. Rather than address the too-global question of whether practitioners use research in general, researchers must examine more closely what *kinds* of research practitioners pay attention to and what kinds they ignore. Practitioners are trying to tell researchers something.

The profession needs a strong research arm, and practitioners need researchers, but the pragmatic reality is that researchers need practitioners as well. University tenure committees are one important "market" for social work research, but they benefit only the individual faculty member and school. The wider market for research endeavors is the world of practice, and practitioners are just not buying at the rate they should be. A business firm whose toasters were not selling would invest some time and money to investigate what consumers did not like about the toasters and then attempt to redesign the product to fit the needs of their market better.

Students in social work research courses at the masters and doctoral levels are usually taught a definition of research that is synonymous with quantitative methods. They think "research" equals numbers crunching. The prevalence of quantitative methods in the curricula of courses on social work research may partly be a reflection of the epistemological stance of the university, which rewards this particular subspecies of research more highly than other forms of scholarship (which may be as valuable or more valuable).

The Limits of Rational Technology

Schon (1983, 1987), a social scientist who has studied professional education in such seemingly different practice professions as architecture, urban planning, psychiatry, and music, characterizes the university's model of the function of the professional school as teaching "rational technology"—the application to practical problems of higher conceptual levels of knowledge developed by university scientists according to the positivist paradigm. However, he sees all the problem-solving professions as undergoing a "crisis of legitimacy rooted both in their perceived failure to live up to their own norms and in their perceived incapacity to help society achieve its objectives and solve its problems" (1983, p. 39). He further believes that this crisis has arisen because rational technology is an inadequate model for the practice professions: It just does not fit what practitioners actually do. Indeed, the perception of rational technology as the lodestar has *created* as many problems as it has solved; examples are the technological ability of medical science to keep alive otherwise dead patients for whom life no longer has any real meaning and the "foolproof" computerized technology of the *U.S.S. Vincennes* that shot down a passenger aircraft.

According to the tenets of rational technology,

given agreement about ends, the question, "How ought I to act?" could be reduced to a merely instrumental question about the means best suited to achieve one's ends. Disagreement about means could be resolved by reference to facts concerning the possible means, their relevant consequences, and the methods for comparing them with respect to the chosen ends of action. Ultimately, the instrumental question could be resolved by

recourse to experiment. . . . It would be possible to select the means appropriate to one's ends by applying the relevant scientific theory. The question, "How ought I to act?" could become a scientific one, and the best
means could be selected by the use of science-based technique. (Schon,
1983, pp. 33–34)

This viewpoint is the same as that espoused by those who think that the
problems of social work practice will be solved if practitioners can only be
made to see that their function is to apply a scientifically validated
rational technology to their clients' problems.

Schon recognized that the view of the practice professions as purveyors of a scientific rational technology to their clients—of practice as a
purely instrumental activity—has resulted in some dramatic successes
for such practice professions as medicine and engineering. These professions and their emphasis on rational technology have been adopted as
role models for the applied social and behavioral sciences. As Schon
(1983) noted,

In such fields as education, social work, planning, and policy making,
social scientists attempted to do research, to apply it, and to educate
practitioners, all according to their perceptions of the models of medicine and engineering. Indeed, the very language of social scientists, rich
in references to measurement, controlled experiment, applied science,
laboratories, and clinics, was striking in its reverence for these models.
(pp. 38–39)

The trouble with rational technology as the definition of a practice
profession is that it assumes that practice is a simplistic process of
problem solving. Rational technology assumes that problems are presented to the practitioner as neat, delimited givens whose parameters are
clear; the practitioner has only to choose from a scientifically validated
theory those instrumental problem-solving techniques whose efficacy for
the problem has previously been demonstrated. The reality, however, is
that practitioners (in whatever practice profession) are only rarely presented with situations that are isomorphic in all particulars with those "in
the books." Rather, they confront "dynamic situations that consist of
complex systems of changing problems that interact with each other. I call
such situations *messes*. Problems are abstractions extracted from messes
by analysis" (Ackoff, 1979, quoted by Schon, 1983, p. 16).

The client system presents the practitioner with a "mess," not with a
neatly circumscribed problem, as some research articles and some rational technology oriented textbooks on practice would make it appear (see,
for example, Fischer, 1978). Such writings give their readers the impression that social work practice consists *only* of selecting and applying

interventions—with, to be sure, a little warmth, empathy, and genuineness mixed in to make the interventive pills go down more easily.

All but rare cases are characterized by what Schon (1983) called "uncertainty, complexity, instability, uniqueness, and value conflict" (p. 17)—characteristics that the rational technology approach ignore, but with which the practitioner must deal, and that describe the *context* of the case.

Extracting a solvable problem from the client's presented "mess" is the practitioner's first crucial level of skill. If the wrong problem is extracted, the wrong problem will be worked on, and the results will be unsuccessful. Or if the client will not accept the practitioner's definition of the problem or "where" the worker is "locating" it because the worker is unaware of or insensitive to the client's perceptions, then the client will not allow the ensuing intervention to work. (Even deliberately "alien" interventions, such as paradoxical directives, still require that the client be willing to follow them. See, for example, Dell, 1981.) Research and rational technology have little to say about this crucial process, but competent and experienced practitioners know a lot about it.

The Diagnostic or Problem Analysis Process

Research and rational technology also have little to offer by way of a better understanding of the diagnostic process, which in rational technology–oriented textbooks on practice is either given short shrift or portrayed as simple and self-evident. In diagnostic assessment (or the author's preferred term *problem analysis*), the practitioner attempts to explore the "shape" of the problem to be worked on to identify those factors that must be changed if the problem is to be ameliorated, judging the accessibility of these factors to efforts to change and separating them from factors that may at one time have been causal but are no longer relevant, factors that exacerbate the problem, factors that perpetuate the problem, and factors that are interesting but peripheral to the problem. Thus, unraveling the Gordian knot of the usual kind of complicated case with which practitioners must deal calls for a good deal of clinical judgment, perspicacity, and both analytic and synthesizing capacities; it is usually not a simple process. Similarly, in the process of defining and locating a problem, if the factors to be targeted for change by this process of diagnosis or problem analysis are incorrectly identified, the intervention applied to them—no matter how scientifically validated—will produce poor results.

These processes transpire, often rapidly, before an intervention even starts. They are processes that involve a kind of research by the practitioner, who is formulating and testing diagnostic and interventive hypotheses. But the practitioner is synthesizing as well: making creative leaps in recognizing patterns and implementing innovative designs to bring about a change in the problem. In doing so, the practitioner must be able not only to feel comfortable with but to utilize creatively the uncertainty, complexity, instability, uniqueness, and conflict in values that characterize all but the unusually simple case.

The foregoing kinds of skills, about which little is known, are at the core of competent social work practice—much more so than is the application of rational technology–prescribed interventions (since the efficacy and appropriate application of interventions is dependent, in large part, on these preceding processual skills).

The "Art" of Practice

The skills involved have been called by various names, including *clinical judgment* and *the art of practice* (Dackorium, 1970, Doelin, 1961; Kaminsky, 1985; Rapoport, 1968; Rothman, 1983; Siporin, 1988). This author confesses to having some trouble with the terms *art* and *artistry* because they sometimes imply an antiscientific stance, or at least a belief in the existence of some mystical quality called "intuition." Because it is by definition interior, intuition cannot be taught to others—which is the task of schools of social work and of agencies that employ neophyte practitioners. However, the problem is solved if one denies that intuition, as was defined, exists and if one redefines what appears to be the intuitive "rightness" of a master practitioner's diagnostic insight or interventive technique as a matter of *knowledge* that is based on the learning accumulated over years of practice experience. It seems intuitive and magical because the practitioner is, at speeds too rapid for him or her even to be aware, dipping into everything he or she has learned previously from books and mentors and practice successes and mistakes, sifting through these experiences for similarities to and differences from the case at hand, and extracting the previous knowledge that applies to this case. Some highly experienced oncologists, for example, can "smell" cancer even before the results of their patients' laboratory tests come in, but 20 years earlier, when they were first-year residents, they were not yet at this level of diagnostic expertise. These physicians acquired an important kind of knowledge, consisting partly of the books they have read and partly of the courses they have taken (and the research reports they have read), but their level of knowledge goes beyond all these sources.

This author prefers the terms *craftsmanship* or *expertise* to *art* (only a difference in semantics). The craftsmanship or expertise of a professional is different from the application of a rational technology by a technician.

As Siporin (1988) pointed out, the "creative person" is

capable of both divergent and convergent thought. He or she needs to possess associative fluency and flexibility, be able to shift perspectives, and use different frames of reference to develop original ideas and solutions. The creative person uses the right and left brain and employs logical as well as nonrational, parallel, lateral, analogical, and intuitive kinds of reasoning.

Creative persons are able to think in Janusian terms; that is, they are able to encompass contradictions and polarities. Similarly, clinicians are able to tolerate and deal with ambiguity, anxiety, disorder, and conflict as well as understand and accept ambivalence and paradox. The clinician's formulations of paradoxical directives illustrates the creative use of imagination to develop original, arresting, ego-involving procedures. (p. 180)

The "ambiguity, anxiety, disorder, . . . conflict . . . ambivalence and paradox" of the practice situation described by Siporin are tantamount to the "uncertainty, complexity, instability, uniqueness and value conflict" of Schon's characterization. It is how the practitioner deals with them, in a way that is truly "creative," that constitutes craftsmanship or artistry. The practitioner's only true instrument is herself or himself. Another hallmark of expertise is the practitioner's ability to shift and be flexible; the worker who is the same person with every client, who uses the same facets of his or her personality and the same mind-set for every case, is not an expert practitioner.

Inexperienced or mediocre practitioners often need to be committed to one theoretical orientation, usually on the basis of its emotional appeal. But Siporin pointed out that the creative practitioner can "shift perspectives and use different frames of reference" without becoming overwhelmed or confused. The creative researcher may, similarly, be the person who can utilize different perspectives or knowledge-building paradigms.

According to Siporin, the artistry of the practitioner involves the use of lateral as well as linear thinking. Linear cognitive processes characterize a logical positivist epistemology and the rational technology approach espoused by many social work researchers. A linear epistemology makes sense for some practice questions as well as for some research questions, but practice utilizes other epistemologies as well. Since Aristotle, logical or linear thinking has been exalted as the epitome of human cognitive process. Logical, linear, or—as deBono (1967, 1971, 1972, 1978) called it— "vertical thinking" is the kind of "thinking" that computers engage in (of course, after they have been programmed). The human programmer defines the problem and indicates the pathways along which the problem is to be explored. The machine then proceeds to work out the problem with unassailable logic and with a degree of speed and efficiency that no human can match. deBono (1967) gave an example of the difference between this and what he called "lateral thinking":

> Just as water flows down slopes, settles in hollows and is confined to riverbeds, so vertical thinking flows along the most probable paths and by its very flow increases the probability of those paths for the future. If vertical thinking is high-probability thinking, then lateral thinking is low-probability thinking. New channels are deliberately cut to alter the flow of the water. The old channels are dammed up in the hope that the water will seek out and take to new and better patterns of flow. Sometimes the water is even sucked upwards in an unnatural fashion. When the low-probability line of thought leads to an effective new idea there is a "eureka moment," and at once the low-probability approach acquires the highest probability. (p. 14)

deBono (1967) insisted that the two types of thinking are not antithetical but complementary:

> When ordinary vertical thinking is unable to find a solution to a problem or when a new idea is required, then lateral thinking should be used. New ideas depend on lateral thinking, for vertical thinking has inbuilt limitations which make it much less effective for this purpose. These limitations of vertical thinking cannot be set aside, for they are its very advantages looked at from a different point of view. (p. 13)

This is another way of stating the point made earlier, that the logical positivist paradigm of knowledge building should not be dispensed with, since it is still useful for certain kinds of knowledge questions that are of interest to the profession. For the kinds of knowledge questions that call for synthesizing rather than analyzing strategies of inquiry, however, the assumptions of logical positivism are inapplicable and the sterility of rational technology as a basis for the profession becomes apparent. Both strategies are needed, but for different kinds of epistemological problems. The central issues seem to be, first, whether the profession is asking the right questions to help us develop practice theory for social work and, second, whether the knowledge-building methodology currently in fashion is the most appropriate way to obtain the answers we need to those questions.

WHO IS RESPONSIBLE FOR BUILDING PRACTICE THEORY?

Karger's (1983) perception is that "in the organizational structure of social work, the researcher-academicians sit on top of the status pyramid" (p. 202). Karger believes that it is

> not the use of quantitative versus qualitative methodology or even the primacy of the scientific paradigm that is at the heart of the debate; rather,

it is the political control of the direction, leadership, and the future of the profession. In essence, it is a struggle between the researcher-academicians and practitioners for control of social work. (p. 202)

The worlds of the university-based school of social work and of the field of practice are different. Schon (1983) examined the relationship between the kinds of knowledge honored in academe and the kinds of competence valued in professional practice. He saw universities as being committed "to a particular epistemology, a view of knowledge that fosters selective inattention to practical competence and professional artistry" (1983, p. vii). In the university's epistemological definition, the function of any of its professional schools is to teach instrumental problem solving, which is made rigorous by the application of scientific theory and techniques. And the development of the scientific, high-level theory on which the professional schools' applications of the rational technology are to be based is the function of scholarly disciplines; it is not really expected of professional schools. The production of respectable scholarship and research by the professional schools is given a kind of surprised and grudging respect, something like Samuel Johnson's famous (or infamous) crack, "Sir, a woman preaching is like a dog walking on his hind legs—it is not done well; but you are surprised to find it done at all."

In their struggle to change this hierarchical distribution of power and status and to prove they were just as "scholarly" as members of the high-status disciplines, social work academics adopted the positivistic epistemology of the university concerning not only science and knowledge but *practice*. Thus, the professional schools are no longer free to set their own knowledge-building agendas and choose their own knowledge-building methods, since only those agendas and methods that fit the university's paradigm will be recognized and rewarded. The result has been the attempt by social work academic researchers to produce a rational technology "theory" for practice, which they expect practitioners to accept and implement unquestioningly. In this design, these researchers have assumed the responsibility, and the right, to create practice theory for the profession. They are attempting to duplicate the same relationship between themselves and practitioners as obtains in their interaction with their superiors at the universities.

This issue was joined, in an explosion of fireworks, a few years ago in the pages of the major professional journal *Social Work.* Fischer (1981) proposed that a "quiet revolution has been taking place in the way social work develops and uses knowledge for practice" (p. 199) in that rational technology—a set of research-validated interventive techniques—was supplanting older social work theory and becoming the new theory for practice (see also Fischer, 1984). In his rebuttal, Gordon (1984) stated that social work practice cannot be permitted to become a "collection of techniques and methods hanging on an empty or shapeless theoretical core" (p. 74), which he believed would reduce practitioners to the level of subprofessional technicians and that would be a "certain route . . . to the demise of the profession" (Gordon, 1983, p. 183). Gordon's argument, basically, was that "theory" must be more than a mere laundry list of interventive techniques.

Perhaps the issue is not so much whether practitioners or researchers, alone, should develop practice theory for a practice profession. Each needs the other: Practitioners need the rigor that researchers demand, and researchers need the relevance that practitioners recognize is essential. The area of expertise of most researchers is research, not practice, in which too often they have minimal experience. The growing tendency of many doctoral programs in social work to prepare social work researchers who have had minimal exposure to practice implicitly assumes that knowledge of the concerns of practice is unimportant. Researchers, working alone, produce artificially segmented "pieces" of knowledge, which do not summatively produce anything that could be called a theory in the technical and scientific definition of that term. They can produce only a rational technology, which has its place but is not the same thing as a theory.

Practitioners, alone, also usually do not produce good theory. Few writers on practice seem to have a grasp of the requirements of a theory, which must be more than the collection of ideas, opinions, or practice experiences that characterize many theoretical books and articles. Practitioners usually are unaware that there are canons and guidelines for the development of theories. Their productions may rate high on relevance, but they are usually short on rigor.

There have been many calls, for many years, for practitioners and researchers to work more closely together. To a limited extent, practitioners and researchers have done so. An outstanding example has been the work of Reid and his colleagues (Reid, 1978, 1985; Reid & Epstein, 1972, 1977), which is based both on the active collaboration of practitioners and on careful research. This kind of theoretical model building, grounded in the teamwork of practitioners and researchers, has had more impact on practitioners—because of its relevance—than abstract albeit rigorous research alone could hope to have.

There probably will never be a "grand" theory for the direct practice of social work—meaning a validated theory that is applicable to every problem of every client in every practice setting. The profession should aim, rather, for what Merton (1949) termed "theories of the middle range"— multiple theories, each applying specifically to the understanding of and intervention in particular, discrete problems of clients. The multiple theories would be bound by social work's particular ecological perspective (so different from the narrow psychotherapeutic focus of psychiatry and psychology) and by the profession's set of values.

Such practice theories should include rational technology, but this is not sufficient. Theory for practice must also address the basic issues of practitioner judgment and the specific skills involved in determining the nature, definition, and location of the clients' problems, the diagnostic and problem-analysis process of the problem-to-be-worked (in the famous phrase of Perlman, 1957), and how expert (that is, effective) practitioners go about selecting and implementing a strategy of intervention. As was noted previously, little is known about these important matters, because social work research has not put them high on its agenda.

But expert practitioners do know a great deal about them. The difficulty is that their knowledge is usually what Polanyi (1967) called "tacit knowledge." It is the kind of knowledge involved when one can identify someone one knows from a photograph, although one cannot explain how it is done. The listing of specific features of the person's physiognomy does not account for this skill, since it is probably a pattern-recognition skill of the right brain, which cannot easily be translated into the verbal, analytic terms of the left brain that most people use pre-dominantly. Or tacit knowledge is the "body" knowledge of how to ride a bicycle, which no one has ever learned by hearing someone describe it or reading a book or research report on it; it can only be acquired by actually doing it.

To the extent that skills like these can be learned only by knowledge in action, they probably cannot be taught didactically (thus, the continued importance of the field practicum in social work) and are not included in a rational technology compendium.

Schon (1983), however, stated that practitioners can be helped to articulate their tacit, experience-based knowledge for their own benefit and that of learners. He described what seem to be some exciting and innovative educational experiments for doing so.

The tacit but often not-well-articulated knowledge of experienced and expert practitioners can be a well spring for practice theory, but it is an area that social work researchers have not considered to be a high priority. The interviewing skills of social work researchers will be in demand in such studies of the actual practice of practitioners.

Although practitioners pay attention to research when they find it relevant to their practice, they tend to pay more attention to people they consider to be knowledgeable about practice, those whom they view as expert practitioners. Researchers tend to decry this tendency because they believe they have more to offer ordinary beginning practitioners than do "expert" mentors. But practitioners are voting with their feet, and researchers may learn that it is in the interest of their survival as a viable force within the profession to begin—finally—to listen to what practitioners have to say.

REFERENCES

Ackoff, R. (1979). The future of operational research is past. *Journal of the Operational Research Society, 30,* 93–104.

Austin, D. M. (1976). Research and social work: Educational paradoxes and possibilities. *Journal of Social Service Research, 2,* 170–176.

Beckerman, A. H. (1978). Differentiating between social research and social work research: Implications for teaching. *Journal of Education for Social Work, 14,* 9–15

Boehm, W. (1961). Social work: Science and art. *Social Service Review, 35,* 144–152.

Brennan, W. C. (1973). The practitioner as theoretician. *Journal of Education for Social Work, 9,* 5–12.

Dell, P. F. (1981). Some irreverent thoughts on paradox. *Family Process, 20,* 37–51.

deBono, E. (1967). *The use of lateral thinking.* New York: Penguin.

deBono, E. (1971). *Practical thinking.* New York: Penguin.

deBono, E. (1972). *P.: Beyond yes and no.* New York: Penguin.

deBono, E. (1978). *Teaching thinking.* New York: Penguin.

Erikson, E. H. (1959). The nature of clinical evidence. In D. Lerner (Ed.), *Evidence and inference.* Glencoe, IL: Free Press.

Fischer, J. (1978). *Effective casework practice: An eclectic approach.* New York: McGraw-Hill.

Fischer, J. (1981). The social work revolution. *Social Work, 26,* 199–207.

Fischer, J. (1984). Revolution, schmevolution: Is social work changing or not? *Social Work, 29,* 71–74.

Geismar, L. L., & Wood, K. M. (1982). Evaluating practice: Science as faith. *Social Casework, 63,* 266–275.

Gordon, W. E. (1983). Social work: Revolution or evolution? *Social Work, 28,* 181–185.

Gordon, W. E. (1984). Gordon replies: Making social work a science-based profession. *Social Work, 29,* 74–75.

Heineman, M. B. (1981). The obsolete scientific imperative in social work research. *Social Service Review, 55,* 371–397.

Imre, R. W. (1984). The nature of knowledge in social work. *Social Work, 29,* 41–45.

Kaminsky, M. (1985). Daily bread: Or, the marriage of art and social work. *Social Work with Groups, 8,* 20–25.

Karger, H. J. (1983). Science, research, and social work: Who controls the profession? *Social Work, 28,* 200–205.

Keeney, B. P. (1982). What is an epistemology of family therapy? *Family Process,* *21,* 153–168.

Kirk, S. A., & Fischer, J. (1976). Do social workers understand research? *Journal of Education for Social Work, 12,* 63–70.

Lincoln, Y. S., & Guba, E. G. (1985). *Naturalistic inquiry.* Beverly Hills, CA: Sage Publications.

Merton, R. K. (1949). Social theory and social structure. In R. K. Merton (Ed.), *Social structure and anomie* (pp. 125–149). Glencoe, IL: Free Press.

Mishler, E. (1979). Meaning in context. *Harvard Education Review, 49,* 1–8.

Perlman, H. H. (1957). *Social casework: A problem-solving process.* Chicago: University of Chicago Press.

Polanyi, M. (1967). *The tacit dimension.* New York: Anchor.

Rapoport, L. (1968). Creativity in social work. *Smith College Studies in Social Work, 38,* 156.

Reid, W. J. (1978). *The task-centered system.* New York: Columbia University Press.

Reid, W. J. (1985). *Family problem solving.* New York: Columbia University Press.

Reid, W. J., & Epstein, L. (1972). *Task-centered casework.* New York: Columbia University Press.

Reid, W. J., & Epstein, L. (1977). *Task-centered practice.* New York: Columbia University Press.

Reid, W. J., & Shyne, A. W. (1969). *Brief and extended casework.* New York: Columbia University Press.

Rosenblatt, A. (1968). The practitioner's use and evaluation of research. *Social Work, 13,* 53–59.

Rothman, J. (1983). The science and art of practice: Joining the two. In M. Dinerman (Ed.), *Social work futures* (pp. 161–182). New Brunswick, NJ: Graduate School of Social Work, Rutgers University.

Ruckdeschel, R. A., & Farris, B. E. (1981). Assessing practice: A critical look at the single-case design. *Social Casework, 62,* 413–419.

Schon, D. A. (1983). *The reflective practitioner: How professionals think in action.* New York: Basic Books.

Schon, D. A. (1987). *Educating the reflective practitioner.* San Francisco: Jossey-Bass.

Siporin, M. (1988). Clinical social work as an art form. *Social Casework, 69,* 177–185.

Strean, H. S. (1978). *Clinical social work: Theory and practice.* New York: Free Press.

Vigilante, J. L. (1974). Between values and science: Education for the profession during a moral crisis, or is proof truth? *Journal of Education for Social Work, 10,* 110–115.

Wood, K. M. (1977). *The impact of social work outcome research on social work direct practice.* Unpublished doctoral dissertation, Rutgers University, New Brunswick, NJ.

Commentary

Epistemology and Research in Advancing Social Work Knowledge

Max Siporin

I very much agree with Katherine Wood's eloquent and trenchant critique of logical positivism and of the rationalist, technological approach to social work research in Chapter 13, as well as with her fair-minded statement that social work needs the rational positivistic technology in addition to the qualitative research and systems perspective for different epistemological problems. There is an increasing, even though still small, body of useful, scientifically validated knowledge, some of it from empirical quantitative research. This research has been well-summarized by Videka-Sherman (1988), Tolson (1989), and by Wood (1978) herself; each contributed useful formulations of practice principles.

Clinical social workers deal with the "messes" of people's lives, as Wood pointed out. To do so, they need to be creative; use left-brain, lateral thinking, as well as right-brain, linear thinking; and be highly skilled practitioners. As Wood suggested, they should do more theory building and make their "tacit knowledge" more explicit. The wide gap between researchers and practitioners should be narrowed; practitioners and researchers should listen to each other better.

In a different Platonic dialogue than the one presented by Bloom in Chapter 12, someone asked: "Can I know what I don't know?" The reply was, "No, you cannot." The first person said, "Well, there is a certain thing that I do not know, and I know that I don't know it. Then don't I know what I don't know?" And the reply was, "I don't know." Clinicians know some things and know that they do not know other things about human behavior and relationships and about helping people effectively. A greater real dialogue between clinicians and researchers would help clarify how and what of the profession's knowledge is known or can be known. This commentary discusses two areas in which further knowledge development would be useful: empirical qualitative versus quantitative methods of research and social work as an art.

USE OF QUALITATIVE AND QUANTITATIVE METHODS

The profession needs to build its knowledge base through the greater use of empirical, qualitative, as well as quantitative, methods. Empirical data should not be associated exclusively with quantitative, positivistic procedures of research. One can empirically and operationally observe and investigate subjective experience, meanings, and feelings without using random samples, controlled experimental group designs, or statistical analysis of quantified data. Hermeneutical dialogue is one such method. If computers can deal specifically with qualitative, "fuzzy" concepts, social workers should be able to do so in ways other than through a positivistic emphasis on quantitative data and statistical analysis.

The current shift now taking place in our field to do more research about the processes of intervention and change in clinical helping situations is promising, for it is in this area that the combined use of qualitative and quantitative methods can be profitable. It is from this approach to knowledge building that the development of humanistic, phenomenological, and hermeneutical methods for research and practice should emerge. Such methods should help social workers understand better how clients construe their reality and experience; how upon the basis of their constructions, meanings, and feelings, objectively and subjectively, individually and communally, they function well or poorly; and how social workers can help clients experience and live their reality more functionally.

A rare example of a process, humanistic approach to both practice and research was provided by Sherman (1984). Sherman reported a creative use of cognitive, phenomenological, and existential helping approaches, through the use of quantitative and qualitative assessment measures and treatment procedures that enabled his clients to gain new experiential, dialogical understanding of their beliefs, behavior, and relationships and to alter them. Thus, he applied such assessment instruments as the I.E. scale, anxiety and depression inventories, semantic differential, locus of control, self-concept, genogram, and role-construct repertory measures, as well as such treatment procedures as experiential focusing, guided imagery, and reminiscing. These measures and procedures provided significant data that could be qualitatively and statistically analyzed and reported.

It is from a concern with process, humanistic research that social workers can discover the kind of practical, sometimes called "intuitive," intelligence that characterizes the practice thinking of many social workers. Schon (1987, pp. 22–26 and 28) referred to an aspect of this thinking as "knowing-in-action"—the dynamic knowing that is immanent in the performance, "in the action," and that is "tacit, spontaneously delivered, without deliberation." It is a knowing, according to Schon, that also is revealed "by our spontaneous skillful execution of the performance" of tasks. Gardner (1983) identified several types of intelligence: personal (intrapersonal self-knowledge and interpersonal, social intelligence), logical-mathematical, linguistic, spatial, musical, and kinesthetic abilities. These cognitive skills and competencies make up a "practical intelligence," which, as Sternberg (1985) and Sternberg and Wagner (1986) explained, goes beyond the abilities measured by IQ tests.

Such practical intelligence refers to a set of competencies for successful functioning in the real world: how to know and manage oneself, relate to and influence others, and accomplish tasks effectively and efficiently. It includes the knowledge and ability to discriminate about what works and what is good work. (See Peters, 1987, for a recent summary of research on and analysis of practical intelligence.) Social workers are particularly strong in this type of intelligence, yet need to learn more about their practical kind of social work knowing and its epistemological foundations.

SOCIAL WORK AS AN ART

Although Wood expressed a high regard for this author's (Siporin, 1988) article on the subject of social work as an art, she stated that she is reluctant to accept this conception and would instead prefer the terms *craftsmanship* and *expertise*. The social worker's creative craftsmanship does apply an expertise of knowledge and skill to produce certain products. I suggest that the process of production and the properties of these products qualify for the designation of social work practice as an art.

Social work is an art when the social worker creates, expresses, and communicates a helping program that evokes or facilitates the achievement of good, true, and beautiful patterns of functioning in clients—in addition to helping clients resolve problems in social living. Effective social work has aesthetic features in its creative use of knowledge, skill, and style; in a dialogic helping relationship, metaphoric communication, and aesthetic form; and in the provision of an aesthetic change experience in an expanded state of consciousness. Dewey (1934/1958) conceived of the creation of art as an aesthetic experience and as the communication of that experience. Social work is an art when there is a felt aesthetic experience, developed reciprocally and shared intersubjectively by the client and the social worker. There is an awareness that what the helping activities are producing is characterized by a harmonious unity of form and content, intensity of feelings, and complexity of ideas; a quality of completion, or, what Dewey called "consummation"; and by an enjoyment of these qualities in an enrichment of consciousness.

Such an aesthetic experience is the dynamic of the process of change that takes place in an effective helping situation. The "critical" or "change events," and what Davis and Reid (1988) called "informative events," in which clients experience change in response to therapeutic intervention, may be understood as aesthetic change experiences. The facilitation or development of such aesthetic change experiences within the art form of clinical social work is both problem solving and a work of art.

Social work has been conceived as an art throughout its history, particularly by practitioners. It also has been claimed to be, or that it should become, a science, though social work will always remain primarily an art. The concept of social work as a scientific art is preferred by some of us because the art does have and should have some base of scientifically validated knowledge. The art of practice is an important area of social work theory and practice, of which little is known and that strongly merits development. It is an area that is suitable for empirical, qualitative, and phenomenological process research. Through this research, social workers can better understand the aesthetic features of the artwork of social work practice and the subjective and intersubjective processes that operate in a social work aesthetic experience. Such knowledge would be directly relevant and helpful to practitioners and would advance the effectiveness of social work practice.

REFERENCES

Davis, I. P., & Reid, W. J. (1988). Event analysis in clinical practice and process research. *Social Casework, 69,* 298–306.

Dewey, J. (1958). *Art as experience.* New York: Capricorn Books. (originally published in 1934)

Gardner, H. (1983). *Frames of mind.* New York: Basic Books.

Peters, R. (1987). *Practical intelligence.* New York: Harper & Row.

Schon, D. A. (1987). *Educating the reflective practitioner.* San Francisco: Jossey-Bass.

Sherman, E. (1984). *Working with older persons.* Boston, MA: Kluwer-Nijhoff.

Siporin, M. (1988). Clinical social work as an art form. *Social Casework, 69,* 177–185.

Sternberg, R. J. (1985). *Beyond IQ.* New York: Cambridge University Press.

Sternberg, R. J., & Wagner, J. (Eds.). (1986). *Practical intelligence.* New York: Cambridge University Press.

Tolson, E. R. (1989). *The metamodel and clinical social work.* New York: Columbia University Press.

Videka-Sherman, L. (1988). Meta-analysis of research on social work practice in mental health. *Social Work, 33,* 325–338.

Wood, K. (1978). Casework effectiveness: A new look at the research evidence. *Social Work, 23,* 437–458.

The Forest or the Trees?

Carol H. Meyer

Observing the self-preservative principle of "let you and him fight," this author will not address directly the controversies among researchers, but will discuss the subject matter she knows best: practice and its implications for research. Since much of Woods's argument in Chapter 13 depends on her appropriate concern with the validation of practice theories, this commentary begins with a mild challenge to her use of terminology. Despite this author's liking of the term *polyocular*, having long relied on the use of *multiple lenses* to pursue the same point that social workers cannot take fixed positions in viewing dynamic and fluid phenomena, the flexibility that is necessary really has to do with perspective, not necessarily theory. An elaboration of this idea may help clarify why practitioners and researchers do not seem to see eye to eye (or ocular to ocular).

PERCEPTUAL BIASES

All social workers would agree with the *Rashomon* idea that everything they choose to work on—practice, research, and the formulation of policy—depends on how they view events. Perceptual biases are what maintain the boundaries of professional disciplines, for what a physician sees as a chronic disease, a social worker views as a problem of home care. Of course, when there is a blurring of boundaries—when the "case" escapes the neat definitions to which the disciplines are accustomed, as is often the case in psychiatric or political events—these "messy" problems often engender battles over "turf" and other controversies.

Sometimes, the discovery of a new phenomenon, a budding theory, or an earth-shaking shock can induce a complete turnaround in traditional paradigms, as Kuhn (1970) explicated. Given that scientific formulations do not appear to be as permanent as they were once thought to be and that "truth" is probably more a function of the way it is beheld, rather than a consequence of pure "objective" fact, it is imperative that social workers identify the perceptions that are at the core of professional social work activities.

The problem in social work is manifested in the continuing disagreements among practitioners and researchers, who seem to have different views of the world, and the existence of these disparate world views creates more dissension than does any conflict about the choice among an array of theories. For example, most practitioners agree on the psychosocial parameters of cases, whether they are of the psychodynamic or sociobehavioral theoretical persuasion. On the other hand, the requirement (insistence?) by researchers that the psychosocial phenomena of a case should be reduced to the narrowest variables for statistical convenience distorts their perception of these phenomena. This difference in what is attended to is a more serious threat to social work's survival than is theoretical overchoice. As Wood suggested, the profession's disarray makes it look ridiculous to the outside world.

One of the consequences of the lack of agreement about perceptions is that cases are variously defined (a priori, even before assessment) as having narrow or broad boundaries. Many researchers and practitioners refer to theories of personality as if they were interchangeable with theories of social work practice. Implicit in this error is the idea that social work practice is interchangeable with counseling or psychotherapy, rather than that counseling and psychotherapy are among a host of techniques in most practice methods. When one views practice in systemic terms, even while relying on the explanatory value of theories of personality, one sees the need for broader based theories that will encompass psychosocial events.

There is a need for research on and the development of a new set of theories that will illuminate interactive events, processes, and the impact of environments. At this point, it is not important to determine which perspective is correct; it is enough to know that social work will remain in serious difficulty as long as social workers cannot agree about whether cases are to be viewed in linear or curvilinear ways. How can the profession answer the questions that Woods raised—"What kind of knowledge is needed, in what areas, from what sources it should come, and what methods should be used to obtain it?"—when social workers have yet to agree on what the "it" is?

It is not theory that is in question here, but perspective. It is not a question of which conceptual lens fits the data of the case but, rather, which conceptual lens allows *in* the data of the case. That is the key perceptual issue; once we social workers have "let in" the data to our vision, there may be multiple ways of doing something about what we see. (The less we see, the less we do.) It would be helpful if social workers could master a full repertoire of theories so they could understand all the phenomena of a case and have several models to use for multiple interventive purposes. But few practitioners or educators can accommodate an integrated view of clients from the ego, behavioral, psychodynamic, and cognitive points of view. Nor are there many who can equally tolerate the repertoire of such social work practice theories as the psychosocial, task-centered, life model, and sociobehavioral, perhaps because the philosophical roots of personality and practice theories are so different and their delineations are so tight and consistent with their orientations.

What is called for is not a unified, professionally agreed-on general theory of people and of practice, but a unified, professionally agreed-on perspective of the tasks of social work; a respect for others' commitments to different theories; and a full repertoire of interventions to accommodate the complexity of psychosocially defined cases. In line with this argument, the dissonance between research and practice will not be resolved by technical fixes, power plays, or claims that one theory is better than another. The task is much more difficult. Researchers and practitioners will have to come to some agreement on grand issues, similar to whether the earth is flat or round. Only as they unite on their view of the world will they find common ground for their theoretical differences, which will and should always remain. How would it be in medicine, for example, if there were fundamental disagreements about the structure of the body? Of course, physicians have theoretical differences about the causes and treatment of diseases, and some of their differences are fierce. But medicine thrives as a discipline because its credibility rests in the public's view of its common ground. Social work has yet to communicate that kind of domain.

DEFINING THE COMMON GROUND

Now comes the hard part: defining the common ground about which there must be a consensus before all credibility is lost. Some relatively easy issues can be dispensed with because the profession has been working on them for about a century, although we social workers have not always acted on them. *Values and ethics* are not in contention here, even though we could do well with a refresher course. The *psychosocial parameters* of social work—methods and goals—have pretty much been determined, although one may wonder about the extension of the psychotherapeutic and social action edges of some practice activities. Perhaps there is even general agreement on *purposes*, although we are often apt to confuse means and ends and in these difficult days are prone to sell our purposes for a mess of potage from the National Institute of Mental Health.

Having found agreement on the simpler issues, the profession is faced with the macro issues. Is its perspective on the world linear or curved? In research and practice, is it possible to identify holistically sectors of the psychosocial unit, rather than to single out the smallest units for attention? Can rational technology in practice or in research address irrational behaviors and processes? Can patterns be found in chaos? Can social workers educate for uncertainty? These questions challenge not only the predictability of life's events, but the sense of certainty that the profession's current empiricist interests seem to reflect.

Social workers can skirt the edges of these questions or retreat to academic bravado, but these approaches will not save us. As Woods said so well, the pressures of university tenure, the pulls of rigor versus relevance, the competition between research and practitioner, and the profession's continuing self-consciousness about the specter of its beginnings in apprenticeship have caused the profession to lean toward (if not to cave into) models of research and sometimes practice that are academic, scientific, and increasingly unrelated to the real world with which it is supposed to be institutionally involved.

How does the profession reach toward a new mission, unified about what it wants to accomplish? We social workers are living in a world of chronic illness, homelessness, child neglect and abuse, substance abuse, teenage pregnancy, family breakdown, poverty, racism, sexism, ageism, and alienation. A view that is unfettered by territorial blinders would be of the phenomena of a case that is in a whirl of dynamic activity. People who are afflicted and oppressed by these conditions cannot and will not stand still to be in control or experimental groups, nor will the study of a sliver of their lives tell us anything of significance. Their social contexts make them richer subjects of study and intervention than social work research and practice are yet prepared to encompass. Their problems, conditions, behaviors, histories, and opportunities are too varied to be classified under any system, such as that of the *Diagnostic and Statistical Manual of Mental Disorders (Third Edition)* (American Psychiatric Association, 1980). The data in cases never really add up linearly; they only interact and become more complex and "curvy."

If this view of the world is even partially realistic, it is fair to ask why researchers do not invent ways of studying it, classifying it, and presenting it in a way that practitioners can comprehend because it reflects the reality that they know. Researchers cannot continue to pursue isolated behaviors and expect this inquiry to help. They cannot persistently (and pretentiously) crunch numbers that reflect only the thinnest veneer of the phenomena under study. If we social workers could only agree on the complexity of things, we might be able to develop qualitative, complex processible instruments that would be original, rigorous, and relevant.

Because a certain degree of intellectual unrest is attributable to chaos theory, this commentary ends by noting that chaos—patterned turbulence—"eliminates the fantasy of deterministic predictability" and demands an analysis of the whole (Gleick, 1987, p. 6). As Thomas (1983) wrote about a single cell and the poets wrote about a grain of sand, chaos theory suggests that because universal properties of systems are built into the simplest representations, research models do not have to be so complex after all: they have only to encompass the whole, in small bites. Even this complex topic of epistemological issues may have the simplest resolution if we have the will to make the wisest choices.

REFERENCES

American Psychiatric Association. (1980). *Diagnostic and statistical manual of mental disorders* (3rd ed.). Washington, DC: Author.

Gleick, J. (1987). *Chaos: Making a new science.* New York: Viking Press.

Kuhn, T. S. (1970). *The structure of scientific revolutions.* Chicago: University of Chicago Press.

Thomas, L. (1983). *Humanities and science. Late night thoughts on listening to Mahler's ninth symphony.* Toronto, Canada: Bantam Books.

Thoughts on Epistemological Issues in Social Work

Aaron H. Beckerman

Chapter 13, by Wood, reveals and challenges many of the preferred ideas and values that are inherent in the conception of social practice knowledge, as well as in the processes that are used in social work to generate this knowledge. This commentary addresses a few of these issues.

LOGICAL POSITIVISM

On the basis of reading articles on social work research, one may conclude that logical positivism is much more alive and active as a topic of ideological debate than as a mode of research in social work. All researchers know, and some try to teach the ideal research model, but as practicing researchers, we adapt the ideal research model to the contextual reality of the problem being investigated. Shils (1957, p. 3), in discussing his study of the primary group wrote:

> [It was] a disorderly movement . . . full of instances of things known and overlooked, unexpected emergencies, and rediscoveries of long known facts and hypotheses which in time of their original discovery had no fitting articulation and which found such articulation only after considerable time.

Perhaps we ought to teach research as we practice it, with all its contextual realities. The world of the practitioner is, as should be noted, shaped and influenced by contextual realities.

KNOWLEDGE

The profession would benefit significantly from a greater sensitivity to the use of language. For example, what is meant by the term *knowledge?* Siporin (1975, p. 363) offered the following definition: "Knowledge is cognitive mental content (ideas and beliefs) concerning reality that we take to be true (perceive with certainty, based on adequate evidence), or that we decide is confirmable and has a high probability of truth."

To compound the issue, one reads about the need for "scientific knowledge." What do the scientists say about knowledge? Bronowski (1973, p. 353), a mathematician, wrote:

> One aim of the physical sciences has been to give an exact picture of the material world. One achievement of physics in the twentieth century has been to prove that aim is unattainable. . . . It turns out that . . . errors cannot be taken out of observations.

In the fantasy land of the future, what if all instructors of social work research began the first class with the following quote from Percy Williams Bridgman, the Nobel prize winner in physics for 1946:

> Finally, I come to what seems to me may well be from the long range point of view, the most revolutionary of insights to be derived from our recent experiences in physics, more revolutionary than the insights afforded by the discoveries of Galileo, Newton, or Darwin. This is the insight that it is impossible to transcend the human reference point. (Quoted in Conant, 1953, p. 86)

Wood quoted Siporin (1988, p. 180) on different ways of knowing. "The creative person uses right and left brain and employs logical as well as nonrational, parallel, lateral, analogical, and intuitive kinds of reasoning." One suspects that researchers and practitioners would be able to communicate much more effectively with each other if they agreed on a continuum of knowledge that included intuition, imagination, hunches, insight, and the like, as well as the thought processes of researchers. These thought processes are critical to competent social work practice.

RESEARCH AND PRACTICE

Early in the chapter, Wood examined the relationship between research and practice. She titled this section Research versus Practice, or Rigor versus Relevance. The significance of this issue is not clear, for unless rigor is an end in itself, what is the relevance of rigor? For example, a young scientist came to Enrico Fermi, excited about an experiment he was about to perform. Fermi is reported to have responded (Deutsch, 1959, p. 105), "Go ahead and perform this experiment. If you are lucky, you will make a discovery. If you have bad luck and your results agree with your theory, you will at least have performed a measurement."

When research is equated with rigor, the power and function of research are severely limited. The preoccupation with rigor stems from a narrow view of research as a method of hypothesis testing—a formulation that is proof-oriented and frequently requires both the selection and reconceptualization of problems that are amenable to traditional research methodologies. This is a familiar problem to practitioners and researchers. Writing more than 30 years ago, Redl (1957, p. 16) commented:

> The practitioner has an odd complaint. He is ready to pay tribute to the long-range usefulness of our fancy formulations, terminology and curves. He politely admits that the research expert produces a lot that is important. His complaint is that the research expert does not answer the question *he* asks.

The problem is serious and endemic in the profession and seems to be fostered and exacerbated by the schools of social work. This problem will continue as long as schools of social work hire instructors of research on the basis of their statistical, methodological, and computer skills, rather than on their knowledge of and interest and experience in practice. Hiring criteria in schools of social work should differentiate between highly sophisticated technicians and competent social work professionals.

INTELLECTUAL "INTERIOR" LIFE OF THE PRACTITIONER

In Chapter 13, Wood drew attention to the "interior" intellectual life of the practitioner, a topic that, with the exception of Lewis (1982), has been almost ignored in the social work literature. Schon (1983, p. 17), a professor of urban studies and education, depicted professional practice as generally composed of "uncertainty, complexity, instability, uniqueness and value conflict."

The first level of skill that is crucial to practitioners, according to Wood, is the ability to extract "a solvable problem from the client's presented 'mess'." This author concurs with Wood's statement that "research and rational technology have little to say about this crucial process, but competent and experienced practitioners know a lot about it." Wood offered an interesting observation that may help explain why this inferential process, which is the sine qua non of competent practice, is so alien to research in general and to social work research in particular:

> These processes transpire, often rapidly, before an intervention even starts. They are processes that involve a kind of research by the practitioner, who is formulating and testing diagnostic and interventive hypotheses. *But the practitioner is synthesizing as well, making creative leaps in recognizing patterns and implementing innovative designs to bring about a change in the problem.* (Italics added.)

ISSUES FOR FURTHER EXPLORATION

Wood raised a number of compelling issues that are essential to understanding and addressing epistemological issues in social work. Given the limitations of space, two issues are noted here.

Scientific rational technology in medicine. Wood wrote: "Schon recognized that the view of the practice professions as purveyors of a scientific rational technology to their clients—of practice as a purely instrumental activity—has resulted in some dramatic successes for such practice professions as medicine and engineering." There is considerable controversy in medical education about the consequences of the phenomenal growth and use of medical technology in the past 20 years. As Gorlin and Zucker (1983, p. 1059), two physicians, noted:

> It is ironic that in this era, dominated by technical prowess and rapid biomedical advances, patient and physician each feels increasingly rejected by the other. . . . The responsibility for dissatisfaction with modern medical care lies not only with the patient but also with the physician.

Polyocular conceptual lens. The introduction of new terms is always intriguing. In Chapter 13, Wood wrote about the ability of practitioners to be "polyocular—to have a variety of lenses through which to see their cases and the clinical judgment necessary to select the conceptual lens that fits best the data of the case." This statement raises two questions. First, what is the relationship between a conceptual frame of reference and a conceptual lens? For example, can one have a single conceptual frame of reference with multiple conceptual lenses?

Second, to what extent is a conceptual frame of reference, as well as a conceptual lens, chosen on the basis of knowledge, values, or both? Although the impact of values on social work practice knowledge was beyond the scope of Wood's chapter, it is important to think about preferred concepts as an expression of values, as well as of knowledge. Furthermore, there are too many situations in which preferred values are conceptualized as if they are knowledge.

REFERENCES

Bronowski, J. (1973). *The ascent of man*. Boston: Little, Brown.

Conant, J. B. (1953). *Modern science and modern man*. Garden City, NY: Doubleday Anchor Books.

Deutsch, M. (1959). Evidence and inference in nuclear research. In D. Lerner (Ed.), *Evidence and inference*. Glencoe, IL: Free Press.

Gorlin, R., & Zucker, H. D. (1983). Physicians' reactions to patients: A key to teaching humanistic medicine. *New England Journal of Medicine, 308,* 1059–1063.

Lewis, H. (1982). *The intellectual base of social work practice.* New York: Haworth Press.

Redl, F. (1957). Research needs in the delinquency field. *Children, 4,* 15–19.

Schon, D. A. (1983). *The reflective practitioner: How professionals think in action.* New York: Basic Books.

Shils, E. (1957). Primordial, personal, sacred and civil ties. In P. Hammond (Ed.), *Sociologists at work: The craft of social research.* Garden City, NY: Doubleday Anchor Books.

Siporin, M. (1975). *Introduction to social work practice.* New York: Macmillan.

Siporin, M. (1988). Clinical social work as art form. *Social Casework, 69,* 177–185.

Synthesis

Themes in the Discussion of Epistemology

Lewayne D. Gilchrist

Overall, three themes emerged from the discussions of epistemology in social work:

- As social workers, we are not quite sure what we know, that is, what knowledge base and intellectual turf are ours.
- In our preoccupation with the acquisition of scientific technologies, we have not considered in useful detail how practitioners know what they know and use what they know in their daily professional practice.
- As educators and researchers, we need to know more about how practitioners think and the key intellectual skills that practitioners bring to social work practice.

With surprising consensus, the discussants emphasized the need to think about thinking in social work and to obtain greater clarity about the fundamental intellectual components of social work practice. They drew from works by Socrates, Plato, Hume, Heisenberg, Einstein, and others to approach the topic of what we social workers know and how we know it.

NEED FOR CRITICAL THINKING

The issue of epistemology in social work is not trivial. We cannot credibly be members of a profession whose practitioners—and educators, for that matter—cannot explain why they do what they do. In several contexts, the discussants noted that practitioners need to know how to think and how to articulate the foundations for their actions. Therefore, a major focus of social work education should be to train students in these key skills of thinking and articulation. The ability to articulate one's decision-making processes is and will continue to be critical to maintain the necessary professional legitimation and will certainly pave the way for more effective professional education. Courses on research and practice, therefore, should go beyond surveying various technical methods to include training in critical reasoning and should teach students how to verify their perceptions so they may correct their own behavior and grow beyond their own subjectivity.

The discussants noted that there is considerable ideological and conceptual inertia on the part of educators and researchers in the area of critical thinking skills and the relation of these skills to professional practice and education. To date, researchers and practitioners have had great difficulty representing and defining the complexities involved in highly competent social work practice. The challenge of defining what we know, how we know it, and what we do with what we know is made more complex by the fact that no single, unitary decision-making process or body of knowledge is consistently at work during practice activities. Various discussants emphasized that professional competence and relevant "knowledge" encompasses cognitive *and* visceral elements, analytic *and* synthesizing capacities, moral *and* intellectual judgments, and scientific *and* esthetic components. Holistic pattern finding and reductionistic focusing on single elements of a problem coexist in constant oscillation. Little attention has been paid to uncovering the nature and implication of these processes. Schon's (1983, 1987) two books were cited by several discussants as valuable aids for understanding complex professional behavior.

To begin to unravel the intellectual and epistemological components of practice, the discussants exhorted researchers to examine carefully the instances of excellent social work practice. The literature on creativity, intuition, the cognitive processing of information, problem solving, decision making, and artificial intelligence were all cited as potential aids to a deeper and more specific understanding of the components of the decisions and actions involved in practice. The discussants also urged researchers to look in controlled ways at the assumptions underlying competent practitioners' everyday decisions, for example, the decision rules they use, so that the profession can more usefully describe what "knowledge for practice" is and how such knowledge develops and is transmitted.

DEFINITION OF PROFESSIONAL KNOWLEDGE NEEDS

Some themes were visible in the discussions on epistemology that were not addressed head-on. When the discussants used the terms *knowledge, practice, practitioner, research,* and *researcher,* they had significant definitional differences but usually talked as if they all agreed on the meaning and significance of these key terms. Furthermore, some discussants used terms, such as *researcher* and *practitioner,* to signal that they were in a particular ideological camp. Several times, these ideological differences stimulated debates that seemed more artificial than real and obscured the recognition of the profession's urgent need to attain conceptual clarity about its mission, work, and methods. It is clear that there is no consensus in the profession on what constitutes expertise or competence.

What constitutes adequate or useful knowledge differs according to one's professional role and pragmatic needs. That the whole idea of effectiveness—the "good" end point—is different, depending on whether one is a "practitioner" or a "researcher," is not a new insight. Yet, we researchers have not gone as far as we might in examining the implications of these different epistemological perspectives. A great deal of professional energy has gone into analyzing why "practitioners" do not read or use the results of *researchers'* empirical studies. The conclusion is usually that *practitioners* need to change their anti-intellectual ways so they will better appreciate and make use of empirical findings. The notion of probabalistic thinking, including assessing the likelihood of a certain outcome, given known base rates and past findings—the intellectual base on which much research is generated and used in other professions—has not been examined with regard to social workers. In their commentaries LeCroy and Ashford presented outlines of this idea as a new direction for the old dilemma of how research should be utilized.

Logical positivism and traditional ways of defining science took a beating from a number of discussants. Although empiricism per se was not seriously challenged, traditional scientific methods—testing a null hypothesis with an analysis of variance, for example—received considerable criticism as being too narrow to address many areas, issues, and dilemmas of social work practice. The discussants seemed to agree that as social work researchers, we need to broaden our technical tools to encompass so-called qualitative methods to improve the validity of our investigations. One direction this broadening should take is the creation of research designs that incorporate and integrate both quantitative and qualitative approaches. Science is not just a handful of recipes. Good science is in-depth thinking about an issue, accompanied by some activities designed to rule out biases and competing explanations. We social workers are not accustomed to thinking about knowledge building in these terms.

Social work research itself is not a unitary term that consistently defines activities with common goals. Activities that are systematically grounded in real events and in previous studies by others—activities that are called by the general term *research*—must be combined with a great deal of creative thinking to meet a wide variety of informational needs. The profession has to generate a new and more sensitive understanding of conditions and problems (using exploratory and descriptive methodologies). It requires innovative thinking and methods to test new and better theories that are derived from a careful synthesis of many descriptive findings. It needs research to verify the effectiveness of practitioners' activities (program-evaluation methodologies) and more, to invent valid methods for examining the effectiveness and efficiency of entire service delivery systems that affect the disadvantaged. New intervention techniques (such as research and development) must be developed to bring about positive changes in disadvantaged individuals, groups, and organizational systems. Methods have to be devised for tracing and predicting the impact of policies on individuals. Each of these research tasks or goals stems from the need for a different type of social work knowledge. Not all research methodologies are appropriate for all these needs. The discussants seemed to approach epistemological issues as if social work practice consisted exclusively of its counseling and psychotherapy functions. However, social work covers a much broader area, much of which requires knowledge, ways of thinking, and empirical methods for which there are no good models. The discussants did not really address the fact that social workers may be called on to develop new empirical methods, rather than just rely on mastering or adapting methods from other fields.

RESEARCH AS A TOOL FOR PERSUASION

Finally, the discussants did not address the notion that social workers pursue empiricism not simply for knowledge, but for the instrumental reason of increasing social work's clout outside the profession. When important decisions are under consideration that will affect our professional constituencies—underserved and disadvantaged groups—social workers should be able to speak a language that is persuasive to others to achieve goals that we think are valuable. In this technocratic society, that persuasive language is the language of science. The epistemological discussions did not address the social contexts and purposes of research and research utilization beyond the level of individual practitioners' evaluations and adaptation of their work in relatively isolated individual practice settings. Research is a tool for persuasion as much as it is a tool for evaluation and knowledge building. It can be used to initiate and sustain planned change in systems, including political systems. The systematic study that we call research is a tool for creation—for discovering new things and moving in new directions. As a profession, we have tended to emphasize only one goal of research—accountability-evaluation—and to ignore the instrumental and creative goals.

REFERENCES

Schon, D. A. (1983). *The reflective practitioner: How professionals think in action.* New York: Basic Books.
Schon, D. A. (1987). *Educating the reflective practitioner.* San Francisco: Jossey-Bass.

Chapter 14

Themes, Issues, and Prospects

Lynn Videka-Sherman, William J. Reid, and Ronald W. Toseland

The articles in this volume express current thinking about the methods and epistemology of clinical social work research. Neither the conference nor the book was intended to provide a state-of-the-art review of all aspects of research in clinical social work. Rather, the topics selected were those that reflected either new developments that merited review or older developments that merited reappraisal. This final chapter considers four of these developments, represented in the four parts of this book: single-system designs (SSDs), the application of research technologies (methodological advances), the utilization of research, and the epistemological debate—and concludes with some observations about the evolution and future of clinical social work research.

SINGLE-SYSTEM DESIGNS (SSDs)

A major goal of the conference was to review developments in one of the hallmarks of the empirical practice movement—SSDs. Various facets of this methodology were explored in the two sessions devoted to it.

A major focus was the use of SSDs by social workers in practice contexts. The notion of practitioner-researchers employing such designs to generate knowledge was reaffirmed by Briar and extended by Nelsen to traditional (nonbehavioral) forms of practice and by Stern to the study of family processes. Still it was recognized that only a few practitioners have been involved in this form of research and that their number is likely to remain small.

The focus of attention was not so much on the knowledge-building function of such designs as it was on their use in the evaluation of ordinary practice. Such evaluations were seen as serving the purposes of assessing clients, determining the effectiveness of interventions, doing case planning, and establishing accountability.

However, there was disagreement over the relative emphasis to be given to these different functions. For example, in Gingerich's opinion, determining the effectiveness of intervention in producing change is an important part of the case-evaluation process. For Blythe, establishing a "causal connection between an intervention and an outcome" is of less concern than ascertaining "client change in relation to previous client functioning and expressed goals."

The difference is not trivial. Determining whether changes in clients are the result of an intervention process normally requires rigorous designs with such control features as extended baselines, withdrawal of the intervention, or multiple baselines. In exchange for such rigor, one gains critical information about the effects of the intervention. Measures of goal attainment or changes in functioning without controls in the design can show change, but, as Thyer pointed out, they lack internal validity, that is, they leave open the possibility that factors other than the intervention may have produced the change.

The disagreement appears to be more about epistemology than about practice. There was little support for the routine use of controlled SSDs as a means of evaluating practice. Various points of view, if not uncertainty, were expressed over what may be surmised about the effects of intervention if there are no controls in the design. There seemed to be agreement, however, that the use of the components of SSDs, especially measures of change in clients or of the attainment of goals, would yield useful evaluative data and establish accountability, at least at the level of determining if the goals of service were being met.

Various obstacles to single-case evaluation even at this level were raised by a number of participants in their struggle to find a fit between the requirements of SSD methodology and the exigencies of social work practice. One set of obstacles, eloquently described by Tolson, has to do with the chaotic nature of many practice situations—multiple problems, brief or episodic contacts, unstructured interventions, the pressing needs of clients, little time for practitioners to conduct evaluations, and so forth. In a similar vein, Wood discussed the difficulties in applying "rational technology" to the "messes" that practitioners must contend with in their daily work. Another set of obstacles, mentioned by Nelsen, has to do with the application of SSDs to such traditional practice modalities as long-term psychosocial treatment, in which immediate targets of change may be multiple, shifting, and difficult to connect to the overall goals of the case. Yet, Blythe, Nelsen, Reinherz, and Tolson suggested reasonable adaptations and compromises for both these types of obstacles.

Even in chaotic practice situations, one can use some elements of SSD methodology, such as the specification of problems or measures of change. Broxmeyer (1978), Dean and Reinherz (1986), Nelsen (1984), and Sodervick (1975), among others, have demonstrated that SSDs are applicable to psychosocial and other forms of traditional practice if the practitioner is willing, at the minimum, to specify goals and to measure the degree to which the goals have been attained.

However, applications of components of SSD methodology raise some definitional issues. At what point does an application become so partial that it no longer makes sense to speak of using SSD methodology? For many practitioners, for example, responsible practice involves specifying goals and assessing the attainment of the goals. They would not necessarily see themselves as using SSD methods. What about differences in terminology? What are the distinctions, if any, among the terms *SSDs* (Stern, Thyer, and Tolson), *single-case evaluations* (Corcoran, Gingerich, and Reinherz), and *single-case research* (Nelsen)? Perhaps proponents of single-case methodology should do what Glisson suggested for qualitative methodology, that is, speak of specific methods, rather than of vaguely defined global entities.

Several participants (Blythe, Corcoran, Gingerich, and Thyer) addressed the utility of SSD methodology for treatment, that is, whether the use of this methodology contributes to the outcome of a case. All agreed that empirical investigations of the utility of SSDs for treatment are needed, but Thyer noted that defensiveness about the lack of research on the utility of SSD methods was hardly justified, given the dearth of research on standard procedures for assessment and recording.

It is not clear, however, how such investigations could be designed to provide a reasonable test of the utility of SSDs for treatment. It is unlikely that one SSD method, such as baselining, or the use of assessment data would be sufficiently decisive to have a demonstrable effect on the final outcome of a case. A package of SSD methods may have an impact on the final outcome, but what should such a package contain? A less ambitious strategy but one that may have a more immediate payoff would be to examine the immediate consequences of SSD methods. For example, what assessment data (not otherwise obtained from the clinical interview) are gained by rapid assessment instruments? How useful are such data in the practitioner's judgment? To what extent do clients comply with self-monitoring procedures? What are the immediate apparent consequences of the use of these procedures for the behavior being monitored? A change-process research approach (Reid) could help establish connections between the use of SSD methods and the consequent events of a case.

Whatever form it takes or whatever results it yields, research on the utility of SSDs for treatment will probably not be sufficient to bring about a marked increase in the use of SSD methods by practitioners. For practitioners, the findings of such research will be less persuasive than will be the perceived benefits derived from the actual use of SSDs. Energy should be put into knowledge diffusion efforts in practice settings (see Robinson, Bronson, & Blythe, 1988), including the promotion of developmental practice in agencies (Thomas). Working with practitioners could also help the proponents of SSDs learn how to refine their methodology to increase its usefulness in practice settings.

APPLICATIONS OF TECHNOLOGY

Several articles in Part 2 considered the applications of research and computer technologies to practice. Hudson asserted that computerized, standardized assessment tools are both easy to use and responsive to the needs of clients and practitioners. Mullen and Schuerman presented expert systems as decision-making tools that integrate empirical knowledge with clinical expertise and opinion. Expert systems have the potential to assist practitioners in making assessments and clinical decisions about important matters, such as whether to place a child in foster care. Reid took a different tack with regard to the application of technologies. He presented change-process research as a rediscovered (and somewhat modified in its newest forms) research technology that has evolved in response to the increased interest in how change in clients comes about.

Theories and Technology

One issue that was addressed is the role of theories in developing and using technologies. Theories are necessary to assign meaning to empirical findings and to provide a basis for explanation and prediction. Knowledge for practice is derived from multiple sources, including research, theories, values, and personal experience (or practice wisdom). There is no fully developed single theory to guide social work research and intervention. The lack of a unifying theory complicates the application of technologies to the practice setting. As Siegel aptly pointed out, theories should determine which problems of clients should be assessed and when these problems should be assessed. She argued that the assessment technologies represented by Hudson's Computerized Assessment System (CAS) may be more advanced than is the profession's conceptual understanding of clients' problems. Proctor and Davis both discussed the importance of theory in defining the "little o's and i's" in change-process research. Under different theoretical frameworks, these little o's and i's may be defined differently, even for the same client. Thus, practice applications of research technologies must take place in a theoretical context.

Theory building is moving forward in some fields. For example, a growing body of research is finding that neither theories of individual psychopathology nor sociological theories are sufficient to explain the occurrence of child abuse and neglect. The most promising theoretical perspective for this social problem is the "ecological" approach, which is a pluralistic mixing of individual, family, community, and social systems theories. The problem with theoretical amalgams, such as the ecological approach, is that they are often articulated at such an abstract level that they are difficult to apply to research or to practice. (In Chapter 1, Briar also criticized systems-based theories as being too abstract to be specified and tested.) Hence, even with ongoing clarification, these theories still raise more questions than they answer. For example, social work is far from identifying the relative contributions of person, family, community, and society variables to the occurrence of child abuse and neglect. In research terms, only a relatively small proportion of the variance of child abuse and neglect can be explained. In clinical terms, there is a great deal of uncertainty about whether the presence of a given, even widely accepted, set of risk factors means that a parent will mistreat a child. This uncertainty leads the practitioner to make semistructured or unstructured decisions. As Mutschler pointed out, computer technology is less readily adapted for unstructured decisions than for structured decisions, such as geographic or income eligibility for services. Uncertainty in prediction, or "imperfect knowledge," as Reamer called it, is one of the reasons that practitioners will be skeptical of expert systems and of computerized clinical assessment tools for decision making.

A promising feature of the change-process approach to clinical research (Reid) is its potential for applying theoretical formulations to individual cases and for operationalizing them in ways that are idiographically meaningful. Another promising feature is that this approach facilitates a clearer articulation of the processes and outcomes of treatment. Clearly specified processes and outcomes can be more readily adopted by other practitioners.

Another example of idiographically operationalizing little o's and i's comes from the field of child abuse and neglect. Recent research has found that specific parent-child interactional patterns are associated with child abuse and neglect and that these patterns are amenable to change with structured training in parenting skills. One might consider parent-child interactions to be "little o's" and elements of the structured-skills learning approach, such as home-based practice of noticing and rewarding compliant behavior, to be "little i's." An alternative would be to consider home-based practice to be the "little o" and client-practitioner planning for the practice to be the "little i." One limitation of this approach is that the theoretical and empirical relationships between the "little o" of parent-child interaction and the "big O's" of child maltreatment and good-quality parenting are uncertain. Continued work on theoretical foundations for practice is necessary to improve the articulation between research technologies and practice.

Context and Technology

Several authors elaborated on the importance of contextual factors in the adaptation of recent research technologies to practice settings. Mutschler discussed the importance of organizational factors, such as the availability of equipment and training and the support of the agency's administration in the adoption of new technologies by practitioners. Proctor delineated the importance of such contextual factors in the therapeutic process as the fee schedule of the agency or whether the office is conducive to privacy. Stein discussed a number of contextual factors that affect and ostensibly could limit the applications of expert systems in different localities. He described decision making in child welfare as already encoded by "statutes, agency policies, and procedural manuals that set forth with precision what workers are to do and by professional standards for practice that narrow the range of variables to be considered in making choices." Statutory differences limit the generalizability of decision making across child welfare jurisdictions. Although legal and regulatory statutes can be built into expert systems, they are also contextual factors that may conflict with other sources of knowledge.

Technology and Social Work Knowledge

A third theme of Part 2 concerns social work practice knowledge. Even those who agree that empirical knowing is relevant and important to clinical social work concur that the empirical knowledge base is incomplete. Mullen and Schuerman allowed for nonempirical sources of knowledge in building expert systems. Expert systems can incorporate the opinions of those with exceptional knowledge or experience. Although Hudson stated that he is comfortable with an empirical epistemology for social work, his CAS allows for case notes and other qualitative records on clients. Siegel proposed the term *computer-assisted*, rather than *computer-based*, practice. Sherman advised social workers to think in terms of dialectical, rather than linear, processes of knowledge building. An epistemological model that allows for partial empiricism and personal knowing is needed, a point discussed in depth in a subsequent section.

Although these ideas may be appealing to most readers, it is also important to acknowledge the dilemmas that are created by technologies that rely on "imperfect knowledge." Consider the possible legal consequences for the child welfare worker who decides to place a child in foster care although the expert system advised against placement. Is the social worker legally vulnerable for making a decision that the expert system advised against? It is incumbent on social workers to use technologies to assist their practice and decision making, but to resist the reification of technologically assisted decision making.

UTILIZATION OF RESEARCH

A theme that runs throughout Parts 3 and 4 is the utilization of research findings for practice. Jayaratne examined the "clinical" meaning of research findings on outcomes for clients. Kirk highlighted the sometimes pejorative view of researchers toward practitioners and raised the provocative issue of whether this pejorative stance has further inhibited practitioners' use of research findings. Fischer's review and critique of meta-analysis as a tool for the integration of research findings emphasized the dilemmas and uncertainties of drawing conclusions from a diverse, often disagreeing, and usually flawed set of research studies. Fischer also discussed the many methodological limitations of the original research studies and quantitative methods for combining them. Nurius, Videka-Sherman, and Nugent all pointed out that most of the problems that Fischer cited are not unique to meta-analysis but also occur with qualitative syntheses of research findings.

Values and Research Utilization

One thrust of the chapters in Part 3 is that values and beliefs affect the extent to which and the ways in which social workers use research findings. Jayaratne presented attribution theory as a context for understanding the role of beliefs and perspective in constructing meaning from empirical findings. Gordon illustrated the irrational elements in decision making, using the selection of a spouse as an example. Levy argued for a broader consideration of clinical decision making by describing clinical data as imperfect and therefore "compromised." Her discussion of the weighted-utility approach in decision theory is a useful framework for further considerations of social workers' applications of knowledge to specific situations. Tripodi's lively case example of the ups and downs of an adolescent client over time made the following point: Values play a critical role in assigning meaning to empirical data. The role of values in knowledge for practice is certainly not a new idea for social work practice. Some writers have asserted that values should be a central determinant in the development of a social work knowledge base for practice (Vigilante,

1974). Many models for the development of social work knowledge explicitly allow for the influence of values in knowledge building (Mullen, 1983; Rothman, 1980). These chapters present ideas for enhancing social workers' understanding and conceptualization of the articulation of theories, personal values, professional values, societal values, research, and experience in developing a knowledge base for clinical social work.

Dissemination of Research Findings

Le Croy and Schilling both criticized the researcher's view of journal articles as the most effective route for the dissemination of findings from studies to practitioners. Le Croy cited De Martini and Whitbeck's (1986) findings that on-the-job training and personal experience are the most influential sources of the knowledge that social work clinicians use to make decisions. Schilling called for social work researchers to present their results through workshops and training programs, rather than through the professional literature alone, and identified managers as important disseminators of practice knowledge. Berlin and Nurius both stated that educators play a central role in the dissemination of new empirical knowledge and new technologies.

Meta-analysis involves the use of highly technical tools for the review of research findings. The technical nature of this data-synthesis approach militates against its use by practitioners. Again, what practitioners require is the substance of the findings.

EPISTEMOLOGY

As Gilgun noted in her synthesis of Chapter 12 and the commentaries on it, "empiricism implies epistemology." Unfortunately, researchers and empirical practitioners have not paid as much attention to the epistemological foundations of their work as they should have, perhaps assuming naively that scientific principles and procedures need no philosophical justification. In attacking the epistemologies of social work empiricists, critics may have compounded this shortcoming with their assumption that these epistemologies fall within the confines of logical positivism. The logical positivists sought to build an epistemology on the foundation of their interpretations of scientific principles and concepts. It is questionable to what extent scientists ever embraced logical positivism or, for that matter, were ever familiar with its tenets.

Researchers, like practitioners, have their own "personal epistemologies," to use Richey's term, but what these epistemologies are is not known. Thus, although it is important, as Woods pointed out, to learn more about how practitioners think, it is equally important to know more about how researchers think.

Proponents of empiricism in social work need to develop formal epistemologies to support the kind of research and practice they advocate. This effort should clearly move beyond logical positivism, which has been largely abandoned by philosophers of science. Rather, it should draw from the many developments in the postpositivist philosophy of science that have appeared in the past two decades. One epistemology that seems to be particularly promising is social constructionism (Gergen, 1985). Social constructionism holds that "knowledge of all kinds, including scientific knowledge, is a construction of the human mind" (Scarr, 1985, p. 499). In contrast to logical positivism, it does not assume that scientific knowledge reflects "a map of the world"; rather, it holds that scientific knowledge is a product of "communal interchange" (Gergen, 1985, p. 266). As a rule, close agreement between observers is possible only when they have "similar personal constructs, similar language, similar social input, similar cultural and historical contexts, and similar motivational structures" (Fishman, Rutgers, & Franks, 1988, p. 327). However, external reality influences observation as one of the ingredients of the construction process. In some circumstances, realities are relatively dominant. All human beings can distinguish between water and sand with near-perfect reliability, regardless of their culture, context, or other factors. But in more complex observations of the types that are of concern in the helping professions—observations of human emotions, for example—factors other than external reality are critical. Within scientific and professional communities, similarities among observers in language, culture, and so forth permit shared assumptions that foster agreement. This epistemological position is close to Bloom's "social epistemological contract in which individuals surrender (agree) to common assumptions about the nature of Knowledge, and work within these assumptions."

The conception of reality as a social construction leads to an emphasis on creating knowledge that may be valid for particular contexts, but not for the generation of general truths (laws). Because of uncertainties about how reality is construed and because of the limiting factors of contexts on valid knowledge, a pragmatic test of what knowledge is useful in particular contexts becomes the criterion for truth.

As Fishman (1988) pointed out, social constructionism has generated two paradigms, one "technological," the other "hermeneutical." Making use of quantitative methods and principles of contextualism and pragmatism, the technological paradigm focuses on getting projects and programs to "work within a particular real-world setting" (Fishman, 1988, p. 264). The hermeneutical paradigm, the more radical of the two, emphasizes the qualitative, interpretative study of natural phenomena.

Social constructionism, with its related paradigms, fits well with the purposes, contexts, and tasks of social work. Its technological paradigm is especially well suited to the developmental research approach proposed by Thomas. Indeed, Thomas's notion of developmental practice provides a means of testing and modifying the kinds of context-specific programs stressed in the technological paradigm.

Although the technological paradigm, as outlined by Fishman (1988), relies on quantitative techniques, qualitative methodology could also be employed. For example, Rose and Farber demonstrated the key role of qualitative methods in a research project that predominantly followed a quantitative technological paradigm. The specification of different types of qualitative methods provided by Glisson and the analyses of their functions and pitfalls offered by Fortune and by Combs-Orme should enable researchers to use these methods with greater clarity and precision within the paradigm. The hermeneutical paradigm would help legitimate more purely qualitative approaches, as well as stimulate the development of this methodology.

These two paradigms could incorporate the different approaches to knowledge building that, as Wood pointed out, have been a source of conflict in the field. Moreover, communication and perhaps a degree of rapprochement between the "technologists" and the "hermeneuticists" would be facilitated by the shared language and assumptions of social constructionism.

Social constructionism is only one possibility, of course. Of greater importance than the choice of any one epistemology is the need for the further development of social work epistemologies in general.

EVOLUTION AND FUTURE DIRECTIONS

Taken as a whole, the articles in this volume are a testament to the evolution of epistemological and methodological thinking in clinical social work research. Although Richmond (1917) described a process of "scientific" fact gathering, diagnosis, and treatment over 70 years ago, little research on the processes and outcomes of clinical social work practice took place until the 1960s. Since the 1960s, there has been a virtual explosion of interest in clinical social work research, spurred by the increasing availability of computers, advances in research methodology, growing calls for accountability, and pressure to publish or perish.

The articles in this volume reflect the rapid developments that have taken place. In the 1960s, much emphasis was placed on large-scale evaluations of social work practice using experimental and quasi-experimental designs. Group experiments, smaller in scale but better controlled, have continued to make an important contribution. However, with the possible exception of Chapter 7, by Rose and Farber, the articles did not address explicitly the methodological developments in this approach to clinical social work research.

In the 1970s, the emphasis, at least at an intellectual level, shifted to SSDs, developmental research, and the training of practitioner-researchers. The articles by Gingerich, Nelsen, and Thomas and the commentaries on them reflect a continued interest in their approaches. But they also reflect the evolution that has taken place, particularly in the area of SSDs. No longer is there a fervent, unqualified, commitment to the strict use of SSDs by all clinical social workers. Instead, these authors have taken a more thoughtful, tempered approach that is based on the experience of a decade.

The 1980s ushered in a number of new developments in research on clinical social work practice, and this volume reflects many of these new developments. Hudson and Mullen and Schuerman described new computer technologies; Fischer, meta-analysis techniques; and Reid, a rekindled interest in process research. Taken as a whole, the articles reflect the evolution that has taken place in clinical social work research in the past 25 years.

This evolution has brought about a number of healthy developments that are likely to influence the direction of clinical social work research into the twenty-first century. Most pronounced among these developments has been the increased expression of concern about the growing schism between clinical researchers and clinical practitioners. As Kirk aptly pointed out, the early years of clinical social work research were characterized by elitism, with clinical researchers looking down on clinical practitioners. As this volume shows, there is a growing realization that clinical research is of little value if clinical practitioners do not use its findings. There is also increased awareness, as the chapters by Bloom and Wood and the commentaries on them clearly showed, that there are many ways of knowing and of knowledge building and that a single-minded, narrowly constructed approach to clinical social work research does a disservice to the profession and to the people that it serves. Although no strategy for healing the schism between researchers and practitioners came out of the conference, there was a refreshing openness to considering clinical research strategies that explicitly take into account the needs and perspectives of practitioners.

A second development, one that received a good deal of attention, has been the growing importance of the computer as a tool in clinical social work research. Expert systems, computerized record keeping, computer-assisted assessment, and the use of computers to analyze clinical evaluation data are all likely to have a profound impact in the years ahead. The challenge to social work educators, and to the profession as a whole, is to prepare clinical social workers to use this tool comfortably and wisely.

A third development has been the increasing pluralism among clinical researchers themselves. Discussions of the value of qualitative and quantitative measurement strategies, of process as well as outcome studies, of issues in determining clinical significance, of adapting SSDs to meet the exigencies of clinical practice situations, and of data derived from case studies and clinical wisdom compared to SSDs and large-scale experimental designs are illustrative of this growing pluralism.

These developments reflect the maturation of clinical social work research. After a fast-paced quarter century, some measure of reality is being added to the dream of creating a scientifically based practice profession.

REFERENCES

Broxmeyer, N. (1978). Practitioner-research in treating a borderline child. *Social Work Research & Abstracts, 14*, 5–10.

Dean, R., & Reinherz, H. (1986). Psychodynamic practice and single system design: The odd couple. *Journal of Social Work Education, 22*, 71–81.

DeMartini, J. R., & Whitbeck, L. B. (1986). Knowledge use as knowledge creation. *Knowledge: Creation, Diffusion, Utilization, 7*, 383–396.

Fishman, D. B. (1988). Pragmatic behaviorism: Saving and nurturing the baby. In D. B. Fishman, F. Rutgers, & C. M. Franks (Eds.), *Paradigms in behavior therapy: Present and promise* (pp. 258–272). New York: Springer Publishing Co.

Fishman, D. B., Rutgers, F., & Franks, C. M. (1988). Paradigmatic decision making in behavior therapy: A provisional road map. In D. B. Fishman, F. Rutgers, & C. M. Franks (Eds.), *Paradigms in behavior therapy: Present and promise.* (pp. 319–338). New York: Springer.

Gergen, K. J. (1985). The social constructionist movement in modern psychology. *American Psychologist, 40*, 266–275.

Mullen, E. J. (1983). Personal practice models. In A. Rosenblatt & D. Waldfogel (Eds.), *Handbook of clinical social work* (pp. 623–649). San Francisco: Jossey-Bass.

Nelsen, J. C. (1984). Intermediate treatment goals as variables in single-case research. *Social Work Research & Abstracts, 20*, 3–10.

Richmond, M. E. (1917). *Social diagnosis.* New York: Russell Sage Foundation.

Robinson, E. A. R., Bronson, D., & Blythe, B. J. (1988). An analysis of the implementation of single-case evaluation by practitioners. *Social Service Reviews, 62*, 285–301.

Rothman, J. (1980). *Social R&D: Research and development in the human services.* Englewood Cliffs, NJ: Prentice Hall.

Scarr, S. (1985). Construing psychology: Making facts and fables. *American Psychologist, 40*, 499–512.

Sodervick, G. J. (1975). *The application of a single-subject design in a psychosocial approach to casework treatment.* Unpublished doctoral dissertation, Smith College, Northampton, MA.

Vigilante, J. L. (1974). Between values and science: Education for the profession during a moral crisis, or is proof truth? *Journal of Education for Social Work, 10,* 110–115.

Index

A

Adoption Assistance and Child
Welfare Act, 85
Applied measurement theory, 105
Artificial intelligence, see Expert
systems
Ashford, José B., 352–358
Assessment devices
see also Computers and clinical
practice
Automated, 107–116, 412
Nonautomated, 105–107
Associative networks, 70
Attribution theory, 273–276, 279,
287, 291, 293, 295, 415

B

Baselines, single system design, 17,
19, 34, 39–40, 43, 411
Beckerman, Aaron H., 400–404
Berlin, Sharon B., 159–162
Best evidence synthesis, 318
Bloom, Martin, 341–349, 350–351
Blythe, Betty J., 29–32
Briar, Scott, 1–10
Bronson, Denise E., 101–104

C

California Department of Correc-
tions survey, 234–235
Case management, automated, 114,
124, 127
CASS system, 108–115, 118–124, 127
Causality issues, meta-analysis,
316–317
Certainty factors, 71

Change-process research
applicability, 144–145, 171, 412–413
background, 131–134
client focus, 134–135, 150, 152,
159–160
client-practitioner interaction,
135–136, 142–144, 163–166, 171
client states, identifying, 140
contextual factors, 136, 154–155,
163, 166, 414
data sources, 137–138, 167
definition, 130–131
hypothesis testing, 140–141, 169–170
interpersonal process recall, 139
methodology selection, 155–157,
166–170
paradigm shift, 141–142, 149–151,
159, 165
quantitative vs. qualitative
approaches, 138, 144, 163
scope, determination of, 153–154
single events vs. aggregates,
136–137, 151, 156–157, 167
sleeper-effect changes, 166
symptom-context methods,
139–140
task analysis, 138–139, 151–152,
160–162
training, 160–162, 171–172
treatment perspective, 134

Chapin Hall Study, 72–75
Child welfare and expert systems,
72–75, 84–86, 414–415
Client-practitioner interaction,
135–136, 142–144, 163–166, 171
Client states, identifying, 140
Clinical significance
actions observation, 274–275
attribution theory, 273–276, 279,
287, 291, 293, 295, 415

decision theory, 290–291, 293
definitions, 272–273, 293–294
dispositional attribution, 276
global change measures, 281,
    287–288, 295–296
goal-attainment scaling, 277–278,
    281
intention, client/practitioner
    assessments, 275–276
maintenance (no change) goals,
    289
mutual goal attainment, 278, 280,
    282
normative categories, 277, 279
outcome components, 277–282,
    293
pretest-posttest comparison, 280
process components, 274–276, 289,
    296
process significance, 275
social comparison, 277, 279
social desirability, 282
statistical significance, 271–272,
    280, 282, 287–288, 293
subjective comparison, 278–280,
    287–288, 294–295

Cognitive-behavioral theory, 175

Combined probability method, 300

Combs-Orme, Terri, 181–188

Commission on Practice, NASW,
    354

Common metric method, 300

Common sense and expert systems,
    77, 83, 95–96

Community Intervention Project,
    223, 226

Computer-Assisted Social Service
    (CASS) system, 108–115,
    118–124, 127

Computers and clinical practice
    see also Expert systems
    assessment devices, administer-
        ing, 109
    assessment devices, interpreting,
        110, 121, 412
    assessment devices, scoring,
        109–110
    case management, 114, 124, 127
    client reaction to computers,
        118–119, 127
    Computer-Assisted Social Service
        (CASS) system, 108–115,
        118–124, 127
    confidentiality, 113–114, 125
    costs, 107, 115
    design flexibility, 108
    forms management, 112–113, 124
    graphs, 110–111, 120, 124, 127
    organizational issues, 125–126, 414
    overuse, 119–122
    single-case designs, 20–21,
        111–112, 120
    storage capacity, 108
    summary, benefits and obstacles,
        127–129, 412–413, 419–420
    tests/examinations management,
        113
    training, 115–116, 120, 124, 129

Conceptual perspectives, 353–354,
    395–397, 403

Confidentiality, computers,
    113–114, 125

Content analysis, 191

Contextual factors
    change-process research, 136,
        154–155, 163, 166, 414
    expert systems, 77–78, 83, 85–86,
        414
    qualitative vs. quantitative
        methods, 182

Control-group experiments,
    174–179, 197

Conventional practice and develop-
    mental research, 204–206, 213,
    218, 228, 230

Corcoran, Kevin J., 54–57

Council on Social Work Education
accreditation standards, 3, 5, 11,
55–56
research utilization issues,
244–245, 268–269

CSWE, see Council on Social Work
Education

D

Data-gathering devices, see
Assessment devices
Data pooling methods, 300–301
Davis, Inger P., 163–173
Decision theory, 290–291, 293
Decision trees, 70
Deductive vs. Inductive, epistemological issues, 356, 371–372,
383–385, 401
Deficient reporting, meta-analysis,
309, 327–328
Developmental research, practice
modes
background, 202–203, 218, 222
conventional practice, 204–206,
213, 218, 228, 230
data collection, 210
developmental practice, activities,
209–212
developmental practice, applications, 212–214
developmental practice, characteristics, 6, 208–209, 219–220
developmental practice, skills
requirements, 212, 229
empirically based practice,
206–208, 213, 218–219
funding constraints, 229
implementation, 210, 219–220,
224–226, 228–229
model vs. method, 219–220, 228
proceduralization, 211–212,
222–224, 226, 229
problem-solving methods, 210–211

practitioner qualifications, 212
sampling procedures, 209–210
single-case methods, 207
testing, 211

Diagnostic assessment, epistemological issues, 382–383
Dispositional attribution, 276
Dissemination of results, 13, 62–64,
235–237, 257–258, 268, 416

E

Eaton, J. L., 234–237
Education, see Training
Educator vs. student perspectives,
359–363, 105–406
Effect size calculation and interpretation, 310–312, 314–316, 328
Empirically based practice and
developmental research,
206–208, 213, 218–219
Epistemological issues
conceptual perspectives, 353–354,
395–397, 403
deductive vs. inductive, 356,
371–372, 383–385, 401
diagnostic assessment, 382–383
educator vs. student perspectives,
359–363, 405–406
gender issues, 345, 347, 352,
366–367
justificationism, 356
limits of empirical data, 353–356
literature base, 342, 363–364, 406
personal epistemologies, 342–348,
360–362, 371–372, 395–397
positivist paradigm, 375–378, 385,
400, 407
"practice wisdom," 383–385,
393–394, 402
pragmatic method, 355
qualitative vs. quantitative
methods, 187, 192, 194–195,
198, 392–394

rational technology, 380–382,
    385–386, 389, 403
reasoning processes, 354
research responsibilities, 385–389,
    397–399, 407–408
research utilization, 374–380,
    388–389, 391, 395–399, 401–402,
    407
review, 416–418
scientific practitioners, 344–346,
    351, 353–354, 369, 372
semantic issues, 366–370, 406
subjective vs. objective, 360–363
validation, 355, 372
value systems, 342–347, 351,
    367–370

Ethnographic analysis, 191
Evaluation research, 237–239, 253
Expert systems
    applications, 68–69, 88–91, 98–100,
        103–104, 412, 419–420
    certainty factors, 71
    Chapin Hall Study, 72–75
    child welfare settings, 72–75,
        84–86, 414–415
    common sense elements, 77, 83,
        95–96
    complexity of knowledge, 78–79,
        82, 90–91, 95–98
    contextual factors, 77–78, 83,
        85–86, 414
    decision trees, 70
    definition, 67, 92
    dependency information, 71–72
    development stages, 73–75,
        102–103
    frame-based languages, 70–71, 75
    inference engines, 70
    knowledge engineers, 70, 74, 99
    knowledge representation, 69–71
    networks, semantic or associative,
        70
    "practice wisdom," 82, 101–104
    problem specification, 73–74

prototypes, 74–75
rule-based systems, 70, 74, 79, 82,
    92–98
social worker shortage, 68–69
story construction, 76–77, 83
symbolic processing, 69
testing, 75, 79–82, 104

F

Family support measures, 184
Family therapy and single-system
    designs, 44–46, 48–53
Farber, Naomi, 174–180
Fischer, Joel, 297–325
Ford Foundation, 238
Forms management, 112–113, 124
Fortune, Anne E., 194–201
Frame-based languages, 70–71, 75
Funding issues, 15, 28, 197, 229

G

Galvanic skin reaction, 132
Gender issues, 345, 347, 352,
    366–367
Gilchrist, Lewayne D., 405–408
Gilgun, Jane F., 371–372
Gingerich, Wallace J., 11–24
Glisson, Charles, 189–193
Global change measures, 281,
    287–288, 295–296
Goal-attainment scaling, 277–278,
    281
Goal identification, 38–41, 49,
    54–55, 411
Gordon, Jesse E., 251–255
Graduate Record Examination, 279
Graphs, computerized, 110–111,
    120, 124, 127
Grounded-theory analysis, 190–192

H

Handicapped children and Medicaid, 185
Hassles Inventory, 176
Homogeneity test, 300–301
Hudson, Walter W., 105–117
Hypothesis testing, 140–141, 169–170

I

Illinois Department of Children and Family Services, 72–75
Imre, Roberta Wells, 366–370
Index of Marital Satisfaction, 106, 107, 110
Index of Self Esteem, 121
Infant illness, contextual factor example, 182–185
Inference engines, 70
Intelligence quotient tests, 279
Interpersonal process recall, 139
Interviews, 106, 119, 127, 177–178
Ivanoff, André, 265–270

J

Jayaratne, Srinika, 271–285
Jenkins, Shirley, 218–221
Justificationism, 356

K

Katie Beckett waivers, 185
Kirk, Stuart A., 233–250
Knowledge engineers, 70, 74, 99

L

LeCroy, Craig Winston, 261–264
Levy, Rona L., 290–292

Literature base
epistemological issues, 342, 363–364, 406
meta-analysis, 298–299, 301–302, 328–329, 335–336
qualitative vs. quantitative methods, 187, 197

Log-linear–based analysis, 191–192

M

Malpractice suits, 84–85
Maluccio, Anthony N., 127–129
Measurement issues, single-system design, 38–44, 52–53, 410
Measurement tools, see Assessment devices
Medicaid and handicapped children, 185
Meta-analysis
background, 297–299
benefits, 301–302, 317–322, 330–333
best evidence synthesis, 318
causality issues, 316–317
combined probability method, 300
common metric method, 300
data aggregates vs. nonaggregates, 314
data nonindependence, 312
data pooling methods, 300–301
deficient reporting, 309, 327–328
definition, 297, 333
effect size calculation and interpretation, 310–312, 314–316, 328
homogeneity test, 300–301
integrating variables, 303–306
literature base, 298–299, 301–302, 328–329, 335–336
methodological variations, primary studies, 306–308, 310
methodologies, 299–301
narrative reviews, traditional, 297–298, 317–319, 333, 335

positive bias, 312–314
problems, 302–317, 326–328,
  334–335, 416
psychometric factors, 310
results interpretation, limits on,
  314–317
sampling bias, unrepresented
  studies, 308–309, 334
sampling error correction, 301
single-system designs, 320
social policy impact, 319–320
statistics, limitations of, 310–314
studies inclusion, criteria, 303–310,
  326–327, 334
study effect meta-analysis, 300
theoretical factors, 310
topics, examples of, 298–299
training, 330–332, 335

Meyer, Carol H., 395–399
Microcomputers, see Computers
  and clinical practice
Model vs. method, developmental
  research, 219–220, 228
Models development, 15
Modes of practice, see Developmen-
  tal research, practice modes
Mount Zion Psychotherapy Re-
  search Group, 140
Mullen, Edward J., 67–83
Multimethod group approach, 175,
  191
Multiple tracking design, 49–51
Mutschler, Elizabeth, 123–126
Mutual goal attainment, 278, 280, 282

N

Narrative reviews, traditional,
  297–298, 317–319, 333, 335
Nelsen, Judith C., 37–47
Neonatal intensive care units,
  182–185

Networks, semantic or associative,
  70
No-change goals, 289
Normative categories, clinical
  significance, 277, 279
Nugent, William, 333–337
Nurius, Paula, 330–332

O

One-dimensional variables, 41–42
Operant theory, 174–175
Orme, John G., 293–296
Outcome components, clinical
  significance, 277–282, 293

P

Paradigm shift, change-process
  research, 141–142, 149–151, 159,
  165
Pattern of implementation, 223
Physiological and Behavioral Stress
  Inventory, 176
Positive bias, meta-analysis,
  312–314
Positivist paradigm, 375–378, 385,
  400, 407
"Practice wisdom"
  epistemological issues, 383–385,
    393–394, 402
  expert systems and, 82, 101–104
  single-system design, 15, 28, 56–57
Practitioner-experimenter concept,
  51–53, 409, 419
Practitioner-scientist role, 2,
  245–246, 269
Pragmatic method, 355
President's Committee on Juvenile
  Delinquency and Youth Crime,
  238

Pretest-posttest comparisons, 280

Problem-solving theory, 175

Procedural descriptiveness, 223

Proceduralization, developmental research, 211–212, 222–224, 226, 229

Process components, clinical significance, 274–276, 289, 296

Process-outcome research, 130–131, 133
see also Change-process research

Proctor, Enola K., 153–158

Profile of Mood States, 176

Psychodynamic approaches, 12, 26–27, 33, 40–41

Psychometric factors, in factor analysis, 310

Psychosocial models, 38

Q

Qualitative vs. quantitative methods
change-process research, 138, 144, 163
characteristics, 181–182, 185–186, 190–191, 420
collaboration barriers, 186–187
contextual factors, 182
data collection, 175–178, 189–192
distinguishing components, 189–192, 194–195
epistemological issues, 187, 192, 194–195, 198, 392–394
funding constraints, 197
generalization of experience, 184–186, 198
guidelines for use, lack of, 196–197
interviews, 177–178
literature base, 187, 197
process factors, 183–184
program development, 178–179
selection of method, 199–200
self-reports, 176–177

single-system designs, 18, 20, 27
time constraints, 197
training, 186–187, 195–196

R

Rational technology, 380–382, 385–386, 389, 403

Reamer, Frederic G., 88–93

Reasoning processes, epistemological issues, 354

Reid, William J., 130–148, 409–421

Reinherz, Helen, 25–28

Research responsibilities, epistemological issues, 385–389, 397–399, 407–408

Research utilization
California Department of Corrections survey, 234–235
Council on Social Work Education, 244–245, 268–269
dissemination of findings, 235–237, 257–258, 268, 416
epistemological issues, 374–380, 388–389, 391, 395–399, 401–402, 407
evaluation research, 237–239, 253
knowledge-based practice, 261–264
obstacles, summary, 266–267
organizational issues, 236–237
practitioner-scientist role, 2, 245–246, 269
practitioner studies, 244
practitioner's view, 239–241
researchers' goals, 251–259
review, 1–7, 234–246, 415, 419
single-subject designs, 245
student studies, 244–245
symbolic vs. substantive functions, 236–237
training, 6–7, 245–246, 258, 267–268
Veterans Administration survey, 234–235

Richey, Cheryl A., 359–365
Rose, Sheldon D., 174–180
Rothman, Jack, 222–227
Rule-based expert systems, 70, 74,
79, 82, 92–98

S

Sampling bias, unrepresented
studies, 308–309, 334
Sampling error, data pooling, 301
Schilling, Robert F., 256–257
Scholastic Aptitude Test, 279
Schuerman, John R., 67–83
Scientific practitioners, 344–346,
351, 353–354, 369, 372
SCL-90-R, 176
Self-monitoring, clients, 42–44,
176–177
Semantic issues, 366–370, 406
Semantic networks, 70
Service vs. research objectives, 12,
14–18, 20, 25, 27, 29–35
Sherman, Edmund, 149–152
Siegel, Deborah H., 118–122
Simmons College School of Social
Work, 26–27
Single-case evaluation
see also Single-case research
applicability, 12–13, 17, 25, 411
baselines, 17, 19, 34, 411
computer systems, 20–21, 111–112,
120
definitions, 13–14
design and development, 16–17,
29–32, 34
dissemination, 13
funding, 15, 28
integration in practice, 11–21, 409,
412
models development, 15
nonbehavioral approaches and, 12

practice-based techniques, 16–18,
31
"practice wisdom," 15, 28
problems with, 12–13, 18
psychodynamic approaches and,
12, 26–27, 33
quantitative vs. qualitative, 18, 20,
27
service vs. research objectives, 12,
14–18, 20, 25, 27, 29–35
Simmons College School of Social
Work, 26–27
training, 15, 25–27
treatment utility, 18–19, 31–32,
34–35, 411

Single-case research
see also Single-case evaluation
baselines, 39–40, 43, 411
data collection, 60–61
developmental research, 207
dissemination of results, 62–64
family member observing another,
44–46
family therapy and, 48–53
goal identification, 38–41, 49,
54–55, 411
improvement in clients, 60–61
information needs, 60
measurement decisions, 38–41, 410
measurement strategies, 41–44,
52–53
meta-analysis, 320
multiple tracking design, 49–51
obstacles in practice, 58–60, 410
one-dimensional variables, 41–42
"practice wisdom," 56–57
practitioner-experimenter concept,
51–53, 409, 419
process measures, 41–42
psychodynamic approach, 40–41
psychosocial models, 38
research utilization, 245
self-monitoring, clients, 42–44
structural models, 38, 40
training, 46, 51–53, 55–56

Single-system designs, see Single-case evaluation; Single-case research

Siporin, Max, 391–394

Sleeper-effect changes, 166

Small-group theory, 175

Social elements, clinical significance, 277, 279, 282

Social learning theory, 175

Social policy impact, meta-analysis, 319–320

Social support measures, 184

Social worker shortage, 68–69

Statistical significance, 271–272, 280, 282, 287–288, 293

Stein, Theodore J., 84–87

Stern, Susan B., 47–53

Story construction, expert systems, 76–77, 83

Stress inoculation, 175

Stress management, 174–179, 183

Structural models, 38, 40

Study effect meta-analysis, 300

Subcommittee on the Working Definition, NASW, 354

Subjective comparison, clinical significance, 278–280, 287–288, 294–295

Subjective vs. objective, epistemological issues, 360–363

Symbolic processing, 69

Symbolic vs. substantive functions, 236–237

Symptom-context methods, 139–140

T

Testing
developmental research, 211
expert systems, 75, 79–82, 104

Tests/examinations management, 113

Theoretical factors, meta-analysis, 310

Thomas, Edwin J., 202–217

Thyer, Bruce A., 33–36

Tolson, Eleanor Reardon, 58–64

Toseland, Ronald W., 228–230, 409–421

Training
change-process research, 160–162, 171–172
computer systems, 115–116, 120, 124, 129
meta-analysis, 330–332, 335
qualitative vs. quantitative methods, 186–187, 195–196
research utilization, 6–7, 245–246, 258, 267–268
single-system designs, 15, 25–27, 46, 51–53, 55–56

Treatment perspective, change-process research, 134

Treatment utility, 18–19, 31–32, 34–35, 411

Tripodi, Tony, 286–289

V

Validation, 355, 372

Value systems, 342–347, 351, 367–370

Variance analysis, 190–191

Veterans Administration survey, 234–235

Videka-Sherman, Lynn, 326–329, 409–421

W

Wakefield, Jerome C., 92–100

Weighted utility, decision theory, 291

Wood, Katherine M., 373–390

Contributors

José B. Ashford is Associate Professor of Social Work, Arizona State University. His research interests are in the areas of law and mental health with a special focus on criminal justice and mental health interactions.

Aaron H. Beckerman is Professor, Wurzweiler School of Social Work, Yeshiva University; Social Work Research Consultant, Long Island Jewish Medical Center; and New York City Research Consultant, New York University Medical Center.

Sharon B. Berlin is Associate Professor and Associate Dean for Academic Affairs, School of Social Service Administration, University of Chicago. Her primary research focus is on developing and testing interventions for depression.

Martin Bloom teaches at the School of Social Work at Rutgers, the State University of New Jersey. He is author of *An Introduction to the Drama of Social Work* (1990) and is currently writing in the areas of evaluation and primary prevention.

Betty J. Blythe has been Associate Professor at the University of Pittsburgh School of Social Work since 1987. She has written numerous articles on evaluating social work practice and recently coauthored, with Tony Tripodi, *Measurement in Direct Social Work Practice*. She is currently doing research on family preservation.

Scott Briar is Professor and Director, Department of Social Work, Florida International University. Formerly he was Dean of the School of Social Work, University of Washington, and a member of the faculty at the University of California, Berkeley. He has served as Editor-in-Chief of *Social Work* and *Practice Digest*, Chair of the NASW Publications Committee, and member of the Editorial Board for the *Encyclopedia of Social Work*. Dr. Briar recently completed a term as Chair of the Commission on Accreditation of the Council on Social Work Education. He has published extensively on clinical judgment, delinquency, poverty, family treatment and policy, child welfare, and practice research.

Denise E. Bronson is Assistant Professor of Social Work, State University of New York at Buffalo. Her interests include practice evaluation, computer-assisted social work, and behavioral methods for family treatment. She is coauthor, with Donald Pelz and Eileen Trzcinski, of *Computerizing Your Agency's Information System* (1989).

Terri Combs-Orme received her MSW degree from the University of Texas at Arlington and her PhD from Washington University in St. Louis. Her practice experience includes work in foster care, and her current research interests include infant mortality and the health of foster children. She has recently published a book entitled *Social Work Practice in Maternal and Child Health.* She serves on the Maryland Governor's Advisory Council on Infant Mortality and as part of a national group to advise on implementation of Public Law 99-457.

Kevin J. Corcoran is Associate Professor, University of Houston. He holds an MA degree in counseling and an MSW and a PhD from the University of Pittsburgh. His current area of emphasis is dispute resolution. He maintains a small private practice on Glenn Cove in Kemah, Texas.

Inger P. Davis is Professor, San Diego State University School of Social Work. His primary interests include clinical social work research in child welfare, family services, and interdisciplinary approaches to family violence.

Naomi Farber is Assistant Professor of Social Work, University of Wisconsin–Madison. Her research interests include adolescent childbearing and family formation among racial and ethnic minorities. She is author of *The Significance of Class and Race in Marital Decisions among Unmarried Adolescent Mothers* (1989) and *The Significance of Aspirations among Unmarried Adolescent Mothers* (1990).

Joel Fischer is Professor of Social Work, University of Hawaii, School of Social Work. His main interests are in the areas of clinical evaluation, effectiveness research, human sexuality, and social actions against apartheid in South Africa and poverty and racism around the world.

Anne E. Fortune holds an AB in anthropology and an AM and a PhD in social work from the University of Chicago. Her interests include treatment process and outcome, termination, short-term treatment, and social work education.

Lewayne D. Gilchrist is Associate Professor and Associate Dean for Research, University of Washington School of Social Work. She has written more than 80 publications, many of which report empirical tests of intervention models for preventing drug use and risky sexual behavior among women and adolescents. She currently serves as grant reviewer and prevention research design consultant for the National Institute on Drug Abuse.

Jane F. Gilgun is Associate Professor, School of Social Work, University of Minnesota. Her research area is the differential effects of child maltreatment, where she uses primarily qualitative, theory-building methods. She teaches research methods, direct practice evaluation, and courses on child welfare. She currently is using a single-system approach in designing an evaluation of a multidisciplinary child abuse evaluation center.

Wallace J. Gingerich is Professor and Associate Dean, Mandel School of Applied Social Sciences, Case Western Reserve University. His primary teaching and research interests are in the areas of clinical practice, clinical evaluation, and computer applications in the human services. Currently he is designing and developing a computer-assisted case monitoring and evaluation system for mental health practitioners. Dr. Gingerich also maintains a small clinical practice.

Charles Glisson is Professor and Chair of the PhD Program in Social Work, University of Tennessee. His major research interests concern the organization and administration of human services and child welfare. Currently he is Principal Investigator of National Institute of Mental Health research grants supporting a three-year study of the coordination of services to children in state custody.

Jesse E. Gordon is Professor of Social Work and of Psychology, University of Michigan. He has published experimental studies of psychotherapy and directed U.S. Department of Labor research and development projects on the utilization of social science research for manpower agencies. His current specialty is psychoanalytic object relations theory.

Walter W. Hudson is Professor, School of Social Work, Arizona State University. He completed his MA and PhD at the School of Social Service Administration, University of Chicago. He teaches research methods, statistics, program and practice evaluation, and psychopathology. He has conducted research in applied measurement theory and has developed assessment tools and case management computer software for use by human service practitioners.

Roberta Wells Imre is an experienced social work practitioner and teacher. She coordinates the Study Group for Philosophical Issues in Social Work, sponsored by the University of Kansas and the Smith College School for Social Work, and is a Visiting Scholar at the Princeton Theological Seminary.

André Ivanoff is Assistant Professor, Columbia University School of Social Work, New York, where she teaches direct practice and practice evaluation. Her research and scholarly interests include the development and testing of interventions for high-risk populations, suicidal behaviors, and empirical clinical practice.

Shirley Jenkins is Professor Emerita, Columbia University School of Social Work, New York, and Director of the Center for the Study of Social Work Practice. She has published more than 50 articles and 10 books, including *The Ethnic Dilemma in Social Services* (1981) and *Ethnic Associations and the Welfare State: Services to Immigrants in Five Countries* (1988).

Srinika Jayaratne is Professor, School of Social Work, University of Michigan. He has authored numerous articles related to practice evaluation and is coauthor with Rona L. Levy of *Empirical Clinical Practice* (1979). His current research includes studies on how practitioners determine clinical significance.

Stuart A. Kirk is Professor, Columbia University School of Social Work, New York. Prior to 1988, he served as Dean of the School of Social Welfare, State University of New York at Albany. His current research concerns the involvement of practitioners in clinical evaluation, psychiatric diagnosis, and case management of the seriously mentally ill. He received his BS and DSW degrees from the University of California, Berkeley, and his MSW from the University of Illinois, Urbana.

Craig Winston LeCroy is Associate Professor and Director of the Doctoral Program, School of Social Work, Arizona State University. He is currently Co-director, National Institute of Mental Health training grant for severely emotionally disturbed children. He is author of *Social Skills Training for Children and Youth* (1983) and *Case Studies in Social Work Practice* (in press). His major research interests include developing and evaluating interventions for adolescents, social competence training, and practice evaluation.

Rona L. Levy is Professor of Social Work, University of Washington, Seattle. In 1979 she coauthored with Srinika Jayaratne *Empirical Clinical Practice* (1979), the first text exclusively on the application of evaluation techniques and single subject designs to clinical practice. She has written extensively and lectured nationally and internationally on clinical social work research.

Anthony N. Maluccio is Professor, University of Connecticut, School of Social Work. He has authored or coauthored a number of books on social work practice and child welfare, including *Permanency Planning for Children* (1986), *Adolescents in Foster Families* (1989), and *No More Partings: An Examination of Long-Term Foster Family Care* (1990).

Carol H. Meyer is Professor, Columbia University School of Social Work, New York. She has been engaged in the development of practice theory through direct practice, teaching, consultation, and writing.

Edward J. Mullen is Professor and Associate Dean, Columbia University School of Social Work, New York. He was previously Professor, University of Chicago and Fordham University. He is currently the Program Director for a National Institute of Mental Health–funded doctoral training program in mental health services research. His research and publications have been in the areas of social intervention research, evaluation research, expert systems development research, and minority leadership development.

Elizabeth Mutschler is Associate Professor, School of Social Work, University of Michigan, Ann Arbor. She has published extensively on evaluation research, research utilization, the development and use of information systems in social work practice, and education. She currently is involved in a research project developing decision support systems for clinical practice in human services.

Judith C. Nelsen is Professor, University of Illinois at Chicago, Jane Addams College of Social Work, where she teaches clinical practice and research courses. Her writings have focused on applications of single case research methods in traditional clinical social work practice.

William Nugent holds an MSW and a PhD in social work from Florida State University. He has worked in a variety of practice settings and has taught at the Graduate School of Social Work, University of Maryland at Baltimore. He is currently Training Director for the Florida Network of Youth and Family Services. He also is an Adjunct Professor, School of Social Work, Florida State University.

Paula Nurius, Associate Professor at the University of Washington, received her doctoral training at the University of Michigan. Her current scholarship interests include the role of cognitive appraisal in stress and coping and in clinical reasoning, the self-concept, and practice evaluation and computer applications in practice.

John G. Orme is Assistant Professor, School of Social Work, University of Maryland at Baltimore. His teaching and research interests are in the area of research methodology and, in particular, applied statistical problems, the development and testing of measurement procedures, and single-system designs.

Enola K. Proctor received her BA from Butler University, her MSW from the University of Texas at Arlington, and her PhD from Washington

University, St. Louis. Her areas of teaching and research include clinical evaluation; treatment planning (including hospital discharge planning); and race, gender, and class effects in practice. She chairs the PhD program in social work at Washington University.

Frederic G. Reamer is Professor, School of Social Work, Rhode Island College. His areas of interest include public welfare, mental health, criminal justice, and professional ethics. His most recent works include *Ethical Dilemmas in Social Service* (1990) and, with Charles Shireman, *Rehabilitating Juvenile Justice* (1986).

Helen Reinherz holds an MSW from Simmons College, Boston, Massachusetts, and an ScD from the Harvard School of Public Health. For the past 20 years she has chaired the research sequence at Simmons. She is the author of articles on the relationship of research and practice as well as the mental health and development of children and youth. She has been the principal investigator of an epidemiological study of youth for the past 14 years.

Cheryl A. Richey has taught graduate courses integrating clinical practice and research for almost 15 years. She has studied hundreds of social workers to determine the extent to which they engage in postgraduate practice evaluation activities. Her current research and writing interests include social network characteristics of and social support interventions with diverse populations.

Sheldon D. Rose is Professor of Social Work, University of Wisconsin–Madison. He has carried out extensive research on the effectiveness of various group approaches for the treatment of children and adults and written a number of articles and books on this topic, including *Working with Children and Adolescents in Groups* (1987) and *Working with Adults in Groups* (1989).

Jack Rothman received his PhD in social psychology from Columbia University, New York. He is internationally known for his seminal work in community organization and his work on social research and development. Other special areas of interest include research utilization, organizational innovation, and diffusion of innovative techniques. His most recent work has included research on chronically mentally ill people, runaway homeless, and youth and health promotion in minority communities. He has received the Gunnar Myrdal Award of the Evaluation Research Society and been granted two Fulbright Senior Research Fellowships for international studies. Dr. Rothman is on several editorial boards of journals emphasizing research and knowledge utilization and has written more than 10 major books.

Robert F. Schilling is Assistant Professor, Columbia University School of Social Work, New York. He has published more than 60 articles and book chapters. His interests include prevention and treatment research in practice settings, substance abuse, developmental disabilities, child abuse, and skills training.

John R. Schuerman is Professor, School of Social Service Administration, University of Chicago; Faculty Associate, Chapin Hall Center for Children; and Editor, *Social Service Review*. He is the author of *Research and Evaluation in the Human Services* (1983) and *Multivariate Analysis in Human Services Research and Evaluation*. His current research involves the development of expert systems in social welfare and the evaluation of programs in child welfare.

Edmund Sherman is Professor of Social Work, State University of New York at Albany, where he teaches courses in clinical practice and theory in the MSW and PhD programs. He is also Director, Center for Social Work Practice Research, School of Social Welfare, State University of New York at Albany.

Deborah H. Siegel is Associate Professor, School of Social Work, Rhode Island College, where she teaches practice and evaluation. She has published research on the teaching of empirically based practice and is now engaged in research on adoption. Her current clinical practice is with families and children.

Max Siporin is Professor Emeritus, School of Social Welfare, State University of New York at Albany. Many of his recent publications have been in the area of social work morality and ethics, and he is revising a set of his papers for a book on this subject. He also is completing a book on the art of social work.

Theodore J. Stein was Director of the Alameda Project and of the Illinois/West Virginia Project. His publications include *Children in Foster Homes: Achieving Continuity in Care*, *Decision Making in Child Welfare Services: Intake and Planning* (1983), and *Child Welfare and the Law* (1990).

Susan B. Stern is Assistant Professor, State University of New York at Albany, School of Social Welfare. She teaches courses on family therapy, clinical research, and treatment of childhood and adolescent disorders. Her primary research interests are in the areas of family and marital conflict, childhood aggression, child abuse, and juvenile delinquency. She has recently completed a study of family anger control and currently is involved in an interdisciplinary longitudinal study of juvenile delinquency. Dr. Stern received her PhD from the University of Chicago and her MSW from the University of Michigan.

Edwin J. Thomas is Fedele F. Fauri Professor of Social Work, Professor of Psychology, and Director of the Marital Treatment Project, University of Michigan. He received an MSW from Wayne State University and a PhD in social psychology from the University of Michigan. He has been a senior Fulbright Scholar, spending one year in England and another in Australia, and has published 120 articles and 12 books, mostly in selected areas of behavioral science and social work, behavior change, marital and family therapy, and assessment and research methods. He currently is conducting research to develop and evaluate unilateral family therapy for alcohol abuse.

Bruce A. Thyer received his MSW from the University of Georgia and his PhD in social work and psychology from the University of Michigan. He is licensed as a clinical social worker in Michigan and Florida. He is currently Professor of Social Work at the University of Georgia.

Eleanor Reardon Tolson is Associate Professor at Jane Addams College of Social Work, University of Illinois at Chicago. She is the author of *The Metamodel and Clinical Social Work* (1988) and coeditor with William J. Reid of *Models of Family Treatment* (1981). She has written numerous articles about social work practice and the use of single-subject designs.

Ronald W. Toseland is Associate Professor, School of Social Welfare, State University of New York at Albany. His areas of interest include social work practice, group work, gerontology, and research. His books include *Group Work With Older Adults* (in press), *An Introduction to Group Work Practice* (1984), and *Working Effectively with Administrative Groups* (1987).

Tony Tripodi is Associate Dean, University of Pittsburgh School of Social Work. He served as a research consultant to the European Common Market and the Zancan Foundation, Padora, Italy. He is currently a member of the Task Force on Social Work Research, National Institute of Mental Health.

Jerome C. Wakefield is Assistant Professor, Columbia University School of Social Work, New York. He specializes in clinical theory and in the philosophical foundations of clinical practice. Current work includes a book on the link between Sigmund Freud and contemporary cognitive science and articles on the nature of mental disorder.

Katherine M. Wood had extensive practice experience before joining the faculty of the Rutgers University School of Social Work, where she is Professor, Coordinator of the MSW Direct Practice Track and a member of the PhD program faculty. She also has taught research. She is the author of a number of articles in professional journals and, with Ludwig L. Geismar, the books *Family and Delinquency* (1986) and *Families at Risk* (1989).